Interpersonal
Communication

Roles, Rules, Strategies, and Games

Interpersonal Communication
Roles, Rules, Strategies, and Games

Dennis R. Smith
Temple University

L. Keith Williamson
Temple University

Wm. C. Brown Company Publishers
Dubuque, Iowa

BOOK TEAM

Ed Bowers, Jr., *Publisher*
Ed Bowers, Jr., *Editor*
Don Walkoe, *Designer*
Ruth Richard, *Manager, Production-Editorial Department*
Mary Jones, *Production Editor*

WM. C. BROWN COMPANY PUBLISHERS

Wm. C. Brown, *President*
Larry W. Brown, *Executive Vice-President*
Ann Bradley, *Director of Marketing Strategy*
Jim Buell, *Director of Information Management*
John Carlisle, *Assistant Vice-President, Production Division*
Robert Chesterman, *Comptroller*
David Corona, *Design Director*
Lawrence E. Cremer, *Vice-President, Product Development*
Richard C. Crews, *Publisher*
John Graham, *National Marketing Manager*
Chuck Grantham, *National College Sales Manager*
Linda Judge, *Director of Personnel/Public Relations*
Roger Meyer, *Assistant Plant Superintendent*
Paul Miller, *Vice-President/Director, University Services*
Roy Mills, *Assistant Vice-President/Plant Superintendent*
Ed O'Neill, *Vice-President, Manufacturing*
Dennis Powers, *Director of Information Services*

Copyright 1977 by Wm. C. Brown Company Publishers
Library of Congress Catalog Card Number 76-41492
ISBN 0—697—04120—4

Fourth Printing, 1980
Printed in the United States of America

To our parents
Marian and Charles, Billie and Bud

Contents

Preface

This textbook is well-grounded in the major historical and contemporary approaches to the study of interpersonal communication. It may be utilized in courses in which the primary emphasis is on building interpersonal skills, or in courses in which the primary emphasis is on communication theory. When the text is used in a skills-oriented course, special attention should be paid to structuring class sessions so that the materials of the textbook are illustrated and amplified by the actual classroom experience. A separate manual to assist instructors has been prepared for this purpose. For theory courses, the book is structured so that it may be used without additional materials or in conjunction with supplementary readings.

The Approach: The study of interpersonal communication has taken a great leap forward in the last ten years. The work of Harry Stack Sullivan, Jurgen Ruesch, William Schutz, R. D. Laing, Paul Watzlawick and Don Jackson, Eric Berne, Gregory Bateson, and similar figures forms a solid core of theory, research, and understanding of the basic processes that govern interpersonal communication. These materials have only slowly been introduced into basic courses in interpersonal communication. By and large they have been reserved for seminars in graduate study. In this textbook, we have attempted to bring these materials together in a way that will make the advancements in interpersonal communication available to the undergraduate student in introductory or basic communication studies.

The approach of this text is in some ways strikingly different from current practices. The main difference between the approach of this text and the dominant current trends lies in our emphasis on communication as both behavior and experience.

We have written, in chapter 10, *"When we are attempting to learn how to improve our own interpersonal communication, it is not enough simply to learn a set of behavioral skills. Rewarding interpersonal communication depends as much upon the way we experience the behavior of self and others as it does upon the way we manipulate our own behavior."*

The giving and receiving of coins is an exercise used in many classes in interpersonal communication to illustrate this point. In the exercise each participant takes four coins: a quarter, a dime, a nickel, and a penny. Each person selects one of these coins to represent himself or herself in some way. During the exercise, each person in turn presents his or her coin to one other person in the group. Some people receive several coins; some receive only one coin; and some receive no coins. The giving of the coin may be viewed as a communicative act. The meaning of that communicative act, however, depends upon the way the individuals experience that act. Let us look at several possible meanings.

Suppose Tom and Sue are very close friends. In the exercise, Tom gives his coin to Sue, but Sue gives her coin to Jerry. Now Tom may interpret Sue's act of communication in many different ways. He may see her act as communicating rejection and say, "Damn her. She didn't think enough of me to give me her coin. Why is she rejecting me?" Or Tom may see her act as communicating interpersonal trust and say, "Sue is so confident in our relationship that she feels free to give her coin to Jerry. That's great." Likewise, there are several ways in which Sue may interpret Tom's giving her a coin. She may see Tom's act as binding and say, "Tom didn't trust me enough to give his coin to someone else. He is trying to bind me to him." Or she may see Tom's giving her the coin as an act of warmth and love and say, "Isn't it great that he communicated his feelings to me by giving me his coin!" *All are perfectly valid experiences of the same communication behavior.*

This book emphasizes communication behavior and communication experience as the structuring and interpretation of communicative interaction with others. To change a person's communication behavior is not enough to improve interpersonal communication. A person's experience, the way he or she perceives the communication of self and of others, must also change. This, we believe, can be done only when a person understands how interpersonal communication is structured and how it functions in interpersonal transactions.

The Level: The materials in this text are written for the introductory course in interpersonal communication or for a second-level course in curricula that require public speaking as a first course. The book has not dodged the complexities of interpersonal communication phenomena. We believe that we do the introductory student a great injustice when we write down to him or her, or when we oversimplify fundamental concepts. The same student who is enrolling in an introductory interpersonal communication course will probably be enrolling in introductory courses in biology, chemistry, physics, economics, and so on. The concepts in these fields are far from simple. Any student who can master the basic concepts in introductory courses in other disciplines will have no difficulties mastering the concepts presented in this textbook. We have, ourselves, taught these materials to freshmen students for five years in an urban university, and we have done so with a high degree of success. In designing this text, we have tried, whenever possible, to draw upon our actual experience with these students.

The Design: The book is structured so that an instructor may cover one chapter per week. Most instructors, however, prefer to spend at least two weeks on the chapter on language. This pacing permits both the instructor and the student to participate in an intellectually exciting and highly diversified course, moving from a review of traditions contributing to the study of interpersonal communication (Historical Perspective), to the introduction of a model of interpersonal communication (Part 1), to the examination of primary message systems (Part 2), and finally, to using the elements of the model to analyze and understand different patterns of interpersonal communication (Part 3). Instructors who wish to omit the historical materials may begin with Part 1.

We wish to thank all of our students and colleagues who have helped us to formulate the ideas that appear in this book, especially John P. Moran III, who researched and wrote the chapter on gesture. Others to whom we are indebted include Ramona Smith and Pat Moran, who helped with the early stages of the manuscript; Dwayne VanRheenen, University of Maine, Orono; Robert Smith, Wichita State University; John Stewart, University of Washington, Seattle; Blaine Goss, University of Oklahoma, Norman; Andrew Wolvin, University of Maryland, College Park; and our editors, Richard Crews and Gail Rosicky. We deeply appreciate their work and their interest in this book.

Dennis R. Smith

L. Keith Williamson

This text, *Interpersonal Communication: Roles, Rules, Strategies, and Games,* is accompanied by the following learning aid:
Instructor's Resource Manual

Acknowledgments

Quotations on pp. 6–7 and 89–90, "John: . . . All those casualties . . . the old mistakes." and p. 293, "Timmy: . . . There was a dream . . . Both in tears, they embrace. . . .)" Abridged from pp. 6–7, 70–71 in *The Subject Was Roses* by Frank D. Gilroy. Copyright © 1962 by Frank D. Gilroy. Reprinted by permission.

Quotations on p. 87, "Michael: . . . I mean . . . truly ashamed. . . ." and p. 87, "Donald: You know . . . Want some?" Reprinted with the permission of Farrar, Straus & Giroux, Inc. from *The Boys in the Band* by Mart Crowley, Copyright © 1968 by Mart Crowley.

Quotations on p. 93, "Martha: (To Nick) Well, did you two . . . upstairs and listen in?"; p. 321, "George: There you are . . . a great big dwink."; and p. 321–22, "Martha: George is not preoccupied . . . (Under her breath). Jesus!" Excerpts from the play *Who's Afraid of Virginia Woolf?* by Edward Albee. Copyright © 1962 by Edward Albee. Reprinted by permission of Atheneum Publishers. All rights, including professional, amateur, motion picture, recitation, lecturing, public reading, radio and television broadcasting, and the rights of translation into foreign languages are strictly reserved.

Diagrams on p. 115. Adapted from *Interpersonal Perception* by R. D. Laing, H. Phillipson, and A. R. Lee. Copyright © 1966 by the authors. Reprinted with permission of Springer Publishing Co., Inc.

Photograph on p. 189. From the CBS Television program "Captain Kangaroo," starring Bob Keeshan. Reproduced by permission.

HISTORICAL PERSPECTIVE

Traditions in the Study of Interpersonal Communication

Our age has been characterized as an age of anxiety—a period in the history of civilization in which the lives of people are dominated by anxiety. This is certainly not a new phenomenon. The end of each of the great periods in history, when the institutions and social structures of that civilization began to collapse, has been dominated by anxiety.

Paul Tillich, a great Protestant theologian, has pointed out that different types of anxiety have marked different eras of Western civilization.[1] At the end of the ancient civilization, the lives of the people were dominated by a great ontic anxiety—an anxiety associated with the fear of death. This anxiety of death, combined with the collapse of the great Greco-Roman civilization, pointed the way to the life-style that was to become known as the Middle Ages. At the end of the Middle Ages, when social institutions such as the Church were losing their influence due to the rise of scientific and democratic thought, the people were confronted with a moral anxiety—anxiety associated with the fear of moral condemnation.

We find ourselves today at the end of another great period in history. For the past 100 years, world civilization has been in upheaval marked by long periods of global war and massive economic change. The institutions of modern scientific civilization are collapsing; virtually all existing social structures, including the family and the state, are being challenged. Tillich sees this as the end of modern civilization.

What is unique about our period in history is the nature of our anxiety. We are no longer dominated by anxiety of death or anxiety of moral condemnation. We are dominated instead by a spiritual anxiety— anxiety associated with the fear of meaninglessness.

1. Paul Tillich, *The Courage to Be* (New Haven: Yale University Press, 1952), p. 41.

The search for meaning leads many people to various kinds of encounter groups and communication training.

This anxiety of meaninglessness is found in all aspects of our lives. Is my life meaningful? is a question we all have asked as we examine our marriages, our family relationships, our friendships, our jobs and our material possessions. Too often we don't know how to grapple with the question; we find ourselves lacking the concepts and techniques for analyzing what meaning is and how meaning is created. In an age dominated by a great anxiety of meaninglessness, it is not surprising that there is intense interest in the study of communication. For in its broadest sense, communication can be viewed as *the process of creating meaning.*[2]

THE SEARCH FOR MEANING

THE SIGNS OF THE SEARCH TODAY

Our popular culture reflects our society's preoccupation with the anxiety of meaninglessness. Listen to any ten of the most popular songs today. At least half of them will likely be concerned with some dimension of communication between people. Examine a list of the current best-selling nonfiction books. The titles of some best-sellers from the past few years are *The Prophet, Games People Play, Between Parent and Child, I'm O.K.—You're O.K., The Joy of Sex, The Sensuous*

2. Dean C. Barnlund, "Toward a Meaning-centered Philosophy of Communication," *Journal of Communication* 11 (1962): 198–202.

Woman, The Sensuous Man, Joy, Alive. Such books are about ways to improve our communication and make our lives more meaningful.

There is hardly a social institution or group in our culture today that is not, in some way, concerned with the study of human communication. The institutions of business and industry, banking and finance, religion, education, medicine, law, labor, government, scientific research, and mental health—all have organized programs of training and research in communication. Each institution seeks to understand how people create meaning in their interaction with others.

We have witnessed the development of numerous programs and movements concerned with problems in interpersonal communication: sensitivity encounters or T-groups, communication training, human growth groups, human potential groups, self-awareness groups, encounter groups, self-disclosure groups, marriage counseling, family therapy, group therapy, Transactional Analysis, Gestalt therapy, social welfare, and guidance and counseling programs. People have turned to these groups with the hope of making their patterns of living more meaningful.

COMING TO TERMS WITH THE CONCEPT OF MEANING

This desire to understand how we create meaning has had an impact throughout our educational system—in the universities as well as in training programs in business and industry. Often people are demanding greater understanding than they are getting. Many people have discovered that it is not enough simply to *encounter* other people, whether they be strangers or close professional associates. Nor are they satisfied merely to get together to reveal themselves within the protection of isolated groups. The anxiety over meaninglessness does not go away even when people lose themselves in "touchy-feely" exercises. Such groups and educational programs are satisfying only if they help us understand how we collaborate to create meaning in our everyday relationships. Most people already have opportunities to communicate with other people. They are looking for ways to make communication more meaningful in the real world of day-to-day living.

But there's the rub, so to speak. For the study of human communication is one of the most complex and difficult tasks ever undertaken by mankind. The stark fact of the matter is that even the complexities of atomic physics and biochemistry have yielded to systematic study faster than have the secrets of communication.

Why should this be so? Two reasons readily appear. First, the process of communication is exceedingly complex. In the evolution of biological systems, communication between human beings is one of the most complex developments. The concept of meaning—possibly the most advanced achievement of animals on the earth—has been reached only by man and perhaps the dolphin.

It is perhaps understandable that we would achieve scientific insight into how people create meaning only after we had gained insight into the biological and physical world. Human communication involves virtually all other levels of biological and physical phenomena. Common sense observation tells us that the chemical effects of alcohol, marijuana, and other drugs alter our concepts of ourselves and our interactions with others. Physiological changes in the body such as puberty, menstruation and menopause may radically affect our communication and relationships with other people. Therefore, knowledge of the physical and biological world appears to be helpful, if not necessary, to understanding communication.

Paradoxically, the second reason understanding has been delayed is that communication may be too simple for our examination. In some ways, the process of communication between people is too obvious, too ordinary to hold our interest for long scientific study. Often our everyday, healthy conversations are not terribly interesting.

Let us look at an actual conversation between two people who have just met at a party at the home of a mutual friend.

> Pat: *I have to leave now. Gotta be up and to work early. Would you like to walk me to the car?*
>
> Jim: *Yes, very much. (They leave the house.) I'm really glad that I had the chance to meet you this evening. I'd like to see you again.*
>
> Pat: *Well, if you're going to be in the city, maybe we can get tickets to the orchestra or go to dinner, if you would like.*
>
> Jim: *Fine, I'll call you sometime next week. Goodnight.*

The setting and the situation of this conversation are potentially interesting. But the actual conversation is very straightforward and undramatic. Nothing goes wrong between Pat and Jim; there are apparently no breakdowns, no hang-ups, no unresolved tensions, no ulterior motives. There is nothing to hold our attention.

Compare the first conversation with one between a husband and wife discussing their son who has just returned home from the army.

> John: *. . . All those casualties and he never got a scratch. We're very lucky. . . . Think he enjoyed the party?*
>
> Nettie: *He seemed to.*
>
> John: *First time I ever saw him take a drink.*

Nettie: *He drank too much.*

John: *You don't get out of the army every day.*

Nettie: *He was sick during the night.*

John: *Probably the excitement.*

Nettie: *It was the whiskey. You should have stopped him.*

John: *For three years he's gotten along fine without anyone telling him what to do.*

Nettie: *I had to hold his head.*

John: *No one held his head in the army.*

Nettie: *That's what he said.*

John: *But that didn't stop you.*

Nettie: *He's not in the army any more.*

John: *It was a boy that walked out of this house three years ago. It's a man that's come back in.*

Nettie: *You sound like a recruiting poster.*

John: *You sound ready to repeat the old mistakes.*[3]

Where the conversation between Pat and Jim is open and spontaneous, the conversation between Nettie and John is filled with tension, double meanings, hidden motives, subtle accusations, evaluation and defensiveness. We are immediately aware that there are problems between Nettie and John; and in the perverse way of all human beings, we immediately become tremendously interested. If ordinary, healthy communication does not usually hold our attention for long, problems in interpersonal communication usually fascinate us.

Most of us instinctively recognize healthy communication in others —communication that is appropriate, satisfying, enriching to individuals and relationships. We also usually notice others' disturbed or unhealthy communication—communication that creates difficulties in living and prevents intimacy. But most of us are only indirectly aware of whether our own communication is healthy or disturbed. We get vague feelings that we may have problems in communication from the long-range effects we have on others.

Jane, for instance, is very attractive; people go out of their way to meet her. Yet Jane slowly realized that few people talked to her for very long and few of her friends continued to see her for much more than a month. Tom realized that he could not keep a secretary for more than a few weeks. John grew discouraged because all of his relationships

3. Frank D. Gilroy, *The Subject Was Roses* (New York: Samuel French, 1962), act 1, sc. 1, pp. 6–7.

ended in arguments. At first he blamed everybody else; then he began to wonder if the problem was in the way he interacted with others.

Much of our understanding of communication tends to be naive or intuitive. Most of us do not have the tools or techniques, the practical knowledge to come to grips with our own communication difficulties. We understand problems in interpersonal communication in much the same way that the Supreme Court understands pornography. We can't define it or say what it is, but we know it when we see it.

Such vague understanding of something so basic to our lives is not good enough. Most of us are vitally interested in better understanding how we communicate. We want to be able to identify communication problems when they occur and to cope with them—to untie the knots in which we so often find ourselves and others bound.

Therefore, this book is designed with two purposes in mind: to help the student understand the basic concepts involved in interpersonal communication; and to help the student develop patterns of behavior that will lead to improved health in communication and interpersonal relationships.

Achieving these goals is not always easy. How people communicate —how they arrive at patterns of mutual influence with one another— has been the subject of intensive study by many disciplines for over one hundred years. Fields as diverse as psychiatry and electrical engineering have contributed to the study. Each field has made its own discoveries and has introduced into the study many of its own concepts and terms. In this text, we have tried to draw these concepts together into a coherent, systematic analysis of interpersonal behavior and experience.

To understand any phenomenon, it is necessary to conceive of some basic unit around which an understanding of the total phenomenon can be built. In biology, for example, the concept of the cell and the concept of the DNA molecule as a double helix were two breakthroughs that rapidly advanced the study of biology. The discovery of the quantum as a structure of nuclear processes permitted the rapid development of atomic physics.

Until very recently, the major concern in the study of interpersonal communication was the search for a basic, integrating unit. Such a unit could be used to study the processes by which two people form relationships and generate meaning within those relationships. Only in the last twenty years has such a concept emerged. The concept of the *transaction* seems to be the long-sought breakthrough in the study of interpersonal communication. To understand the nature of this central concept, it is useful to understand the historical traditions from which it emerged.

THE PSYCHOANALYTIC TRADITION

Probably the oldest and most important scientific study of interpersonal communication is the field of psychoanalysis. Speech communication behavior was one of the primary interests of Sigmund Freud, the "father" of psychoanalysis. Freud focused his attention on communication problems—the difficulties that people have in living. Freud was fascinated by the communicative function of dreams. He also spent much effort on understanding the meaning of slips of the tongue, unconscious speech behavior, the power of language in producing hypnosis, the communicative function of hysteria, and the relationship between language and physical illness. Freud applied his scientific training to the study of the communicative dimensions of symbols and symbolic behavior with more success than anyone before him.

Freud's emphasis upon understanding the communicative function of pathologies in behavior shaped the study of interpersonal communication for the half century following his initial work. Until the last decade, very little attention was paid to the dynamics of healthy communication *per se*. Again it has been a case of the pathological holding our fascination much more than the healthy, of the abnormal and unusual interesting us while the normal and usual eludes our study.

In analyzing pathological behavior, Freud discovered that some illnesses may be attempts to communicate with others when the more normal channels of communication become blocked. When there is no damage to the nerves or muscles, the paralyzed arm of a hysterical soldier may be a message expressing his fear or moral revulsion of battle. A mother who compulsively washes her hands or looks through drawers might be communicating her fear of failure in raising her children. A suicide attempt might be diagnosed as a desperate cry for help. In each case the act may be seen as having meaning.

Freud based his entire analysis of human behavior on the principle of *psychic determinism*—perhaps his most significant contribution to the study of communication.[4] The principle of psychic determinism is the assumption that *all behavior, and therefore all communication, is purposeful.* From the psychoanalytic point of view, no behavior is accidental. Every behavior has an underlying connection with previous behavior. The "slip" of the tongue is never random; the "slip" actually reflects deeply held beliefs and attitudes of the speaker. Likewise, hysteria and schizophrenia represent certain specific and identifiable traumatic experiences in the earlier life of the patient. They are communication behaviors related to past experiences.

4. Charles Brenner, *An Elementary Textbook of Psychoanalysis* (New York: International Universities Press, 1955; Garden City, N.Y.: Doubleday & Co., Anchor Books, 1957), pp. 2–3.

Thus Freud's basic approach was the belief that all behavior, even irrational behavior, possessed an underlying, identifiable logic. Yet looking at moment-to-moment sequences of behavior, Freud noticed that many behaviors do not seem to relate to anything in the immediately surrounding stimuli or to immediately previous behavior and experience. This observation led to his postulation of the *theory of the unconscious*.[5]

Freud believed that the behavior a person displays at a given moment does not necessarily follow from an immediately previous behavior. What appears in a person's behavior at one time might be related to an event that occurred at a much earlier time. A trauma occurring in childhood might surface in the behavior of the person as a young adult. Stimuli encountered in the morning might not be responded to until late in the afternoon. The connection between the two events lies in the unconscious.

A familiar example of this unconscious connection is the experience of humming a tune but not knowing why you are humming it. For instance, one morning Helen's clock radio awakened her playing "Bridge Over Troubled Waters." That early in the morning, she was not fully aware of what was on the radio; she was concentrating on waking up. But five hours later, she was sitting in her office humming "Bridge Over Troubled Waters." There seemed to be no stimulus in her immediate environment or experience to account for her humming that particular song. The radio was tuned to a news broadcast. There was nothing on her desk to remind her directly of the song. No one had just mentioned the song. It seemed to be coming out of nowhere.

From a psychoanalytic point of view, Helen's behavior does make sense. Her clock radio was the stimulus directly connected to "Bridge Over Troubled Waters." The stimulus entered her unconscious in the morning; her response in the afternoon is directly connected to that earlier experience.

The theory of the unconscious explains other types of behavior common to us all. One professor reported to us the following incident: "A student was discussing with me his term project on the rhetoric of modern folk music. Suddenly he looked a little blank, then blurted out 'Mary Tyler Moore,' shook his head, and returned to the conversation we were having. I asked him what Mary Tyler Moore had to do with anything we were talking about. He smiled and explained that coming to school several hours earlier, he had sat facing an advertisement with a picture of someone he recognized but whose name he could not remember. Suddenly, during our conversation, the name of the person in the picture popped into his mind and he felt that he needed to verbalize

5. Ibid., pp. 2, 4–15.

it because he had been thinking so hard to remember who it was."

In both these examples, much other behavior and experience had intervened between the stimulus and the response. But the theory of the unconscious accounts for a direct connection between a stimulus at one time and a response at some later time; it also allows for the intervention of other behaviors between the stimulus and the response.

The two principles—psychic determinism and the unconscious— together form the basic framework of psychoanalytic theory. During his lifetime, Freud developed several models of the unconscious and was in the process of revising his famous concepts of id, ego, and superego when he died.[6] Students and followers of Freud, such as Jung, Horney, Sullivan, Fromm, and others, modified the principle in various ways to account for the complexity of mental illness. Freud's theory of the unconscious remains an important principle in Freudian psychology and in understanding communication behavior. Theorists who were primarily concerned with diagnosing and treating pathologies in communication (such as hysteria, schizophrenia, paranoia, and compulsive behaviors) tended to emphasize the principle of the unconscious in their research and clinical treatment. Yet very little has been done even today to apply the principle of the unconscious to the study of normal, healthy interpersonal communication.

On the other hand, Freud's principle of psychic determinism has been incorporated into the study of normal, healthy communication. The initial discovery that all communicative behavior is purposeful has led to some of the most important breakthroughs in our understanding of human communication. The principle of psychic determinism, and its modifications, led to the discovery of the principle that one cannot not communicate, and from there to the discovery of communication paradoxes, double binds, paradoxical injunctions, and the concept of games—concepts that we will discuss in later chapters.

6. Ibid., pp. 34–37; and Calvin S. Hall, *A Primer of Freudian Psychology* (New York: World Publishing Co., 1954; reprint ed., New York: New American Library, Mentor Books, 1954), p. 17.

The principle of psychic determinism as discussed by Freud held that there is a single, simple cause for every behavior. In recent years, the concept has been modified to take into account probability theories associated with quantum theory and general system research. In this form the principle of psychic determinism holds that there may be more than one condition that leads to the same response, or conversely, that the same condition may lead to more than one response. In both cases one can calculate the probability of a particular condition and a particular response becoming associated. A detailed example of this is presented in the section on information theory in this chapter.

Freud demonstrated that the theoretical and methodological tools of science could be fruitfully applied to the study of communication behavior. He firmly established that communication could be studied scientifically in any setting—in the clinics, in hospitals, in the street, in families. He showed, in fact, that we must consider communication in its context. For out of context, the communication makes no sense. The paralysis of the rifle arm of a soldier is meaningful within the context of battle. The same behavior isolated in the laboratory makes little sense. We cannot experiment upon the soldier's behavior; we cannot reproduce the conditions of the trauma that led to the soldier choosing hysteria as his means of communication; we do not have the capability in our laboratories of blocking all other channels of communication. As scientists, we must look to the individual in his or her real life context and, like Freud, draw upon all of our scientific knowledge to try to make sense out of what we observe.

Finally, we should not ignore Freud's contributions to the study of language. In his early studies, Freud became fascinated with hypnosis. Why could language used in a certain way induce hypnotic states? Why could hypnosis, induced by words, help the patient give up his or her symptoms? In his later studies, Freud discovered that hypnosis was not necessary to obtain the same results. A person engaged in discussion with the analyst might be able to give up the symptoms of a neurosis or psychosis simply by encountering the problem through communication.

Although Freud failed to discover a basic integrating unit for the study of interpersonal communication, he laid the groundwork for its discovery. It is unfortunate that psychoanalytic studies have been separated from the study of normal, healthy communication for so long, since one cannot begin to understand the transactional process without reference to psychoanalysis. Although Freud and his followers were more concerned with the dynamics of intrapsychic processes, the foundations of the concept of the transaction lie within Freud's principle of psychic determinism. We shall see this developed more fully later in our discussion of the nature of a transaction.

THE SYMBOLIC INTERACTION TRADITION

From the psychoanalytic theorists, the search for basic concepts in interpersonal communication moved to a group of people who became identified as *symbolic interaction theorists*. Symbolic interactionism arose as a school of thought led by key figures such as George Herbert Mead, Charles Cooley, John Dewey, and Harry Stack Sullivan. Like Freud, these men greatly influenced many disciplines—particularly sociology, social psychology, and American psychiatry. Individually and collectively, these men and their followers advanced our knowledge of the nature of interpersonal communication and its relationship to society.

Symbolic interactionists held that the chief integrating concept in interpersonal communication was the *self* or the self-system.[7] They observed that the self is created and maintained through social interaction. In turn, the concept of self modifies all interaction of the individual with society.

These theorists observed that human infants are born not with a developed langauge, but with the capacity to learn human languages. Infants do not speak English or Chinese when they emerge from the womb; they learn the language of the group in which they are reared. Likewise, infants are not born with an already formed gestural system; they have the capacity to learn the set of gestures used by their society. Thus each person learns language, gestures, and the roles and rules for using these communication systems from the society in which he or she is reared.

In early infancy the child learns communication skills from the family and culture by sheer imitation. From imitation the infant progresses to imitation with understanding. Then through extensive play, the child learns a variety of roles within the society and begins to comprehend the rules associated with each role played. With experience the child begins to internalize certain roles which eventually come together to form what the child finally experiences as the self. With the further development of language, the child begins to understand how other "selves" would react in situations similar to the child's experiences. Finally, each child develops the ability to empathize with others in situations that he or she has not experienced.[8]

While the psychoanalytic theorists were primarily concerned with psychic processes within the individual, the symbolic interactionists were focusing attention upon the social dimensions of our communication behavior. Although the psychoanalysts and the symbolic interactionists disagreed on certain aspects of communication theory, theorists such as Harry Stack Sullivan demonstrated the important relationship between the two approaches to interpersonal communication.[9] Their analyses often focused upon the concept of *role*.

7. Jerome G. Manis and Bernard N. Meltzer, eds., *Symbolic Interaction: A Reader in Social Psychology* (Boston: Allyn and Bacon, 1967).

8. For a concise description of this role-taking theory of empathy, see David K. Berlo, *The Process of Communication: An Introduction to Theory and Practice* (San Francisco: Rinehart Press, 1960), pp. 124–29.

9. Harry Stack Sullivan, *The Interpersonal Theory of Psychiatry,* ed. Helen Swick Perry and Mary Ladd Gawel (New York: W. W. Norton & Co., 1953).

Psychoanalytic theory, especially under the influence of Carl Jung, focused upon the use of symbols and symbolic behavior in maintaining the continuity of the personality of human beings within the framework of societies and cultures. It is obvious that societies may exist for three or four hundred years, and cultures for two or three thousand years, while an individual usually lives for less than eighty years. Jung believed that symbols exist in a collective unconscious. *The collective unconscious transcends the individual, yet each individual draws his or her use of symbols from it.*

The symbolic interaction theorists also viewed symbols as the fundamental elements of society. However, they were more concerned with how societies and cultures operate to create the individual personality or self experienced by the individual as "I" or "me." In this sense, the psychoanalytic theorists and the symbolic interactionists may be seen as studying different faces of the same coin, one telescoping from symbols to culture, the other from symbols to the self.

The concept of *role* has been a unique contribution of symbolic interaction theories of communication. In the research and literature, the term *role* has been used in two ways, designating essentially two different aspects of the same concept. In general, the symbolic interaction theorists use the term *role* to designate the *sociological role*—a particular set of behaviors associated with a particular function within a society. A person could assume various roles, such as mother, father, son, daughter, teacher, doctor, lawyer, or peacemaker. The functions of a sociological role are prescribed by the society. The specific nature of the role, however, may vary from society to society. Every society has a role it calls father; yet the functions and definitions of a father may differ greatly. In our society the role of father is usually based on a genetic relationship with the child. In other societies, genetic relationships may be unimportant. The father may simply be the person who assumes primary responsibility for a younger person.

Each person may be expected to play many roles either at the same time or at different times during his or her life. A person may simultaneously be a mother, a daughter, a sister, a counselor, and a businesswoman. In general, all mothers in our society behave similarly because of the social expectations associated with the role they are playing. The same is true for all daughters, all sisters—in short, for every role. We call a person mother because she *assumes* the role of mother. If she violates the social expectations of the role, social wags will say, "Look at her, she's no mother. Those children just don't have a mother." These statements refer to the sociological role a person plays in relationship to other people in the society and not to any particular physiological or genetic relationship associated with birth or conception.

The term *role* is also used to refer to the *psychological role*. The psychological role is based on the sociological concept of role but refers more to the attitude one assumes in fulfilling a given role. Gary may be a professor (sociological role). It is possible for him to assume different psychological roles within the acceptable behaviors of his sociological role of professor. Gary may be a demanding professor, a sympathetic professor, an absentminded professor, an aloof professor. Each of the psychological positions (demanding, sympathetic, absentminded, aloof) indicate an attitude or style that Gary could adopt in translating his role of professor into behavior in relation to other people.

In this book the term *role* usually refers to both the sociological and the psychological roles a person adopts in interactions with others. When we analyze Gary's interpersonal communication, we analyze his communication role as an absentminded professor or a sympathetic advisor or whatever combination of sociological and psychological roles he assumes at the time.

Both the concept of the self and the concept of role have proven to be valuable contributions and are now seen as integral parts of interpersonal communication. Yet neither concept can explain complex communication behavior and experience sufficiently to serve as a basic unit of communication analysis.

Throughout our study we shall see the influence of the symbolic interaction theorists. The concept of the self and the processes that create and maintain the self are the central concerns of the study of interpersonal communication. In fact, we might observe that the study of interpersonal communication is actually a study of how we obtain our self-concepts through our interaction with significant others in the family, the society, and the culture.

THE CYBERNETIC TRADITION

About the time that the symbolic interaction theories were having their greatest influence in sociology and social psychology, the center of study of communication shifted away from the social sciences to the field of electrical engineering—a field that would seem at first to be quite unrelated. For a period of almost twenty-five years, the study of human communication was dominated by various areas of engineering: first by information theory, then by cybernetics, and finally by general system theory.

The sudden emergence of the engineering sciences as a means of studying interpersonal communication produced a sharp turn in the

Research in the engineering sciences led to great advances in communications technology.

direction of research—a turn away from the concept of meaning.[10] The engineering sciences considered it irrelevant to examine whether there was anything meaningful betwen two objects engaged in interaction. They were more concerned with the effects that one person or object had on another person or object through the exchange of messages.

The period between 1940 and 1965 produced amazing advances in communications technology: the creation of guided missile systems, automatic guided weapons, and high-speed computers. The discoveries in the electrical engineering sciences led people to speculate upon the possible relationships between machine communications and communication between human brains.[11] Striking analogies between the mechanics of the computer and the switching mechanisms of the human brain led some scientists to conclude that the brain was simply an advanced computer. If the brain could be studied as a complex computer, then the interpersonal communication between two brains could be seen as essentially the same as the communication between two me-

10. Claude E. Shannon and Warren Weaver, *The Mathematical Theory of Communication* (Urbana, Ill.: University of Illinois Press, Illini Books, 1949), p. 31.

11. W. Ross Ashby, *Design for a Brain: The Origin of Adaptive Behavior* (London: Chapman & Hall, 1952; Science Paperbacks, 1965).

chanical computers. Rather than studying people in interaction, it would be easier to study two computers in interaction and generalize the findings to all complex automata, including human beings.

Information Theory. In the early stages of research, engineering scientists, led by Claude Shannon of the Bell Laboratories, conceptualized the communication system as a collection of elements identified as sender, message, and receiver.[12] The function of the sender was to encode and transmit a message to some other point in space. The function of the receiver was to decode the message and to act on the information contained in the message. For all practical purposes, information theorists considered the receiver to be simply a machine that engaged in the reverse functions of the sender. A message was defined as a measurable unit of overt activity capable of transmission over some channel. Every message was seen as being time-bound; a message had an observable and well-defined beginning and an observable and well-defined end.

To the information theorists, the basic unit of communication had little to do with the sender and the receiver. The basic unit of communication was not even the message; it was a particular characteristic of the message—*information*. With the discovery of the concept of information, many theorists believed they had at last discovered the secret of the complex processes of communication. At first, advances in communication research came quickly. Great strides were made in computer design, the processing, storage, and retrieval of information, and the high-speed transmission of information over complex radio, microwave, and laser beam networks.

Although the concept of information eventually showed itself to be unsatisfactory for analyzing and understanding communication between two human beings, the concept remains important and appears in much of the research on interpersonal communication. It is important, therefore, that we obtain at least an elementary understanding of the concept of information and its role in the search for a basic unit of human communication.

The concept of information grew out of a theory of probability put forth by Willard Gibbs to explain some of the contradictions appearing in the research in various areas of physics.[13] Gibbs broke with the idea of simple causation which formed the framework of Newtonian physics and was the basis of Freud's analysis of human communication behavior. Gibbs joined Werner von Heisenberg in postulating that there is

12. Shannon and Weaver, *Mathematical Theory of Communication*, pp. 33–34. *Information source,* which is Shannon and Weaver's term for sender, emphasizes their information-centered (rather than meaning-centered) orientation.

13. Norbert Wiener, *The Human Use of Human Beings: Cybernetics and Society* (Boston: Houghton Mifflin Co., 1950; New York: Avon Books, 1967), pp. 14–21.

always an uncertainty in the actions of the universe.[14] This uncertainty arises because the universe has a natural tendency to move toward disorganization. The sun is burning itself up, the earth is losing its heat into space, hot water tends to become cool when left standing, etc. This tendency of nature to move toward disorganization is known as *entropy*.

Information theorists discovered that it was possible not only to measure the amount of disorganization that occurs naturally in the physical universe, but also to measure the amount of uncertainty (caused by this disorganization) that could be reduced by human action. *Information* was conceived as the measure of uncertainty reduced through the exchange of messages. The measure of uncertainty, and therefore the measure of information, was called a binary unit, or a *bit*.

We can illustrate the concepts of information, bit, and redundancy in the following situation. Suppose that we know there is an x somewhere in this diagram, but we do not know the location of the x.

It is possible systematically to reduce the uncertainty in our knowledge about the location of the x by asking questions about the diagram that can be answered with a binary response. A binary response is the answer to a question that can have two and only two possible answers. Thus, the first step in applying information theory to the problem is to phrase all possible questions so that they can be answered with a simple yes or no.

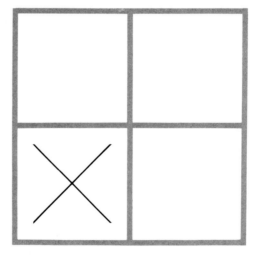

Locate the x through binary questions. How many binary questions does it take to find it?

14. Werner von Heisenberg, *Philosophy and Physics* (New York: Harper Torchbooks, Science Library, 1958).

Having limited the possible answers, we may ask the question, Is the x in the top half of the diagram? The answer is no. We have obtained one binary unit, or one bit, of information and we have reduced the uncertainty over the location of the x by exactly one-half. We may next ask, Is the x in the left half of the diagram? The answer is yes. We have once again reduced the remaining uncertainty by one binary unit, or by one-half of the remaining uncertainty, and we have located the x.

If the second question we had asked had been, Is the x in the bottom half of the diagram? we would have received the answer yes. But since we already knew that the x was not in the top half of the diagram, the answer to this question would not have reduced our uncertainty by any additional amount. Instead of producing information, the answer to that question would have produced *redundancy*.

The concept of information was applied to research in human communication by studying messages in terms of both the amount of information exchanged and the probability associated with the information exchanged.[15] For example, we can study the exchange between two persons who meet each other every morning in the hallway outside their offices.

> Jones: *Good morning.*
>
> Smith: *Good morning. How are you?*
>
> Jones: *Fine. Have a good day.*

In the broadest sense of the method, we can divide the exchange of messages between Jones and Smith into binary units to determine whether there was any information exchanged. We could posit that Jones had at least a binary choice in answering the question, "How are you?" He could have said, "Fine." Or he could have said, "Terrible." If we assume that these were the two choices available to Jones, then we could say that Smith gained one bit of information in the exchange.

Our common sense tells us, however, that the exchange was mostly ritual and had very little to do with conveying information. There is something more going on in the exchange than the transmission of information—something that appears to be meaningful in some way to both Jones and Smith.

Although information theory does not deal with the concept of meaning (and in fact is totally incapable of dealing with it), it is possible to make a little more sense out of the exchange between Smith and Jones than we get from simply counting the bits of information ex-

15. A typical example of such research is provided by G. A. Miller and E. A. Friedman, "The Reconstruction of Mutilated English," *Information and Control* 1 (1957): 38–55. An extensive review and analysis of this type of research appears in Wendell Garner, *Uncertainty and Structure as Psychological Concepts* (New York: John Wiley & Sons, 1962).

Suppose we observe Smith and Jones on 100 different mornings and compile data on their behavior.

1. On three out of four mornings Smith initiates the conversation; on one in four mornings Jones initiates the conversation.

2. When Smith initiates the conversation, he asks, "How are you today?" two-thirds of the time; the other one-third of the time he asks, "How are things going?"

3. When Jones initiates the conversation, he always says, "Nice day, isn't it?" to which Smith always responds, "Yes. How are you today?"

4. When Smith asks, "How are you today?" Jones always responds, "Fine."

5. When Smith asks, "How are things going?", Jones says, "So-so, I guess."

When Smith and Jones meet each other today, what is the probability that Jones will say, "Fine," in the exchange?

What is the probability that Jones will say, "So-so, I guess"?

Answers: The probability is .75 that he will say, "Fine," and .25 that he will say, "So-so."

---

changed. The exchange can be interpreted by introducing the concept of probability into the framework of information theory.

We could observe that Jones and Smith meet each other almost every morning and almost always use the same kind of greeting. If Jones says "Good morning" first, then Smith almost always asks "How are you?" But if Smith says "Good morning" first, then Jones usually says, "Nice day, isn't it?" By observing the patterns of interaction between Smith and Jones, we can begin to predict the probability of Smith initiating the exchange and the probability of Jones initiating the exchange. We can also measure the probability of the question "How are you?" appearing and the probability of the question "Nice day, isn't it?" appearing. In information theory, the probabilities of given patterns of activity appearing give the scientist important *information* about the interaction between the sender and the receiver.

By carefully measuring the amount of information and redundancy in a message, and then systematically controlling the ratio between information and redundancy in the messages, a scientist or engineer can control the probability of a given message being correctly received and decoded by a receiver. This discovery has been important in the engineering of complex telephone exchange systems and in the engineering of radio, television, radar, and microwave networks. It has also been useful in genetics and neurological research.

Cybernetics. The information theorists were primarily concerned with constructing messages that could be transmitted with precision. Cybernetic theorists (principally Norbert Weiner) focused not only on the transmission of the message, but also on the receiver's response to

People in a control room must receive feedback in order to maintain control over guided missiles and spacecraft.

the information contained in the message.[16] Cybernetics is the study of of the theory of control, and control can be achieved only if a sender knows that the receiver has decoded the message and is responding to the message as intended.

The importance of the receiver's response can be seen in the design of the Apollo rocket that took three men into orbit for the moon landing. The scientists and engineers on that project were not just concerned with whether the rocket was activated or not activated. They were much more concerned that, once in motion, the rocket would follow a very precise, predetermined course. If the senders of the control messages could not determine whether the rocket was responding correctly to their messages, they would lose control. They would be unable to keep the rocket on a course capable of achieving the orbits and the landings.

16. Wiener, *Human Use of Human Beings*, pp. 23–39.

Control over guided and self-regulating machines was achieved by introducing the concept of feedback into the communication system. For most early communication theorists, *feedback* was defined as a materially evident response of a receiver to a message. By studying the responses of the receiver, the sender could vary the information transmitted to assure that control was effected over the receiver—that the receiver was responding as the sender intended.

There are fairly obvious similarities between the communications of guided and self-regulating machines and human communication behavior. In one sense, human beings are self-regulating machines that control one another through the sending and receiving of messages. The influence of cybernetics upon the study of interpersonal communication was therefore profound. The study of information and feedback as control mechanisms in human communication led to the discovery of important laws concerning channel capacity, message transmission, and punctuation of message. These laws apply not only to two-person communication systems, but also to small groups and large societies.[17]

General System Theory. Information theory and cybernetics were eventually integrated into a broader field called general system theory.

General system theory was started by Ludwig von Bertalanffy in the 1930s as an attempt to produce theoretical concepts capable of explaining the rapid and revolutionary developments then occurring in biology, genetics, and embryology.[18] In later years, von Bertalanffy and his followers were more concerned with utilizing the concept of general system theory to demonstrate relationships between what appeared, on the surface, to be widely different fields such as biology, physics, electrical and computer engineering, and mathematics.

General system theory integrated the concepts of information and feedback into the broader concept of a system. A system usually is defined as a set of elements and their interrelationships.[19] In general system theory, information and feedback are viewed as part of the interrelationship between various elements within a system. General system theorists conceive of communication as a simultaneous process between elements of a system.

The application of general system concepts to the study of interpersonal communication finally led to the long-sought breakthrough—the discovery of a basic unit of communication. The discovery emerged

17. W. Ross Ashby, *An Introduction to Cybernetics* (London: Chapman & Hall, 1956; University Paperbacks, 1964), esp. pt. 3.

18. Ludwig von Bertalanffy, *General System Theory: Foundations, Development, Applications* (New York: George Braziller, 1968).

19. Ibid., p. 55. See also Paul Watzlawick, Janet Helmick Beavin, and Don D. Jackson, *Pragmatics of Human Communication: A Study of Interactional Patterns, Pathologies, and Paradoxes* (New York: W. W. Norton & Co., 1967), pp. 120–21.

from the unique combination of insights derived from psychiatry, electrical and computer engineering, and general system research. Instead of trying to analyze communication between two people as a series of discrete messages exchanged between a sender and a receiver, theorists such as Jurgen Ruesch, Gregory Bateson, David Berlo, Paul Watzlawick, Don Jackson, and Virginia Satir evolved the concept of interpersonal communication as a system. When these theorists started viewing communication in this way, they discovered the concept of a transactional system, or simply a *transaction*.

In a transaction, two people are never seen as discrete elements. They are always studied in relationship to each other. Within a transaction we may "exchange messages," but the "exchange" is largely an artificial breaking down of what is actually happening. For in reality, I do not send a message and wait for you to receive and respond to it. When you and I mutually perceive each other, we both *simultaneously* assign meanings to our behavior. Then, with the passage of time, we modify or change the meanings.

Using the concept of the interpersonal communication transaction, communication theorists have been able to analyze the complex dimensions of human communication in ways that were too difficult or impossible to handle through the linear approaches of information theory and feedback analyses.

RETURN TO MEANING

Meaning, of course, is a concept that lies outside of the theories of information and feedback. The concept of meaning was irrelevant to theorists interested in controlling behavior. Such analyses are perhaps useful, but they do not satisfy us that that is all there is to interpersonal communication. We can analyze the greeting between Jones and Smith; we can discover in it measurable amounts of information and calculate the probabilities of the occurrence of this information. But we are left with the feeling that Jones and Smith have engaged in something that cannot be explained in terms of information and probabilities alone.

There is something *meaningful* about the exchange between Jones and Smith as they meet in the hall every morning. Jones and Smith are establishing their identities as persons in relationship to each other, and perhaps in relationship to their jobs. They are invoking certain well-established rules that govern social interaction within their society and within the subgroup of employees in their office. Smith and Jones do not greet each other because they wish to transmit and receive information; they greet each other because it is meaningful for them to do so—and would be meaningful for them not to do so. In real life most of us find the question, How much information did you convey? to be largely irrelevant to anything we consider important. We are much more concerned with the question, What do you mean?

CONTRIBUTIONS FROM RHETORICAL TRADITIONS

Dramatism and general semantics, two branches of contemporary rhetorical theory, have made significant contributions to the study of meaning in interpersonal communication theory. Both of these traditions are concerned primarily with the nature of language and the effect of language on behavior.

Dramatism stems from the writings of Kenneth Burke, Hugh Duncan, and Erving Goffman. Dramatistic theory views human behavior as drama, especially as tragedy.[20] The most important aspect of dramatism for interpersonal communication theory is its emphasis upon the concept of role.[21]

Naming creates roles. Burke and Duncan both held that naming something implies a particular course of action toward the thing named. To call someone an enemy dictates an implicit course of action that is different from action toward someone called an ally. Thus language not only creates roles, but contains within it the implicit rules for action toward those roles.

Language, by its very nature, divides society into a hierarchy of roles; this hierarchy becomes established as social order.[22] Social order is maintained by processes of *mystification* (using words to surround a role with mystery and therefore maintain its authority) and *victimization* (using words to keep certain roles lower in the hierarchy). In both mystification and victimization, the hierarchy is created and maintained through the natural properties of language.

General semantics is the study of the relationship between words and behavior.[23] This tradition has profoundly influenced the teaching of speech. The aim of general semantics is to get people to look at the way they are using language and to try to correct some of the more damaging uses of language in society.[24] General semanticists have contributed

20. Kenneth Burke, *Permanence and Change: An Anatomy of Purpose*, 2d rev. ed., with an Introduction by Hugh Dalziel Duncan (Indianapolis, Ind.: Bobbs-Merrill Co., 1965).
21. A dramatistic approach to interpersonal communication is found in Erving Goffman, *The Presentation of Self in Everyday Life* (Garden City, N.Y.: Doubleday & Co., 1959).
22. See Hugh Dalziel Duncan, *Symbols in Society* (New York: Oxford University Press, 1968). See also Hugh Dalziel Duncan, *Communication and Social Order* (New York: Bedminster Press, 1962; London: Oxford University Press, 1968).
23. John C. Condon, Jr., *Semantics and Communication*, 2d ed. (New York: Macmillan Co., 1975).
24. Alfred Korzybski, *Science and Sanity: An Introduction to Non-Aristotelian Systems and General Semantics*, 4th ed., with new preface by Russell Meyers (Lakeville, Conn.: International Non-Aristotelian Library Pub. Co., distributed by Institute of General Semantics, 1962).

most to our present understanding of the processes of abstraction and inference.

According to general semanticists, all language is an abstraction from reality. When we name something, we do not capture the totality of the thing named. We merely call attention to certain aspects of the object. The same person may be both an enemy and an ally. The Chinese for instance may be our enemies in the struggle against communism, but they may be our allies in our efforts to contain the expansion of Russia in Asia. Either name, *enemy* or *ally,* is an abstraction associated with particular ways of behaving. This idea is similar to Burke's statement that naming is a predisposition to action.

General semanticists are also concerned with the nature of inference.[25] All naming implies drawing inferences because naming is by nature an abstraction. The inferential processes associated with the use of language are particularly important in the formation of the self and in the selection of the appropriate role for each interpersonal communication transaction. Later we will explore the concepts of abstraction and inference in greater detail.

RECENT CONTRIBUTIONS

Two other significant contributions have been made in very recent years to further our understanding of meaning in the interpersonal communication transaction. The first contribution comes from the currently popular field of Transactional Analysis developed by Eric Berne and Thomas Harris. The second comes from a large group of clinicians and therapists who might best be recognized under the label of the Human Potential Movement.

Transactional Analysis. The label applied to this branch of psychiatry founded by Eric Berne is somewhat misleading. The "transaction" in Transactional Analysis is really an interaction as we use the term in communication theory—a sequence of messages rather than a simultaneity of messages. Care should be taken not to confuse Transactional Analysis with the analysis of communication transactions. There are, of course, great similarities between the two, but the differences are significant.

Although Transactional Analysis is in some ways closely related to psychoanalytic theory, Transactional Analysis itself has grown primarily as a reaction against the strict, often dogmatic structures imposed by psychoanalytic theory on therapy. While both theories recognize unconscious motives in expressed behavior, Transactional Analysis

25. William V. Haney, *Communication and Organizational Behavior Text and Cases,* rev. ed. (Homewood, Ill.: Richard D. Irwin, 1967).

emphasizes understanding communication behavior without reference to the unconscious. In applying Transactional Analysis to the study of interpersonal communication, we limit ourselves to the study of the expressed communication. The message expressed does not necessarily represent some deeper, unconscious motivation. All of the data required to understand the relationship between the two communicants is present in the observable interaction between them.

By carefully observing and recording the ways people talk to each other, Eric Berne was able to discern strict regularities in patterns of interaction. He discovered certain patterns that simply occupy time and other patterns that progress toward intimacy between the two communicants. Still other patterns are inherently dishonest and are structured so that one of the communicants obtains a *payoff* in the interaction. Berne used the term *games* for these complementary patterns of interaction leading to payoffs.[26]

Berne observed that it always takes two people to play a game, to engage in a pastime or ritual, or to achieve intimacy. Equally important, the two people must collaborate to achieve their goal. In order for two people to be intimate, both must agree to follow the rules of their interaction for achieving intimacy. Likewise in a game, one person can achieve a payoff only if the *victim* agrees to play by the rules of the game that eventually lead to his own victimization. Games require both communicators to follow the rules very strictly for either party to partially fulfill the need to establish intimacy with another human being. If one of the persons in a dyad (a two-person communication situation) refuses to participate in the game or refuses to follow the rules of the game, the result is often despair for one or both individuals involved. In extreme cases, despair could even lead to death.

Later we will discuss the concept of games as rule behavior in much greater detail. The concept of games is probably the most significant contribution of Transactional Analysis. Even though it is still in its infancy, this theory has greatly advanced our understanding of the way most of us communicate with those we love. It is conceivable that Transactional Analysis will in turn be influenced by other advances in interpersonal communication theory.

The Human Potential Movement. In the 1960s a large number of people became associated with using sensitivity training, T-grouping, and small group therapy techniques to achieve interpersonal growth.[27]

The great strength of the Human Potential Movement is its existential position—its insistence upon our experience as human beings in our

26. Eric Berne, *Games People Play: The Psychology of Human Relationships* (New York: Grove Press, 1964), esp. pp. 48–65.

27. Kurt W. Back, *Beyond Words: The Story of Sensitivity Training and the Encounter Movement* (New York: Russell Sage Foundation, 1972; Baltimore: Penguin Books, 1973).

communication with others. Working from a basic interest in what it means to be human, writers and therapists such as Carl Rogers and William Schutz brought to interpersonal communication studies a new concern for values, courage, and freedom.[28] Institutions such as the National Training Laboratories and the Esalen Center developed techniques for use in small groups.[29] When properly applied these techniques often helped group participants to reduce their own defensiveness in communication, to disclose the self more, and to discover more of their own potential for dealing with people both at work and in personal situations.

The Human Potential Movement is primarily an attitude toward human communication behavior and experience. Its emphasis upon the role of experience in communication has helped shape the direction of interpersonal communication theory. The concern for what is human in communication will remain with us for many years to come.

TOWARD AN INTERPERSONAL THEORY OF COMMUNICATION

The range and diversity of the fields that have contributed to the study of interpersonal communication are impressive. Indeed, the subject matter itself virtually prohibits comprehensive study within the boundaries of a single field or discipline. Nevertheless, a general consensus on the nature of interpersonal communication seems to be emerging among scholars, theorists, and researchers. From the solid core of theory and research, we can formulate specific principles and integrate them into a systematic theory of interpersonal communication.

In concluding our review of the contributing traditions, it might be useful to outline in a different form the various stages through which interpersonal communication theory has progressed. We then may be better able to see where interpersonal communication theory is today— and how it got where it is.

ACTION MODELS OF COMMUNICATION

The first stage in the development of communication theory has been called the *action* stage.[30] Between 1890 and the early 1930s, the general

28. See Carl Rogers, *On Becoming a Person* (Boston: Houghton Mifflin Co., Sentry Edition, 1961), esp. pp. 273–359. See also William C. Schutz, *Joy: Expanding Human Awareness* (New York: Grove Press, 1967).

29. Back, *Beyond Words*, esp. pp. 103–16.

30. Dennis R. Smith, "Mechanical and Systemic Concepts of Feedback," *Today's Speech* 21 (Summer 1973): 23–28; John Stewart, "Introduction," in *Bridges Not Walls: A Book about Interpersonal Communication,* ed. John Stewart (Reading, Mass.: Addison-Wesley Publishing Co., 1973), pp. 8–10; Karen Rasmussen, "A Transactional Perspective," in *Persons Communicating,* ed. Donald K. Darnell and Wayne Brockriede (Englewood Cliffs, N.J.: Prentice-Hall, 1976), pp. 28–31; and Joe A. Munshaw, "The Structures of History: Dividing Phenomena for Rhetorical Understanding," *Central States Speech Journal* 24 (Spring 1973): 29–42.

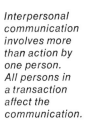

Interpersonal communication involves more than action by one person. All persons in a transaction affect the communication.

orientation to the study was drawn from linear mechanics. The first serious attempts to study systematically the way people communicate focused primarily on what the sender of a message must do in order to establish control over a receiver. The main question of interest was, How must a speaker *act* in order to persuade his listener? In psychiatry and psychology the question would be phrased, What is causing the patient to communicate in abnormal channels? or What must a therapist *do* in order to change a patient's behavior? In business the question would be, How must a salesman *pitch his product* to make a sale? In religion it might be, How must a minister *speak* in order to convert his listeners?

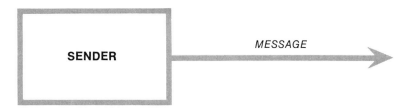

Action Model of Communication

The questions of interest in these early studies were all sender oriented. They emphasized how the sender must structure a message or a pattern of communication in order to secure a desired result. Little attention was paid to the receiver of the messages.

INTERACTION MODELS OF COMMUNICATION

The second stage in the development of interpersonal communication theory has been called the *interaction* stage.[31] As communication theorists and researchers became more and more concerned with control, they added the concept of linear feedback to communication models. Control could be achieved only if the sender knew how the receiver was responding to the message. Thus, it was necessary for the receiver to feed back to the sender certain cues about the reception of the messages. Then the sender could adjust future messages accordingly and maintain control over the receiver.

In some of the early interaction models of interpersonal communication, the interaction process was diagrammed in this form:

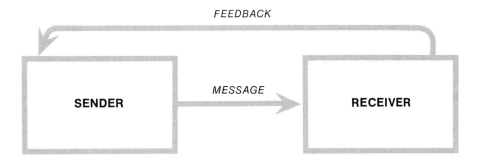

Early Interaction Model with Feedback Loop

31. Diagrams of the interaction model are derived from Smith, "Mechanical and Systemic Concepts," pp. 24–25.

However, when the dimension of time was included in the model, the linear qualities of the model became more apparent. A more accurate diagram of the basic interaction models would look like this:

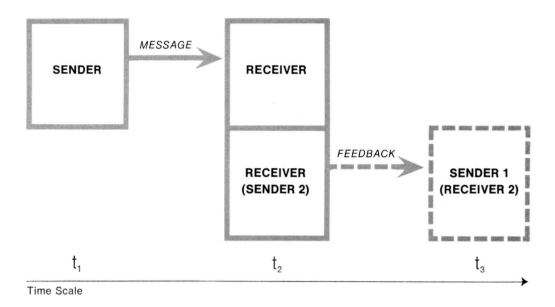

Interaction Model with Linear Feedback

In this later diagram, it is easier to see that the exchange of messages is taking place over a period of time and that the interaction actually consists of a continuity of responses between the sender and the receiver. The sender is alternately sending a message and receiving feedback from the receiver; and the receiver is alternately receiving a message and sending feedback to the sender.

Because of the alternation between sending and receiving, there is a sense in which the interaction model violates our sense of true interaction. Within the model diagrammed here, there is a continuous, sequential line of action and reaction between the sender and the receiver. There is little sense of *interaction* between them. This has been one of the major points of criticism against the interaction models of interpersonal communication.

The interaction model of interpersonal communication is best suited to the analysis of verbal messages, or of language interaction between two people. The model becomes cumbersome and loses clarity when applied to the analysis of multiple message systems operating simultaneously. While John is speaking, Mary is generating messages in many ways—through her body posture, her distance from John, her use of touch, her maintaining or avoiding eye contact, etc. If we attempt to diagram the flow of messages and potential messages generated by each person through each of their message systems, the overlapping lines begin to merge into a simultaneity of interaction which is characteristic of the transactional model. Though insufficient as a model in itself, the concept of interaction still is useful as an analytic tool within the context of the transactional model of communication.

TRANSACTIONAL MODELS OF COMMUNICATION

Models of interpersonal communication have now entered the *transactional* stage.[32] Rather than focusing upon the linear feedback which is central to the interaction model, the transactional model views communication as a *simultaneity* of responses.

The difference between the interaction and the transaction models can readily be seen in this diagram of the transactional model.

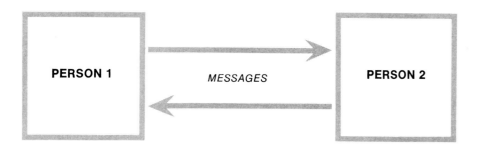

Transactional Model

The arrows indicate that both persons in the communication situation are participating simultaneously. They are mutually perceiving each other; and both persons (not just a sender) are making adjustments to messages exchanged within the transaction.

In the transactional model we observe the entire communication situation rather than isolating out an arbitrary sender and an arbitrary receiver. Because we view the entire transaction, we observe the prog-

32. Ibid. pp. 24–25 (including diagrams of the transactional model); and Rasmussen, "A Transactional Perspective," pp. 31–37.

ress of the communication by reexamining the transaction at a later time. The element of time may be diagrammed in the transactional model like this:

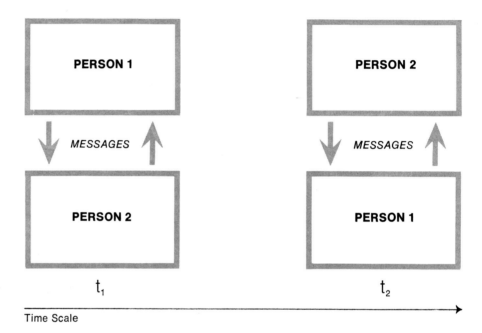

Transactional Model over Time

While the action models are adequate for describing the communication components of something like a telephone switching system, they are inadequate for describing a phenomenon as complex as two people engaged in a discussion. The interaction models have been useful for the development of guided missile control systems and even for experimentation in human communication. The transactional model presently appears to be the only model capable of describing communication between two perceiving and adapting human beings.

The transactional model is based in the historical development of the action and interaction models and thus possesses the capacity for testing and research both in the laboratory and in real life situations. Because of these strengths and its usefulness for describing the complexities of communication simply and directly, we have selected a transactional model as the basis for the theory of interpersonal communication presented in the following chapters.

SUMMARY

The study of interpersonal communication is interdisciplinary. People with an extremely diverse set of backgrounds and interests have been drawn to the study. The scientist, philosopher, psychiatrist, theologian, physician, engineer, poet—each has contributed in his or her own way to the growing body of knowledge of how human beings communicate.

There have been five basic approaches to the study of interpersonal communication. The psychoanalytic tradition is the oldest scientific study of communication processes. Much of our present theory and research is still based upon Freud's principles of psychic determinism and the unconscious. No study of interpersonal communication could be complete without incorporating the insights of psychoanalysis.

The symbolic interactionists were oriented toward the concept of the self. These theorists, with the exception of Sullivan, were more concerned with social interaction in "normal" contexts, than with abnormalities in human communication and behavior. The classroom, the family, and social groups provided the settings for the data observed by the symbolic interactionists. Out of their studies we have derived important understandings of the concept of the self and how it is created and maintained through interpersonal communication.

The cybernetic tradition began in the engineering sciences rather than the social sciences or medicine. The study of automata led engineers to speculate about the similarities between machine behavior and human behavior. From the engineering point of view, communication can be equated with control. When communication occurs, someone or something is being controlled by some other person or thing.

Cybernetics and information theory rigorously applied the concepts of information and redundancy to the study of behavior. While these fields of engineering greatly advanced our knowledge of communication processes, they appear to be limited. General system theory has sought more general applications of the basic concepts of cybernetics and information theory. General system theory moved these branches of science toward studies of processes unique to living systems, such as the creation of meaning.

Two rhetorical traditions, dramatism and general semantics, focused primarily upon the use of language. Dramatism contributed significant insights into the way language creates and maintains roles. Naming implicitly establishes a role relationship between the user of the language and the person or object named; naming also dictates a course of action toward the person or object named. General semantics expanded our understanding of the concepts of abstraction and inference and their effect on our interpersonal behavior.

Transactional Analysis and the Human Potential Movement are both relatively recent branches of mental health which have been highly influenced by psychoanalytic theory and symbolic interaction theory. Each of these new movements provides us with refinements on basic concepts—refinements that are necessary to develop a complete model of communication behavior.

Looking at the traditions in the study of interpersonal communication, we can trace the development of the lines of thought that lead to the model presented in the following chapters. The first models of interpersonal communication were action oriented, focusing primarily upon the sending of messages. These models were followed by the interaction models, which focused upon the concept of feedback. While the interaction models provided important advancements over the strictly action models and are analytically useful within the broader context of the transaction, they did not provide the degree of understanding obtainable through application of the transactional model. The transactional model appears to be uniquely suited for the study of interpersonal communication.

QUESTIONS FOR REVIEW

1. What are the two principles that underlie psychoanalytic theory? Explain each.
2. How does the symbolic interaction tradition contribute to the study of interpersonal communication?
3. What is information according to information theory? How is it related to uncertainty and redundancy?
4. What role do control and feedback play in cybernetic theory?
5. How is a system defined in general system theory? Explain how this concept advances our understanding of interpersonal communication.
6. What is the essential contribution of dramatistic theory to the study of interpersonal communication?
7. What is the importance of rules in interpersonal communication according to Transactional Analysis?
8. Characterize the chief contribution of the Human Potential Movement to the study of interpersonal communication.
9. Diagram and explain the action model of interpersonal communication.
10. Diagram and explain the interaction model of interpersonal communication.
11. Diagram and explain the transactional model of interpersonal communication.

EXPLORATIONS

1. Throughout this book we will make specific suggestions for compiling a communication journal. A loose-leaf notebook or writing pad which is to be used exclusively for the journal is best. Entries should be made in the journal at least once each week, summarizing specific events, observations, and exercises suggested in the Explorations following each chapter in this book. We suggest that the first entry in your journal be a brief essay (about 600 words) on the topic "Who am I?"

   Many people who do this exploration find it disturbing. The "I" is a very difficult thing to pinpoint and describe. In the explorations for chapter 2 we will process some of the aspects of this exploration that are more commonly (frequently) disturbing to people.

2. Take a box of children's tinker toys or a bag of odd-shaped pieces of wood. Label each major piece with the name of one of the elements of interpersonal communication that you can identify from your own experience. Now take the linking pieces or differing lengths of string and link the various labeled elements together to form a three-dimensional model of the elements of interpersonal communication.

3. Use the tinker toys or pieces of wood and string described above to construct a model of an important interpersonal relationship that you presently have—perhaps with a close friend, a husband, a wife, a lover, a parent, etc.

4. As a second entry in your journal, write a brief paragraph explaining what the word *meaning* means to you. When you have completed the paragraph, list five things that are meaningful to you at this point in your life. Closely examine each of the things that you have listed. What makes them meaningful? Does the meaning of each thing listed come from the thing itself or from the fact that the thing is associated with significant relationships with others?

5. Divide a sheet of paper in half. On one side of the page list *at least* five things that you consider to be strengths that you have in your interpersonal communication right now. On the other side of the page, list *at least* five things that you consider to be weaknesses in your interpersonal communication right now. Be honest and realistic in your assessment. When you have completed this self-inventory, construct at least five specific goals that you will seek to attain by the end of this course. State your goals in terms of specific, observable behaviors or events so that at the end of the course you can measure the degree to which you have attained these goals.

FOR FURTHER READING

Ashby, W. Ross. *An Introduction to Cybernetics.* London: Chapman & Hall, 1956; University Paperbacks, 1964.

The basic nature of cybernetics, its major concepts and themes, are detailed with technical accuracy and clear prose. Cybernetics, or the art of steermanship, is explained in terms of mechanism (an ordered system), variety (the set of possibilities for a given system), and regulation and control (order in systems, biological or otherwise). This book is probably one of the best introductions to cybernetics for anyone wanting a technically accurate view of the subject.

Brenner, Charles. *An Elementary Textbook of Psychoanalysis.* New York: International Universities Press, 1955; Garden City, N.Y.: Doubleday & Co., Anchor Books, 1957.

Brenner provides a clear, concise, and comprehensive introduction to the complex and often confusing world of psychoanalysis. The breadth of his view is indicated by the range of topics he covers, including the two fundamental hypotheses of psychoanalysis, drives, psychic apparatus, dreams, and psychopathology. Brenner presents psychoanalytic theory in a way understandable to the layperson without sacrificing its essential features.

Koestler, Arthur. *The Ghost in the Machine.* Chicago: Henry Regnery Co., 1967.

This book is a challenge to a mechanistic philosophy of the nature of man. Koestler proposes an open systems philosophy of man, built on the idea of the holon: an entity that is at one and the same time a complete, functioning unit at one level of examination, and a component in a larger unit at another level of examination. Because man is a holon, his consciousness ("the ghost in the machine") cannot be satisfactorily explained by mechanistic thinking.

Manis, Jerome G., and Meltzer, Bernard N., eds. *Symbolic Interaction: A Reader in Social Psychology.* Boston: Allyn and Bacon, 1967.

This collection of readings, comprised of journal articles and reprints of chapters from books, remains one of the best collections of literature on the symbolic interaction viewpoint. The articles summarizing and contrasting Mead and Freud, as well as the articles by Cooley, Dewey, Mills, Strauss, and Goffman, are still considered to be classics in the field.

Wiener, Norbert. *The Human Use of Human Beings: Cybernetics and Society.* Boston: Houghton Mifflin Co., 1950; New York: Avon Books, 1967.

Wiener, one of the founding fathers of the science of cybernetics, writes here in a most readable fashion about the relevance and implications of that discipline for human society and for the social sciences. Each chapter is actually an essay on some aspect of the relevance of cybernetics for history, for the study of language, for the theory and practice of law, for secrecy in society, for economics, etc.

PART I

A Transactional
Model of
Interpersonal
Communication

Chapter 1

The Structure
of an Interpersonal
Communication
Transaction

COMMUNICATION—THE CREATION OF MEANING

Ask any three or four of your classmates why they are studying inter-personal communication. Their answers may include statements such as: "I'm trying to find out who I am"; "I'm having difficulties with my husband (wife, parents, children)"; "I can't relate to my friends the way I want to"; "I want to be able to relate to my customers better"; "Maybe I can learn to stop playing games and make my relationships more meaningful." Such typical answers indicate that people often turn to the study of interpersonal communication as a means of coping with the feelings of loneliness and alienation so characteristic of our age of anxiety. The search for personal meaning somehow leads people to look more closely at their communication with others. Such a turn of events should not be surprising. For *communication is the behavior and ex-perience of organisms involved in creating meaning.*

For a period of nearly twenty years in the study of communication, no distinctions were made between human communication and machine communication. During this time, communication was seen as the proc-ess of transmitting information from one point to another. Yet the problems of interest in machine communication are fundamentally different from the problems of interest in human communication. To avoid confusion over terminology, most writers today reserve the term *communications* (spelled with an s) for the transmission of information and use of the term *communication* to designate the process of creating meaning between organisms.

When we define communication in terms of meaning, three important distinctions set it apart from information transmission between machines, automata, or living organisms.

1. *Meaning arises out of relationships between organisms.*

Unlike machines, living organisms form relationships. The process of creating meaning involves an act of union or merger between organisms. The word *communicate* literally means 'to make common'; sharing, or communion, joins different elements into a community of relationships.[1] The process of communication draws individuals together into a social unit and makes them one.

The creation of meaning involves more than making common. That which is meaningful to human beings is also that which is different. To communicate with another person it is first necessary that there be some difference. If there is absolute union, if commonness has already been achieved, then communication is not necessary. Thus meaning also arises in acts that divide or differentiate between organisms. In the broadest sense, meaning arises from the relationship between differing organisms.

In the act of communicating two people share something in common; they lose their individuality and merge into a dyad, a two-person unit. At the same time, they take on unique differences from each other within that relationship. If they are communicating as teacher and student, for instance, one becomes teacher and the other becomes student only in relation to each other. If they are communicating as friends, they take on a different set of commonness and differences and their relationship changes.

When information is being transmitted from one point to another, the idea of a relationship is not important. Two computers may be connected by a telephone hookup and the information on one tape may be transmitted to another tape across country. The data on the tapes has no meaning to either computer because the computers are incapable of perceiving relationships between them.

2. *The process of creating meaning involves both behavior and experience of oneself and another.*

Communication must always involve some behavior that can be perceived by at least one other member of the community. The human being is born behaving; in fact, it is impossible for a living individual

---

1. The notion of communication as involving both commonness and difference is taken from Kenneth Burke, *Permanence and Change: An Anatomy of Purpose*, 2d rev. ed., with an Introduction by Hugh Dalziel Duncan (Indianapolis, Ind.: Bobbs-Merrill Co., 1965).

not to behave. The behavior may be either intentional or accidental, but communication exists when some other organism perceives and interprets that behavior.

Yet the analysis of behavior, in and of itself, is inadequate for describing the process of interpersonal communication. *Experience* is as fundamental to communication as behavior. You behave; you act. But your actions cannot become communicative until I or some other organism perceives and interprets them. In this sense, all communication arises out of our experience of behavior—our perception and interpretation of actions engaged in by ourselves and others.[2]

Experience is a private phenomenon. The experience of each individual is different from the experience of every other individual. Just as no two fingerprints, eyes, ears, noses, nerve endings, or senses of balance are the same, there is a sense in which each person can say, "I am uniquely me." The fact that my body is different from your body is sufficient to explain why my experience is uniquely mine and your experience is uniquely yours.

On the other hand, experience also has a communal or shared dimension to it. The idea of *reality* is an idea of some shared experience. When you and I and others can share our experiences, we say that our experience is based in reality. When it is not possible to share one's perception and interpretation of events, we say that one's experience is based in fantasy. The difference between fantasy and reality, then, depends on the degree to which others can and do confirm or share in our experience.[3]

The idea that reality lies in the sharing of common perceptions does not rule out the possibility of dyadic, group, or national fantasies. George and Martha, in the play *Who's Afraid of Virginia Woolf?*, agree to fantasize the existence of a son; for twenty-one years they both act as if the imaginary son were real. This is a dyadic fantasy, which is an essential part of their relationship. The ancient Roman belief in Roman invincibility, the Nazi belief in the reign of the Third Reich, and the nineteenth century American belief in Manifest Destiny are examples of national or group fantasies.

When we say that communication involves both behavior and experience, we are speaking of experience that can be shared or confirmed by others—not fantasies. When others can share our experiences, it becomes possible for us to see both our own behavior and the behavior

2. R. D. Laing, H. Phillipson, and A. R. Lee, *Interpersonal Perception: A Theory and a Method of Research* (New York: Springer Publishing Co., 1966; New York: Harper & Row, Perennial Library, 1972), p. 15.

3. Shared experience (*interexperience*) and fantasy are discussed by R. D. Laing, *The Politics of Experience* (New York: Ballantine Books, 1967), pp. 17–45; and also by Laing, Phillipson, and Lee, *Interpersonal Perception*, pp. 12–45.

of others as meaningful. When we communicate, we must experience each other's behavior in a way that can be validated by others.

3. *Meaning involves the experience of loneliness and love.*

Love is a four-letter word that is neither popular nor fashionable in the scientific community today. Our universities have chosen to leave the discussion of love primarily to theologians and others concerned with religious and humanistic matters rather than with scientific truth. In some ways it is easier to discuss sex in the classroom than it is to talk about love. We can make our talk about sex seem to be scientific and objective; but it is very hard to be objective and scientific about love.

It is difficult if not impossible, however, to discuss communication as the process of creating meaning between living organisms without coming face to face with the concept of love. Interpersonal communication seems to be rooted in the need to love and be loved. In fact, interpersonal communication appears to be motivated, in large part, by the need of human beings to overcome loneliness and alienation from others through the establishment of intimate relationships.[4] Meaning seems to be involved with finding merger or union with at least one other human being.

We should not underestimate the power of the experience of loneliness or alienation in human affairs. Many psychologists believe birth is traumatic because it is a violent separation of the infant from its physical and psychological oneness with the mother. The traumatic loss of union experienced at birth may be felt by the adult as severe loneliness or alienation. The individual forever seeks to regain such union in interaction with others.

It is interesting to note that people often seek to change or improve their interpersonal communication as a means of transcending loneliness and alienation. How can I meet people? How can I relate to others? How can I find meaningful relationships? All such questions are about finding union with others. People seek to communicate well in order to enhance their ability to commune with others—to be a part of the human community.

Later in this book we shall see the influence of loneliness and alienation, and its counterparts, love and intimacy, at work in two ways. First, it is virtually impossible to understand certain kinds of difficult interpersonal relationships without postulating that fear of loneliness is a basic motive in interpersonal communication. Some people seem to

4. For a discussion of loneliness and the need for intimacy, see Harry Stack Sullivan, *The Interpersonal Theory of Psychiatry*, ed. Helen Swick Perry and Mary Ladd Gawel (New York: W. W. Norton & Co., 1953), esp. chaps. 16–17. See also Eric Berne, *Games People Play: The Psychology of Human Relationships* (New York: Grove Press, 1964), esp. the introduction and pts. 1 and 3.

*The experience of loneliness
and the need for love
motivate us to communicate
with other people.*

endure the most difficult patterns of interaction—constant put-downs, vicious and destructive games, etc.—rather than simply parting or finding others with whom they can have more pleasant and healthy relationships. These people choose to continue to play games and engage in unproductive communication because they fear that they might experience loneliness if they let go of their present relationships and patterns of communication. Ironically, people who have the courage to break off their game-ridden relationships and seek other healthier relationships rarely experience the degree of loneliness they had imagined. Nevertheless, it takes great courage to risk changing interpersonal relationships when loneliness appears to be the alternative.

Second, we will see that healthy communication is related to the way people handle their need to transcend loneliness through patterns of love and intimacy. When people are able to communicate in ways that establish intimacy with others in appropriate contexts, their communication is healthy.

In summary, we have seen that communication is the process of creating meaning through the behavior and experience of living organisms. Meaning arises out of relationships that involve not only union but also differentiation between the communicants. Communication involves overt behavior as well as common or shared experience between organisms. Communication is motivated by a need to transcend loneliness and alienation through love and intimacy. Communication health is determined to a large extent by the way a person handles intimacy in relationships with others.

INTERPERSONAL COMMUNICATION—BETWEEN ROLES

Communication may occur among any number of people. It appears that the number of people has some specific influences upon the way meaning is created and conveyed. Studies of communication have therefore focused upon four basic levels of social integration—social units initially defined on the basis of the number of persons involved.

The *dyad* is a two-person unit. The *small group* has at least three and usually not more than approximately fifteen to eighteen people. Generally, the *public* or large group is a collection of many people gathered together at one time in one place as in a convention or lecture or political rally. The *mass* is usually defined as a diffuse audience, such as readers of a newspaper or listeners of a radio station who are located in various places.

Each of these levels of social integration has unique characteristics. When we study the process of communication, we should keep in mind the level of social integration. In studying small groups, for example, it is important to observe the group phases (stages of group development) as well as the group climates and group leadership. While these concepts are critical to understanding the communication process of the small group, they make little sense when applied to the dyad or to the public and mass levels of social integration.

Interpersonal communication occurs in the dyad—the simplest level of social integration. Interpersonal communication may occur within the context of a small group, the public or even the mass. The reverse, however, is not true; small group, public, or mass communication cannot occur in the dyad.

We can better grasp the nature of interpersonal communication if we consider the components of the word *interpersonal—inter* and *person.*

Inter. The prefix *inter-* means 'between'; communication occurs between people. Meaning requires a social situation or a social context and the minimum social unit is a dyad.

Person. The word *person* is derived from the Latin word *persona* which means 'mask.' In contemporary social theory, the term *persona* or *person* refers to the concept of role—both the sociological and psychological roles that people assume in any social situation.[5]

Meaning is dependent upon the personas, or masks or roles, of the people within a particular situation. For example, the act of Mary kissing John's ring could have various meanings depending upon their roles. If Mary is John's mother, the gesture of kissing John's ring could be a communication of comfort to an injured child. If Mary is a bride and John is the groom, Mary's act becomes a communication of love

5. In contrast, sociological and psychological roles are separated (with interpersonal communication identified only with the latter) by Gerald R. Miller and Mark Steinberg, *Between People: A New Analysis of Interpersonal Communication* (Chicago: Science Research Associates, 1975), esp. pp. 12–30.

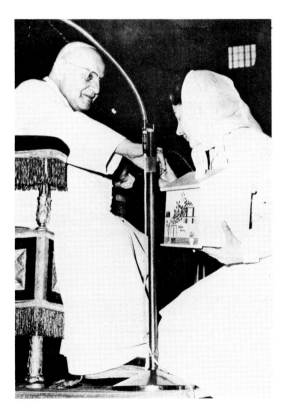

The meaning of any act depends on the roles of the people involved in the transaction.

and matrimonial fidelity. The gesture evokes quite a different meaning if John is the Pope and Mary is a devout Catholic.

The communicants can determine what constitutes a message and what a message means only after they have established their roles in relation to each other. Thus interpersonal communication may be viewed as communication between roles.

THE STRUCTURE OF A TRANSACTION

When we look at communication within role relationships, we discover a process of creating and conveying meaning that can best be described with the term *transaction*. We present a model of interpersonal communication using the transaction as the basic integrating unit. Any model or theory rests on axioms—basic assumptions about the nature of the phenomenon, working premises that cannot be proved or disproved. We introduce our transactional model of interpersonal communication with our first axiom.

Axiom I: *The basic unit for the analysis of interpersonal communication is a transaction.*

The transaction is the central concept used to study interpersonal communication. A transaction can most simply be defined as *two people engaged in mutual and simultaneous interaction.* When we speak of an interpersonal communication transaction—a transaction in which meaning is created—we are referring to *a specific kind of system in which two persons mutually perceive each other, differentiate role relationships between them, and interact by a specific set of rules for a measurable period of time.*

Every interpersonal communication transaction has certain structural elements—certain underlying processes characteristic of all transactions. There appear to be four such processes that make up the structure of an interpersonal communication transaction.

1. *A transaction requires mutual engagement in a social situation.*

Because a transaction is a system, it requires the mutual engagement of two people. Mutual engagement, in its simplest sense, requires what David Berlo has called *physical interdependence.*[6] A transaction can exist only when two people are in some way physically interacting. They need not be engaged in face-to-face conversation (much interper-

6. David K. Berlo, *The Process of Communication: An Introduction to Theory and Practice* (San Francisco: Rinehart Press, 1960), p. 108.

sonal communication occurs in transactions carried out over the telephone), as long as there is some level of physical interaction. A transaction does not exist if one person is fantasizing the existence of the second person in the dyad.

Mutual engagement is more than just physical interdependence. It requires the perception of the other person's perceptions.[7] Two people are standing across the room from each other at a party. Their eyes meet. They acknowledge each other's glances. Contact has been established. Each person perceives the other and perceives the other's perception of him or her. A transaction has been established and there is meaning in the interaction between them.

A group of people are standing in line at the box office of a movie theatre. A voice behind John says, "What is this line for when there is another line over there?" John turns and replies, "This one is for buying tickets. That one is for people who have their tickets." "Oh, hello, John," Mark says, "I didn't recognize you from behind." When John turns to speak, he and Mark mutually perceive each other and a transaction is established.

When there is physical dependence without mutual perception, a transaction cannot occur. John is walking down the street with his head turned away from Jane. Even though Jane waves at him, John cannot perceive the act. In this case mutual perception cannot exist; therefore a transaction cannot be established.

Sometimes, however, we have reason to believe that other people perceive us but choose to ignore us. In such cases we may reasonably say that mutual perception or mutual engagement in a social situation could exist; we may also say that a transaction has been formed. We can then analyze the behavior and experience (the ignoring and the perception of being ignored) to discover their meaning.

> 2. *In a transaction there is a simultaneous assignment of roles so that the communicants may interpret the interaction.*

In a transaction people simultaneously assume roles in relation to each other. The roles they assume determine which behaviors are to be interpreted as messages and what the messages mean within the context of those roles.[8] In some transactions there may be a relatively large number of roles that each of the participants may legitimately assume.

Suppose Father Gerald is a student of Dr. Smith. They are good friends and occasionally enjoy dining and drinking together. Dr. Smith sometimes attends masses celebrated by Father Gerald. Even if we dis-

---

7. Jurgen Ruesch and Gregory Bateson, *Communication: The Social Matrix of Psychiatry* (New York: W. W. Norton & Co., 1951; reprint ed., 1968), pp. 23–24.
   8. Ibid., pp. 27–28.

regard the psychological roles, there are still at least three sociological roles that each man may assume in relation to the other.

Dr. Smith	Father Gerald
professor	student
supplicant	priest
friend	friend

When Dr. Smith and Father Gerald enter into an interpersonal communication transaction, there are at least nine different *role relationships* that they may assume with each other: professor-student, professor-priest, professor-friend, supplicant-student, supplicant-priest, supplicant-friend, friend-student, friend-priest, friend-friend. Some of the role relationships, such as those of professor-student, supplicant-priest, and friend-friend, are obviously appropriate. They are role relationships that are regularly encountered in social situations. Other role relationships, such as supplicant-student, would appear to be inappropriate except under very unusual circumstances.

The role a person chooses to assume when he or she forms an interpersonal transaction with another person depends upon at least three factors: the person's imagination of the role the other person is going to assume; the context in which the communication is occurring; and the person's perception of the behavior of the other person.

Imagination of the Other Person. When we engage another person in an interpersonal communication transaction, we usually have some image of how that person is going to behave. We form some idea of what role the person will assume and how we are to act toward that role. Our imagination or expectation of the other's behavior is based on our prior experiences with that person or with people in similar situations. If Mr. Jones is a sales representative calling on a new customer, Mr. Jones will imagine that the new customer will behave in about the same manner as his previous new customers have behaved in similar situations. Mr. Jones will then assume his role of sales representative anticipating that the other person will assume the role of customer based on his or her previous encounters with sales representatives.

Context of the Transaction. The context in which a transaction occurs is probably the strongest guiding factor in the assumption of roles.[9] At a funeral one is to be comforting and supportive of the family. One does not make amorous advances to the widow or try to collect bills. Such communication blatantly violates the roles dictated by the occasion.

Most people are adequately guided by cues in the context of a communication transaction that determine what roles are appropriate. When people meet in a singles bar, they assume roles that might be inappropriate in the university classroom or in the office, but are entirely appropriate in the context of a bar, and vice versa.

People sometimes seek social situations that are very different from those they normally encounter. In different contexts, they can escape roles that are usually imposed on them by the context of their occupations or their families. Often doctors, members of the clergy, and professors refuse to be recognized by their professional titles in bars or at parties or other social occasions. These men and women have discovered that when other people know their titles and professions, there is a tendency for others to assume certain stereotyped behaviors toward them. To be truly healthy individuals, Dr. Smith, Father Gerald, and Professor Allen need to communicate in roles different from their professional roles. They need to be able to form transactions in which they can play the roles of Roger, Gerry, and Barbara. To a certain degree, we judge people to be healthy in their communication if they can easily assume a variety of roles and choose roles that are appropriate to the context of the communication.

9. For a discussion of communication context (including the social situation), see ibid., pp. 23–44.

Behavioral Cues. Finally, we assume roles in interpersonal communication transactions on the basis of behavioral cues given off by the other person as we enter into a transaction with that person.

Suppose a man of about thirty, dressed in a suit and tie, enters the office of Dr. Holms, a single, thirty-three-year-old associate professor of speech. Since they have not met before, a number of role relationships are possible between them. The man extends his hand and says, "Hi. I'm Bill Fraser." Even before the man can say, "I'm the new representative of Wm. C. Brown Company Publishers," Dr. Holms has read many significant cues in the man's behavior. The way the man is dressed, the way he extends his hand (students usually wait for a professor to initiate a handshake), the way he enters the office—any of these behaviors might be cues that guide Dr. Holms in establishing role relationships.

There is a possibility that the book representative has admired Dr. Holms from a distance and is now attempting to make a social contact with her rather than trying to sell her the latest textbook by Smith and Williamson. But given the sincerity and dedication of the Wm. C. Brown representatives, we can be reasonably confident that the salesman is probably giving Dr. Holms a line—about the book.

The word *probably* is very important in discussing the accuracy with which we assume appropriate roles in our transactions. Often, human behavior can be predicted with a high degree of accuracy; but there is always an element of uncertainty built into human behavior. This uncertainty provides us with a measure of creativity necessary for survival in an ever-changing world. When we predict how another person is going to behave in a given communication transaction, we can indicate only the pattern of behavior that is most probable.

Difficulties in communication arise when the roles assumed by the two people in the transaction are not mutually compatible, such as when Dr. Smith assumes the role of supplicant and Father Gerald assumes the role of student. These difficulties may be readily resolved if one or both persons modify their roles; but their initial encounter may be disturbing to them. If they fail to realize that they are assuming incompatible roles, more serious problems may arise in their relationship. These problems could be the basis for the expectation of further difficulties in future encounters, leading to a spiral of increasingly unhealthy or unproductive communication between them.

Since two people in a transaction assume roles *simultaneously,* there is an element of risk involved. They can minimize the risk of difficulties in communicating to the extent that they are guided by their expectations of each other, the context of their communication, and the behavioral cues present in the social situation. Considering these factors will help them choose the appropriate roles, or personas, for the particular communication transaction.

> 3. *A transaction possesses an implicit set of rules that govern the interaction of the communicants.*

The more one studies interpersonal communication transactions, the more one sees the tremendous regularity in the structure of interactions. Every time two communicants in an interpersonal transaction assume roles in relation to each other, they adhere to a set of rules that governs their subsequent interaction.[10] The rules for interaction are usually implicit in the social situation. In a few cases, some rules are explicitly defined, such as in communication between nurses and patients in a hospital, or between guards and inmates in prisons, or between judges and lawyers in a courtroom. There the rules that govern interpersonal transactions are a part of the institutional settings. In interpersonal transactions outside of such institutional settings, the rules for interaction are derived implicitly from social codes, from cultural restrictions and taboos, from tradition, and from social etiquette and manners.

The specific rules operating in a transaction are dependent upon the roles assumed by the communicants. The rules that govern Dr. Smith and Father Gerald's transactions as supplicant and priest would be different than those that govern their transactions as friend and friend or professor and student. When the personas are associated with formal institutions such as the Church or the university, the rules tend to be more formal. When the roles or personas are less institutionalized, the rules tend to be more informal.

The same principle seems to apply within business organizations. When the interpersonal communication transaction is taking place between positions defined by the formal structure of the organization (as for example between a corporate vice-president and a plant manager), the rules governing their transactions will be much more explicit and rigidly felt than when the transaction involves two employees of the same rank.

When people meet outside of their office settings, there is often an ambiguity in role relationships which permits greater freedom of interaction. If an office secretary meets his or her boss in a neighborhood supermarket, the roles in the transaction may be either those of boss and secretary or of shopper and shopper. While playing the role of a shopper talking to a fellow shopper, the secretary might be able to communicate things to the boss about the operations of the office that he

---

10. The nature of rules is explained in ibid., pp. 27–28, and in Paul Watzlawick, Janet Helmick Beavin, and Don D. Jackson, *Pragmatics of Human Communication: A Study of Interactional Patterns, Pathologies, and Paradoxes* (New York: W. W. Norton & Co., 1967), pp. 132–48.

The rules governing transactions between a principal and his secretary change with the context of their communication.

or she would not communicate while more clearly in the role of a secretary in the context of the office. Many businesses have found that the most productive and creative suggestions for improving working conditions come from employees in these out-of-office settings. There both the supervisor and the employee feel less constrained by the rigid rules associated with their positions at the office.

The rules that govern the flow of interpersonal transactions cover all aspects of our communication. Roles not only restrict what we feel we can say to the other person; they also govern our expressions, body language, and social actions—even eye contact, as in the following example.

David and Judy are walking down the street toward each other. They do not know each other. Their eyes meet. Judy promptly looks away; she senses that she has established eye contact for the correct amount of time for casual social recognition of a stranger. A moment later, she allows her eyes to glance back at David; his eyes are still intently meeting hers. Judy probably feels that David is violating the implicit social rules that govern length of eye contact for two people in the role of strangers meeting each other on the street.

At this point Judy is faced with a choice. She may continue to interpret David's gesture as staring and consider it a rude violation of social rules; or Judy may change her interpretation of the roles in light of the rules David seems to be using. She might assume that David is making a sexual advance through his prolonged glance and relabel the roles to those of "boy interested in meeting girl," and "girl interested in meeting boy." Then the two people will probably find some excuse for stopping to speak to each other and continue in these new roles. Otherwise, Judy may pass David by as a rude person who violates the rules of proper social interaction on the streets.

Over a period of time, each dyad develops its own unique rules for various aspects of interaction. A husband and wife who have spent a few years together have their own implicit rules for dealing with problems; they reach implicit agreements about what may be discussed and how it may be discussed. Children and parents also evolve rules for communicating. One family we know has an implicit understanding that they will not discuss politics or personal income among themselves. If the father should initiate a discussion of politics, the rules are that the son will refrain from making any counter statements. If these rules are not followed, everyone in the family knows that there will be heated arguments, hurt feelings, and misunderstandings which simply make life more difficult than it needs to be. To preserve harmony in relationships, people implicitly create sets of rules that forbid certain kinds of behaviors by certain people in their transactions.

4. *An interpersonal communication transaction occurs over a period of time.*

Every transaction exists for a measurable period of time; *specific transactions* have a beginning and an end. The time involved in any specific transaction is indefinite; it may be a matter of a few seconds or of several hours. During a transaction, the two people exchange messages, create meaning through mutual social interaction, and either strengthen or modify the roles and rules of their relationship.

The rules governing interaction in a particular relationship operate over a period of time. Both parties may modify their roles in relation to each other and their rules in order to keep their relationship intact. In long-standing relationships (such as between husband and wife or parent and child), interpersonal transactions may become highly structured, with precise, definable, recurring patterns of interaction. It is possible to analyze any interpersonal communication transaction in terms of *how* the patterns of interaction are generated and *what function* the patterns serve for the communicants.

Look at the following conversation between a husband and wife discussing their son who is home from college for Thanksgiving holidays.

> Husband: *There was a hell of a lot of noise here last night.*
> Wife: *Really?*
> Husband: *The car woke me up. Then there was noise in the garage. And all that carrying on downstairs. Some people have to work, you know.*

> Wife: *Johnny brought a couple of friends home. I fixed some cake and coffee.*
>
> Husband: *It figures. It's no wonder he's gotten outta hand. The way you encourage him to carry on he probably never even goes to bed at night when he's away from here.*
>
> Wife: *I thought it was nice that he came back here after the party.*
>
> Husband: *Well, I didn't get much sleep. You could have been more considerate.*

To analyze this transaction, we must observe the relationship between the husband and the wife throughout the entire transaction. The full significance of the conversation is that the transaction is a game of "If It Weren't For You."[11] The game emerges not by breaking the dialog apart, but by analyzing the transaction as it occurs over time.

We can observe that the husband's comments have an ulterior quality. He is not expressing genuine irritation about the noise or the visitors of the night before. He is indirectly saying, "If it weren't for you I could sleep at night. If it weren't for you our son wouldn't carry on like that. If it weren't for you . . ." The wife is responding in an extremely neutral way. Her response of "Really?" (line 2) indicates that she perceives that he is not really talking about the noise; therefore she shows neutral concern about the noise disturbing her husband. (She does not say, "Oh, that's too bad," or "Oh, I'm sorry.") The response of "Really?" is an open-ended question that permits the husband to continue interaction along the same lines. Thus, the wife indicates that she understands the rules for their interaction and is willing to continue the game. We would have to see the conclusion of the transaction to discover the significance of the game and the function it serves in their relationship.

Because of the regularity of certain recurring patterns in interpersonal communication transactions, we may analyze these patterns according to a relatively precise system for classifying interpersonal communication behavior. These recurring patterns of interpersonal communication have been called strategies and games.

SUMMARY

In this chapter we have defined three key components of the words *interpersonal communication*. Communication, as a transactional concept, is defined as the behavior and experience of organisms involved

11. Berne, *Games People Play*, pp. 50–58.

in the process of creating meaning. Interpersonal communication limits the area of study to communication within a dyad, or a two-person unit. The concept of persona implies that communication occurs between roles or "masks" assumed by people in their transactions with others. In interpersonal communication, the focus of study is on the creation and unification of differences in the role relationships between two people.

An interpersonal communication transaction has four structural characteristics. First, the two people in the transaction must experience some act or behavior as a response to their mutual engagement in the social situation.

Second, the two people simultaneously assign role relationships that permit them to interpret their communication. Each person chooses role relationships based upon his or her imagination of the other's behavior, the context of the transaction, or behavioral cues displayed by the other. The assignment of roles is usually based on all three of these factors.

Third, a transaction has an implicit set of rules that govern the interaction between the communicants. These rules may be derived from the society, from the culture, or from past transactions between them. Regardless of their origin, these implicit rules are manifest in regularly recurring patterns of interaction in particular role relationships. These patterns of interaction may be studied and the rules that govern the transaction may be explicitly stated, as in the analysis of communication strategies or interpersonal games.

Fourth, a transaction endures for a period of time, varying from a few seconds to several hours. During the passing of time, the communicants may modify the roles and rules governing the interpersonal transaction. In long-standing relationships, transactions may become highly structured recurring patterns of interaction.

QUESTIONS FOR REVIEW

1. What are the three distinctions between communication (the process of creating meaning) and communications (the process of transmitting information)?
2. What is a dyad? What relevance does it have for the study of interpersonal communication?
3. What does the word *person* mean in its historical context? What does it mean today? How are the two meanings similar?
4. How is *transaction* defined?

EXPLORATIONS

1. The answer to the question "Who am I?" (with which you began your communication journal) depends upon the specific role relationships that you have had. Look back at your essay. Note how many times you defined who you are in relationship to other persons. This exploration is an extension of defining the self in terms of roles. Draw a time line that begins with birth and ends with the present. At each appropriate point on the line, indicate the most significant role relationships at that time in your life. For example, at birth the critical role relationships were with the mother or mothering one. At age five the significant role relationships may have been between you as a student beginning kindergarten and the teacher. Try to complete a time line for yourself; then examine it to see how much "who you are" depends upon the significant people with whom you are communicating. (This is also a good exercise to share with a small group of classmates; it may be used as a point of discussion of the materials in this chapter.)

2. Choose a person whom you have known for a long time and with whom you communicate frequently. List at least three sociological roles that each of you are normally capable of assuming. Which of these roles go well together (i.e., if you "paired" in the roles, could you communicate compatibly)? Which do not go well together? Why? What happens if the two of you assume conflicting or incompatible roles?

3. Imagine one specific social situation (such as a family dinner at home on a holiday, a business interview, a religious ceremony, etc.). List at least ten implicit rules that govern the interpersonal communication in that situation. Choose a quite different situation, list rules for it, and contrast these rules with the rules listed for the first situation.

4. Time is an important variable in interpersonal communication, as in any other system. Think of any long-standing relationship you have had (parent-child, friend-friend, etc.). How has the passage of time affected your communication in this relationship? What roles and/or rules have changed through time? Be as specific as possible in your answer.

5. Think of three weaknesses that you perceive in your present interpersonal communication (e.g., I don't talk enough, I don't introduce myself to strangers, I don't initiate conversations.) List these on the left-hand side of a page. Now in a center column, translate these "weaknesses" into "should statements" (e.g., I should talk more, I should introduce myself to strangers, I should initiate conversations.)

In the right-hand column try to identify the source of the "should." Who says that you should talk more? What rule indicates that you ought to initiate conversations? How do we come to establish "shoulds" and "oughts" that govern our communication behavior?

FOR FURTHER READING

Burke, Kenneth. *Permanence and Change: An Anatomy of Purpose.* 2d rev. ed. Introduction by Hugh Dalziel Duncan. Indianapolis, Ind.: The Bobbs-Merrill Co., 1965.

The first major work of the sociologist-critic, this book is both exciting and challenging for the student interested in the origins, functions, and uses of language. Most of Burke's techniques for dealing with language analysis are discussed or used in this book, which sets forth both a theory of language and a theory of social criticism.

Goffman, Erving. *The Presentation of Self in Everyday Life.* Garden City, N.Y.: Doubleday & Co., Anchor Books, 1959.

Using a dramaturgical or theatrical metaphor, Goffman describes how a person presents his or her self as a kind of characterization or mask which others will acknowledge, like a performer before an audience. Goffman makes frequent reference to his observations in a Shetland Island farming community to illustrate how individuals form teams that help define and support characterizations of self, how discrepant roles are enacted, and how impressions are managed.

Laing, R. D. *The Politics of Experience.* New York: Ballantine Books, 1967.

The importance of experience and modern society's misunderstanding of it are the central themes of this little book. Laing maintains that behavior is necessarily a function of experience and that both behavior and experience are social, always related to people or things besides the self. According to Laing, our social experience (our interexperience with others in contemporary society) tends to blind us to the reality of the inner world, to alienate us from ourselves and others, and to lead to destruction. Despite its controversial nature, this book raises issues that deserve attention.

Ruesch, Jurgen, and Bateson, Gregory. *Communication: The Social Matrix of Psychiatry.* New York: W. W. Norton & Co., 1951; reprint ed., 1968.

In this pioneering volume comprised of a series of essays, Ruesch and Bateson interpret psychiatric theory and practice from the point of view of communication theory, especially of cybernetics and information science. They show how the communication process is the social foundation of psychiatry—how values, social conventions, mental illness and its treatment, etc., are all shaped by communication.

Wilmot, William W. *Dyadic Communication: A Transactional Perspective.* Reading, Mass.: Addison-Wesley Publishing Co., 1975.

As the title indicates, the book focuses upon two-person communication systems. After defining a dyadic transaction and contrasting it with a triad, Wilmot shows how the perceptions of self and others are socially influenced and how relationships are perceived and maintained. Wilmot provides a very readable overview of many essential elements in a transactional theory of human communication.

Chapter 2

The Ecological Nature of an Interpersonal Communication Transaction

The idea that the interpersonal communication transaction may be looked at as an ecological system is not new; yet it represents a significant departure from the action and interaction models. Instead of looking at senders and receivers, the transactional model looks at role relationships.

The creation of meaning in role relationships in social situations has probably been most fully investigated by Gregory Bateson and his colleagues. Bateson has also been widely recognized for his work in human ecology.[1] It is not surprising, then, that the concept of interpersonal communication has been merged with the concept of ecological systems. For in a very important sense, interpersonal communication is an ecological phenomenon.

Until the mid-1960s relatively few people outside of the universities had even heard of the word *ecology*. Before that time, ecology was primarily the concern of biologists who studied wildlife patterns. When they began to notice important relationships of various animals to one another and to their environments, biologists discovered ecological systems.

Some scientists observed, for example, that the wolf population and the rabbit population in a given area were highly interdependent.[2] When the population of wolves increased, they ate more rabbits. As the rabbit population dwindled, a large number of wolves would die of starvation.

1. Many of his essays in this area are found in Gregory Bateson, *Steps to an Ecology of Mind* (New York: Ballantine Books, 1972).
2. V. C. Wynne-Edwards, *Animal Dispersion in Relation to Social Behavior* (New York: Hafner, 1962).

Then as the number of wolves decreased, the population of rabbits would increase. These alternating patterns of growth and decline kept the numbers of wolves and rabbits in balance.

Since the wolves and rabbits were so closely interrelated, any other element in their environment that affected one would eventually affect the other. When vegetation became scarce during a period of drought, fewer rabbits would survive and more wolves would starve. If hunters killed a large number of wolves, the rabbit population would increase and destroy more crops in the area. Thus other elements in the environment could upset the natural balance between the wolves and the rabbits.

Scientists also discovered that animals adapt to changes in their environments. Certain moths, for instance, adapt to the color of vegetation in their habitat.[3] In central England, gray moths blend in with the color of certain birch trees to protect themselves from birds. At one point, factories in the area so polluted the air that the trees turned from gray to black. Over a period of years, the gray moths adapted to become black moths. Then economic recession shut down the factories. Gradually the trees returned to their natural color. The moths, then black, became endangered as a species because they were readily visible against the gray of the trees. In a few years, however, the moths again turned gray. The various elements of the ecological system—the birds, moths, trees, humans, and even the air—were all affected by a change in one of those elements. The moths adapted to that change and restored the ecological balance.

These examples illustrate two important principles of ecology. First, *in an ecological system every element is affected by an event in any part of the system.* Wolves are affected by a shortage of grass; the color of moths is affected by an economic recession in the human population. The second principle is very closely related to the first. *Living organisms adapt to changes in their environments.* When one organism changes its behavior, other organisms will adapt to the change in order to restore balance in the ecological system.

Interpersonal communication transactions operate upon the same principles as wildlife ecological systems. When two people enter into a transaction, each becomes an important part of the other's environment. Whatever affects one person affects the other person and affects the relationship between them. When one changes, the other must adapt to the change to restore balance in their relationship. This simultaneous,

3. Anthony Wilden, "Epistemology and the Biosocial Crisis: The Difference that Makes a Difference," in *Coping with Increasing Complexity: Implications of General Semantics and General Systems Theory,* ed. Donald E. Washburn and Dennis R. Smith (New York: Gordon and Breach Science Publishers, 1974), pp. 249–70.

mutual influence and constant adaptation in a transaction are characteristic of an ecological system.

What are the advantages of an ecological model of interpersonal
communication? How does it help us understand our own communication? By looking at the interpersonal communication transaction as an
ecological system, we discover two important principles that cannot be
derived from the action and interaction models. First, we discover that
we cannot not communicate. Second, we learn that all difficulties in
communication arise from incongruency somewhere within the structure of a transaction.

IMPOSSIBILITY OF NOT COMMUNICATING

Axiom II: *In an interpersonal communication transaction*
one cannot not communicate.

Within a transaction, neither person can stop behaving; and each
adapts to the other's behavior. Whether they are talking or remaining
silent, being active or being passive, they are behaving. Each person
perceives the other's behavior and attaches meaning to some of it.

*The principle that one cannot not commu-
nicate is probably the most important
theoretical advance in nearly a half century
of study of human communication. The
idea was fully developed only as recently
as 1967 by Watzlawick, Beavin, and Jackson in their book* The Pragmatics of Human
Communication. *Although the principle
seems to be a restatement of Freud's
concept of psychic determinism, there are
important differences. According to Freud,
all behavior is meaningful; no behavior is
random or accidental. The axiom that one
cannot not communicate does not go as
far as stating that all behavior is meaningful. It does imply, however, that all
behavior may be meaningful.*

*To the student of interpersonal commu-
nication, the axiom that one cannot not
communicate is more useful than Freud's*
*principle of psychic determinism. Freud's
analysis of behavior linked meaning to an
unconscious psychic structure. What appeared on the surface to be random or
accidental behaviors derived their meaning from processes occurring in the unconscious portions of the id, ego, or superego.
The reconceptualization of this principle
into the statement that one cannot not
communicate does not require a concept
of the unconscious. All behavior may be
meaningful simply because it may be
assigned meaning by the other person
within the transaction. To discover meaning, we need not understand what lies in
the unconscious. We need only examine
the behavior and experience between
two people in the context of an
interpersonal transaction.*

Those behaviors to which meaning is assigned become messages. Since any behavior may become a message, it is impossible to keep from generating meaning within a transaction. In this sense one cannot not communicate.[4]

Suppose that John is picking Mary up for a date. Mary comes out to the car, opens the door, and gets in. John is in the driver's seat. John and Mary mutually perceive each other. Now that a transaction is established, it is impossible for either of them to not communicate. If Mary says, "Hi," she communicates; if she says nothing, she communicates. If Mary moves closer to John, she communicates one thing; if she remains seated against the door, quite another. The precise meaning of these behaviors depends upon the culture and upon the roles and rules in John and Mary's transactions. But neither of them can act without the other person assigning some meaning to those acts—meaning that modifies the role relationship between them. Communication has occurred whether it was intended or not.

4. Paul Watzlawick, Janet Helmick Beavin, and Don D. Jackson, *Pragmatics of Human Communication: A Study of Interactional Patterns, Pathologies, and Paradoxes* (New York: W. W. Norton & Co., 1967), pp. 48–51.

The axiom that one cannot not communicate gives us insight into how people communicate—what kinds of behavior they may use to generate specific meanings within a transaction. When we look at actual examples of interpersonal communication, we can see what the axiom implies about particular kinds of communication behavior and experience.

COMMUNICATION WHEN ONE MODE IS BLOCKED

The experience of a university student and his counselor illustrates that one cannot not communicate. The student's feelings of frustration in communicating with his mother, teachers, and friends are similar to frustrations we have all probably experienced to one degree or another.

Albert was an eighteen-year-old student in his second year at the university. He had been rushed through high school and pushed against his will into a prestigious college. He was awarded scholarships that paid for both tuition and living expenses. His father had been dead since Albert was three; Albert's mother had been unable to complete college during the depression. Therefore the mother was extremely proud and happy that her son had done well and was able to attend college. The high school counselor was pleased with Albert's admission and scholarships; the school was pleased with his success.

Everyone was happy except Albert. He did not want to go to college. He felt too young to be in such an intensive study program. He had no goals for his life; he had no professional or job orientation. He felt swamped by events that he believed were beyond his control.

After the first few weeks of college, Albert felt extremely frustrated with himself, his school, his family, his situation. He began to be moody. He would begin practicing the piano and suddenly pound the keys violently. He abruptly left conversations with close friends and slammed the door on his exit. Something even trivial that went wrong could send him into a rage; he would pound walls and throw things.

At this point, Albert was persuaded to visit a counselor. The counselor quickly determined that there was no deep maladjustment in Albert's personality. He began to examine Albert's behavior from the standpoint that one cannot not communicate. Within the framework of the interpersonal communication transaction, Albert's strange behaviors—slamming doors, having temper tantrums, throwing objects—are clearly forms of communication. They are, in fact, messages, with meaning almost as precise as if Albert were using language. In Albert's case, language—sitting down and talking out the problem—was blocked. At least Albert believed he could not use language to communicate his feelings to someone who would understand him.

Albert felt that he could not speak to his mother about his frustrations. She was happy and proud that he was in school. He could not bear to tell her that he was unhappy. He felt that telling her his feelings would create more problems than he was capable of solving. Neither did he wish to talk to his high school counselors and friends. He believed that speaking to them about his frustrations would change their image of him as a successful student. In each of these relationships, Albert was cast into a role he did not like. But he was afraid of the consequences of trying to change that role by speaking frankly about his feelings. Albert needed a way to communicate his frustrations without directly hurting his mother or his image in the eyes of others. Albert chose, consciously or unconsciously, to communicate by gestures—by throwing objects, hitting walls, slamming doors.

Albert's experience suggests the first implication of the axiom that one cannot not communicate.

1. *When a person perceives one mode of communication as blocked or dysfunctional, the person will use alternate forms of behavior to convey meaning.*

Although their behavior may not always be as extreme as Albert's, children, adolescents and adults may all communicate this way in the presence of frustration. When people perceive that something in their transactions makes their usual communication behavior inappropriate or dysfunctional to convey the meaning they want to convey, they will seek other ways to communicate. People may communicate through behaviors such as excessive drinking, heavy use of marijuana, drug abuse, or deviant or criminal behavior. Although these forms of communication are probably not as efficient as language would be, they may be properly understood as messages. They are behaviors to which we may attach meaning within a transaction operating on the principle that one cannot not communicate.

Children, students, and employees often feel that they cannot use language to express certain ideas or frustrations. Obedience is expected in each of these roles; one is not supposed to tell parents, teachers, and supervisors what to do. Thus children, students, and employees commonly use alternate forms of communication.

In business settings, people do not usually throw tantrums, beat walls, or throw things. That kind of behavior would clearly violate the role expectations of an employee and could lead to prompt dismissal. Employees may communicate their frustration with their jobs or their supervisors in more subtle ways—"accidentally" delaying projects or reports that are important to the supervisor, forgetting conferences or meetings, ignoring memos, or not returning phone calls. Whenever such behaviors begin to form a clear pattern in a business setting, an alert supervisor should recognize that the employee has chosen, consciously or unconsciously, to communicate by some form other than language. The health of the organization and the health of the employee-supervisor relationship depend on understanding that communication.

Whenever communication takes a form other than language, it is important for both persons to realize that one cannot not communicate. Then they may identify the communicative behavior and explore their meanings as messages. They may discover why the person chose to communicate in that manner. Sometimes the two people are capable of moving the communication into open discussion between them. At other times the situation may require the intervention of a third person —one who is skilled in handling interpersonal communication problems, such as a communicologist, an expert in organizational communication, or a psychologist.

The first implication of the axiom that one cannot not communicate explains that people use an alternate form of communication when they

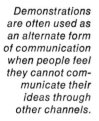

Demonstrations are often used as an alternate form of communication when people feel they cannot communicate their ideas through other channels.

perceive one form as blocked. A second implication of the axiom applies when people attempt to conceal their actual feelings.

2. *Once a transaction has been established, attempts to conceal meaning in order to defend the self-image are themselves communicative.*

Throughout our discussion of interpersonal communication we will come upon the concept of self-image. The self-image does not usually refer merely to the physical body, but to a complex set of role images. The self-image includes not only a person's own image of himself or herself, but also the images that the person believes others have of him or her.

The self or self-image is the center from which all communication occurs. When there is a perceived threat to the self-image, communication will be characterized by defensiveness.[5]

Defensive communication involves a person's attempt to conceal some significant meaning in order to protect his or her self-image. Since one cannot not communicate, the attempts to conceal feelings or reactions are themselves communicative.

Suppose Barbara says to Mike, "You're an incompetent businessman." Mike may conceal his immediate feelings and reactions to Barbara's comment by becoming defensive. He may be feeling, "Maybe I am incompetent," but he says, "What do you know about business?" Mike's defensiveness may be seen as a valid message about Barbara's criticism. The message may be, "I don't want you to judge me." We can understand Mike's response as an attempt to defend his self-image. His attempt to conceal his meaning communicates something to Barbara and to us as observers.

Unblocking Communication. All the illustrations in this section have dealt with the ways we create meaning when we experience our usual ways of communicating to be inappropriate or blocked. It is possible to unblock modes of communication and to change basic communication patterns. To open a blocked mode, it may be necessary to seek new role relationships and redefine established role relationships.

In order to get Albert to use language to communicate feelings of frustration, the counselor suggested that Albert establish new friendships and talk out his feelings with these new friends. Since the new friends did not have a preconceived image of who Albert was or should have been, he was able to use langauge to express himself without fear of damaging a particular self-image. Eventually he was able to discuss his problems with his old friends and his family.

5. Jack R. Gibb, "Defensive Communication," *Journal of Communication* 11 (September 1961): 141–48.

*In new role rela-
tionships, people
are often able to
communicate in new
or different ways.*

College students who move away from home have opportunities to explore a variety of ways of communicating in new role relationships. These students frequently find that, once they have been away, their communication with their parents changes. They can discuss things with their parents that they could not have discussed had they remained at home.

Most of us use new role relationships to help us deal with difficulties in communication. We often try to solve problems by talking things over with a third person—someone outside of the relationship in difficulty. With this outside person we create role relationships different from our existing relationships such as parent-child, husband-wife, lover-lover. People sometimes find they can express themselves (both verbally and nonverbally) in sensitivity groups with complete strangers. Often they express what they would never dream of expressing in their more intimate, long-term relationships.

In new role relationships, people are often able to communicate in ways they previously perceived as blocked. Once they realize these modes are not blocked, they can transfer these ways of communicating back to their day-to-day transactions. The freedom to use all modes of communication in new role relationships usually leads to growth in the self-concept. The individual can then redefine previous role relationships according to his modified self-image.

The two implications discussed in this section show the central role of the self-image in communication and the strong need people have to defend that self-image. In chapter 10 we will discuss defensiveness as a natural barrier to intimacy in interpersonal communication.

ATTEMPTS TO DENY COMMUNICATION

From the following illustration we will see the implications of the axiom that one cannot not communicate when one party in the transaction attempts to deny communication with the other.

A doctoral student of ours, whom we will call Tom, works as a volunteer at a state mental hospital. One afternoon Tom was assigned to work with a female patient. He was told to try to get her to enter into a discussion with him. When Tom began speaking to the woman, she did not acknowledge his presence. Tom asked questions, made comments, and generally conversed as if she were responding. During all of this time, the woman, seated no more than three feet away from Tom, was withdrawn into herself. She gave no overt sign that she heard Tom or was even aware of his presence except for carefully avoiding looking at him.

After a half hour of this one-sided conversation, Tom maneuvered himself into a position where the patient was virtually forced to estab-

This umpire's refusal to communicate is actually a clear message to the manager about the umpire's opinion.

lish eye contact with him. At this point, Tom asked the woman a direct question. She answered the question and from then on engaged in normal conversation. When the conversation was going fairly well, Tom casually asked, "Why didn't you talk to me earlier?" The woman replied, "I didn't hear you."

It is unreasonable to believe that the woman did not hear Tom. Yet, as long as she could avoid establishing direct eye contact with Tom, she denied that he was communicating with her. Once eye contact was established, she could no longer deny Tom's presence and began to talk. The woman later acknowledged things Tom had said during the time that she claimed she did not hear him.

This incident illustrates another implication of the axiom that one cannot not communicate.

> 3. *Once a transaction has been established, attempts to deny communication become communicative and meaningful in themselves.*

The concept of the interpersonal communication transaction becomes very important to understanding this incident. The woman's attempts to deny communication are meaningful only if a transaction existed. If the patient did not hear Tom or if the patient did not know he was there, he could not be said to be communicating with her before she began to speak.

There is evidence, however, that the woman perceived Tom as soon as he began to speak; and she knew that Tom knew she perceived him. Since there was a mutual perception of perception, a transaction existed. The woman was not *failing to perceive* Tom's presence; she was *refusing to acknowledge it.*

The woman's behavior becomes *meaningful* within the framework of a transaction. By trying to deny communication with Tom, the patient was in fact communicating with him. Her denial becomes a message that Tom or any other interested observer can interpret. Once a transaction is established, one cannot not communicate.

The woman's behavior is an extreme form of the communication behavior of many children. There is hardly a family that has not experienced such communication. A mother calls a child to come to dinner. The child is watching a favorite show on television. While the volume is pretty high, both the mother and the child know that she called for dinner. In five minutes, Mother calls a little louder and a little more forcefully. The child does not respond. In another minute or two, Mother says in a much softer voice, "If you aren't at the table in ten seconds, you are going to get your bottom warmed." Presto! The child heard that message and is at the table. Children do the same thing when there are dishes to be done, trash to be emptied, eggs to be gathered, chickens to be fed, dogs to be bathed—anything children don't want to do. The same kind of communication happens between husbands and wives over the same issues and over issues such as picking up clothes, going to parties, doing the laundry, taking the children to piano lessons, washing the car, mowing the lawn, and trimming the hedge.

When communication is denied, both parties actually hear each other; and both are aware of the other person's perceptions of the situation. The failure to respond to a request or suggestion is meaningful behavior within a transaction. The behavior is not simply a failure to act. It is a message that says something about the person's view of the task, about the request, or about the person making the request. The message may be: "I don't *like* taking the trash out"; "I don't like *being told* to wash the car"; "I don't like *you* telling me that the laundry is piling up."

UNINTENTIONAL COMMUNICATION

The two previous sections dealt with behavior that was designed, either consciously or unconsciously, to generate meaning. The principle that one cannot not communicate also works in another way. It is possible to communicate through behavior that is not intended to be meaningful. People failing to recognize what their own behavior communicates may find themselves in the typical misunderstandings that occur in interpersonal communication. Often these misunderstandings must be resolved before other productive communication may occur. The following example illustrates unintentional communication.

A husband forgets that it is his wedding anniversary. The entire day goes by and he does not mention it, bring flowers, or acknowledge the event in any way. The wife may interpret his forgetting to mean that he no longer considers their marriage important. Whether or not the husband intended to generate this message to his wife is unimportant in understanding the communication between them. What is important is that the wife attaches meaning to the absence of flowers and the absence of language about their anniversary. To her, the husband's silence and forgetfulness are gestures that generate meaning about their relationship.

This brings us to the final implication of the axiom that one cannot not communicate.

4. *Once a transaction has been established, one person may assign meaning to behaviors that the other person does not intend to be communicative.*

Each of us can probably think of many examples of unintentional communication. A daughter forgets to send her father a birthday card; he is offended and sees her forgetting as an indication that she is unhappy with him. Mr. Jones sees his boss on the street; his boss looks at him and continues on without speaking. Mr. Jones immediately begins to worry about what he has done wrong at the office to make his boss turn on him like that.

The fact that the husband, the daughter, and Mr. Jones's boss did not intend to communicate those messages is largely irrelevant. What is important is that one person in the transaction assigned meaning to some significant behavior. Assigning meaning to this behavior changed or modified the relationship between the two persons. This change in relationship may affect all future communication between them.

In later chapters of this book we will look at ways we can use the principle that one cannot not communicate for generating healthier interpersonal communication, especially in dealing with interpersonal acceptance and interpersonal rejection.

INCONGRUENCY—THE SOURCE OF COMMUNICATION DIFFICULTIES

Axiom III: *All difficulties in interpersonal communication*
arise from incongruency somewhere within the structure
of the interpersonal communication transaction.

We use the term *incongruency* here much the same way that we use the term in everyday language.[6] When things are incongruent, they don't jibe; they don't fit; they are different from, disjunctive from, or contradictory to one another. Two or more elements of a transaction are incongruent when they function to create meanings that are in some way contradictory. If what you said was incongruent with how you said it, the meaning created by what you said contradicts the meaning created by how you said it.

The idea that incongruency is the source of communication difficulties derives from the ecological nature of interpersonal communication. Incongruency causes problems because of the adaptive nature of living organisms. Within the ecological system, each person is con-

6. The concept of incongruency is described by Virginia Satir, *Conjoint Family Therapy: A Guide to Theory and Technique,* rev. ed. (Palo Alto, Calif.: Science and Behavior Books, 1967), pp. 82–83. Incongruency is highlighted in its most serious form (the double bind) by Don D. Jackson, "Family Interaction, Family Homeostasis and Some Implications for Conjoint Family Psychotherapy," in *Individual and Family Dynamics,* ed. Jules H. Masserman (New York: Grune & Stratton, 1959), pp. 122–44; reprinted in *Therapy, Communication, and Change: Human Communication,* vol. 2, ed. Don D. Jackson (Palo Alto, Calif.: Science and Behavior Books, 1968), pp. 185–203.

stantly reacting and adapting to the other's behavior. If two or more elements of the transaction are creating contradictory meanings, one or both of the persons will not know how to respond. To which of those contradictory meanings should they adapt their behavior? If the two people have difficulty adapting, they will have difficulty maintaining balance in the ecological system of the transaction.

One of the great advantages of the ecological model of interpersonal communication is that it provides us with the means to discover the sources of communication problems. By keeping in mind the various elements of the transaction, a sensitive observer may identify the different types of incongruency that may occur among those elements. Two major kinds of incongruency may occur in the basic structure of a transaction, which may cause problems in communication.[7]

INCONGRUENCY BETWEEN ROLE AND CONTEXT

Major difficulties in interpersonal communication occur when a person assumes a role that does not fit in the context of the transaction.

Suppose two army buddies go out drinking as they do on occasion. Their evening is going pleasantly when Frank (a sergeant) says to Bob (a corporal), "Get me another drink." "Get it yourself. I've had enough," replies Bob. Frank threatens, "Listen, I outrank you. Don't you forget that. And I ordered you to get me another drink."

The role Frank assumes is appropriate within the context of conducting military business but incongruent with the context of two buddies out for a good time. Whether Frank spoke in seriousness or in jest, Bob will probably feel hurt and resentful. The incongruency between role and context, therefore, becomes the source of difficulties in communication between Frank and Bob.

INCONGRUENCY BETWEEN ROLES

Difficulties in interpersonal communication arise when two people in a transaction assume roles that are incongruent. If Danny is trying to talk to Mary as a friend and Mary is responding to Danny not as his friend but as his supervisor, their roles are clearly incongruent.

The case of Tom and the patient discussed earlier also illustrates incongruency between roles. The woman's behavior may be seen as congruent with the context of their transaction; unusual behavior is

7. These sources of incongruency are rooted in Haley's formula about messages: "I (source) am communicating (message) to you (receiver) in this context," appearing in Jay Haley, "The Family of the Schizophrenic: A Model System," *Journal of Nervous and Mental Disease* 129 (1959): 357–74; reprinted in *Communication, Family, and Marriage: Human Communication*, vol. 1, ed. Don D. Jackson (Palo Alto, Calif.: Science and Behavior Books, 1968), pp. 171–99 (esp. pp. 188–99).

Obviously these women notice that the man's appearance is incongruent with the situation.

expected in her role as a patient in a mental institution. But her role as an unwilling communicator is incongruent with Tom's role as a therapist. When it is time for therapy, the rules of the transaction indicate that patients and therapists are supposed to communicate verbally and nonverbally. The woman violates these rules by attempting to deny communication with Tom. When she violates rules that govern patient-therapist transactions, she fails to fulfill her role as a patient. This incongruency between Tom's role and the woman's role is the major source of difficulties in their communication.

Incongruency between roles usually results in a violation of the implicit rules that govern transactions. The violation of the rules becomes the source of difficulties in further communication within that transaction. Difficulties in communication may be overcome or reduced by redefining the rules and the role relationship between the communicators. Notice that when Tom interpreted the woman's attempt to deny communication as a message, he redefined the rules for communication between them. The redefined rules allowed denying communication to be a form of communication in their transaction. The woman was then communicating according to the redefined rules and fulfilling her role as a patient in therapy. Redefining the rules governing communication also redefined the roles. The woman had been checkmated, so to speak, and would have to make a different move to create a different set of roles and rules in order to try to avoid communication with Tom.

When people realize that they are assuming incongruent roles, they may redefine their roles and eliminate difficulties. If, however, they fail to realize that their roles are incompatible, the difficulties they encounter may lead to increasingly unproductive communication in future transactions.

There are many other kinds of incongruency that can occur in transactions. After we discuss other elements of the transactional model in the following chapters, we will examine the particular kinds of incongruency that may occur among them. We will then suggest ways to eliminate those incongruencies and the problems they create.

IMPROVING COMMUNICATION—A WORD OF CAUTION

When we are trying to improve our own interpersonal communication, it would be easier if we had a nice, neat set of rules—guidelines to follow in changing our communication behavior. Unfortunately, the very fact that interpersonal communication occurs within an ecological system makes it difficult, if not impossible, to write universal prescriptions for improving communication.

First, it is difficult to prescribe what one person should do. Communication is not something that one person does alone; it takes two to communicate. One person is only one part of the ecological system and is affected by all the other elements in the system. What we should do depends upon the person with whom we are communicating and the context in which we are communicating.

Second, while the ecological model helps us identify sources of difficulties in communication, it does not provide universal solutions to those difficulties. For each communication problem, we must take into account the unique combination of elements in that particular transaction. Once all the elements in the system are considered, then the transactional model can be extremely useful for suggesting specific ways to improve communication in that particular transaction.

SUMMARY

In this chapter we considered two axioms derived from the ecological nature of transactions. The first axiom is that one cannot not communicate once an interpersonal communication transaction has been established. Applying this axiom to various interpersonal communication transactions, we arrived at four implications of the axiom. We discovered that when a person perceives a usual form of communication behavior as blocked or dysfunctional, he or she will create meaning through other forms of behavior. These alternate means of communicating may not be as efficient as language, but they are nevertheless important ways of communicating. To open blocked modes or to change patterns of communication, it is often necessary to create new role relationships. Challenges to one's perceived self-image are met with resistance or defensive communication. Attempts to conceal meaning in order to defend the self-image are themselves communicative. Attempts to deny communication once a transaction has been established will themselves become messages. Finally, once a transaction has been established, one person may assign meaning to behavior that the other does not intend to be communicative. Misunderstandings may arise from the incongreuncy between one person's interpretations of particular behaviors and the other person's interpretations.

The second axiom states that all difficulties in interpersonal communication arise from incongruency somewhere within the structure of the interpersonal communication transaction. Two major forms of incongruency are incongruency between roles and the context of a transaction and incongruency between two roles within a transaction. Because of the ecological nature of communication, solving communication problems depends on careful consideration of all elements in the ecological system of the particular transaction in difficulty.

QUESTIONS FOR REVIEW

1. What does it mean to say that an interpersonal communication transaction is an ecological system?
2. Why is it impossible to not communicate?
3. In what sense.can a "block" be said to occur in communication? Why does the existence of a block only hinder, but not prevent, communication?
4. What does defensive behavior defend?
5. Why is the attempt to deny communication within an interpersonal communication transaction always unsuccessful? Explain.
6. How can unintentional or unconscious behavior be communicative?
7. What is the significance of incongruency within an interpersonal communication transaction?

EXPLORATIONS

1. In your journal make a list of 5 situations in which you attempted to not communicate in the last two or three days. Examples might include such things as refusing to return a telephone call, not answering a memo as requested, pretending that you didn't hear your husband (wife, parent, roommate) asking you to help with the dishes

or take out the garbage. Be specific in identifying these situations. After each entry, jot down how your attempt to not communicate was probably interpreted by the other person in the transaction. What meaning did the person probably attribute to your behavior? What message did you actually generate by trying to not communicate?

2. Reverse the process outlined in the first exploration. List three instances in which you felt people were trying to not communicate, either with you or with someone you were observing. What did their noncommunicative behavior really communicate? Why? Perhaps you want to cite some examples from history in which people have tried unsuccessfully to not communicate.

3. Try to recall three situations in which you unintentionally communicated something to someone else. Was the meaning created through language, gesture, space, or sexuality? How did you find out that the other person saw your behavior as meaningful?

4. Identify one or two situations in which people tried to explain misunderstandings by saying, "We had a breakdown in communication," or "Well, I just didn't get any feedback from you." How can breakdowns in communication be explained in transactional terms? If one cannot not communicate, is it possible to not receive feedback from someone? For example, what is the nature of the feedback that one receives when a person fails to return a telephone call?

FOR FURTHER READING

Jackson, Don D., ed. *Communication, Family, and Marriage: Human Communication.* Vol. 1. Palo Alto, Calif.: Science and Behavior Books, 1968.

This book is comprised of a series of articles originally published in various journals but happily collected here. Grouped into four sections, the articles deal with generalizations from clinical data, with the double bind theory (including the original essay presenting that theory), with communication and pathology (including the concept of incongruency in a communication system as explained by Haley), and with approaches to research involving communication systems. The result is a useful volume of important articles of interest to any student of human communication.

Jackson, Don D., ed. *Therapy, Communication, and Change: Human Communication.* Vol. 2. Palo Alto, Calif.: Science and Behavior Books, 1968.

Like volume one, this book is a collection of articles by scholars related to the Mental Research Institute. The four sections of the book focus upon the interactional context of psychotic as well as other behavior and upon the nature of therapy and change through psychotherapy and conjoint family therapy. Contributors such as Gregory Bateson, Jay Haley, and the editor provide keen insight into the nature of interactional communication systems.

Smith, Dennis R. "Fallacy of the Communication Breakdown." *Quarterly Journal of Speech* 56 (December 1970): 343–346.

This article discusses the errors in our thinking that arise from looking at difficulties in communication as breakdowns in a linear system rather than as pathologies operating continuously and simultaneously within a dyadic system.

Watlzawick, Paul; Beavin, Janet Helmick; and Jackson, Don D. *Pragmatics of Human Communication: A Study of Interactional Patterns, Pathologies, and Paradoxes.* New York: W. W. Norton & Co., 1967.

Undoubtedly one of the most significant recent books on communication theory, this volume presents a theory of human communication grounded in information theory, cybernetics, general system theory, and game theory. The authors offer some axioms of communication, describe pathological communication as an interactional phenomenon, apply their theory in a communicational analysis of the play *Who's Afraid of Virginia Woolf?,* and investigate the impact of paradox upon communication in general and psychotherapy in particular. Anyone seriously interested in interpersonal communication should read this book.

Chapter 3

Messages:
Communication
Behavior

Everybody is familiar with the idea of messages; they are obviously central to interpersonal communication. "May I take a message?" "He left a message for you." "I didn't get your message." A hundred similar sentences and phrases appear in our everyday conversation. Most people think of messages in terms of information. Information is the answer to the question, What is new? That which is old in a message is called redundancy. In our everyday use of the word *message,* we tend to emphasize the information capacity of messages.

The action and interaction models of interpersonal communication were concerned primarily with the relationship between messages and information. Meaning was of little concern and was specifically excluded from consideration in cybernetics and information theory. The transactional approach moves the emphasis from information back to meaning. An ecological model of interpersonal communication is concerned with how behavior becomes messages and how these messages generate meaning in human interaction.

AN ECOLOGICAL VIEW OF MESSAGES

Since two people have an ecological relationship in an interpersonal communication transaction, all of the behavior of each person has the potential of influencing the other person and the relationship between them. In actual practice, however, we do not attend to all of the behavior of other people. We choose to notice certain behaviors and adapt our behavior only to those behaviors we select. *Messages are those selectively perceived behaviors to which each person in an interpersonal transaction adapts his or her own behavior.*

Each culture tends to codify and regulate the behaviors to which members of that culture attend. We can classify these selected behaviors as belonging to specific *message systems*—sets of behavior to which we assign meaning.

These message systems may vary from culture to culture, from society to society, and from subgroup to subgroup within the society. They are usually governed by the implicit rules of the culture, society, and subgroups. What may be a message for one person may not be a message for another person. Yet if both persons are acting by the same rules within the transaction, they will have a tacit agreement as to which behaviors are to be interpreted as messages and which are not.

IDENTIFYING FOUR PRIMARY MESSAGE SYSTEMS

Axiom IV: *Within an interpersonal communication transaction meaning is conveyed through four primary message systems. These message systems can be identified as language, gesture, space, and sexuality.*

There is little consistency among scholars about how many message systems people use to create meaning. Some writers have limited the discussion to two message systems—verbal and nonverbal messages. This viewpoint seems extremely restrictive and fails to distinguish between nonverbal messages. Gesture and space, both nonverbal, function in quite different ways in interpersonal transactions.

The extreme narrowness of the verbal/nonverbal dichotomy was demonstrated several years ago by the anthropologist E. T. Hall in *The Silent Language*. Hall studied communication in many cultures. He concluded that there may be as many as ten primary message systems used in every culture to generate meaning. He identified these ten primary message systems as interaction, association, subsistence, bisexuality, territoriality, temporality, learning, play, defense, and exploitation (use of material).[1] Hall's message systems suggest that we can manipulate almost every aspect of our environment to create meaning.

Cody Sweet has discussed nine nonverbal message systems: gestures, postures, voice tones, physical appearance, clothing, touch and touching, use of space, surroundings, time and timing.[2] Sweet's message systems indicate that we can use virtually every aspect of the body to create meaning.

1. Edward T. Hall, *The Silent Language* (Garden City, N.Y.: Doubleday & Co., 1959; Greenwich, Conn.: Fawcett Publications, 1959), pp. 42–62.
2. Cody Sweet as interviewed by Bess Winakor, "Can Understanding Body Language Change You?" *Philadelphia Sunday Bulletin,* 14 March 1976, p. WA 3.

It is extremely difficult, however, to deal with nine or ten separate message systems in the study of interpersonal communication. Moreover, many of Hall's categories are similar; the distinctions he draws between some categories are more relevant to the study of anthropology than to the study of communication. Sweet's categories are restricted to the use of the body. Therefore, we have merged the categories into four primary message systems: language, gesture, space, and sexuality. We believe that these four message systems are adequate for understanding the nature of messages in interpersonal communication.

Language is self-explanatory. It consists of the verbalizations of human speech as well as the linguistic structures and rules for using these verbalizations. *Gesture* is defined as any act that can be assigned significance by one or both parties in a transaction. *Space* includes the use of territoriality, distances, and angles of interaction and inclination to create meaning. *Sexuality* is a general classification that designates the use of the body to integrate interpersonal transactions. Critical elements of this message system are touch and touching, body image, and body rhythms.

We make no claims that these categories are definitive. In fact they are highly tentative, and may overlap with categories identified by other authors. However, we do believe that these four categories are very useful for understanding the primary codifications of communication behaviors from culture to culture and from society to society. While sexuality may be somewhat controversial as a message system, it has been identified as such in anthropological and psychoanalytic studies of human communication.[3] Even though it has received little attention in the field of speech, there is enough significant research on how aspects of human sexuality affect interpersonal communication to warrant its inclusion.

THE ENVIRONMENT/INSTRUMENT DUALITY OF MESSAGES

Messages are certain structured combinations of the behavior of another person to which we attend and assign meaning. In the ecological system of a transaction, the other person and the person's behavior are part of the environment. In this sense, messages are environmental to the person perceiving the message in much the same way that air, clothing, automobiles, houses, etc., are environmental.

3. Anthropologist Hall, for example, maintains in *The Silent Language*, pp. 49–51, that bisexuality is a primary message system. Some speech communication authors who discuss sexuality as an important aspect of interpersonal communication are George A. Borden and John D. Stone, *Human Communication: The Process of Relating* (Menlo Park, Calif.: Cummings Publishing Co., 1976); also Gerald M. Phillips and Nancy J. Metzger, *Intimate Communication* (Boston: Allyn and Bacon, 1976).

*Can you read the
message in this man's
face? If you don't see
him in context (see opposite
page) you may misinterpret
the message: the pain
of physical effort.*

Language is one set of behaviors that surrounds us as an environment. Human infants acquire their language from the environment in which they are reared. Likewise, the particular gestures we use to communicate are learned from our social environment. How we use space and even our bodies comes from outside ourselves. These are dimensions of our total social and cultural environment that become important for communicating with others.

The concept of message as environmental to the human being leads to considerations about how messages function as environments, how they shape us, and how we adapt to them. As communicative environments, messages and message systems are the ground out of which meaning is created. By studying the environmental dimensions of messages we can better understand how our message systems limit us, guide us, enhance or hinder our development of the self, and, when we are fortunate, lead us to the potentials of self-transcendence.

Messages are instruments as well as environments. In ecological systems everything that is a part of the environment of a living organism has the potential of becoming an instrument in the service of that organism.[4] Someone once created a hammer, which became a part of the environment of its creator. The person adapted to his own creation. But the hammer was also an instrument within the environment that the person could use to some purpose. The same is true of message systems. Language, gestures, significant spaces, and body images have all been embodied with certain meanings by our culture and our society. They have become a part of the environment and we adapt to them. But we also use these message systems as tools to generate and convey meaning in our own interpersonal transactions. We use message systems for our own purposes.

4. Hall argues in *The Silent Language* that the cultural environment controls our lives (p. 38), but that awareness of cultural patterns can loosen their grip and put them more at man's instrumental usage (pp. 165–68). This argument is further elaborated in Edward T. Hall, *Beyond Culture* (Garden City, N. Y.: Doubleday, Anchor Press, 1976).

The environment/instrument nature of all messages allows us to identify an important relationship between meaning and messages, specifically: *The meaning of the message depends on the context in which it occurs; the meaning of each element (word, gesture, act) in the message is determined by the culture.* We can illustrate this relationship by looking at the meaning of the phrase, "you dirty dog." The word *dog* has a cultural meaning associated with four-legged animals. *Dirty* describes an unclean condition. *You* is a pronoun that identifies the subject. Each element of the phrase has a relatively specific meaning within our culture.

The meaning of the phrase, "you dirty dog," however, is context specific; it changes from context to context. It is one thing to shout, "Get off the sofa, you dirty dog," and quite another to snarl at an enemy, "You dirty dog." When one businessman slaps a colleague on the shoulder and laughingly says, "You dirty dog," the phrase generates an altogether different meaning. Any given set of behaviors may have

The worker's hand gesture has a literal meaning. It tells the crane operator what to do. The gesture has meaning on the denotative level.

several meanings derived from the cultural and societal codes. In a particular transaction, the meaning of the behaviors depends on the specific context in which the behaviors are used.

LEVELS OF MEANING

Axiom V: *In interpersonal communication transactions,*
messages have three levels of meaning:
the denotative level, the interpretive level,
and the relational level.

Besides having many possible meanings, messages have different levels of meaning. These levels of meaning help us discuss the relationship between messages and meaning. Every message system generates meaning on all three levels—the denotative, interpretive, and relational levels.[5]

5. These categories are adapted from Virginia Satir, *Conjoint Family Therapy: A Guide to Theory and Technique,* rev. ed. (Palo Alto, Calif.: Science and Behavior Books, 1967), pp. 75–76; and Paul Watzlawick, Janet Helmick Beavin, and Don D. Jackson, *Pragmatics of Human Communication: A Study of Interactional Patterns, Pathologies, and Paradoxes* (New York: W. W. Norton & Co., 1967), pp. 51–54. Our subsequent definition of each of the three levels of meaning relies upon these sources.

DENOTATIVE LEVEL OF MEANING

The *denotative level* of meaning is *that to which the message literally refers.* Virginia Satir illustrated the denotative level of meaning by a situation in which a wife says to her husband, "The dog is on the couch."[6] The individual words of this sentence and the sentence as a whole have denotative meaning.

The words *dog* and *couch* in the English language define or designate two general classes of objects to which both people can refer. The dog may range from the mangiest mutt to the most pedigreed; but a person hearing the word *dog* in the context of this sentence has some rather specific idea of the class of objects referred to by the speaker. The couch may be a simple board with covering and pillows or an expensive, elaborately designed leather or velvet piece of furniture. Regardless, the *class* of objects referred to by the speaker and listener is well defined by the society and the language of the communicants.

Some linguists limit the concept of denotation to specific properties of nouns of a language.[7] They maintain that adjectives, adverbs, etc., cannot be denotative. We believe that a much broader view must be taken. The words "is on the" would appear to have a denotative level of meaning. The words themselves designate or refer to a class of behavior in which the dog is engaged. The words denote the state of the dog as being on the couch rather than running under the couch, clawing the couch, or doing whatever else dogs do when they come into contact with couches.

Likewise, the entire sentence "The dog is on the couch" has a denotative level of meaning. The sentence in its totality specifies a class of objects, behaviors, and experiences for the communicants. Obviously, the class of objects, behaviors, and experiences designated by the sentence "The dog is on the couch" is different from the class of objects, behaviors and experiences designated by the sentence "The baby is crying."

The denotative level of meaning is not limited to the language message system. Within most cultures, gestures and space have denotative levels of meaning as precisely defined as those of language. Suppose two American businessmen have an appointment to meet at a specified place at 3:00 P.M. If one of them has not arrived by approximately 3:20, the failure of the person to arrive denotes that he or she is not going to make the appointment or is rude or irresponsible; the other person will probably go on with other activities. In Latin American societies, the

6. Satir, *Conjoint Family Therapy*, pp. 78–81.
7. John C. Condon, Jr., *Semantics and Communication* (New York: Macmillan Co., 1966), pp. 33–35, 57–59.

failure of one party to arrive for a business appointment within twenty minutes of the specified time would not provide the same denotative meaning; such "lateness" in arrival times is expected and normal there.[8] Despite differences in the meanings attached to these gestures by the differing cultures, the gesture of arriving within culturally prescribed time limits (or failing to arrive within those limits) has a denotative level of meaning in both cultures in the same way that words and sentences of words have a denotative level of meaning.

INTERPRETIVE LEVEL OF MEANING

The *interpretive level* of meaning in a message system is generated by a complex set of cues within the message itself. These cues tell the other person in the transaction (as well as observers of the transaction) *how the message is to be interpreted.* Is the message to be taken seriously or lightly? Does the message mean what it literally denotes? Or could the message mean exactly the opposite of its literal content?

8. Hall, *The Silent Language*, pp. 15–30, 128–45 (esp. pp. 17–18).

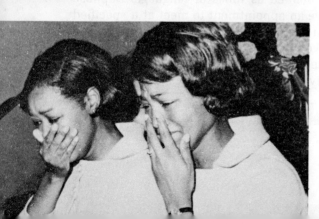

Facial, hand, and body gestures may have literal meanings or may tell us how to interpret messages.

The interpretive level of meaning in interpersonal transactions is easier to discuss when we actually see or have an audiovisual recording of the exchange. Obviously many mannerisms, facial, hand and body gestures, as well as inflections and tones of voice give us clearer indications of how a given transaction is to be interpreted.

An interpersonal communication transaction drawn from the play *The Boys in the Band* may help us understand more fully what is meant by the interpretive level of meaning. In the play Michael and Donald have been lovers for almost one year. Michael is expecting eight of his homosexual friends for a birthday party when he receives a call from an old college friend who is in town and must see Michael immediately. When Michael announces that his friend is on his way over, Michael and Donald have this conversation:

> Michael: . . . *I mean, they look down on people in the theatre— so whatta you think he'll feel about this freak show I've got booked for dinner? . . .*
>
> Donald: *What the hell do you care what he thinks.*
>
> Michael: *Well, I don't really but . . .*
>
> Donald: *Or are you suddenly ashamed of your friends?*
>
> Michael: *Donald, you are the only person I know of whom I am truly ashamed. . . .*[9]

Michael's tone of voice, the inflection placed on the words *you, only,* and *truly,* as well as his body movements should indicate whether Donald, his lover, was the only person of whom he was truly ashamed (a possibility even if said in jest), or whether Michael intended for Donald to interpret the remark as a facetious affirmation of their love in a society they perceive as hostile to their homosexuality. Donald's response indicates that he interpreted the message with all of its inflections and gestures to be understood as a facetious remark.

> Donald: *You know what you are, Michael? You're a real person.*
>
> Michael: *Thank you and Fuck you.* [Michael crosses to take a piece of crab and nibble on it] *Want some?*[10]

The interpretation of the meaning of Donald's statement revolves around the word *real.* In sensitivity groups, self-encounter groups, and related activities, it is a compliment to call someone a "real person." *Real* in that context means genuine, open and honest, warm and loving. In some groups, however, calling someone a "real person" implies that

---

9. Abridged from Mart Crowley, *The Boys in the Band* (New York: Farrar, Strauss & Giroux, 1968), act 1, pp. 28–29.
   10. Ibid., p. 29.

the person is "plastic"—false, artificial, without a center to his or her life. When Donald says to Michael, "You're a *real* person," Donald's statement indicates that it is to be interpreted in both senses *at the same time.*

In some transactions it is dangerous to assume that one level of meaning is somehow more authentic than the others. Donald means a certain warmth and affection for Michael and admires him as "real" in that sense. Donald also means that Michael is plastic, cold, and artificial and lacks real values in his own life. Michael understands that the sentence is to be interpreted as having both meanings—and he responds to both the compliment and the ridicule in his rejoinder "Thank you and Fuck you."

While the nonverbal aspects of communication are certainly important in providing cues for accurately interpreting meaning, language conveys an interpretive level of meaning as much as the other message systems. The choice of words and the arrangement of words often indicate how the words are to be interpreted.

A message might consist of four words: *I, you, only,* and *love.*[11] The mere arrangement of these words in a sentence changes the way the words are to be interpreted.

> I only love you.
> You, only I love.
> Only you I love.
> I love you only.
> Only I love you.

We can, of course, alter the inflection in each of the above arrangements of words. By changing the word accented by the voice, we change the interpretation of the sentence. For example, in the first sentence we can alternately emphasize each word.

> <u>I</u> only love you.
> I <u>only</u> love you.
> I only <u>love</u> you.
> I only love <u>you</u>.

Every sentence, gesture, manipulation of space, time, dress—every behavior that can have meaning for another person within an interpersonal communication transaction possesses cues that indicate how the perceiver is to interpret the message. Regardless of which primary mes-

11. This example, called to our attention by Prof. Charles R. Petrie (Department of Speech Communication, State University of New York at Buffalo), is taken from John W. Black and Wilbur E. Moore, *Speech: Code, Meaning and Communication* (New York: McGraw-Hill, 1955), p. 184.

Many everyday gestures say something about our relationships with others.

sage systems are involved, those dimensions of the message that indicate how the message is to be interpreted constitute the interpretive level of meaning.

RELATIONAL LEVEL OF MEANING

The *relational level* of meaning is the complex set of cues within the message itself that *indicate the relationship between the two communicants.* Every message in an interpersonal transaction either reinforces the existing relationship or modifies the relationship between the two persons involved.

In the play *The Subject Was Roses*, there is an excellent illustration of how messages indicate the relationship between the communicants, even when the denotative level of meaning is not about the relationship itself. Timmy, age twenty-one, has returned home to his parents after being in the army for three years and fighting overseas in World War II. Nettie and John, his parents, throw a homecoming party for him. The next morning before Timmy has awakened, Nettie and John are talking.

> John: . . . *All those casualties and he never got a scratch. We're very lucky. . . . Think he enjoyed the party?*
>
> Nettie: *He seemed to.*
>
> John: *First time I ever saw him take a drink.*
>
> Nettie: *He drank too much.*
>
> John: *You don't get out of the army every day.*

Nettie: *He was sick during the night.*

John: *Probably the excitement.*

Nettie: *It was the whiskey. You should have stopped him.*

John: *For three years he's gotten along fine without anyone telling him what to do.*

Nettie: *I had to hold his head.*

John: *No one held his head in the army.*

Nettie: *That's what he said.*

John: *But that didn't stop you.*

Nettie: *He's not in the army any more.*

John: *It was a boy that walked out of this house three years ago. It's a man that's come back in.*

Nettie: *You sound like a recruiting poster.*

John: *You sound ready to repeat the old mistakes.*[12]

The dialogue between Nettie and John is ostensibly about their son Timmy. Even a brief reading of the dialogue tells us that the denotative meaning is pretty far removed from the important relational meaning. The conversation is a stark discussion of their own relationship.

Nettie's initial statement to John conveys the denotative information that Timmy drank too much. Nettie's choice of words, her blunt, direct, attacking statement immediately implies, however, that she is not as concerned with Timmy's drinking as she is with blaming John for Timmy's being sick. The starkness of the statement, "He drank too much," immediately removes her from responsibility (even though she was obviously at the party also) and implies to John, "It was your fault."

John is aware that the statement is not designed to simply convey information about the state of Timmy's stomach. He perceives that Nettie's remark is directed at his relationship with her and his relationship with Timmy. John's response is a defensive maneuver. He removes himself from the implied responsibility by providing a rationalization for Timmy's enjoying himself and drinking.

Notice that Nettie is unwilling to allow the transaction to move to a state of balance in which she and John are equals. She continues to put John down, to place blame on him, even though she denotatively is talking strictly about Timmy. "He was sick during the night. . . . I had

12. Abridged from Frank D. Gilroy, *The Subject Was Roses* (New York: Samuel French, 1962), act 1, sc. 1, pp. 6–7.

to hold his head." Nettie is clearly saying that she considers herself to be a responsible mother. Her son was ill during the night, but John did not see fit to get up to take care of his son. At the relational level, Nettie's messages are designed to structure a relationship in which she is superior to John.

John's response, "No one held his head in the army," is another defensive maneuver to restore balance to the relationship. He is unwilling to accept blame and remain "one down" from her. His defensiveness is also an attack on their relationship. He clearly implies that their son is capable of taking care of himself now and that Nettie is needlessly interfering with Timmy for the purpose of trying to put John down.

Having been unable to firmly establish her superiority in their relationship with her earlier statements, Nettie brings her implied meaning into the open when she says, "It was the whiskey. You should have stopped him." Notice that all three statements—"He drank too much," "I had to hold his head," and "You should have stopped him"—are really saying the same thing in different words. They are all assertions about the relationship between Nettie and John; and they are all assertions about the relationships between Nettie and Timmy and between John and Timmy. But only in the last statement are the denotative and the relational levels of meaning congruent.

CONTENT AND METACOMMUNICATION AS SUMMARY CATEGORIES

The denotative level of meaning is *content* oriented. It conveys the meanings associated with specific objects, behaviors, or experiences. The interpretive and relational levels of meaning are about the nature of the message itself. They tell us how to interpret the content; they tell us how to modify our roles in relation to each other in order to understand the content. Because the interpretive and relational levels are communication about communication they have been referred to as *metacommunication*.

Because of the distinction between content and metacommunication, it is easy to make a somewhat misleading association of content with verbal communication and metacommunication with nonverbal communication. As we have indicated earlier, we feel that such an equation leads to more difficulties than it solves.[13]

In the broadest sense, all messages within interpersonal communication transactions are comprised of content and metacommunication.[14]

13. This equation is made by Watzlawick, Beavin, and Jackson, *Pragmatics of Human Communication*, pp. 60–67.
14. Ibid., pp. 39–43; and Satir, *Conjoint Family Therapy*, p. 76.

General semanticists often divide the content level of the message into the denotative and connotative meanings of words.[15] Connotation refers to the set of associations that a person has for any given word. One person may associate the word dog with friendliness, love, or memories of childhood. For another person the word may call forth fear, reactions of panic from asthma, or recollections of pain from dog bites. Likewise the sentence "The dog is on the couch" may have the connotations of pleasant moments shared with a lover before an open fireplace or memories of bitter arguments about who will discipline the dog.

There is a sense in which the associations or connotations we attach to lan-guage may be divided among the three categories of meaning—the denotative, the interpretive and the relational levels. Also connotations are purely experiential; they are attached to a message by the perceiver of the message and cannot be directly communicated in the behavior of either person within a transaction. You cannot directly experience my experience of a situation; you can only experience my behavior from which you infer my experience. A transactional model of communication, therefore, does not deal directly with the connotative level of meaning. It is handled via the other three levels which are behavioral and therefore open to direct observation.

The content level—denotation—conveys or reports information. The metacommunication levels—interpretation and relationship—indicate how the information or the relationship between the communicants is to be understood.

HOW WE USE LEVELS OF MEANING IN INTERPERSONAL TRANSACTIONS

Though all interpersonal communication involves content and meta-communication, sometimes we choose to attend to the content of our communication and other times we attend to the metacommunication (especially the communication about our relationships with others). Most interpersonal communication transactions are rich in the many levels of meaning that we weave in the bonds of our relationships. The fact that we have at least four primary message systems, each of which can generate three levels of meaning, creates complex and intricate transactions. The sheer number of message systems and levels of meaning allows ample room not only for the extreme variety of interaction we enjoy with others but also for the many pathologies and confusions in communication that so often occur.

15. This distinction is succinctly explained by family therapist Satir, *Conjoint Family Therapy,* pp. 64–65.

Although an exhaustive analysis of any interpersonal transaction is extremely complex, it is useful to examine the various levels of meaning that might be generated in a single exchange.

George and Martha are the central characters in the play *Who's Afraid of Virginia Woolf?* George is a professor of history at a small college of which Martha's father is the president. George and Martha return home late from a cocktail party for new faculty at the home of Martha's father. Martha has invited Nick and Honey to visit after the party. Nick is a young, virile biology professor; Honey is his naive, phlegmatic wife. After some introductory conversation when they arrive Martha and Honey go upstairs where Martha changes into a very seductive dress. George and Nick talk until Honey and then Martha rejoin them.

> Martha: (To Nick) *Well, did you two have a nice little talk? You men solve the problems of the world as usual?*
>
> Nick: *Well, no, we . . .*
>
> George: (Quickly) *What we did actually, if you really want to know, what we did actually is try to figure out what you two were talking about.*
>
> (Honey giggles, Martha laughs)
>
> Martha: (to Honey) *Aren't they something? Aren't these* (cheerfully disdainful) *. . . men the absolute end?* (to George) *Why didn't you sneak upstairs and listen in?*[16]

In analyzing this dialogue, we must remember that one cannot not communicate; that there are many message systems utilized in the transaction; and that there are multiple levels of meaning generated within even a brief conversation.

To discover the many levels of meaning, let us make the following observations:

a. George makes a declarative statement that denotatively reports what he and Nick were doing while the women were upstairs. The statement clearly indicates, however, that it is to be interpreted as a question, directed at Martha, about what she and Honey were talking about.

b. In gestural response to George, Martha addresses her remarks to Honey. Martha refuses to respond directly to George with language; gesturally Martha is giving him a put-down which is reinforced by the content (the denotative meaning) of her comment to Honey.

c. On the denotative or content level, Martha's remarks to Honey assert a kind of feminine conspiracy—"Aren't they something? Aren't

16. Edward Albee, *Who's Afraid of Virginia Woolf?* (New York: Atheneum Publishers, 1962; reprint ed., New York: Simon and Schuster, Pocket Books, 1963), act 1, p. 48.

these *men* the absolute end?" On the relational level, however, Martha is placing herself one up on Honey. Martha does not even acknowledge Honey as a person. Honey becomes a very convenient object to which Martha may address her remarks. Honey is not given a chance to respond either to Martha or to George. She is totally subordinated to the scene Martha is creating through one strategic statement.

d. Even though Martha is apparently addressing her remark about men to Honey, there are many cues that indicate that the remark is intended for Nick and George, and is a comment about Martha's relationships with both men.

With these initial observations in mind, we can look more closely at the various levels of meaning generated in the transaction.

George and Martha. In the transaction between George and Martha, what is not said, what is not directed to George, and what is implied in the interaction are more important than what actually is said. In this transaction, the gestural behavior takes on tremendous meaning.

The denotative message between George and Martha appears to be Martha's *behavior rather than Martha's words.* The literal content of Martha's interaction with George has two components. First, the content of Martha's behavior is her gesture of speaking to Honey, not to George. This action is a very literal indication to George that Martha is answering his question by ignoring it. Secondly, Martha confirms the content of her gesture toward George by uttering a statement to Honey that does not answer George's question.

On the interpretive level, Martha's gesture of refusing to answer George's question, combined with the nonrelevance of her words to Honey clearly indicate that George is to interpret Martha's actions (the gesture and the statement) as a put-down. In other circumstances the failure to respond to a question posed by one's spouse might carry cues that the gesture is accidental or insignificant. In this case, however, Martha has given numerous cues to indicate that the message is to be interpreted as a deliberate and calculated action.

The relational level of the message in the transaction between George and Martha is perhaps the most interesting. At this level, Martha's apparently irrelevant response to George's implied question takes on special meaning. Martha is making a sexual advance toward Nick. Her refusal to answer George is flirtatious, coquettish—designed to attract Nick to her. At the same time, the flirtation is designed to arouse George sexually and provoke him into asserting himself in their relationship. She is challenging George to overpower and dominate her. (This set of relationships eventually leads to Nick and Martha "Humping the Hostess" on the kitchen table.)

The relational level of interaction between George and Martha is almost a prototype of the kind of flirtatious and teasing sexual behavior between couples almost anywhere. Observe the interaction as a guy picks up a girl for a date on a college campus. The behavior they exhibit in the dorm lobby often makes George and Martha look like amateurs in manipulating the relational level of meaning. Listen to a husband and wife when they are entertaining one or more guests who might be sexually attractive to one of the partners. Carefully observe the behavior in an office or between teachers and students. In almost all of these situations, one will find widespread use of the same technique employed by Martha in her transaction with George—a technique of nonresponse at the content level for the purpose of evoking sexual dominance or attraction at the relational level.

Martha and Honey. The interpersonal communication transaction between Martha and Honey presents us with a very different set of meanings.

Denotatively, Martha's statement to Honey—"Aren't they something? Aren't these . . . *men* the absolute end?"—literally refers to Nick and George. The two husbands are the apparent content of Martha's transaction with Honey.

Probably the most important level of meaning in the transaction between Martha and Honey is the interpretive level. The statement, and the fact that Martha's response to George's question is directed to Honey, indicate that Martha's message probably should be interpreted to mean "Keep your mouth shut, Honey! Do *not* tell George what we were talking about." By refusing to allow Honey to say anything, Martha absolutely preempts any attempt Honey might make to answer George.

On the relational level, Martha's implied instructions place Honey in a subordinate position. Both the interpretive level and the relational level indicate to Honey what she is to do.

Martha and Nick. Since Martha's statement to Honey is made in Nick's presence, a transaction is established between Martha and Nick also. The content of the communication transaction between them is their relationship.

There are two clear cues within the situation which indicate that Martha's statement to Honey is to be interpreted by Nick as a sexual come-on, a flirtation, or an invitation to Nick to make a sexual advance. First, the way Martha emphasizes the word *men* indicates that she is referring to Nick as well as George. Second, Martha's behavior is more consistent with the rules of flirtation, picking up a sexual trick, and sexual games than with the rules of healthy, long-time, husband-wife relationships. Flirting and sexual sparring in front of others by people who have been married for twenty years, as have George and Martha, usually indicates problems in the sexual relationship. Such interactions are usually sexual games. The rules of such interaction are very different from the implicit rules of behavior for a happily married couple when they are with other people.

The relational level of meaning within the Martha-Nick transaction is thus the establishment of Nick in the role of a possible seducer and Martha in the role of the seduced. These roles may be reversed as Martha and Nick continue to communicate. Since Martha is making the first move, she may prove to be the seducer.

WHAT DOES IT ALL MEAN?

We have risked belaboring this brief conversation to emphasize the importance of the multiple levels of meaning generated by messages. This short exchange between George and Martha is in many respects quite typical of transactions that occur frequently between husbands and wives entertaining guests in their home. We cannot overemphasize the fact that this particular conversation is neither unique nor unusual. One can find precisely the same richness of meaning, the same manipulation of the multiple levels of meaning of our message systems on almost any day, almost anywhere—on a street corner, in the elevator of an apartment building, in the lobby of a dormitory, at a cocktail party. Each and every one of us engage in similar patterns of one-upmanship, social put-downs, sexual come-ons, and double and triple meanings. We do this in our exchanges between husbands and wives, between lovers, between friends, between businessmen and secretaries, between salespeople and customers, between women and hairdressers, and so on.

Every interpersonal communication transaction generates meaning on all of the levels of meaning. Every interpersonal transaction has both content and metacommunication. Every transaction is ostensibly about something; and every transaction involves communication about how the communication is to be interpreted, what relationships exist within the transaction, and how those relationships are modified through continued communication. Because every interpersonal transaction is so complex, there are numerous possibilities for incongruency within the transaction that can lead to problems in communication.

PUNCTUATION

The dialogue between George and Martha illustrates the ecological nature of interpersonal transactions. Nick and Honey are a part of the ecological system; thus George and Martha adapt their communication behavior to Nick and Honey. The dialogue would have very different meanings on various levels if either Nick or Honey were not in the environment of the George-Martha transaction. The sixth axiom of our communication model is derived from this concept of a communication transaction as an ecological system.

Axiom VI: *The meaning of messages*
depends upon the punctuation of
the interaction by the communicants.

Punctuation has been defined as the way two communicants in an interpersonal transaction break up the flow of messages between them into meaningful units.[17] Communication itself is a process, an ongoing activity occurring in time; it has no beginning and no end, and is not reversible. Once something has been communicated, it is impossible to take back the communication. Like any moment in time, once a communication event has happened it cannot happen that way again. Similar communication events may occur in the future, but no two events are ever precisely the same.

The perceptual organs of the human being function to filter out a very large portion of the stimuli that impinge upon them at any given moment. We *selectively* attend to the stimuli in our environments. Behavior of others becomes meaningful only when we select out certain parts of the behavior as important and ignore other parts of behavior as unimportant. The function of punctuation is to divide or organize the continuous stream of behavior into segments or units of perception and experience. People punctuate interpersonal communication transactions in three ways: sequencing, labeling the social situation, and establishing complementarity or symmetricality in the relationship.

SEQUENCING

Sequencing is the way we divide up the continuous stream of behavior into meaningful units by imposing beginnings and endings on communication events.[18]

In looking at interpersonal communication as a transaction, we begin to approximate our naive experience of communication. On the one hand, we experience our communication with other people as a

17. Jurgen Ruesch and Gregory Bateson, *Communication: The Social Matrix of Psychiatry* (New York: W. W. Norton & Co., 1951; reprint ed., 1968), p. 24; also Watzlawick, Beavin, and Jackson, *Pragmatics of Human Communication,* pp. 54–59.

18. Watzlawick, Beavin, and Jackson, *Pragmatics of Human Communication,* pp. 54–59, 93–99.

constant flow—an uninterrupted stream of behavior. On the other hand, we experience communication as a series of events, or transactions, which have beginnings and endings. Janice is sitting at her desk working on some papers. Paul comes by, stops, talks to her for five minutes, and leaves the office. Since Janice and Paul have talked to each other hundreds of times, their interpersonal communication is ongoing. Janice and Paul have a relationship that exists whether they are in each other's physical presence or not. Yet when Paul stops at Janice's desk to chat for a while, both Janice and Paul experience the beginning of a transaction. They assume particular role relationships and communicate by a particular set of rules appropriate to their roles and the social situation in the office. When Paul leaves Janice's office, both persons experience the end of this particular transaction.

Two points should be made regarding the punctuation of communication by sequencing. First, it is important to distinguish between the relationship that exists between two people and the interpersonal transaction in which they are engaged at any particular time. A relationship may endure through many transactions. Janice and Paul may assume a variety of roles in their relationship. They may be co-workers on one project in the office, boss and subordinate in another, friends at the company picnic, or lovers on a date. The relationship between them endures through many different transactions, even though they may be assuming different roles in their relationship at different times.

Second, the duration of a particular transaction may include several different encounters. Suppose that Janice and Paul are working on a project together. Their transaction can be seen as beginning when they greet each other in the morning, lasting through a series of encounters, and ending when they finish the project in the early afternoon. During all of this time, both persons maintain their roles in relation to each other and communicate according to the roles and rules appropriate to the context of that transaction.

If, later in the afternoon, Paul comes back into Janice's office and invites her out to dinner and over to his apartment later in the evening, we might assume that this encounter falls within a different interpersonal communication transaction. The communicants would certainly be assuming different roles and following different rules than they had in their previous encounters that day.

There is a certain degree of arbitrariness in the punctuation of transactions by sequencing. People may legitimately differ on the beginning and the ending of the transactions. In fact, difficulties in communication often arise when two people cannot agree on the beginning of their transaction. A dialogue typical of many brother-sister relationships between children illustrates different sequencing.

"Mommy, Johnny hit me."

"I did not. Janey knocked me off my scooter."

"Well, Johnny ran over my doll."

"If she hadn't had her doll on the sidewalk, I wouldn't have hit it. It's all her fault."

"Johnny doesn't want me to play on the sidewalk. He doesn't want to play with me at all. He tries to run away from me."

Johnny and Janey have a relationship which endures through many, many transactions. In this particular transaction, Johnny and Janey are sequencing the event differently; they do not agree on the beginning of the transaction. It is very important to both children that their own version of the beginning of the transaction be accepted by the mother. In this case, whoever "began" the transaction will probably be blamed for the problems that followed. And somebody may be sent to bed without any supper.

LABELING THE SITUATION

Labeling the situation is another way we punctuate interpersonal communication. Every interpersonal communication transaction is labeled by both of the participants.[19] Sometimes we explicitly discuss the labels we place on encounters ("Drop by for a cup of coffee," "We'll discuss that issue at the committee meeting tomorrow," "Let's take the night off and go out on the town," etc.). Or the label may be applied implicitly, often by the social context of the communication.

The social context usually provides us with directions for labeling a social situation. People dressed somberly, in mourning, gathered together to bury someone who has died, labels the social situation as a funeral. This label, in turn, indicates a specific set of rules for inter-action which the society or culture deems appropriate. Social norms are equally strong in other social situations, such as weddings, dances, banquets, worship services, church socials, dates, business meetings, office conferences, and classrooms.

In social situations less formally defined, there is a greater chance for two people to label the social situation differently. Tom had known Janet and Bill for several years. Since Janet and Bill had never met each other, Tom invited them to a party for the purpose of introducing them. Since Janet was seriously dating another person, she labeled the situation as a social party and her encounter with Bill as a platonic meeting. Bill, however, labeled the social situation as a sexual encounter and his interaction with Janet as sexual advance. Janet and Bill punctuated the

---

19. Ruesch and Bateson, *Communication*, pp. 28–29.

In every culture, specific rules govern behavior in particular social situations.

transaction differently because the cues provided by the social context were ambiguous. Both persons could have been perceiving the social situation accurately, and both were acting according to the rules appropriate to their perceptions of the social situation.

In every interpersonal communication transaction, the nature of the relationship is affected by the label placed on the situation. John and Mary will probably assume different role relationships if they meet as man and woman in a singles bar than if they meet as professor and student in the classroom. The same two people will interact differently when they meet at a bar mitzvah or church social than when they meet on a street downtown.

ESTABLISHING COMPLEMENTARITY OR SYMMETRICALITY

We also punctuate interpersonal communication transactions by establishing and maintaining complementarity or symmetricality of relationship.[20] A symmetrical relationship is one in which the communicants perceive themselves as equals within that transaction. A complementary relationship is one in which the communicants perceive an inequality between them within the transaction—a hierarchy in which one is superior to the other in some sense.

The complementarity or symmetricality between two people may arise from their role relationships. The two authors of this book have maintained several combinations of relationships for several years. Den-

20. Watzlawick, Beavin, and Jackson, *Pragmatics of Human Communication*, pp. 67–70; also Jay Haley, "Control in Psychotherapy with Schizophrenics," *A.M.A. Archives of General Psychiatry* 5 (October 1961): 340–53; reprinted in *Therapy, Communication, and Change: Human Communication*, vol. 2, ed. Don D. Jackson (Palo Alto, Calif.: Science and Behavior Books, 1968), pp. 146–68 (esp. p. 151).

nis and Keith have been friends since their undergraduate days at college. As friends, they have a symmetrical relationship. While Keith was doing his graduate work, Dennis was his advisor and major professor. As student and professor, they had a complementary relationship; Dennis was in a one up position in their transactions concerning academic matters. Keith is an ordained minister and has sometimes served as Dennis's pastor and counselor. In that complementary relationship, Keith is in a one up position when advising, counseling, and providing pastoral care and concern. The nature of their relationship is complementary or symmetrical depending upon the social context of a given transaction between them.

Thus the same people can maintain a diversity of complementary and symmetrical relationships depending upon the roles they assume in various social situations. The ease with which a person assumes different complementary and symmetrical relationships under appropriate social circumstances is undoubtedly one measure of the healthiness of that person's communication.

DIFFICULTIES IN COMMUNICATION ARISING FROM INCONGRUENT MESSAGES

Axiom III stated that all difficulties in interpersonal communication may be seen as arising from incongruency somewhere within the structure of an interpersonal transaction.[21] Incongruency between message systems, between levels of meaning, and between ways of punctuating transactions are probably the most common sources of difficulties in interpersonal communication.

INCONGRUENCY BETWEEN MESSAGE SYSTEMS

People often express one meaning with their language, another with their gestures, and perhaps a third meaning with their sexuality or their manipulation of space. When a person with whom we are interacting uses multiple message systems that generate incongruent messages, we experience difficulties in communicating with that person.

A speech therapist had been working with a nine-year-old girl whom we will call Barbara. Barbara was straining her voice to such an extent that the therapist feared continued abuse would require major surgery.

Near the end of the first year of therapy, Barbara sent the therapist a card with a picture of a puppy on the cover. Inside the card Barbara had printed this message:

21. See chapter 2 for a definition of *incongruency* and some bibliographic sources for the concept.

"To the best speech teacher anyone could ever have. Here is
something I know you will not like but I am going to tell you
anyway. Roses are red, violets are black, you would look better with a knife in your back. Love, Barbara."

We are at once struck by the many problems in communication
arising from the incongreuncy between messages in the sending of this
card. There is not only incongruency between message systems, but
also incongruency between various parts of the same message system.

Sending the card is an act within the gestural message system. It is
usually a friendly gesture—one that shows affection, concern, or sympathy. In this case, the cute puppy on the cover indicates that the card
is a gesture of friendship or affection. The opening lines of the language
message and the signature are congruent with the gestural meaning of
the card. "To the best speech teacher anyone could ever have" and
"Love, Barbara" confirm our initial interpretation of the gestural message as one of friendliness and affection.

The stark incongruency between the opening lines and the verse
is most striking. "You would look better with a knife in your back" is
an open expression of hostility. One could hardly be more direct. This
part of the language message system is obviously incongruent with the
other parts of the language message system and with the gestural
message.

By breaking the transaction down into its various elements, the
therapist can readily determine the several dimensions of message and
pinpoint the location of the incongruency in the message systems. The
difficulty in communication for the therapist is pragmatic. How should
she respond to Barbara's highly complex and incongruent message?

While the card and its contents communicate affection, perhaps even
love, they also communicate hate and aggression. If the therapist
chooses to assume a role in which she acknowledges only Barbara's
affection, the therapist would be denying Barbara's expressed hostility.
To deny the hostility would be, in effect, to fail to confirm Barbara as a
person who needs to express hostility and aggression. If the therapist
chooses to assume a role in which she acknowledges only Barbara's
hostility, the therapist would then be denying Barbara's affection and
failing to confirm Barbara as a person who needs affection.

Communication like Barbara's is neither unique nor unusual. Although the incongruencies are not usually as sharply defined, many
people engage in this kind of communication frequently. A person may
often say one thing with words but indicate quite the opposite meaning
with their bodies. A husband might say, "Of course I love you very
much," while actually pushing his wife away from him. A son or daugh-

ter can tell a parent, "I think of you every day," and forget to send a birthday or anniversary card.

In all such cases the problems in communication lie in the incongruency between message systems. To which message should the other person respond? Is it possible to respond to both messages at the same time? What is the role relationship created in the transaction? Which message system is the more important? When one or both communicants have difficulty handling the incongruency within a transaction, there will inevitably be difficulties in their relationship.

INCONGRUENCY BETWEEN LEVELS OF MEANING

The transaction involving George, Martha, Nick, and Honey from *Who's Afraid of Virginia Woolf?* illustrated several incongruencies between one or more levels of meaning. This kind of incongruency is probably the most frequent incongruency in interpersonal transactions. Incongruency may arise, for example, between the denotative and the interpretive levels of meaning; a person may say something but indicate that it is not to be interpreted literally. Humor, sarcasm, facetiousness, cattiness, self-deprecation—all are forms of incongruency in which one level of meaning negates another level of meaning.

In general, people are able to deal with incongruencies between levels of meaning without encountering major difficulties. Problems arise when one or both persons in the transaction assign meaning to the incongruency itself. Jane may jokingly say to Joe, "I'm so ashamed to be seen with you." The interpretive level indicates that the denotative level is to be taken as a sarcastic or facetious remark. If Joe interprets the message as sarcasm and responds to it in a way Jane sees as appropriate, then their relationship remains the same.

Joe, however, might begin to attend to the fact that there was incongruency between the various levels of meaning. He might begin to wonder whether Jane was really joking or whether the interpretive level of meaning (indicating that the remark was facetious) was a cover for her real meaning (that she actually is ashamed of him). If Joe assigns meaning to this incongruency, then the message becomes incongruent instead of sarcastic; Joe will have difficulty determining the appropriate role relationship to assume in his transactions with Jane.

INCONGRUENCY IN PUNCTUATION OF TRANSACTIONS

Many people run into difficulties in living because they persist in sequencing interpersonal transactions differently from the people with whom they are communicating. One such person, who can be called the perpetual critic, is always wary of agreeing with anyone about the mutual and simultaneous nature of transactions. He or she finds it necessary for some reason to place blame on the other person for difficulties in their interaction. Such persons build their interactions with others on the assumption that if they can always fix the blame on the other person for beginning the transactions that lead to difficulties in living, they have somehow absolved themselves.

People who constantly try to punctuate their transactions so that other people can be blamed for problems are people who have adopted a life position of "I'm O.K.—You're Not O.K."[22] These people take their life positions with them into their communication transactions. They tend to be untrusting and therefore are generally unable to establish strong relationships with other people based on trust.

Such interpersonal communication behavior is both dishonest and unhealthy. Interpersonal communication transactions are mutual and simultaneous. It takes two people to communicate; it takes two people to agree on the roles and the rules of their communication. Both people are responsible for problems in the transaction that lead to difficulties in living.

Watzlawick, Beavin, and Jackson illustrated this mutual responsibility with the now classic example of the withdrawing husband and the nagging wife.[23] On the one hand, we can sequence the interaction by saying that the husband withdraws because the wife nags. According to that punctuation the wife is to blame because we assume she began the interaction by nagging. On the other hand, it is equally likely that the wife nags because the husband withdraws. She may believe it is the only way she can continue to interact with him. If we punctuate their interaction in this way, we assume that the husband is to blame because he withdrew first, causing the wife to nag in order to maintain communication with him.

From the transactional point of view, the husband and the wife are engaged in transactions that require mutual response. The wife could not continue to nag as easily if the husband did not withdraw; nor could the husband continue to be withdrawn as effectively if the wife suddenly stopped speaking to him. The husband and wife have implicitly collaborated to create patterns of behavior that would be destroyed if either of them acted differently.

In healthy interpersonal communication, people enter into their transactions with the understanding that the roles and rules of the

22. Thomas A. Harris, *I'm O.K.—You're O.K.* (New York: Harper & Row, 1967; Old Tappan, N.J.: Fleming H. Revell Co., Spire Books, 1973), esp. pp. 72–73.
23. Watzlawick, Beavin, and Jackson, *Pragmatics of Human Communication*, pp. 56–58.

transactions are mutual. They are willing to share the responsibility for their transactions. In healthy communication, people are willing to risk assuming an inappropriate role or violating some implicit rule without feeling that they have to blame other people for misunderstandings. They strive to punctuate their transactions with mutual beginnings and mutual endings.

Incongruent punctuation may also occur when two people label the social situation differently. One might see the situation as a time for joy while the other person sees it as a somber occasion. One might see the situation as sexual while the other deems sexual advances to be completely inappropriate. One might see the situation as strictly business while the other sees it as a social event.

In other cases, one person may deliberately manipulate the labeling of the situation for personal advantage. Many of us have experienced situations in which a person leads us to believe that he or she is taking a survey in order to gain our participation in the transaction. After getting us to cooperate, the person suddenly relabels the situation as a sales encounter. This relabeling (an entirely different punctuation) significantly changes the relationship between the communicants. Instead of having an interviewer and interviewee, with the corresponding behaviors of seeking information and providing information, we suddenly are confronted with the roles of salesperson and customer. The two parties of the transaction are punctuating the situation differently if one is labeling it sales encounter and is playing the role of salesperson while the other is still labeling it a survey and continuing to behave as interviewee. The deliberate manipulation of labeling the event to create disparate punctuation often gives one of the parties a significant advantage over the other.

Two people may punctuate a transaction differently regarding complementarity and symmetricality. In the relationship between Keith and Dennis, there were undoubtedly times when the social situation called for a symmetrical relationship, yet one or the other would strive to assert a one up position.

> Dennis: *Where did I leave the manuscript?*
>
> Keith: *You've lost it again? Why don't you ever make a note of where you leave things? It would save you time, you know.*

Let's assume they are both communicating as friends and are both punctuating the social situation with the same label. Dennis is asking a direct question, which Keith should answer in a way that maintains a symmetrical relationship within the transaction. If Keith had simply said, "I don't know," he would have kept the relationship symmetrical, and they would have punctuated the transaction the same. Instead Keith asserts superiority over Dennis and punctuates the transaction differently.

INCONGRUENCY BETWEEN MESSAGE AND CONTEXT

One other form of incongruency falls outside of our previous analyses of incongruency. In this case there is incongruency between the content of the message and the context or social situation in which the message is produced. Suppose a wife has burned the dinner on several different evenings. Each time the wife burns the dinner, the husband says, "The meal is really very good." On other evenings, the wife fixes tremendous meals; everything turns out perfectly. The husband says, "The meal is really very good."

In this case, the wife is left with a set of messages that cannot be interpreted clearly. Is the husband serious when he says, "The meal is very good," when it is really burned? Is he being facetious when he says, "The meal is very good," when it turns out as she wants it to? Because the husband uses the same message in contradictory contexts, she cannot distinguish when he "means" his statements and when he does not. The wife is left with messages that are incongruent with the contexts of their transactions. Because of this incongruency, the meaning of the message is undecidable.[24]

SUMMARY

Whenever two people enter into an interpersonal communication transaction and become parts of an ecological system, all their behavior has the potential of being communicative. In actual practice, however, only a few behaviors are attended to and assigned meaning. These behaviors are usually selected on the basis of cultural codes that determine which sets of behavior are message systems. These message systems exist as environments to every person within a culture. These systems also become instruments—parts of the environment that each person can manipulate to generate meaning. When people communicate, they generally manipulate four primary message systems—language, gesture, space, and sexuality. At least these four message systems are necessary for understanding interpersonal communication.

Regardless of which message system or combination of message systems persons use, they generate meaning on three levels: the denota-

24. The concept of undecidability is discussed by Watzlawick, Beavin, and Jackson, *Pragmatics of Human Communication*, p. 224.

tive, interpretive, and relational levels. Denotation is the content level of meaning. The interpretive and relational levels of meaning are about the nature of the message itself and are therefore described as meta-communication.

The meaning of messages is also determined by the way the communicants punctuate the transaction. Punctuation is the way individuals break up the continuous stream of behavior and experience into meaningful units. Punctuation may occur through sequencing (assigning beginnings and endings to individual transactions within the flow of communication), labeling the social situation, and establishing complementarity (inequality) or symmetricality (equality) between the communicants.

Incongruencies between message systems, between levels of meaning, and between ways of punctuating transactions are often the source of difficulties in communication.

QUESTIONS FOR REVIEW

1. What are the four primary message systems?
2. Distinguish between the environmental and the instrumental dimensions of messages.
3. What are the three levels of meaning? Give an example of each.
4. What is the definition of *punctuation*? What are the three ways in which people punctuate interpersonal communication transactions?
5. Contrast complementarity with symmetricality.
6. What are the various kinds of incongruency discussed in this chapter. What kinds of difficulties in communication arise from each kind of incongruency?

EXPLORATIONS

1. If you are keeping a communication journal, this exercise may serve as a valuable guide to this week's entry. If you are not keeping a journal, you may find this to be an extremely valuable exercise to do on your own.

People often kill a conversation by making comments that mean something other than what the statements literally say. These "killer statements"[25] may take the form of a put-down ("Are you serious?") or a dismissal reaction ("That's stupid"). Take a specific two or three hour period during the day, and conscientiously jot down each

25. Jack Canfield and Harold C. Wells, *100 Ways to Enhance Self-Concept in The Classroom: A Handbook for Teachers and Parents* (Englewood Cliffs, N.J.: Prentice-Hall, 1976).

killer statement that you hear. Note the situation in which it arose. At the end of the day, carefully examine each statement, and write out what you think the intended meaning of the statement was. For example, a dismissal reaction at the denotative level ("That's stupid") may be an expression of jealousy at the relational level ("I am jealous that I didn't think of that idea because it makes you one up on me and I have to put you down in order not to feel inferior"). Or it may be a self-denying statement on the interpretive level, indicating that the speaker does not want the statement to be interpreted literally. After analyzing four or five such statements, you will begin to see the value of looking at the multiple levels of meaning that people generate in interpersonal transactions.

2. Consider one or two of the most important personal relationships in your life right now. How do you use each of the four primary message systems to maintain those relationships?

3. A father and his son are talking at a family dinner. If they both label the situation as a friendly discussion, what kinds of roles and implicit rules are they likely to adopt?

4. If the father labels the social situation as a friendly discussion while the son sees it as a reprimand situation, there would be incongruency in the punctuation. Identify the implicit rules of communication that each would be using to guide his communication in the transaction. What specific difficulties in communication would most likely emerge?

5. Think of the last upsetting argument or confrontation you had with someone. How can you explain the difficulty in communication with that person in terms of the types of incongruency discussed in this chapter? What was the incongruency that was the source of the difficulty? What could have been done to eliminate the incongruency and remove the difficulty in communication?

FOR FURTHER READING

Hall, Edward T. *Beyond Culture.* Garden City, N.Y.: Doubleday & Co., Anchor Press, 1976.

Hall's book examines the power of our cultural environment, the difficulty of discerning or studying that power because of the nature of our lives and language in culture, and the importance of context in giving meaning to symbols in any culture. Hall offers a perspective on how culture and communication can be better understood.

Hall, Edward T. *The Silent Language.* Garden City, N.Y.: Doubleday & Co., 1959; Greenwich, Conn.: Fawcett Publications, 1959.

Anthropologist Hall reports on the pervasive silent (nonverbal) message systems which affect human behavior. Conceiving of culture as a form of communication, Hall shows how various cultures use time, space, sexuality, and other message systems differently. His analysis emphasizes the importance of recognizing cultural differences in communicating with people of other cultures.

Johnson, Wendell. *People in Quandries: The Semantics of Personal Adjustment.* New York: Harper and Row, 1946.

This is a highly readable, practical book dealing with the way people use language to create difficulties in living. Johnson presents many "solutions" to these problems based upon the principles of general semantics.

Satir, Virginia. *Conjoint Family Therapy: A Guide to Theory and Technique.* Rev. ed. Palo Alto, Calif.: Science and Behavior Books, 1967.

This readable book, straightforwardly written in an outline format, presents family theory and communication theory from the systems and clinical perspective of the so-called Palo Alto school (which includes Watzlawick, Jackson, and others). The theory and practice of therapy is then explained from within this framework. Therapy with the entire family (and not just with the identified patient) is shown to be necessary and desirable because of the interrelatedness of all family members and the impossibility of not communicating.

Chapter 4

Perspectives: Communication Experience

All communication between persons involves the creation or discovery of meaning. The meaning of the communication between two parties in a transaction depends not just on their behavior (generating messages) but also on their experience (perceiving and interpreting messages). Meaning, in other words, is rooted in how people experience each other. Our transactional model helps clarify the role of experience in communication in the following ways. First, it defines experience. Second, it maintains that experience exists on multiple levels. Third, it demonstrates that the patterns of experience that shape interpersonal communication—whether for good or ill—are transactional in nature.

What is experience? As conceived within our transactional model, *experience* is the process of perceiving and interpreting some stimuli—what someone does, says, etc.[1] Suppose Charles and Mary are out on a date and have seen a movie. Upon leaving the theater, they talk about where to go and what to do next. At one point in the conversation, Mary says, "We can do anything you'd like to do." Charles perceives her behavior; he pays attention to what she says and does. He must also interpret what he has perceived; he must ask himself, "What does she mean by that?" Charles's experience of Mary's comment consists of what he perceives (what he actually hears and sees) and how he interprets it (what he thinks it means). Charles's reply to Mary will be based on his experience (perception and interpretation) of her comment within the transaction and within their relationship. Communication between Charles and Mary will probably proceed smoothly (other factors being equal) as long as *Charles's* experience of Mary's comment is essentially

1. R. D. Laing, H. Phillipson, and A. R. Lee, *Interpersonal Perception: A Theory and a Method of Research* (New York: Springer Publishing Co., 1966; New York: Harper & Row, Perennial Library, 1972), p. 15.

the same as *her* experience of her comment—that is, as long as any given behavior is experienced similarly or congruently by both participants in a transaction. Problems begin to arise, however, when the two parties' experiences are incongruent or dissimilar. Such experiential congruency and incongruency can be seen best from within the framework provided by the seventh axiom of the transactional model of interpersonal communication.

Axiom VII: *Interpersonal communication transactions involve multiple levels of experience, or perspectives.*

EXPERIENCE OF PERSONS VS. EXPERIENCE OF OBJECTS

The analysis of levels of experience in communication must begin with an awareness of the difference between experiencing an inanimate object and experiencing another person. Experiencing an object involves perception (gathering data through the five senses about the object's size, shape, color, etc.) and interpretation (deciding what kind of object it is—a book, a pencil, etc.—and what significance it has at the present moment). Note that in experiencing an object, we are unconcerned with how the object experiences us. Books and pencils do not experience! Any reader who wonders how this book is perceiving him or her should probably take a break!

Experiencing another person is perceptually and physiologically like perceiving an inanimate object, since gathering sense data is much the same regardless of whether we are looking at a book or a person. But interpretively and psychologically, the difference between experiencing another person and an inanimate object is tremendous![2] People, unlike objects, are experiencing us as we are experiencing them. That is, *they* are perceiving and interpreting what *we* say and do at the same time that *we* are perceiving and interpreting what *they* say and do.[3] The experiential process is no longer unilateral (a person experiencing a book); it becomes transactional (two persons simultaneously experiencing each other). Thus, experience of persons is transactional; experience of objects is not.

In analyzing interpersonal communication transactions, we must be concerned with the experience of persons—how two parties in a dyad

2. The physical similarity and psychological difference between person perception and object perception is discussed by Fritz Heider, *The Psychology of Interpersonal Relations* (New York: John Wiley & Sons, 1958), p. 21; and Renato Tagiuri, "Person Perception," in *The Handbook of Social Psychology*, Vol. 3, ed. Gardner Lindzey and Elliot Aronson, 2d ed. (Reading, Mass.: Addison-Wesley Publishing Co., 1968), pp. 395–96.

3. Laing, Phillipson, and Lee, *Interpersonal Perception*, p. 34.

experience each other.[4] When Mary tells Charles that they can do anything he would like, his communicative response will be appropriate
only if he figures out what she meant. He must try to interpret her
comment as she herself interprets it; otherwise, his response could get
him in big trouble! Mary's experience is not something that Charles can
see, exactly; it is physically invisible to him. Nevertheless, Charles
experiences Mary as an experiencing person (and vice versa). Thus,
each person in a dyad experiences events, and experiences (more or
less accurately) the other person's experiences of those same events.

So we are led to postulate the existence of multiple levels of experience, or *multiple perspectives,* within every interpersonal communication transaction. This basic theory of multiple perspectives and its related concepts are based upon Laing, Phillipson and Lee's book, *Interpersonal Perception.*[5] There are three levels of perspectives with which
we (like Laing et al.) are most concerned: (1) the direct perspective—a
person's direct view of an issue; (2) the metaperspective—one person's
view of another person's view of an issue; and (3) the meta-metaperspective—one person's view of another person's view of the first person's view of an issue. In order to understand how these multiple levels
of experience function in interpersonal communication, we must first
recognize the possible relationships and issues that can exist in dyads.

RELATIONSHIPS AND ISSUES

In any dyadic transaction, there are four possible relationships involving the two members.[6] For purposes of explanation, we use a husband-
wife dyad, although any dyad that has existed for a relatively long
period of time could also be used.

In a marital dyad, the two centers of experience can be labeled the
husband (H) and the wife (W). Each of these persons has a relationship
with self and with spouse:

> Wife has a relationship with her husband (WH)
> Husband has a relationship with his wife (HW)
> Wife has a relationship with herself (WW)
> Husband has a relationship with himself (HH)

These are the only four possible relationships involving just the husband and wife within the dyad.

There is virtually no limit, however, to the number of content issues
upon which the four relationships can focus. An *issue* may be defined

4. R. D. Laing, *The Politics of Experience* (New York: Ballantine Books, 1967), pp. 17–22.
5. Laing, Phillipson, and Lee, *Interpersonal Perception.* The various perspectives are explained
on pp. 68–75.
6. Ibid., pp. 70–71.

as some content aspect of the relationship between the two people in the dyad. A few sample issues are respect, love, responsibility for, honesty, forgiveness, worry, dependency, kindness, blame, humiliation, disappointment, doubt, hate, deception, and spoiling.[7] For instance, the husband has a relationship with himself (HH) regarding the issue of respect (his respect for himself). The husband also has a relationship with his wife (HW) regarding respect (his respect for her). Similarly, the wife has a relationship with herself (WW) regarding the issue of respect (her respect for herself) and a relationship with her husband (WH) regarding respect (her respect for him). The four relationships can focus upon any issue. Since all relationships involve issues, we can speak of *issue relationships*.

PERSPECTIVES

The four relationships exist for any given issue, regardless of who is looking at the dyad. The husband, the wife, or some third party (such as the reader or any other observer) can view each of the four relationships regarding any issue. These views of issue relationships may be called *perspectives*.

THE DIRECT PERSPECTIVE

Each of the four relationships in any given dyadic interpersonal communication transaction can be viewed *directly* by each member of the dyad.[8] For example, the husband has a direct perspective on his wife's relationship with him. His direct perspective (his experience of that relationship) can be represented diagrammatically as $H{\rightarrow}(WH)$. The wife, of course, also has a direct perspective on her relationship with her husband, diagramed $W{\rightarrow}(WH)$. Notice that *each* partner (husband and wife) has a direct perspective on the *same* relationship—in this case, the wife's relationship with the husband (WH).

The illustration of direct perspectives on the opposite page focuses on the issue of respect in the wife's relationship with the husband. At the left is the husband's direct perspective. At the right is the wife's direct perspective. In this case, the partners' direct perspectives are congruent; each reports the direct view that the wife respects the husband. Obviously, in actual experience, direct perspectives (or certain other perspectives) are often incongruent. Such an incongruency would exist in the direct perspective illustration if he would have said, "She does not respect me."

7. Sixty issues are classified in ibid., pp. 66–68.
8. Ibid., pp. 68–71.

For purposes of notation in analyzing perspectives in transactions, the husband's direct perspective on each of the four relationships can be diagramed as follows:[9]

H's view of his wife's relationship with him   H→(WH)
H's view of his relationship with his wife   H→(HW)
H's view of his wife's relationship with herself   H→(WW)
H's view of his relationship with himself   H→(HH)

Likewise, the wife's direct perspective on each of the same four relationships can be diagramed as:

W's view of her relationship with her husband   W→(WH)
W's view of her husband's relationship with her   W→(HW)
W's view of her relationship with herself   W→(WW)
W's view of her husband's relationship with himself   W→(HH)

These two diagrams can be combined into one by placing the husband's direct perspective to the left of the relationship notation and the wife's direct perspective to the right. Their direct perspectives on the four relationships would then be diagramed as follows:

$$H→(WH)←W$$
$$H→(HW)←W$$
$$H→(WW)←W$$
$$H→(HH)←W$$

9. The diagrams are adapted from ibid., pp. 70 71.

Direct Perspectives

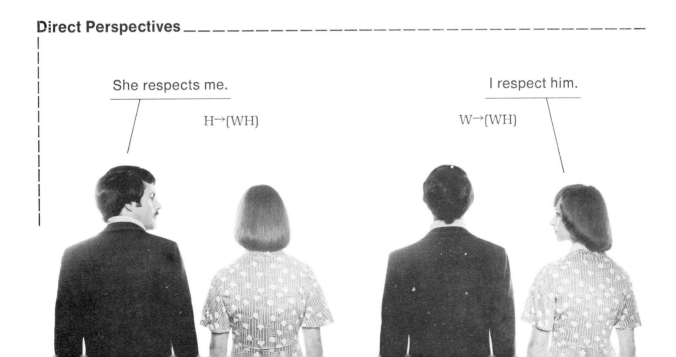

She respects me.

H→(WH)

I respect him.

W→(WH)

THE METAPERSPECTIVE

Each partner in a dyad has not only a direct perspective but also a metaperspective on each relationship.[10] The *metaperspective* is one person's view of the other's view of a given relationship. In other words, each person has a view of the other's direct perspective. For example, the husband has a metaperspective of his wife's relationship with him. This can be diagramed as H→W→(WH). The husband's metaperspective is his view of his wife's view of her relationship with him. The metaperspective always involves *one* person's imagination of how the *other* person is viewing the relationship.

In the metaperspective illustration, the relationship is still the wife's relationship with the husband (WH) and the issue is still respect. The left side pictures his metaperspective—what he thinks she thinks regarding her respect for him. The right side shows *her* metaperspective— what she thinks he thinks of the relationship.

Each dyadic partner will always have a metaperspective—a view of the other's direct perspective—on any given issue relationship. Whenever we try to figure out how other people view things, we are forming metaperspectives.

For purposes of notation, it is possible to represent the metaperspectives as W→H→(WH)←W←H. This diagram would be read in the following manner: (reading from left to center) the wife imagines the husband's view of her relationship with him; and (reading from right to center) the

10. Ibid., pp. 71–76.

Metaperspectives _____

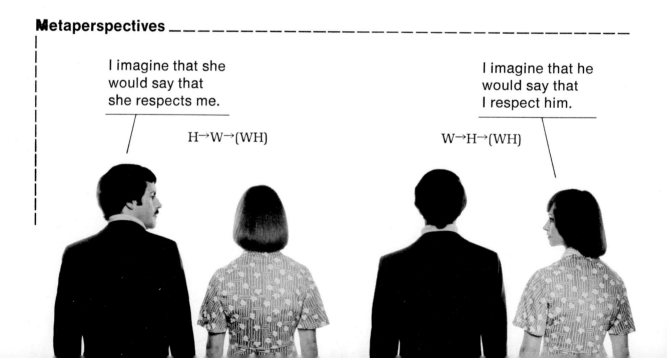

I imagine that she
would say that
she respects me.

H→W→(WH)

I imagine that he
would say that
I respect him.

W→H→(WH)

husband imagines the wife's view of her relationship with him. The diagram may be constructed in a similar manner for each of the other three relationships in the dyad.

THE META-METAPERSPECTIVE

In addition to having a direct perspective and a metaperspective, each partner also has a meta-metaperspective on each relationship.[11] That is, each person has a view of the other's view of the first person's view of the issue relationship. In other words, each person has a view of the other's metaperspective.

In the meta-metaperspective illustration, the same relationship (WH) and issue (respect) are shown. At the left is his meta-metaperspective; he thinks that she thinks that he believes that she respects him. The right side indicates her meta-metaperspective; she thinks that he thinks that she believes that she respects him.

While higher levels of experience (such as the fourth level of experience, the meta-meta-metaperspective) are theoretically possible, they are too complex for most of us to understand. We will deal with the first three levels of experience because they are essential elements in our transactional model of interpersonal communication. They are necessary concepts for understanding how communication is influenced by experience.

11. Ibid.

Meta-metaperspectives ——————————————————————————————

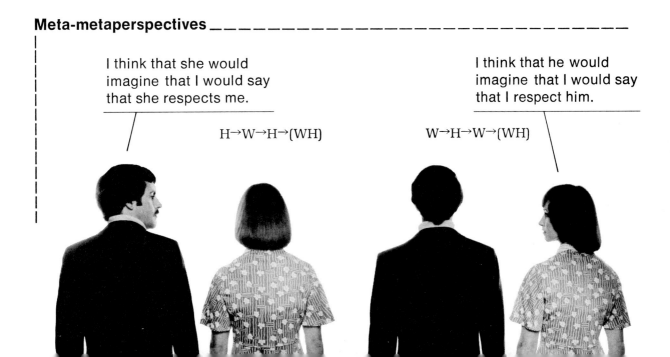

I think that she would imagine that I would say that she respects me.

H→W→H→(WH)

I think that he would imagine that I would say that I respect him.

W→H→W→(WH)

As communicators, we are always trying to estimate how others see things. Our success or failure at this task is reflected in our patterns of perspectives. Various patterns of congruency and incongruency between perspectives have important implications for interpersonal communication.

PATTERNS OF CONGRUENCY AND INCONGRUENCY BETWEEN PERSPECTIVES

Having identified issues, relationships, and three levels of perspectives, we can now precisely discuss the most common terms people use to describe their interpersonal communication: agreement, disagreement, understanding, and misunderstanding.[12] These terms have a very precise meaning within the transactional model of interpersonal communication. They are described as certain patterns of congruency and incongruency between perspectives.

AGREEMENT AND DISAGREEMENT

Agreement and disagreement are concepts associated only with the direct perspectives that two people have in their relationships. By comparing two people's direct perspectives on an issue relationship, we can determine whether the two people agree or disagree.

Agreement may be defined as the congruency of the direct perspective of one person with the direct perspective of the other person in the

12. These and other patterns of perspectives are explained in ibid., pp. 76–92.

Agreement _____ _____

I respect her.

H→(HW)

He respects me.

W→(HW)

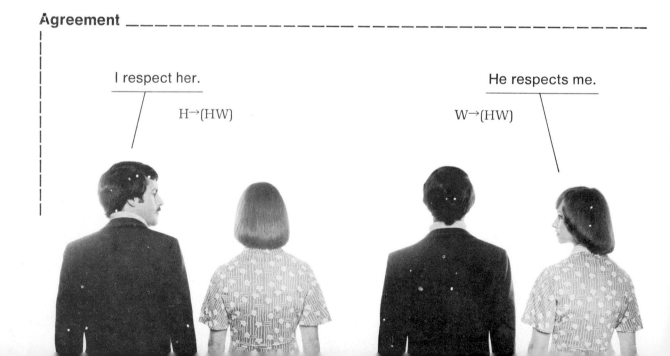

dyad. In the illustration of agreement, the issue is again respect, but this time the relationship is the husband's relationship to his wife (HW). Since the direct perspectives are congruent, the two people agree on this issue relationship.

Disagreement may be defined as the incongruency of the direct perspective of one person with the direct perspective of the other person in the dyad. In the illustration, the issue is honesty, and the relationship is the wife's relationship to her husband (WH). Since the direct perspectives are not congruent, the two people disagree on the issue of honesty in her relationship to him.

In the illustration of disagreement, the wife feels that she is not honest with her husband in her relationship to him. The husband, however, feels that she is honest with him. On the basis of the information given, neither person can be judged right or wrong. The illustration merely shows that they are in disagreement on the issue.

Much has been written about problems of agreement and disagreement in interpersonal relationships. While agreement and disagreement undoubtedly affect interpersonal communication, they are relatively unimportant in themselves. Whether two people agree or disagree on an issue within their relationship is largely irrelevant to their relationship as a whole. Husbands and wives, close friends, and lovers manage to live happily together with various areas of disagreement. Employers and employees can maintain good relationships and good communication in spite of substantial areas of disagreement. To improve interpersonal communication, it is not necessary to achieve agreement; it is more important to achieve understanding.

Disagreement ———————————————————————————————

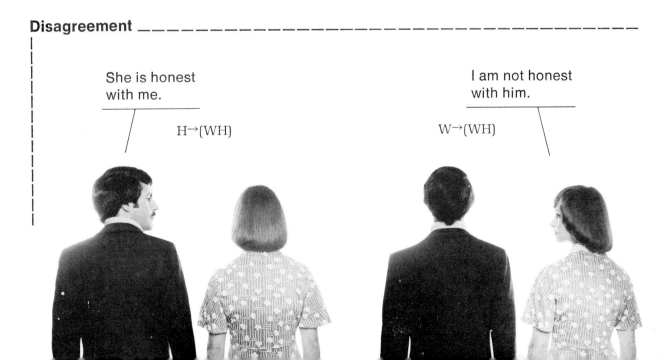

She is honest with me.

H→(WH)

I am not honest with him.

W→(WH)

UNDERSTANDING AND MISUNDERSTANDING

While the concepts of agreement and disagreement involve only the direct perspectives, the concepts of understanding and misunderstanding involve both the direct perspectives and the metaperspectives. To determine whether there is understanding or misunderstanding, it is necessary to compare one person's metaperspective with the other's direct perspective.

Understanding may be defined as congruency between the metaperspective of one person and the direct perspective of the other person in the dyad. To find out if the wife understands the husband, we compare the wife's metaperspective with the husband's direct perspective. Another comparison—of the husband's metaperspective with the wife's direct perspective—determines if he understands her.

In the illustration of understanding, the wife correctly imagines what the husband actually thinks. She understands her husband on the issue of honesty in her relationship with him (WH).

Misunderstanding is incongruency between one's direct perspective and the other's metaperspective. In the illustration of misunderstanding, the husband does not correctly imagine what his wife actually thinks on the issue of honesty in the (WH) relationship.

In determining patterns of understanding and misunderstanding, it is important to remember that the person whose metaperspective is being examined is the one who is *doing the understanding or misunderstanding.* The person whose direct perspective is examined is, of course,

Understanding _

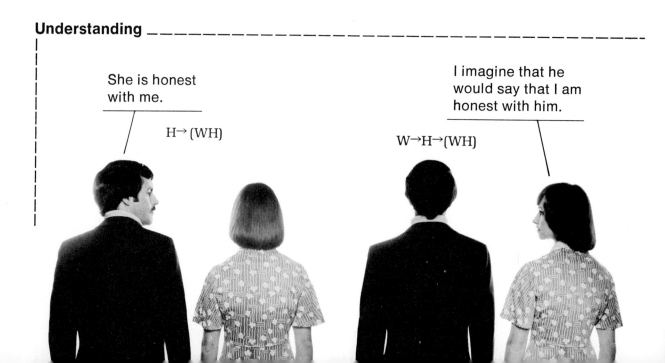

She is honest with me.

H→(WH)

I imagine that he would say that I am honest with him.

W→H→(WH)

the person who is *being understood or misunderstood.*

Understanding and misunderstanding are more important to healthy interpersonal communication than simple agreement or disagreement. When two people disagree but understand that they disagree, they minimize their difficulties in communication.

On the other hand, problems in communication arise when two people agree but one or both do not understand that they agree. A husband and wife may actually agree that he is honest with her (HW relationship), but the husband may misunderstand and feel that she disagrees with him. Or the wife may misunderstand that he agrees with her; or they may both misunderstand. We have all seen two people engaged in animated argument in which both people agree, but they simply don't understand that they agree. These patterns of incongruency between perspectives usually lead to arguments and bad feelings between people.

Likewise, difficulties arise when two people disagree, but one or both think they agree. Bob and Bill work in the same office. Bob thinks Bill agrees with him on a critical issue. Bill, however, knows that he disagrees with Bob on this particular issue. Bill has even tried to explain to Bob that he disagrees. But Bob seems unable to understand what Bill is talking about, because Bob fails to see that there is disagreement between them. When the critical vote on the issue comes and Bill votes against Bob, Bob may feel like he has been knifed in the back. Within that particular relationship, Bob and Bill disagree; while Bill understands that they disagree, problems arise because Bob misunderstands.

Misunderstanding

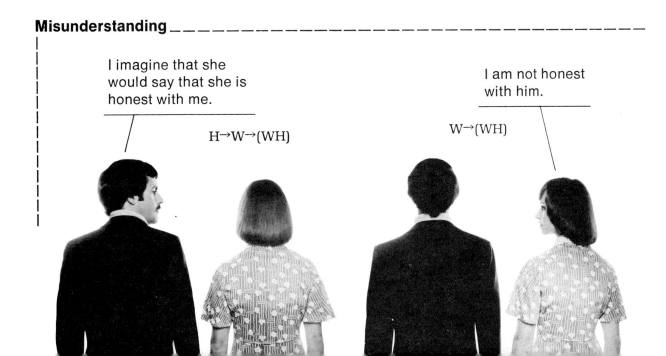

I imagine that she would say that she is honest with me.

H→W→(WH)

I am not honest with him.

W→(WH)

People may improve interpersonal communication by striving to reduce the amount of misunderstanding that exists over the various issue relationships in the dyad. The people involved in the transaction may do this themselves, or they may seek the help of a therapist, counselor, social worker, minister, management consultant, or other skilled professional. A major goal in interpersonal communication is not so much that people agree with each other, but that they understand whether they agree or disagree.

REALIZATION AND FAILURE OF REALIZATION

The next patterns of congruency and incongruency between perspectives are realization and failure of realization.[13] The members of a dyad do not just agree or disagree. Nor do they merely understand or misunderstand their agreement or disagreement. They also realize or fail to realize that they understand or misunderstand each other. To determine realization or failure of realization, we compare one person's meta-metaperspective with the other person's metaperspective on the same issue.

Realization occurs when one person's meta-metaperspective is congruent with the other's metaperspective. The illustration of realization shows the husband's meta-metaperspective at the left. The wife's metaperspective is shown at the right. If we compare these two perspectives, we see that:

his meta-metaperspective	$H \rightarrow W \rightarrow H \rightarrow (WH)$
is her metaperspective	$W \rightarrow H \rightarrow (WH)$
as viewed by him	$H \rightarrow W \rightarrow H \rightarrow (WH)$

In other words,

his meta-metaperspective	(he thinks
	  she thinks
	    he sees
	      her respecting him)

and her metaperspective	(she thinks
	  he sees
	    her respecting him)

are congruent.

13. Ibid., pp. 80–92.

Realization has occurred. He realizes that she understands him on the issue of her respect for him.

Failure of realization is the incongruency of one person's meta-metaperspective with the other's metaperspective. Such failure of realization would occur if their perspectives were as follows:

his meta-metaperspective   (he thinks
         she does *not* think
            he sees
               her respecting him)

her metaperspective   (she thinks
         he sees
            her respecting him)

These two perspectives are incongruent. He fails to realize that she understands him on the issue of her respect for him.

Realization and failure of realization, the highest patterns of perspectives, are perhaps the most significant. It is important to know not only whether two people understand or misunderstand each other, but also whether they realize or fail to realize that they understand or misunderstand. If a husband and wife agree on an issue but misunderstand that they agree, they cannot begin to correct their misunderstanding until they realize that they misunderstand. An incongruency on any given level of experience can only be grasped from the next higher level.

Realization _

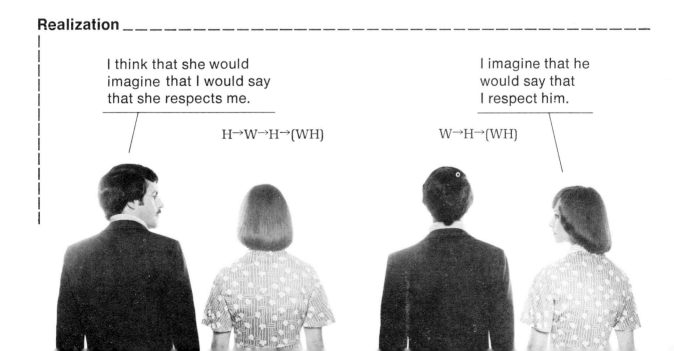

I think that she would imagine that I would say that she respects me.

H→W→H→(WH)

I imagine that he would say that I respect him.

W→H→(WH)

These patterns of congruency and incongruency between perspectives are admittedly complex to analyze, but they are commonplace in our everyday experience. We experience relationships and issues on multiple levels and intuitively sense (accurately or inaccurately) whether our experience is congruent with another person's experience —i.e., whether we agree or disagree, understand or misunderstand, realize or fail to realize.

FEELING OF BEING UNDERSTOOD OR MISUNDERSTOOD

The final patterns of congruency or incongruency between perspectives considered here involve the feeling of being understood or misunderstood.[14] These patterns are seen by examining the same person's direct perspective and meta-metaperspective. For example, Charles thinks that Mary respects him (his direct perspective). He also believes that she sees that he thinks she respects him (his meta-metaperspective). Since his direct perspective on the issue relationship is congruent with his view of her view of his direct perspective, he has the feeling of being understood. Conversely, if his direct perspective ("I think she respects me") is incongruent with his meta-metaperspective ("I think she believes that I think she does not respect me"), he has the feeling of being misunderstood. Obviously, it is more gratifying to feel understood.

THE TRANSACTIONAL SPIRAL OF PERSPECTIVES

These multiple perspectives and the various patterns of congruency and incongruency between them are important indicators of how communicators experience their relationship. The significance of these perspectives is heightened by their spiral quality. Each level on one person's side is intended to reflect the next lower level on the other person's side. (His metaperspective, for example, is intended to reflect her direct perspective.) The multiple perspectives of two dyadic partners are therefore like a spiral staircase. The spiral is evident in the progression of perspectives from side to side (each person viewing the *other's* experience) and up and down (each *higher* level of one person's experience being an estimation of the other's *lower* level experience). In other words, the spiral of perspectives is transactional (both parties simultaneously experiencing issue relationships as well as the other's experience of these issue relationships) and hierarchical (through multiple levels of experience). Therefore, we can speak of the transactional spiral of perspectives.[15]

14. Ibid., pp. 38, 80.
15. Laing, Phillipson, and Lee develop the basic notion of spiraling perspectives, which they call "the spiral of reciprocal perspectives," in *Interpersonal Perception*, pp. 30–45.

Such spirals can be completely congruent, completely incongruent, or somewhere in between.[16] The most harmonious, healthy spiral is probably characterized by mutual (that is, bilateral) congruency: agreement between the two people, understanding of each by the other, and realization of understanding by each. With such bilateral understanding and realization—such highly congruent experience—their communication is likely to be characterized by mutually accurate perception and correctly interpreted behavior. This kind of spiral tends to bring two people together, to increase their solidarity, to heighten their empathy.

In contrast, probably the most disruptive, unhealthy spiral features mutual incongruency: disagreement between partners, misunderstanding of each by the other, and failure by each to realize that they misunderstand. In such a case, each person's experience and related communication behavior would probably spiral off in the opposite direction from the other's. Since each one fails to see what the other sees and also fails to see that he fails to see it, each would react to the other inappropriately. This type of spiral leads to increasingly confused communication, reciprocal alienation, and relational problems.

Spirals can, of course, have some congruency and some incongruency. One such type of spiral exhibits a one-sidedness. For instance, he might understand her, even though she misunderstands him on the same issue relationship. Furthermore, he might realize that she misunderstands him, but she fails to realize that he understands her. In such a case, her inaccurate experience of him spirals off lopsidedly. The more he tries to correct her impressions, the more she misunderstands and fails to realize. This spiral would be extremely frustrating for him (he can never get through to her) and baffling to her (she cannot see why he is disconcerted, if she is even able to notice that).

Regardless of the type of spiral, the upper levels are the most significant in analyzing health or disturbance in the dyad's experience and communication.[17] Mere disagreement is not usually too serious in a dyadic relationship. Even though he says he respects her and she says he doesn't, a couple can conceivably discuss and eventually resolve such a disagreement. To do so, they need to understand that they are in disagreement. Likewise, misunderstanding is not too serious if the partners realize that they misunderstand; without such realization they are unable to deal with any misunderstanding.

Thus, the transactional spiral of perspectives offers important insight into the various ways in which members of a dyad can experience issues and relationships—insight into what those issues and relationships mean to each of them.

16. Ibid., pp. 76–92. Complete congruency is discussed on pp. 90, 139–41, with various less congruent patterns explained on pp. 90–92, 141–44.
17. Ibid., pp. 90, 146.

SUMMARY

Experience is as important as behavior in interpersonal communication. Experience includes both perception and interpretation. Unlike the experience of objects, the experience of persons is transactional in nature. There are three essential levels of experience: direct perspectives, meta-perspectives, and meta-metaperspectives. Various patterns of congruency and incongruency between perspectives involve agreement and disagreement, understanding and misunderstanding, realization and failure of realization, and the feeling of being understood or misunderstood. These patterns form transactional spirals of perspectives that have implications for ongoing interpersonal communication.

QUESTIONS FOR REVIEW

1. What is the difference between experience of persons and experience of objects?
2. What is an issue? a relationship? an issue relationship?
3. What are three different levels of perspectives? Diagram and give an example of each.
4. What perspectives are compared to determine each of the following:
   agreement or disagreement
   understanding or misunderstanding
   realization or failure of realization
   feeling of being understood or misunderstood
5. What is the transactional spiral of perspectives? Distinguish between healthy and unhealthy spirals.

EXPLORATIONS

1. Write a brief essay describing yourself as you think you would be seen by another person, such as your brother, sister, parent, close friend, etc. Then write another brief essay selecting a different person. Finally, compare the way you think each of those people sees you with your own image of yourself.
2. Consider the fact that somebody would like to be you. It might be a younger person who looks up to you; it might be an older person who sees something promising in you; it might be one of your peers— perhaps somebody in this class with you. After carefully reflecting on this fact, write a brief essay or series of paragraphs trying to describe why someone would want to be you. This is an excellent way to see your strengths as others see them. We particularly recommend this exercise for people keeping a communication journal.

3. Focusing upon a close personal relationship you have with someone, list three issues in your relationship on which you think the two of you agree. Next list three issues in your relationship on which you think you disagree. Ask the other person to do likewise. Compare your lists. Are you really in agreement or not? What other perspectives are evident in this activity? (Hint: Is your view of the other person's view involved?) Do you understand each other?

4. Choose two main characters from a television series, a movie, or a novel. Try to decide what kind of transactional spiral of perspectives exists between them. Typically do they agree or disagree? Does the first understand the second while the second misunderstands the first, or is understanding or misunderstanding mutual? What could be done to make their spiral healthier?

FOR FURTHER READING

Kotkas, L. J. "Informal Use of the 'Interpersonal Perception Method' in Marital Therapy." *Canadian Psychiatric Association Journal* 14 (February 1969): 11–14.

This article briefly summarizes the essential features of Laing, Phillipson and Lee's interpersonal perception method in its relevance to marital counseling. The author then suggests how the method could be adapted for informal use in marriage therapy.

Laing, R. D.; Phillipson, H.; and Lee, A. R. *Interpersonal Perception: A Theory and a Method of Research.* New York: Springer Publishing Co., 1966; New York: Harper & Row, Perennial Library, 1972.

In the first part of the book the authors present a theory of interpersonal perception involving multiple levels of perspective, dyadic interaction and interexperience, and the spiral of reciprocal perspectives. In the second part, they present their interpersonal perception method (IPM), review its historical antecedents, and describe it by reference to a study in which they use the IPM to investigate disturbed and nondisturbed marriages. The third and final section of the book contains the IPM questionnaire for "he" (in a male-female dyad). This is probably the most comprehensive and insightful single contribution to the study of interpersonal perception in recent years.

Laing, R. D. *Knots.* New York: Random House, 1970.

Knots is both a book of poetry and an application of the author's theory of interpersonal perception. The knots of which he speaks are tangles in the process of interpersonal perception, tie-ups between various perspectives held by different people. These knots are both funny and serious, for they illustrate the perceptual binds that are a part of living.

Williamson, L. Keith. "An Investigation of Perspectives on a Person's Relationship with Himself within Dyadic Marital Interpersonal Communication Systems." Ph.D. dissertation, Temple University, 1975.

After providing a theoretical and methodological rationale for studying interpersonal perception, Williamson reports on a study of seventy married couples using Laing, Phillipson and Lee's IPM. One finding was that when husbands and wives were in disagreement, wives tended to feel agreed with significantly more frequently than husbands.

Chapter 5

The Self in
Interpersonal
Communication
Transactions:
An Ecological View

In interpersonal communication transactions, the question, What does it mean? cannot be answered until we know the answer to two other questions, Who am I? and Who are you? The meaning of any message depends upon the roles of the communicators within the transaction. Every message generates a relational level of meaning that helps to establish and maintain the roles of the two persons communicating. Therefore every message is an attempt to define who I am in relationship to who you are. Every message is a request for the other person to confirm one's *self* within the role relationships of the transaction. Thus, whether we are concerned primarily with the study of messages, meaning, transactions, or any other dimension of interpersonal communication, we must squarely confront the concept of the self. The self is central to the study of interpersonal communication.

Each section of this chapter deals with a particular aspect of the ecological view of the self within interpersonal communication transactions. The first section shows how the self begins to form out of the patterns of communication between the mother and the infant. These patterns of communication (beginning immediately after birth and remaining throughout life) function to create and maintain the self of the mature adult. The second section presents four stages in the development of the self and shows how the experiences of the self become unified into a concept of "me" through communication with significant others. The third section introduces the concept of inference and explains the role of inference in feeling empathy with others. The fourth section analyzes *intrapersonal* communication as a complex form of interpersonal communication transactions.

TRANSACTIONAL THEORY OF THE SELF

Axiom VIII: *The self is created and maintained through interpersonal transactions.*

In the ecology of interpersonal communication, the self is a set of roles that a person may assume in a variety of social situations. One's self, and one's own perceptions of one's self, are shaped in relationships with other people. The self requires interaction with other human beings for its formation, development, and maintenance. The transactional nature of the self and its relationship to interpersonal communication processes are probably best explained by examining the formation and growth of the human self, beginning in infancy and continuing into adult life.

PREPERSONAL COMMUNICATION— ORGANIZATION OF EXPERIENCE

Both the symbolic interactionists and the psychoanalytic theorists stress the importance of the very early development of the human infant. Many people view this psychiatric emphasis on the first few weeks of life as an "obsession" of the whole field of psychiatry. Yet psychiatrists emphasize birth and the period immediately following because the infant's patterns of interaction with significant others in the environment become established during that time. These patterns *become the basic patterns of organizing and integrating experience and behavior in all future transactions.* As the child grows and develops, significant modifications can occur in these patterns of forming transactions with others. The basic patterns, however, generally remain with the individual throughout his or her life.

These very early patterns of organizing experience and behavior may be called prepersonal communication—that is, communication that occurs between the infant and its environment before the infant has acquired fully developed perceptual systems or the ability to behave according to the roles and rules that govern interpersonal communication transactions.

Prepersonal communication refers to the transaction patterns between the human infant and a mothering one from the moment of birth until sometime between two to four weeks after birth. The terms *mother* and *mothering one* do not refer to a sex distinction but to a role relationship. The role of mother or mothering one may be played by either a male or a female, by the natural mother, the father, an older brother, sister, cousin, wet nurse, etc. As long as the role of mothering one is properly fulfilled, the basic patterns of interaction will evolve naturally regardless of the sex or genetic relationship of the adult involved.

Most mammals are born with more fully developed nervous systems and perceptual mechanisms than are humans. At birth, the human infant cannot see. Focusing the eyes and visual recognition often take as long as six weeks to develop. The sense of hearing is often not fully functional. Gross bodily sensations are present, but the sense of touch as experienced by the human adult is not yet developed. This "premature birth" requires an extremely close relationship between the human infant and another human being to assure the infant's survival. The infant is incapable of caring for its needs.

PHYSIOLOGICAL NEEDS

What psychologists have often called *physiological needs* require interpersonal interaction for their satisfaction. The infant has needs for food, warmth, touch, and cleanliness; unless these needs are satisfied, the human infant will die. But the infant cannot fulfill its own physiological requirements. It cannot feed itself, clean itself, or keep itself warm. It cannot massage the body and satisfy its need for touch. During the lengthy period required for the full development of basic survival abilities, the human infant must have social interaction with other human beings.

INTERPERSONAL NEEDS

As the infant develops, it acquires other needs; the unfulfillment of these needs can also lead to harm or death. These needs are rooted in the social interaction between the infant and other people in its environment. They have been called *interpersonal needs* to distinguish them from the needs immediately manifest at birth. To separate physiological needs from interpersonal needs is somewhat artificial, however, since both require appropriate interpersonal interaction for their satisfaction. Schutz has identified the interpersonal needs as the need for affection, the need for inclusion, and the need for control.[1]

The *need for affection* is probably the earliest of the interpersonal needs to appear. This is the need to be loved and to love. In adult behavior and experience the need for affection is expressed as the need

1. William C. Schutz, *FIRO: A Three-Dimensional Theory of Interpersonal Behavior* (New York: Rinehart, 1958); reprint ed., *The Interpersonal Underworld* (Palo Alto, Calif.: Science & Behavior Books, 1966), esp. pp. 13–33.

to establish intimacy with at least one other human being. According to Schutz, the need for affection may be satisfied only in a one-to-one relationship. Love is a dyadic or transactional relationship.

The *need for inclusion,* in contrast, is satisfied in a many-to-one relationship; it can be fulfilled only by many persons. The need for inclusion is the need to be viewed by others as a member of a group, society, or tribe. It is a social need that is not usually part of the behavior of the newborn infant. By the time the child has learned to walk and talk, however, the need for inclusion is evident in the child's behavior. Inclusion behavior can be seen particularly in preschool nurseries; the children are strongly motivated by a need to be included in the activities of the group, to be recognized as a part of the group, and to feel the support of cooperative behavior with both the teachers and the other children.

The *need for control* is the need to manipulate others and to be manipulated by others. It is a need satisfied by power in interpersonal relationships. Roles in interpersonal transactions embody implicit power relationships between the two persons. This complementarity arises in transactions from the need to control and the need to be controlled by others.

Although these three interpersonal needs do not arise until after the first few weeks following birth, the mechanisms for integrating interpersonal transactions are the same for fulfilling interpersonal needs (for affection, inclusion, and control) as for fulfilling physiological needs (for food, warmth, touch, and cleanliness).

PATTERNS OF INTEGRATING DYADIC EXPERIENCE

Two important observations may be made about the human infant at birth. First, the experience of the infant may be said to be one of *prehension* rather than *perception.*[2] Since the infant is neurologically incomplete and the perceptual organs are not fully functional, the infant does not yet perceive and interpret the world as the adult does. In the preperceptual or prehensive state, the infant, insofar as we can tell, has no experience of self. Except for experiencing isolated tensions associated with physical needs, the infant has no perception even of its own body *per se.* Nevertheless the infant is physiologically capable of establishing and maintaining interactions with others appropriate and necessary for its survival (assuming the cooperation of the mothering one).

The second important observation is that the human infant is capable of feeling discomfort or tension when its basic life needs are not

2. Harry Stack Sullivan, *The Interpersonal Theory of Psychiatry,* ed. Helen Swick Perry and Mary Ladd Gawel (New York: W. W. Norton & Co., 1953), p. 76.

fully satisfied. We may call this discomfort, or absence of fulfillment, a *tension arising from needs*.[3] This tension creates behavior by the infant that is designed to obtain satisfaction of needs. When the infant experiences tension arising from hunger, it cries. When the infant experiences tension arising from lack of warmth, it cries. When the infant experiences tension from a lack of touch, it cries. And when the infant experiences tension from a lack of cleanliness (caused by excretion or urination), it cries. The cry is designed to evoke a response from a mothering one to satisfy the need and reduce the tension arising from that need.

This basic pattern of interaction may be diagramed as follows:

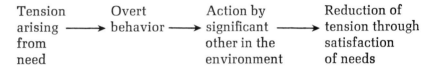

Tension arising from need ⟶ Overt behavior ⟶ Action by significant other in the environment ⟶ Reduction of tension through satisfaction of needs

Since the human infant cannot itself satisfy the need for hunger, warmth, touch or cleanliness, *the infant can meet the needs only through the integration (or formation) of an interpersonal transaction with a mothering one.*

Sullivan has observed that the infant organizes (or arranges) its experience of interactions into three forms. Since the prototype of infant-mother interaction is feeding the infant, Sullivan labeled the three types of experiences of interpersonal situations "good nipple," "wrong nipple," and "bad nipple."[4] The word *nipple* in these terms has little to do with the actual physical nipple of the mother since the mothering one might as easily be a male as a female. The terms refer to patterns of organizing (or arranging) interaction in the infant's experience. The good, wrong, and bad nipple situations are, in fact, the very earliest and most simplified role relationships experienced by human beings.

Good Nipple. The *good nipple* is a pattern of experience in which the infant and the mothering one integrate or form an interpersonal situation in such a way that the tension arising from needs is reduced and the needs are satisfied.

The typical pattern of interaction leading to a good nipple situation between the infant and the mothering one begins with the experience of tension arising from needs, such as hunger. The hungry infant cries, evoking a response from the mothering one which produces the experience of "nipple in lips" for the infant. The sucking reflex is present at birth and is automatically activated by the presence of the nipple in the lips. The infant sucks, milk or appropriate liquid is present, and the

3. Ibid., pp. 37–39.
4. Ibid., pp. 79–80.

need is fulfilled. The tension arising from the need is reduced. The interaction necessary for the infant's survival has been successfully integrated.

Wrong Nipple. The wrong nipple refers to a pattern of experience in which the infant and the mothering one integrate (form) an interpersonal situation in such a way that needs are not satisfied and tension is not reduced because of incorrect or inappropriate conditions or responses by the mothering one.

In the typical wrong nipple situation, the infant experiences tension arising from a need (hunger) and cries. The mothering one produces a nipple in the lips, but when the infant sucks, there is no fluid. Perhaps that breast does not give milk. Or if an artificial nipple is used, it may be blocked or too strong for the infant's sucking. In the case of the wrong nipple, the interpersonal situation between the infant and the mothering one is integrated or structured poorly. The conditions presented by the mothering one are not appropriate to the satisfaction of the infant's needs. The tension arising from the need remains. Further interaction between the infant and the mothering one is needed to reduce the tensions and satisfactorily integrate the situation. The wrong nipple might be seen as a very early, simplified case of the assumption of an inappropriate role by one of the participants within an interpersonal transaction.

The good nipple situation is the earliest successful interpersonal transaction.

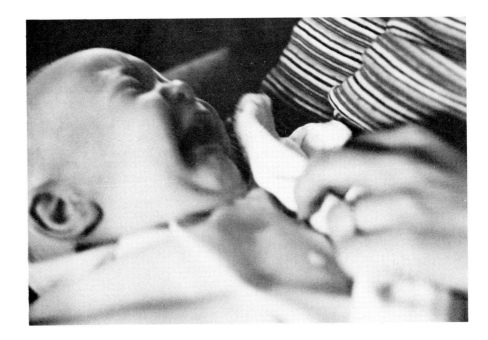

The bad nipple situation is unsuccessful because of the presence of anxiety in the transaction.

Bad Nipple. The bad nipple refers to a pattern of experience in which the infant and a mothering one integrate an interpersonal situation in such a way that the needs are satisfied, but tension is not reduced because of the presence of anxiety in the situation.

Anxiety is induced in the infant by a mothering one who is anxious. The infant experiences the anxiety within its field of interaction. But the infant can do nothing to reduce or eliminate the anxiety since it is produced outside the infant.

In the bad nipple situation the infant experiences tension arising from needs, cries to evoke the appropriate response from the environment, experiences the nipple in the lips, and begins sucking. Milk or appropriate food is present, and the tensions arising *from the needs* are reduced. The tension *within the interpersonal situation,* however, is not reduced because of the presence of anxiety. While needs are satisfied, the tensions remain.

The experience of anxiety is devastating to the infant; extreme physiological changes occur in its system unless the anxiety is relieved or the source of anxiety is removed. Sullivan described the presence of anxiety in these early interpersonal situations as having the same effect as a blow to the head of the infant. When an infant is in the presence of an anxious mothering one, the infant usually cries and may experience anoxia, cholic, gas in the stomach, or vomiting. If the anxiety is not rapidly removed from the infant's ecological field, the infant will go into a state of apathy and then into an anxiety-induced sleep.

The influence of anxiety in the relationship between a mothering one and an infant may be seen in the case of one of our former students. She gave birth to her first child the week after completing her master's degree, while she was still working on her doctorate. She was a rather nervous woman and occasionally experienced periods of anxiety. A few months after birth, the baby began to experience periodic illnesses. The pediatrician diagnosed these illnesses as symptoms of a spastic colon. In treating the child for spastic colon, the doctor prescribed no medication for the son, but tranquilizers for the mother. By using medication to reduce and control the mother's anxiety, the doctor was able to eliminate the baby's problem with the spastic colon. The anxiety came from outside the infant; it existed within the ecological system. To treat the infant, the pediatrician treated the system.

Many of our interpersonal communication problems are similar to this mother-baby example. To improve our own interpersonal communication we must often improve relationships within the complete system. What is unhealthy is not necessarily in ourselves, but in our patterns of relationships with others.

Similar patterns occur with each activity involving the infant and a mothering one. There are good, wrong, and bad patterns of forming interactions in regard not only to feeding, but also to changing the diaper, washing the baby, holding the baby, or rocking it to sleep.

The infant's experiences are never in isolation from the environment. Tensions arise within the infant and are experienced. But those tensions always lead to the integration or formation of an interpersonal situation with a mothering one to resolve the tension. The early experiences, whether good, wrong, or bad, are transactional (except in the earliest stages, when the infant is preperceptual and the experiences are interactions rather than transactions). Thus, *the experience of the infant is always one of a relationship with at least one other human being.*

ZONES OF INTERACTION[5]

As it develops, the infant uses various zones of the body to interact with the environment. For almost two months after birth, the infant's patterns of integrating experiences center primarily around the mouth. The pictures presented here were all taken within fifteen minutes. They show a variety of ways in which the infant uses the mouth to explore and interact with the environment. The experience of "me" is focused around that zone.

5. Ibid., pp. 62–66, 124–45.

As the infant matures, other zones of interaction begin to play more prominent roles in integrating the infant's experience. The infant begins to discover that the toes are a part of the body. This usually happens when the infant first sticks the toes into the mouth and bites down. Until this happens, the toes are some strange looking objects "out there." They are not associated with the infant's body. With the discovery that the toes are a part of the body, what the infant perceives as "me" expands to include both the mouth and the toes.

Through random play, the hands of the infant touch the genital area. This area is sensual and pleasurable to touch. The penis, clitoris, and anus become critical zones of interaction at the onset of toilet training. At this point in development the child enters what psychoanalysts call the anal stage. In this stage the child begins to organize its interaction around the need for defecation, urination, and cleanliness. The child experiences the genitals as zones of interaction with the environment—especially as zones of the body that require interaction with significant others in the family or society.

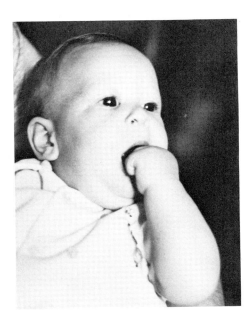

During the first months of life, the mouth is the primary zone of interaction with the environment.

It is important to note that the infant perceives the zones of interaction as relatively discrete. The human infant has no concept of its own body as a complete entity. The infant initially experiences the self as the mouth; then "me" begins to incorporate the toes, the fingers, and a few other parts of the body that can be explored by the mouth. Later, the genitals and their functions become zones of interaction that evoke great interest and occasional anxiety in other people. The various zones of interaction lead to good, wrong, or bad experiences in the integration of interpersonal situations between the infant and others.

An interesting pattern of behavior (associated with the zones of interaction) emphasizes the relationship between healthy interpersonal communication and the development of a healthy self-concept. A child may knock over a vase and send it smashing on the floor. The child may cry and be remorseful and slap the offending hand. To the child, the "I" did not knock over the vase; the hand did. Viewing this behavior from a strictly adult perspective, parents often become irritated and punish the child not only for breaking the vase but also for "pretending" that the hand—not the child—was responsible.

Such punishment is misinformed. The child is not deceitfully separating the hand from the self in order to avoid punishment. At that point, the child actually does not experience the hand and the self as parts of the same unit and does not perceive the hand as being under the will of the self. The hand and the self are discrete in time, motive, and behavior. Gradually the child begins to combine more and more elements of the self into a self-concept. Usually it is not until sometime after puberty that a child actually views the body, experiences, and social roles as a totality or as "me."

Another behavior associated with discrete zones of interaction is a form of dissociation of certain parts of the body from the total personality. This dissociation is prominent in certain types of schizophrenia, but crops up with amazing frequency in people who are not in need of extensive psychiatric treatment.

In the most extreme forms of this dissociation, certain parts of the body are perceived as discrete from the rest of the body or certain roles are perceived as discrete from the other roles the person

assumes. For many adults, such dissociation began in early infancy. For example, a mothering one may have brought extreme anxiety into the interpersonal situation whenever the genitals were touched, either in diaper changing or in the child's play with the genitals. If this occurred frequently enough or if the anxiety was strong enough to have an effect comparable to a blow to the head, the infant may have dissociated the offending part of the body from the rest of the body. That area of the body and those patterns of behavior that provoked extreme anxiety in early interpersonal relationships became a part of a "not-me." The parts of the body were obviously still there, but they were not experienced as an integrated part of the body. Likewise, within the repertoire of roles an individual assumes certain roles necessary for survival in the particular society are simply not perceived as belonging to "me." Like the anxiety-producing parts of the body, these roles are relegated to a system of behavior that is "not-me." When engaging in these roles, the person becomes, in effect, "different" persons. The person is assuming roles in relationships in which the "not-me" is involved.[6]

Some adults, for instance, cannot culminate a satisfactory sexual relationship because extreme patterns of anxiety have led to experiencing the genitals as "not-me." In such cases, the individual involved is basically saying, "How can I function satisfactorily in a sexual transaction when my genitals are not-me?" For some homosexuals, the entire system of sexuality and sexual orientation has been relegated to an area of "not-me." The results are often disastrous confusions of role relationships, self-concept, and self-esteem.

Counselors working with students and young adults (either in the university, the church, or clinical settings), frequently find people whose patterns of interpersonal communication possess this strange dimension of a "not-me." In some cases, by carefully avoiding anxiety-provoking discussion, the counselor can initiate a series of interpersonal transactions that leads to the person's discussing the experience. The primary problem facing the counselor in these situations is to get the individual to complete the process of integrating all parts of the body, bodily experiences, and roles into the self-system. Optimum interpersonal communication depends on such integration. The process of integrating the perceptions of the body and the self follow relatively distinct patterns of development, for the adult as well as for the child.

»

FORESIGHT AND RECALL

The basic patterns of experience—good nipple, wrong nipple, and bad nipple—are organized on the basis of *foresight* and *recall*.[7] These two mechanisms become operative in the infant's experience in the first hours after birth—well before the perceptual organs are fully developed and functioning. In the infant, foresight and recall are very simple. The infant can experience a wrong nipple a few moments after birth, reject it and begin searching for a good nipple. In the next couple of feedings, the infant will begin immediately to reject the wrong nipple without fully testing it. He *recalls* what it is, and *foresees* that it will not be satisfactory, now or in the future. This is an early form of learning. Later, the infant's behavior indicates that it may be anticipating the presence of the wrong nipple and is already prepared to search for the good nipple. In the case of the bad nipple, there is clear evidence that

6. Sullivan discusses the "good me," the "bad me," and the "not me" in *The Interpersonal Theory of Psychiatry*, pp. 161–64.
7. Ibid., pp. 38–39, 71–72.

the infant engages in a wide variety of behaviors to attempt to prevent the bad nipple's introduction into the interpersonal situation.

While these processes are relatively simple in the infant, foresight and recall become very complex when adults use them in their interpersonal communication behavior. In the following dialogue, a father is rehearsing to himself what he is going to say to his son when the son comes into the room. The father's role rehearsal is a type of foresight (anticipating the son's role) based upon recall (of previous transactions with the son).

> Father: *Jimmy, what do you mean by hurting your mother like that? Have you no decency? Your mother is upset with you, do you know that? Damn it, I told you that if you ever snapped back at your mother you've had it. Didn't you believe me?*

And when the son comes to the father for the conference, the father may see his rehearsed role as inappropriate and the transaction may actually come out like this:

> Father: *Jimmy, I understand you and your mother have had problems again. Would you tell me about them?*

From the very beginning of our interaction with other human beings, we develop mechanisms of foresight and recall. These mechanisms become the basis for all future interpersonal experience and behavior. They eventually lead to role playing and symbolic role taking, which are so important to interpersonal communication.

DEVELOPMENT OF THE SELF AS A PERSON

The operation of foresight and recall in the communication patterns of an infant in its earliest interpersonal situations—good, bad, and wrong —form the basis for the development of roles that constitute the self-system.

In the good nipple, wrong nipple, and bad nipple situations, the infant experiences and later perceives the zones of interaction as discrete. It also perceives each stimulus in the environment as a discrete stimulus. Thus the good nipple and the bad nipple are experienced as two entirely different physical objects, even though they may very well be the same physical nipple. As the perceptual mechanisms of the infant develop and mature, the infant begins to react more selectively to stimuli in the environment on the basis of foresight and recall. This selective attention is accompanied by a process of generalization of stimuli. The nipple becomes generalized into mother. The particular "mother" that engages in an interpersonal situation with the infant is at first (like the nipples) not integrated. Sometimes there is a good mother, sometimes the wrong mother, and sometimes the bad mother.[8] When the infant perceives the approach of the bad mother, for instance, it will try to escape from the situation in order to avoid the experience of anxiety.

The communication patterns of good nipple, wrong nipple and bad nipple eventually give way to four stages. Each stage is characterized by a different communication process and each advances the development of the self. These stages in the development of the self are personification, imitation, role playing, and symbolic role taking.

PERSONIFICATION

The process of *personification* is the first stage in the development of the self-system of the human being. This stage begins around the sixth to ninth month after birth and lasts until about the eighteenth to twentieth month.

The beginning of language acquisition has a tremendous impact upon the experience of the infant, especially in its experience of interpersonal relationships. The acquisition of language has the effect of slamming together experiences, stimuli, and perceptions which had previously been discrete. With language, there is no longer a good mother, a bad mother, and a wrong mother. There is only mother. Thus, the effect of language acquisition is to unite discrete stimuli into a more generalized stimulus.[9]

But at the same time, the effect of language acquisition is to differentiate various aspects of that stimulus into different roles. The infant begins to perceive mother as a set of roles. Mother is sometimes good, mother is sometimes wrong, and mother is sometimes bad. Mother is always the same physical object; but the role mother assumes in interaction with the infant changes.

Similar transformations occur in the child's perception of self. Where the child had previously perceived the good me, the bad me, and the "not-me," the acquisition of language has the effect of slamming all of the "me's" together into one. The child begins to perceive himself as "me." Sometimes "me" assumes the role of "good me" in interaction with the mothering one; sometimes "me" assumes the role of the "bad me" in interaction with the mothering one; but in every case, the "me" is a combination of roles that can be assumed.

This transformation of discrete perceptions of stimuli into perceptions of a single other capable of assuming many roles and of discrete

8. Ibid., pp. 85–91.
9. Ibid., pp. 111–24, 188–89.

selves into a single self capable of assuming many roles is called *personification*.[10] In the process of personification, the human being quite literally begins to experience himself and other people as a collection of "masks" or roles rather than as unrelated stimuli, zones of interaction, and discrete experiences. The collection of roles that may be assumed in a variety of interpersonal interactions constitutes the *person* or the *personality* of the individual human being.

Personification of self is a transactional concept. The infant's definition of self as good or bad is, in the early stages, totally dependent upon the interpretations that others in the environment place upon the child's behavior. Knowing this, parents and others should take great care in the language they select to discipline and correct very young children. A parent should avoid criticizing the child with the words "You are a bad boy" or "You are a naughty girl." It is not the boy or the girl who is bad or naughty. It is the act or the role assumed by the child that is offensive to the parent. The criticism should not be directed at the child but at the child's actions. While parents may say that the child is too young to know the difference between words directed at the child and words directed at the child's actions, a very few minutes working with mentally disturbed or delinquent children can remove any such doubts. Children are tremendously affected by this important but subtle distinction between criticism of the child and criticism of the role behavior the child has assumed in a given situation.

Personification involves more than roles. In the process of personifying self and others, the child acquires the implicit set of rules appropriate to each personification, or role. Most of the child's socialization from the age of about nine months to seven years involves the child's acquisition of the appropriate set of rules for each *persona* or role that he or she is able to assume.

IMITATION

The second stage in the development of the self is *imitation*.[11] From the age of about ten months through eighteen months, the child begins to simply repeat the activities and the words of others; there is no understanding involved. In this stage, the child acquires the roles and rules of its environment by imitating what it sees, hears, and experiences in interaction with the environment.

The child imitates whatever it perceives as significant. Many parents are astounded at the behavior that the child imitates in the interper-

---

10. Ibid., pp. 118.
11. Bernard N. Meltzer, "Mead's Social Psychology," in *Symbolic Interaction: A Reader in Social Psychology*, ed. Jerome G. Manis and Bernard N. Meltzer (Boston: Allyn and Bacon, 1967), p. 10.

*Much of what
a child begins
to experience
as the self comes
from imitating
the behavior
of adults.*

sonal environment of the home. One of our laboratory technicians was extremely proud of his new daughter and reported her actions to us regularly. He and his wife decided to give up smoking when they discovered their daughter, less than two years old, putting pencils in her mouth and saying, "'moke, 'moke." Another parent told us how. embarrassed she was when her child of about the same age began uttering the expletives *damn* and *shit* to everything that didn't go right. She was about to punish the child when she remembered that both parents used the expletives frequently in their daily routines.

Imitation is a potent part of the development of the child's concept of self. In the course of any week, the child will probably imitate most of the behaviors of adults in the environment. Some behaviors will become reinforced and will survive; other behaviors will be imitated once and will pass out of the child's repertoire. Those behaviors that survive are added to the set of roles that form the self of the child. The influence of imitation on the development of the child's self-concept demonstrates the ecological nature of role acquisition.

Children learn to act out the many different roles of adults they encounter—such as doctor, police officer, teacher, parent, and sports hero.

ROLE PLAYING

The third stage in the development of the self is role playing.[12] *Role playing* has been defined as imitation with understanding. In this stage, the child also begins to associate specific meanings with the roles being imitated. The child becomes particularly conscious of the rules that govern the patterns of interaction associated with particular roles. The child learns what is appropriate and what roles should be avoided in specific situations.

Children from the ages of three to five years engage in role-playing behavior as a spontaneous extension of their imitation behavior. Given toys or the proper setting, children of this age play house or play store.

12. Ibid., pp. 10–11.

The ecological influences on the self may be clearly seen in the behavior of a child who is learning to pull itself up in the early stages of learning to walk. As the child pulls itself up to its feet, it oftentimes loses its balance and falls to the floor. Sometimes the child will take quite a fall. What happens next is most instructive. In most cases the child neither cries nor laughs. It looks around to the significant persons in its environment to see how it should respond. If the adult present laughs and makes a happy occasion out of the fall, the baby usually responds by laughing and pulling itself up again. If the adult expresses horror or anguish and seems very serious about the fall, the baby usually begins to cry and becomes distraught itself. In a very real sense, the baby looks to its environment to see whether it is hurt or not. Its experience of the fall depends upon the behavior of others in the environment.

The adult's experience of defining self is essentially the same as that of the baby. We all look to others in our social environments to tell us who we are and how we should behave. Our selves are defined in terms of relationships with others in the environment.

A three-and-a-half-year-old girl or boy can skillfully play the role of a father or mother bathing or dressing a doll. Since this behavior is an extension of imitation, it often cannot be distinguished from it. As the child develops in this stage, however, the child begins to understand the dimensions of the role that he or she is assuming. The child can begin to develop creativity within the role based on an understanding of the implicit rules that govern interaction within the role. This ability to experience a role abstractly usually does not develop until language functions become more fully developed near the end of this stage (age four to five years).

The following is an actual dialogue between a father and his three-and-a-half-year-old son, David:

> Father: *You play like you're Mommy and I'll play like I'm David, O.K.?*
>
> Son: *You're Mommy? That's my Mommy* (pointing to her).
>
> Father: *No, you're Mommy. You be Mommy.*
>
> Son: *No!*
>
> Father: *Why not?*
>
> Son: *Because I want to listen to that thing* (a tape recorder).
>
> Father: *No. You be Mommy and I'll be David, O.K.? I'm David.*
>
> Son: *I'm David.*
>
> Father: *No, I'm David.*
>
> Son: *I am.*

> Father: *Now wait a minute. You be Mommy and I'll be David, O.K.?*
>
> Son: You're Daddy.
>
> Father: *No, I'm not Daddy. I'm David.*
>
> Son: *I don't like that. I'm going to run away from you.*
>
> Father: You're going to go where?
>
> Son: *I'm going to run away from you.*
>
> Father: *You're going to run away? Why?*
>
> Son: *'Cause I'm . . . 'cause I'm . . . going to run away. Bye now.*

In this transaction, the father is trying to get David, the son, to handle the concept of role at a level above that of mere imitation. It is obvious that the situation is anxiety provoking for David; he resolves his anxieties by simply fleeing from the situation with a final "Bye now." David is quite capable of playing house or playing that he is going to the store; but he has difficulties in the abstract understanding of roles.

Our work with four-year-old children in a wide variety of role-playing situations has led us to the observation that a child's ability to handle the role-playing stage is directly related to the level of development of the child's language abilities.[13] Four-year-old children who have an exceptionally advanced facility with language have little difficulty with complex and abstract role playing. In contrast, five-and-a-half-year-old children with language skills below the norm for their age have great difficulty moving into the role-playing stage.

In role playing with understanding, the child begins to imagine how another person would act in a specific set of circumstances.[14] When a girl begins to role-play a mother, she begins to behave as she imagines a mother would behave in a particular situation. *The imagination of how another person would behave in a given situation is an extension of the processes of foresight and recall and is ultimately the basis for all further role behavior in interpersonal communication transactions.* It is the critical point in the development of the child's concept of self and of his other communication skills.

Until the child can successfully recreate, in its own imagination, the behaviors that others would manifest in given social situations, the child cannot successfully imagine its own behavior in relationship to those persons. In interpersonal transactions, we are not dealing with

13. Dennis R. Smith, "The Effect of Four Communication Patterns and Sex on Length of Verbalization in Speech by Four-Year-Old Children," Office of Economic Opportunity, Washington, D.C., Contract No. B99-49801, Final Report, March 1970.

14. David K. Berlo, *The Process of Communication: An Introduction to Theory and Practice* (San Francisco: Rinehart Press, 1960), pp. 125–26.

An interesting relationship between touch (which is a part of the sexual message system) and language seems to be important in the transition from imitation behavior to role-playing behavior. Children in preschool nurseries (regardless of their racial or ethnic origins) display a fascinating pattern of behavior, bordering upon innate ritual behavior. A child may be playing alone with some blocks or a truck or a sandpile. Then, without any apparent stimulus from the environment, the child suddenly gets up, runs to the nearest adult, and hugs or clings to the adult. If the adult embraces the child firmly until the child wishes to free itself, the child will break loose in about five or ten seconds and immediately go back to playing. Sometimes the child will not go to an adult, but will seek out another child, hug that child for a few seconds, and then return to play as though the interruption had never occurred. The need to be touched overcomes interest in the blocks or cars or sandpile.

Every nursery and preschool teacher is familiar with this pattern of behavior. Although we have been unable to locate controlled clinical studies on this particular phenomenon, it is fairly clear now that this pattern of hugging, or the need for touching, is more frequent in children who have not yet acquired advanced development of language than in children with more advanced language skills. Children with fewer acquired language skills tend to be in the imitation stage of self-development.

As a child acquires more advanced language skills and begins to assume a greater variety of roles with understanding, verbal interaction appears to substitute for physical touching or stroking to a large degree. Although the need for physical touch continues, the need to be reassured by others appears to be satisfied through verbal interaction. It was partially upon this observation that Eric Berne called the verbal interaction between adults in interpersonal transactions a form of "stroking."[15] In the imitation stage of self-development, the need for intimacy must be fulfilled with greater physical contact, with actual physical stroking. When the child develops the ability to assume roles with understanding, the child also develops the ability to fulfill some of the need for intimacy through verbal stroking.

unchanging objects. We are interacting with other people. And the other people in the transactions are also imagining how we are going to act in relationship to them. When we interact with objects, we don't have to imagine what objects think of us. But when we interact with people, our behavior must include our imagination of what the other people think of us. That interpersonal perception determines what constitutes a message and the meaning of a message in our interactions.

SYMBOLIC ROLE TAKING

The final stage in the development of the self is *symbolic role taking.*[16] In symbolic role taking, the child does not need to assume a role directly. The child begins to develop the ability to assume a role symboli-

15. Eric Berne, *Games People Play: The Psychology of Human Relationships* (New York: Grove Press, 1964), pp. 15, 37–38.
16. Berlo, *Process of Communication*, pp. 126–27.

cally—to act mentally as if he or she were assuming the role without physically doing so.

In symbolic role taking, we develop the ability to see a situation as we imagine other people would see it. John begins not to play the role of a policeman, but to imagine how he would do something if he were a policeman. Mary begins not to play the role of a businesswoman, but to imagine how she might act toward a problem if she were a businesswoman.

As a part of symbolic role taking, we begin to imagine how others see us. In other words, when John develops the ability to imagine how he would see a situation if he were a policeman, he can also imagine how the policeman would see John. Mary can symbolically imagine not only how she would act toward a problem if she were a businesswoman; she can extend the process and imagine how the businesswoman would act toward Mary.

In symbolic role taking we begin to see ourselves as we imagine other people in general see us. Our communication behavior is tremendously influenced by this development. We begin to act on the basis of what we believe others think of us. We become concerned with our self-images or what we imagine others think of our behavior. We incorporate into our own communication behavior all of the rules and role restrictions that we imagine others expect of our behavior in any situation we are capable of imagining symbolically.

To a very large extent, the socialization of the child occurs through this process, which has been called the *generalized other*.[17] The generalized other is the set of role behaviors that a child imagines others in general expect of the child in a social situation. These are not the role behaviors that a specific parent might expect; they are the role behaviors that others in general might expect.

The effect of the generalized other on the self is not limited to children. In fact, the implicit rules that govern all transactions are rooted in the concept of the generalized other. We behave in a given social situation, not only on the basis of how we perceive the situation, but also on the basis of our imagination of how other people in general expect us to act.

Writing a textbook is extremely difficult. When an author sits down to draft a chapter, he or she must imagine the generalized reader. It is impossible to write in the abstract; one must communicate with some audience. The problem is to write in a way that you imagine this generalized other will find understandable. Suppose that the author imagines that the generalized reader will be a student in the first year of college, with little experience with children, only vague professional

17. Ibid., p. 127. See also Meltzer, "Mead's Social Psychology," p. 21.

goals, and an interest in few things other than sports, sex, and running around all weekend. It might be possible to write a textbook in inter-personal communication that would be of some interest to that imagined stereotyped student.

Now suppose that the author imagines that the generalized reader is a more serious student, or a veteran returning to school, or a parent, or a person seeking professional skills, such as for counseling younger people in trouble with the law. The behavior of the author that would be appropriate for the first generalized student would probably turn off this second generalized student.

Or suppose that the author imagines that the generalized student reading his textbook is a Catholic sister of unknown age who has been teaching an introductory communication course since before anyone can remember. Is it possible that the examples and language that would be acceptable behavior for the author in the first two situations would even be tolerated in this situation?

As the author sits down to write, he or she is guided by a fusion of all three generalized readers. The author writes for readers in general who have all of the characteristics of all of the imagined readers. This example illustrates the way the generalized other actually functions. In most instances, a generalized other is a composite of social stereo-types from which we formulate our own behavior. These social stereo-types provide us with the rules that govern our interpersonal trans-actions.

The generalized other is extremely important in the formation of the self-concept. If you have a strong self-concept—if you have high self-esteem—you will tend to imagine that others in general view you positively. If you have low self-esteem, you will tend to imagine that others in general view you negatively or unfavorably. In either case, you are not necessarily dealing with how others *actually* do view you. You are dealing with your *imagination* of how others view you. In changing your self-concept, then, you do not focus your attention upon the behavior of others, but upon your own experience of their behavior. In changing your self-concept, it is necessary for you to change your imagination of how others in general view you.

Insofar as we now know, the four stages in the development of the self are sequential; the child does not skip one stage and later go back to pick it up. But the stages in the development of the self are not lim-ited to the child's development of the self. Changes in an adult's self-concept or self-image must follow the same sequence. The first stage in changing patterns of interpersonal communication associated with the self-concept is to change the individual's way of personifying roles. Communication designed to improve the self that takes into account the sequential nature of the development of the self has greater chances of success.

EMPATHY: INFERENTIAL PROCESSES IN THE DEVELOPMENT OF SELF

The development of the self is based upon the potentials and limitations of the body that are shaped through interpersonal transactions with others. In the early stages, the child imitates others, and thus learns to be like others, act like others, experience like others. As the child matures, imitation alone is an inadequate basis for social interaction. The child must acquire the ability to imagine the behavior and the experience of others in a variety of social situations. Later, effective social interaction requires that the child not only imagine how other people see themselves, but how other people see the child. This complex process of imagination of the other has been called empathy.

Empathy is a complex process in which one person imagines the experience of another person, including the other's feelings, perceptions of social situations, and orientations toward people in his or her environment.[18] Empathy involves symbolically recreating in one's own experiences the experiences of others. When we empathize, we place ourselves in other people's shoes—try to see the world as they see it, feel it as they feel it. The role-taking theory of the development of the self is thus a role-taking theory of empathy. But role taking is based on processes of *inference*. To understand empathy we must combine the role-taking theory with an inferential theory of empathy.

THE INFERENTIAL THEORY OF EMPATHY[19]

Inferential explanations of empathy begin with the assumption that a person has firsthand knowledge only about his or her own internal states and only secondhand knowledge about the internal states of others. For example, Michael can directly experience his own internal states of hunger or thirst or anger. Jennifer cannot directly experience Michael's internal states. She can only indirectly know how Michael is experiencing them. Jennifer can only infer Michael's experience on the basis of her own experience.

Two problems arise when we try to explain how people empathize when they can have firsthand knowledge only of their own experiences.

First, how can a person empathize with an experience of another that he or she cannot directly experience? How can Michael empathize

---

18. Berlo, *Process of Communication*, pp. 116-21.
19. Ibid., pp. 122–24. Berlo acknowledges that his major source for the inference theory of empathy is Solomon Asch, *Social Psychology* (New York: Prentice-Hall, 1952), pp. 139–69.

with Jennifer when she is in menstruation? How can Jennifer, who is white, empathize with Michael, who is black, in dealing with racial problems in their interaction with friends? Even though people may never have firsthand knowledge of others' experiences, we know that it is possible for Michael to empathize with Jennifer about menstruation and for Jennifer to empathize with Michael on racial problems.

The second problem is that different people may associate different behaviors with the same internal states. For example, when Keith is angry he tends to let everybody within hearing distance know about it. When Dennis is angry, he tends to withdraw into himself and become very quiet. Both people have the internal state of anger, but they behave differently in expressing that internal state. How can we empathize with others when behaviors associated with internal states may differ from person to person?

Psychologists answer these questions by noting that the inferences we draw about the experience of others are fairly strictly governed by the rules governing social situations. Inference is a process that exists in and is affected by the ecological system of interpersonal relationships. We can usually make fairly accurate inferences about another's internal states, their perceptions and experiences, because the relationship between behavior and experience is highly probable. Although you and I may behave differently when we are angry or hungry or tired, the *range* of our behavior that expresses those states is very strictly governed by the rules of interaction in our society. If this were not so, social interaction could not exist.[20]

An infant cries when it is hungry, but it also waves its hands and kicks its feet when it is hungry. Why does a mother produce food when the infant cries rather than when it kicks its feet? Because the implicit rules of social interaction dictate that one produces food when a baby cries. When the child grows older, it learns to ask for food when hungry. It may say, "Can I have a peanut butter and jelly sandwich?" We can note that this behavior is some variation on the range of acceptable patterns of behavior for hungry children in our society. It is also a fairly predictable behavior. Thus, we learn to associate only certain behaviors with our own internal states. It is thus possible to infer a person's internal states from their outward behavior. By combining sets of inferences, we reconstruct in imagination the roles of others and we empathize with their experiences.

20. A number of ecological studies of communication have concluded that the genetic survival of a species or biological subgroup depends upon the absence of variation in signal-meaning relationships when there are competing biological groups in the same territory. Signals may vary more widely in form and meaning without danger to the group when there are no competing genetic or biological subgroups. An excellent example of this kind of research is found in Peter Marler, "Developments in the Study of Animal Communication," in *Darwin's Biological Work: Some Aspects Reconsidered,* ed. Peter Robert Bell (Cambridge: University Press, 1959), pp. 185–91.

THE ROLE OF "ME" IN EMPATHY

In the earliest stages of imitation, role playing, and symbolic role taking, the person can assume a wide range of behaviors with comparative ease. As the person matures into various roles, the range of roles that the person can assume with ease becomes more and more limited. After puberty, in late adolescence and early adulthood, an individual's set of roles becomes fairly well defined. Each person selects certain roles and styles of enacting roles. The individual comes to experience these selected roles as "me." In trying out various roles the person says, "This is me," or "This is not me." For example one person might imagine himself or herself experiencing a homosexual relationship while another person would be horrified at such a role relationship. One might see himself or herself as a priest or missionary while another could not imagine being in such roles.

From a transactional point of view, the "me" is not some "inner man" or "inner woman" locked within trying to get out. The "me" is a set of role relationships that are developed and maintained through interpersonal communication with others. The "me" can exist only in relationship to someone else.[21]

For some people, the "me" becomes a point of reference that permits them to empathize easily with others. These people feel secure in their own concepts of self and can readily imagine how others would experi-

21. Manis and Meltzer, *Symbolic Interaction*, pt. 3, pp. 215–97.

Teenagers especially try out many different roles and images in search of the self. Each person keeps some roles as a part of "me" and rejects other roles as "not me."

ence various role relationships. For others, the "me" becomes a problem. These people tend to get a "hardening of the categories" which prevents them from being able to put themselves in the roles of others and view the world from different frames of reference. People who are insecure in their concepts of "me" tend to lack empathy and tend to be overly defensive in their communication with others.

In healthy interpersonal relationships a person is not so locked into his or her own experience of self that he or she is unable to imagine the world as others experience it. The healthy self always permits the individual a wide range of inference in role relationships. The healthy use of inference permits a man to empathize with a woman's menstrual experience and a white person to empathize with a black person's experience in our society. In healthy interpersonal communication, people maintain a balance between their own sets of roles and the process of inference. Through their own experiences of "me" and their imagination of others' experiences of "me," they can empathize with the roles others assume in their interpersonal transactions.

INTRAPERSONAL COMMUNICATION AS A TRANSACTIONAL PROCESS

Developing the ability to act toward a person's own set of roles as the person acts toward the roles of others marks an extremely critical point in the development of the communication process. It is only after an individual develops the ability to act toward the self with a set of expectations of the self that the individual can engage in what has been called *intrapersonal communication.*[22]

Almost every adult experiences intrapersonal communication. We seem to be able to communicate with ourselves. We dialogue with ourselves; we debate with ourselves; we even sometimes talk aloud to ourselves—and answer ourselves. When we carefully analyze this intrapersonal communication behavior, we discover that the communication occurs between two roles that we enact in our imagination.

Since it occurs between roles, the process of intrapersonal communication is a very complex form of interpersonal communication transactions. In intrapersonal communication a person not only acts toward the self as the person would toward others, but also imagines how he or she would act toward the self if he or she assumed other roles. An intrapersonal communication experience is a transaction in which one

22. Manford H. Kihn, "Major Trends in Symbolic Interaction in the Past Twenty-five Years," *The Sociological Quarterly* 5 (Winter 1964): 61–84; reprinted in Manis and Meltzer, *Symbolic Interaction*, pp. 46–67 (esp. pp. 57–58). See also Harry Stack Sullivan, "The Illusion of Personal Individuality," *Psychiatry* 13 (1950): 317–32.

When we are holding a dialogue or debating with ourselves, we are imagining communication between two different roles of the self.

role in the dyad is the experienced self and the other role is the self projected into a different imagined role. The dialogue that a person carries on with himself or herself is a dialogue between two imagined roles.

Child psychologists and psychiatrists are fairly certain that the human infant is capable of experiencing a vast amount of dream, reverie, and preperceptual activity that extends into childhood and even into adulthood. Since these activities are not subject to consensual validation, they fall outside of the realm of experience that we associate with intrapersonal communication. Dreams, reveries and private fantasies are noncommunication behaviors. The kind of imagination important in the analysis of intrapersonal communication is the imagined experience that can be confirmed by the experience of other people and that has its manifestations in the person's overt behavior. When a person is communicating with himself, the person is imagining possible future (or possible past) behaviors that might occur while assuming certain roles or engaging in certain communication behavior with other persons. This kind of imagination is simply a more complex form of the kind of imagination each of us uses when we anticipate the appropriate roles to assume every time we enter into interpersonal communication transactions.

Let us take the case of Andrea debating with herself about moving from one apartment to another apartment. When Andrea begins debating with herself about moving to a new apartment, she selects particular roles on which to base her intrapersonal dialogue. She might begin her debate with herself by being "Andrea the housekeeper," "Andrea the socialite," "Andrea the lover," or "Andrea the professional woman." Whichever roles Andrea assumes as her self for this particular intrapersonal communication will, of course, give a particular slant to the kind of intrapersonal communication that follows. The kind of debate that "Andrea the housekeeper" will carry on with "Andrea the socialite" may be quite different from the kind of debate "Andrea the professional woman" would carry on with "Andrea the lover." Each role would have different reactions to moving or not moving to a new apartment.

In the imagined transaction, the two roles may be roles that the person has actually experienced or roles that the person imagines are typical of the way other people view him or her. In other words, when "Andrea the housekeeper" begins to communicate with "Andrea the socialite," she can either enter into an imagined transaction with roles based on her own *direct experience,* or she can imagine herself as she believes *other people might see her* in given roles. The self of "Andrea the socialite" may be concerned primarily with how "Andrea the housekeeper" perceives "Andrea the socialite," or with other people's expectations of "Andrea the socialite." In such a transaction, the imagined interaction is between a role directly experienced by the person (as "Andrea the housekeeper") and a role made up of the imagined expectations others have of the person (as "Andrea the socialite").

Both the psychoanalytic and the symbolic interactionist traditions have stressed the importance of social interaction in the formation of the self-system. Intrapersonal communication must be analyzed with proper recognition of the self as a role. Therefore, intrapersonal communication is always transactional and can develop only after the basic interpersonal communication skills have been established. To improve intrapersonal communication, one must therefore develop an understanding of the nature and function of roles and rules in interpersonal communication transactions. One can apply the basic skills of interpersonal communication to the improvement of intrapersonal communication.

Even in the area of intrapersonal health, the concept of the transaction as the basic unit of communication has proven to be of immense value in diagnosing communication problems that create difficulties in living. Careful application of the concepts in the following chapters have often led to great success in reducing problems people have in intrapersonal communication as well as in their communication with others. Roles, rules, strategies, and games—whether intrapersonal or interpersonal—are best understood via the transactional model of communication.

SUMMARY

The self is an ecological phenomenon that arises out of and is maintained through interpersonal communication transactions.

The foundations of the self-system arise from the patterns of organizing experience of interpersonal interactions between the infant and the mothering one. These patterns, present immediately after birth, remain as basic patterns of organizing interpersonal communication throughout life. These patterns have been classified into three categories: good (needs are satisfied and tensions reduced); wrong (needs are not satisfied and tensions are not reduced); and bad (anxiety in the environment prevents the reduction of tension even though needs are satisfied). These three situations are experienced around discrete zones of interaction and are integrated on the basis of the mechanisms of foresight and recall. Foresight and recall, the earliest forms of learning, become the basis for role differentiation in later interaction with the environment, especially in the role-playing stage of the child.

Personification is the first stage in the development of the self as a set of roles through which a person interacts with others.

The development of language has the effect of merging what had been perceived as discrete stimuli into generalized concepts. The good nipple, wrong nipple, and bad nipple become generalized into the good mother, the wrong mother, and the bad mother, then simply into the concept of mother who assumes good, wrong, and bad roles in relation to the infant. The second stage is imitation. In imitation, the child simply replicates the actions of others without understanding. In the third stage, role playing, the child learns to assume the roles of significant others in the environment. Role playing also appears to be related to the child's acquisition of language skills. Finally, in the stage of symbolic role taking, the child acquires the ability to perceive the roles others in general expect the child to assume. The child learns to act toward the self as the child imagines others would act toward him or her or as the child imagines others expect him to act toward himself or herself. Symbolic role taking is the most advanced stage in the development of the self.

The development of a set of roles that form the self-system is accompanied by the development of the process of inference. The acquisition of a role requires inferring the experience of others in similar roles. Empathy in interpersonal communication involves placing oneself in the roles experienced by others. As such, empathy is a complex process that combines role playing with the process of inference. An inferential theory of empathy assumes that each individual has first-hand knowledge of his own internal states and secondhand knowledge of the internal states of others. Although two people may associate different behaviors with the same internal state, the social environment provides each person with appropriate models of behavior for expressing various internal states. Thus, there is remarkable consistency in the way individuals within the same society combine the role playing and inferential processes.

Intrapersonal communication is a highly complex form of interpersonal transactions. Intrapersonal communication requires the development of both the inferential process and symbolic role taking. In intrapersonal communication, the individual imagines assuming two roles and carries on a silent dialogue between the two roles.

QUESTIONS FOR REVIEW

1. What are the three interpersonal needs? Characterize each.
2. What is the good nipple experience? the wrong nipple experience? the bad nipple experience?

3. What are zones of interaction? Why are they significant in the development of the self?
4. What are the four stages in the development of the self as a person? Describe each.
5. What is the inferential theory of empathy?
6. How can intrapersonal communication be seen as a transactional process?

EXPLORATIONS

1. Who we are depends in part upon the person(s) we are with at the time. Try to complete each of the following sentences.

When I am sad, I talk with _____
When I'm happy, I talk with _____
When I'm depressed, I want to be with_____
When I celebrate, I want to go with_____
When I travel, I like to be with_____
When I want to talk about intellectual things, I seek out_____
When I want to talk politics, I talk to_____
When I discuss religion, I talk to _____

2. Nicknames often tell us who we are, in both a positive and a negative sense. Many nicknames are names that call attention to negative aspects of the self, such as Runt, Skinny, Fatso, and Dumbo. Other nicknames call attention to talents, such as Ringer, Hawkeye, and Speedy. Think back through all the situations in which you have had nicknames. Make a list of them. Are they positive or negative? Now make a list of the nicknames that you would have liked to have had or that you might like to have in your present situations. What do these two lists of nicknames tell you about yourself?

3. Who are your heroes and heroines? What do you admire about these people? In what ways did (does) each hero or heroine influence who you would like to be and what you would like to become? Why did you select this group of people?

4. Most people have difficulty expressing their pride. A good journal exercise is to write an essay beginning with the statement "I'm proud that I . . ."

5. An exercise that is widely used in groups dealing with strengthening and enhancing the self-concept involves a series of imaginings. This exercise takes about thirty minutes, but has proven to be a positive way of changing one's concept of self through changing one's relationship with generalized other concepts.

Begin the exercise by thinking about the various ways in which you tend to underrate yourself. As each item comes to mind jot it down in your communication journal. Reflect on each of the ways you underrate yourself. Close your eyes and take a few moments to translate each of the words you have used to describe yourself into images in your imagination. Reflect on your feelings about the ways you underrate yourself.

Next imagine the way you would like to be perceived by others, such as, athletic, "with it," romantic, sexy, etc. Imagine how you think others want you to be. Notice that these images tend to vary with each relationship; your family may hold one ideal, your friends another ideal, your lover another. Reflect on your feelings on each of these role relationships.

Finally, select from these images those qualities that you would most like to incorporate into your own communication behavior and interpersonal relationships. Close your eyes and begin to imagine your relationships with others if you possessed these ideal qualities —if you were your ideal. Begin to redefine your self-image. As you near the end of the exercise, begin to reflect on ways to incorporate these ideal qualities into your own communication. *It can be done.* You have already taken the first step!

FOR FURTHER READING

Berlo, David K. *The Process of Communication: An Introduction to Theory and Practice.* San Francisco: Rinehart Press, 1960.

This book makes an important contribution to communication theory, for it provides a *process* orientation, stressing the ongoing, interactional nature of communication. Berlo relates his process model of communication to both the rhetorical and communication traditions, and emphasizes the importance of meaning and perception.

Brown, Barbara B. *New Mind, New Body; Biofeedback: New Directions for the Mind.* New York: Harper & Row, 1974.

While this book views intrapersonal communication differently than we have in this chapter, it is a most valuable resource. Defining biofeedback as interaction with the interior self, Brown explores the ways a person communicates with himself or herself via the skin, the muscles, the heart, the brain, etc. Her readable and authoritative book underscores the importance of awareness of biofeedback in our lives.

Canfield, Jack, and Wells, Harold. *100 Ways to Enhance Self-concept in the Classroom: A Handbook for Teachers and Parents.* Englewood Cliffs, N.J.: Prentice Hall, 1976.

This book consists of 100 exercises, which may be used by students of all ages, from elementary school through college, that are designed to enhance the development of some aspect of the self. It is interesting and highly readable and should prove to be a useful resource book for parents and teachers interested in exploring the development of the self in children.

Schutz, William C. *FIRO: A Three-Dimensional Theory of Interpersonal Behavior.* New York: Rinehart, 1958; reprint ed., *The Interpersonal Underworld,* Palo Alto, Calif.: Science and Behavior Books, 1966.

Sullivan, Harry Stack. *The Interpersonal Theory of Psychiatry.* Edited by Helen Swick Perry and Mary Ladd Gawel. New York: W. W. Norton & Co., 1953.

Schutz presents formally and in detail his theory of human behavior. The first part of the book focuses upon his theory of interpersonal needs—inclusion, control, and affection. The second half of the book applies the theory of interpersonal needs to various communication settings, particularly to the small group.

This book presents psychiatrist Sullivan's systematic theory of the mental development of the individual in and through his interpersonal relations with others. Taking a developmental approach, Sullivan traces the growth of the self in infancy, childhood, the juvenile era, adolescence, and adulthood. Inappropriate as well as appropriate or healthy growth patterns are considered, all within the framework of the interpersonal world of the individual.

PART II

Primary Message Systems

Chapter 6

Language a
Primary Mes
S

The use of language as a means of communication has often been seen as one trait that makes us uniquely human.[1] Every human society, from the most technologically advanced to the most primitive, employs language. These languages range from the gutteral articulations of German and English to the intoned and highly inflected Chinese-based languages to the whistle and click languages used by certain African tribes. Regardless of the variety of human languages, all language shares certain basic characteristics: (1) language is an important part of the social environment of every individual; (2) the language environment is important in creating and socializing the self of every person; and (3) language is a part of the environment that every individual uses as a tool or instrument for shaping and changing the world around him.

LANGUAGE AS ENVIRONMENT: THE EFFECTS OF NAMING

Although born without a language, every normal and healthy human infant has an innate capacity to learn any of the languages spoken by human societies. The infant experiences the language of its society as an environment. The particular language environment of that society shapes and molds the personas of the child as it develops. This shaping or molding of the self by language is not limited to childhood; it continues into adulthood and affects each of us to the end of our lives.

1. The definition of man as the creature who responds to language and other symbols is offered in Kenneth Burke, *A Rhetoric of Motives* (New York: Prentice-Hall, 1950; Berkeley, Calif.: University of California Press, 1969), p. 43; and Kenneth Burke, *Permanence and Change: An Anatomy of Purpose,* 2d rev. ed., with an Introduction by Hugh Dalziel Duncan (Indianapolis, Ind.: Bobbs-Merrill Co., 1965), p. 275. See also Harry Stack Sullivan, *The Interpersonal Theory of Psychiatry.* ed. Helen Swick Perry and Mary Ladd Gawel (New York: W. W. Norton & Co., 1953), pp. 24–25, quoting Edward Sapir, *Language: An Introduction to the Study of Speech* (New York: Harcourt, Brace and Co., 1921), pp. 7–23.

LANGUAGE AND THE SELF

The way a person experiences the self is highly influenced by the language of the society in which that person was raised. In fact, the very concept of self varies widely from society to society and from language to language. In Anglo-American and western European cultures, language emphasizes the self as an *individual*. To be a person is to be unique—different from the other persons in society. In the Chinese langauge, however, the self is subordinated to family and society. There is no concept of individualism as we know it in our culture; the self is a part of the family. In the last century, for example, many Americans were appalled by the Chinese system of justice which allowed any member of one family to be tried and executed for the murder of a

The language in different cultures affects the way a person experiences the self and the environment.

Some language theorists believe that all languages follow similar patterns of development. They think, for example, that English has some of the same patterns of thought as the "primitive" aboriginal languages of Africa and Asia. Even today, for instance, we use certain phrases that invest objects in nature with human powers. A driver skids from the highway toward a steep cliff and is stopped when the car crashes into a tree. In telling about the accident later, the driver may say, "That tree saved my life." Notice the similarity between this use of language and that of primitive languages which link the self or soul to natural objects. The driver is saying that the tree intervened for a purpose— i.e., to save the driver's life.

Contrast the phrase "That tree saved my life" with the expression "Thank God for that tree being there." Instead of attributing the intervention to the tree, the speaker of the latter phrase is viewing the tree as an instrument of the intervention of God or a higher power. Both of these phrases are different in important ways from the statement "I saved my life by crashing my car into that tree." Here the speaker is crediting himself with saving his own life.

We should not dismiss these differences in language usage as trivial. By listening carefully to the language people use, we gain important insights into the ways they perceive reality. People in our society probably use most phrases like the ones in this example unconsciously. But whether we use them consciously or not, such statements are important indicators of our predispositions to act.

person from another family; the person found "guilty" may have had no connection with the crime other than a familial relationship to the actual murderer. The guilt was upon the family and not upon the individual. Given such language concepts of the self, the Chinese under the communism of Mao do not "miss" the absence of individual freedom and initiative any more than Americans "miss" the absence of collectivism and family dominance. The Chinese concept is simply absent from the American language environment and vice versa.

Another interesting relationship between language and self is found in some of the Australian, Indonesian, and African languages. In these languages, the self is conceived of as a part of nature. A person raised in such a language environment may speak of part of his or her self as located in a tree or waterfall or stream.[2] The person sees his or her own self, or soul, as linked to the fate of the natural object; what happens to the tree or stream happens also to the self or the person.

Language is a critical environmental influence on the nature of the self. How one perceives and experiences the self is derived from the particular language environment of his or her culture.

2. Ernst Cassirer, *Language and Myth,* trans. Susanne K. Langer (New York: Harper and Brothers, 1946; New York: Dover Publications, 1953), pp. 49–54; and Claude Levi-Strauss, *The Savage Mind* (Chicago: University of Chicago Press, 1966), pp. 112–13.

LANGUAGE AND PERCEPTION

The relationship between language and perception remains one of the more controversial issues in the study of human communication.[3] At best, we can say that there appears to be a twofold relationship between language and perception. Language both helps us to perceive and prevents perceiving.

We attend to events and things for which we have names and fail to attend to things for which we have no names. When we describe someone's face we call attention to the nose, the lips, the eyes, moles, scars, hair—aspects of the face for which we have common names. But we almost never call attention to those two funny-looking ridges of skin running between the nose and the lips. In fact, if you try to remember what these little ridges look like on the face of your best friend, you probably cannot recall. We do not attend to things for which we have no names. In English we have only one name for snow and we perceive snow as being snow. But an Eskimo may have many different names for snow, each one indicating an important difference.[4] The Eskimo language allows the Eskimo to attend to differences in snow that we normally do not perceive. Language provides us with names for those things that are important for us to perceive. Naming something helps us to perceive it.

Language also prevents us from seeing certain aspects of things or events that we have named. Once we have applied a label to something, we tend to react to that object or event *in terms of the name* or the label rather than *in terms of the object* or act itself. This has the effect of making us perceive selected aspects of an object or an event and miss other, perhaps equally important aspects of the same object or event. If we call something a cup, our tendency is to see only those features that make the object a cup. We forget that the object might also be a portable toilet, packing material, a pincushion, or any number of things.

Why is this twofold relationship between language and perception important? Because naming directs human behavior.[5] What we call

3. Harry Hoijer, "The Sapir-Whorf Hypothesis," in *Language in Culture,* ed. Harry Hoijer (Chicago: University of Chicago Press, 1954), pp. 92–105; reprinted in Larry A. Samovar and Richard E. Porter, eds., *Intercultural Communication: A Reader* (Belmont, Calif.: Wadsworth Publishing Co., 1972), pp. 114–23. See also Edward Sapir, "The Status of Linguistics as a Science," in *Selected Writings of Edward Sapir in Language, Culture, and Personality,* ed. David G. Mandelbaum (Berkeley: University of California Press, 1949), pp. 160–66 (esp. p. 162); and Benjamin Lee Whorf, "Science and Linguistics," in *Language, Thought, and Reality: Selected Writings of Benjamin Lee Whorf,* ed. John B. Carroll (New York: Wiley; Cambridge, Technology Press, 1956), pp. 207–19.

4. Edward T. Hall, *The Silent Language* (Garden City, N.Y.: Doubleday & Co., 1959; Greenwich, Conn.: Fawcett Publications, 1959), pp. 101, 103.

5. Hugh Dalziel Duncan, Introduction to *Permanence and Change,* by Kenneth Burke, p. xv. The relationship between language and perception is also discussed by John C. Condon, Jr., *Semantics and Communication,* 2d ed. (New York: Macmillan Co., 1975), pp. 36–38.

something determines not only how we perceive it, but how we are predisposed to act toward it. You might see your parents' inquiries about your activities as meddlesome, while they view them as showing concern. You might think you were assisting your friends and find yourself arrested for interfering with a police officer in executing his duties. George Carlin has observed that in New York subways you can be fined fifty dollars for spitting, but vomiting is free. Some people saw Lt. Calley of the My Lai incident as a war hero who should be decorated, while others saw him as a criminal who should be jailed. Sometimes the difference between calling an act an accident or self-defense or murder determines the course of a person's life.

THE FUNCTIONS OF NAMING

Naming or labeling is undoubtedly the most important single aspect of language. Naming has several different functions that affect us as an environment. The seven functions of naming are: signification, definition, polarization, stereotyping, socialization, transformation, and reification.

Signification. Probably the first aspect of naming that we experience in our lives is *signification*.[6] This function of naming has sometimes been called *ostensive definition*. Most of the infant's early experiences with naming take the form of signification, which is constantly reinforced by adult behavior. Signification is the process of identification by pointing to something.

An infant experiences signification when a mother leans over the cradle, holds a doll in front of the baby, and says, "doll." In doing this the mother has identified the object without use of a description. The mother has signified the object by *pointing* to it.

But signification is not limited to objects in the child's environment. For example, Shawna, an eight-month-old girl, was often left in the care of her grandmother. Grandmother, as grandmothers are prone to do, would take Shawna's hands, clap them together, and sing, "Pattycake, Pattycake, Pattycake." The grandmother repeated this a number of times over a period of two or three weeks. Then one day when the grandmother was singing, "Pattycake, Pattycake, Pattycake," the baby began clapping her hands together. For Shawna, the word *Pattycake* had come to signify or point to a specific pattern of behavior.

Signification in the infant involves only the grossest kinds of distinctions or differentiation between objects and events. Refinements in differentiation are learned only slowly. A child may learn the word *cat*

6. Sullivan, *Interpersonal Theory of Psychiatry*, pp. 77–87.

and then use the word to signify all sorts of objects in the environment, such as dogs, horses, and cows. As perceptual mechanisms develop and the child acquires increasing facility in manipulating language, the word *cat* gradually comes to signify only cats, the word *dog* to signify dogs, and the word *cow* to signify animals that moo.

Definition. A more socially complex function of naming is *definition.* To define an object or event is to mark the boundaries of such an object or event.[7] Definition occurs when we name in terms of relationships. As the child matures and begins to distinguish between cats and dogs, the child has begun the process of using naming for definition. The child has begun to distinguish sets of elements or sets of characteristics that distinguish one object or event from another object or event. The child has begun to generalize the sets of elements into relationships or to form categories. Definition is related to the processes of abstraction and inference and is one of the most significant aspects of adult use of language.

Definition, the marking of boundaries, serves two opposite yet complementary functions: division and unity.[8] When we define something we engage in an act of division. We distinguish one thing from another. It is the divisive aspect of definition in naming that sets us apart from one another, that leads to name-calling, to slander, to the put-down, and to subordination of groups that we identify as different from ourselves.

Severe divisions in the American society arose in the 1950s between groups who perceived themselves as "loyal, dedicated Americans" and groups that they identified as "subversive, Communist, fellow travelers, or unwitting dupes of the Communist conspiracy." Severe divisions in the American society of the 1960s emerged between those who called themselves "patriotic Americans" and those they called "radicals and liberals." Divisions arose between those who were anti-Communist and those who were antiwar, between those who perceived themselves as the Movement and those they perceived as the Establishment.

But even as we are led to despair over the divisiveness that arises from naming, we are led to hope in the unity of naming. To define something, to mark the boundaries, is not only to *exclude* but also to *include.* To name is also to unify, to make one, to stress that which is common among us.

People seek unity by defining their groups through names. Last names arose as a way of indicating unity in the clan. First names arose to signify differences. Thus, the name Smith served to unify the Smith

---

7. Kenneth Burke, *A Grammar of Motives* (New York: Prentice-Hall, 1945; Berkeley, Calif.: University of California Press, 1969), p. 24.
8. Burke, *Rhetoric of Motives,* p. 22.

clan as well as to distinguish it from the Jones clan; the name Dennis served to distinguish Dennis from the other members of the Smith clan. Democrats, Republicans, radicals, liberals, Kiwanians, Lions, Boy Scouts, Girl Scouts, Catholics, Baptists—all of these terms may become definitions of groups in which people seek unity. People also seek unity in the use of god terms such as "in the name of justice" or "in the name of democracy." When the North Vietnamese were fighting for victory, the United States was committed to "peace with honor." Thus naming defines the boundaries of great movements or calls to action; it can be an extremely powerful force in generating and guiding social action.

Polarization. The tendency to use sets of terms with their opposites or counterparts is called *polarization.* We use language in such a way that it is difficult to construct a continuum of concepts between the extremes. Consider the following set of terms: male, female; black, white; good, bad; young, old; hot, cold; kind, cruel. Now stop for a moment and try to fill in three or four terms between each of the polar terms. For each there is perhaps a middle term, but it is very difficult to construct a continuum of terms.

black	?	?	gray	?	?	white
masculine	?	?	neuter	?	?	feminine
young	?	?	middle-aged	?	?	old

It is difficult to conceive the gradients between polarities in the English language. Even the middle terms are somewhat ambiguous.

The research of Charles Osgood and his colleagues indicates that polarization in language may be a universal phenomenon.[9] Osgood has tested bipolar sets of adjectives in over fifty different languages and has tentatively concluded that polarization is a fundamental characteristic of the human use of language. Regardless of the language studied, Osgood and his associates discovered that the polarizations of language center around three dimensions of what they called *semantic space.* These polarities were identified as *evaluation* (represented in English by good/bad), *potency* (represented by hard/soft), and *action* (represented by fast/slow). Osgood's studies indicate that every word or concept evokes one or more sets of polarities which lie in the areas of evaluation, potency, and action.

9. Charles E. Osgood, G. J. Suci, and P. H. Tannenbaum, *The Measurement of Meaning* (Urbana, Ill.: University of Illinois Press, 1957).

Although polarization appears to be a universal dimension of naming, there are significant differences between cultures in the use of polarization. In Western cultures the polarities in language are used as discrete categories. Categories are conceived as being "either/or." Something is either *A* or Not *A*. Something is either good or bad, black or white, right or wrong, weak or strong, male or female, hot or cold. The languages are constructed so that if category *A* applies, category Not *A* cannot apply.

Where Western languages tend to use polarities in a categorical "either/or" fashion, Eastern languages use them in a "both/and" fashion. Where the Westerner sees polarities as discrete, the Easterner sees polarities as two aspects of a unity. The most famous expression of this polarity within unity is the concept of *yin* and *yang*—the opposing forces in the universe that combine to form all that exists. The principle of *yin* and *yang* conceives objects and events as manifesting aspects of both polar qualities. Thus, to the Eastern mind each person is both male and female possessing qualities of both maleness and femaleness; an event is both good and bad; food is both sweet and sour; a person is both weak and strong.

This difference in the use of polarity in language is one of the most significant variants between Eastern and Western cultures. A Western mind which thinks of polarities as separate categories has difficulty coping with Eastern thought which perceives polarities as two aspects of a unity. Marshall McLuhan has discussed the Easternization of Western thought and finds our language is undergoing significant changes.[10] In order to discuss the process features of the world, to grasp atomic science, quantum physics, and the intricacies in socialization created by electricity and electrical circuitry, Western man is having to reconceive his use of polarities in langauge.

The child of the electrical age, the progeny of television, has little trouble conceiving an event as existing both now and then. A child today can juxtapose time as his parents or grandparents cannot do. The child raised on television lives in a world of both here and there, simultaneously experiencing events in Los Angeles, New York, London and Paris. Under such influences the Western categorical use of the polarities of language is undergoing significant changes. We are witnessing the Orientalization of Western language and thought. Perhaps we will also live to witness a decrease in the polar stereotyping that occurs in our use of language.

Stereotyping. The categorical use of polarization in language often leads to *stereotyping*. Stereotyping has come to have very negative con-

10. Marshall McLuhan and Quentin Fiore, *The Medium is the Massage* (New York: Bantam Books, 1967), pp. 125, 145.

notations. The phenomenon of stereotyping is neither good nor bad in itself. People may use stereotyping for good or bad ends, but the phenomenon itself is neutral. There are three basic kinds of stereotyping: allness, indiscrimination, and time binding.

Allness is the tendency of people to use language in such a way that they characterize an entire object, event, or person in terms of only one of its aspects. Allness occurs when people use one attribute of an object as if that one attribute were all there is to say about that object.[11]

When people say, "Oh, she's just a woman," or "He is a Jew," or "Charles is a Negro," or "Well, you know, he's Irish," they are selecting one feature of the person and acting as if that one feature were all there is to say about that person. Mary is a woman, but she is hardly *just* a

11. William V. Haney, *Communication and Organizational Behavior Text and Cases*, rev. ed. (Homewood, Ill.: Richard D. Irwin, 1967), pp. 253–79.

The behavior of individuals often breaks the traditional stereotypes that exist in our language.

woman. She may also be a professional person, a mother, a daughter, a sister, a typist, a fine decorator, a charming person, etc. Saul may be a Jew, but he may also be a father, a son, a custodian, a respected member of his community, etc. Charles may be a Negro, but he may also be a banker, a citizen, a philanthropist, a shrewd businessman, etc.

The corrective for the allness syndrome in stereotyping is to remember that whatever one says about a particular person or object, there is always more that can be said. To keep from falling into the allness trap in stereotyping, remember to add an *et cetera* (and so forth) to every description, as we have done in the previous paragraph.[12] This serves to remind everyone that the characteristics mentioned do not constitute *all* there is to say about the person. There are always other characteristics, qualities, or attributes, etc., that may be added.

Indiscrimination is another categorical use of language. Indiscrimination arises when people use language in such a way as to take the attributes of one element of a set and generalize those characteristics to all elements of the set.[13] The phrase "Negroes are lazy" is one such use of indiscrimination, as are "Blonds are dumb," "Jews are rich," etc. In each of these phrases, the characteristics of one member of the category are generalized to all members of the category indiscriminately. It may be that a person has met one Negro who was lazy, one blond who was dumb, and one Jew who was rich. But it is certainly a misuse of language to indiscriminately apply attributes of one person to all persons in the category.

The corrective for indiscriminate stereotyping is to apply a kind of *category indexing.*[14] This indexing serves to remind us that person$_1$ is not identical to person$_2$. While Mary, Jane, Joan, and Carry are all blonds, blond$_1$ is not blond$_2$ is not blond$_3$ is not blond$_4$.

Time binding is very similar to indiscrimination. In time binding the user of the language fails to recognize that people, objects, and events change over time.[15] Heraclitus's statement that "one cannot step into the same stream twice" warns us against time binding.

Difficulties in communication arise when people fail to remember the simple fact that people change over time. When a person becomes time-bound in the use of stereotyping, that person's language often fails to correspond to reality. Parents may become time-bound and fail to recognize that their children are no longer youngsters who need parental protection and constraint. When John is twenty-four and Jane is

12. Stuart Chase, *Power of Words* (New York: Harcourt, Brace & World, 1953, 1954), pp. 139–40.
13. Haney, *Communication and Organizational Behavior*, pp. 281–93.
14. Chase, *Power of Words*, pp. 140–41. See also Haney, *Communication and Organizational Behavior*, pp. 291–92.
15. This definition of time binding is quite different from that offered by Korzybski, who identified it with man's ability to progress by building on past knowledge—i.e., by "binding" time.

twenty-two and both are married and have children, they are not the same people they were when John was seven and Jane was five. Yet, in many cases, parents act as if John and Jane were still seven and five. This, of course, creates problems in communication. Roles change, and the use of language must accommodate the changes in roles.

Time binding can be corrected by mentally time indexing in much the same way that indiscrimination is corrected by category indexing. When we are communicating, we should remember to index our stereotypes. $John_{1978}$ is not the same person as $John_{1958}$.[16] Time indexing permits us to recognize in our use of language that roles change—that the individuals with whom we communicate become different persons or personas with the passage of time.

Socialization—the Self-fulfilling Prophecy. One of the primary functions of naming is the *socialization* of individual members of a group, society, or social order. Naming or language has the capacity to shape our actions and perceptions in accordance with social values. One aspect of the socializing function of naming has become known as the *self-fulfilling prophecy*.[17] Naming something is a prophecy that fulfills itself; people become what they are called. There is, in short, a tendency for people to try to live up to a name. When people with red hair are perceived socially as having tempers, they frequently find themselves living up to the social perception whether or not they feel comfortable in such a role.

The self-fulfilling prophecy also operates in living down a name. Because of the phenomenon of stereotyping, people are frequently forced to live down names or labels that others in the social environment have placed upon them. Probably the best known and most thoroughly described example of living down a name is that of Hester Prynne in Hawthorne's *The Scarlet Letter.* A person's behavior is constantly related (either positively or negatively) to the self-fulfilling prophecy of labels. Whether a label is accurate or not, an individual must deal with it as long as others apply the label.

The extremely powerful consequences of the socializing effects of the self-fulfilling prophecy are illustrated in a book entitled *Pygmalion in the Classroom.*[18] In that study, a computer randomly labeled children as having certain academic abilities. Even though the labels were purely arbitrary, children whom the teachers expected to be "late-bloomers" and show abnormally high developments in I.Q. actually did so. The study tends to provide empirical evidence of the great power of labels; they affect the basic concept of self through interpersonal interaction.

16. Chase, *Power of Words,* pp. 141–42.
17. Condon, *Semantics and Communication,* pp. 63–66.
18. Robert Rosenthal and Lenore Jacobson, *Pygmalion in the Classroom: Teacher Expectation and Pupil's Intellectual Development* (New York: Holt, Rinehart and Winston, 1968).

Transformation. The use of naming to transform individuals or objects from one state to another may be called *transformation*. In transformation, naming serves as a rite of passage; the changing of the name is associated with the changing of the state or status of an object or individual.[19] One of the most common uses of transformation in our society occurs in marriage when the wife typically adopts the name of the husband.

Naming also serves as a rite of passage in the conferring of titles. When a person has earned a doctoral degree, he or she also earns the title Doctor. When Mr. Jones is ordained as a minister, he is addressed as the Reverend Mr. Jones. In British society, the conferring of titles of address, such as Sir and Lord, indicates a transformation from one status to another. Election to office is often accompanied by changing names and forms of address such as Senator or Bishop or President. Once a person has held an office he or she frequently continues to be addressed by the title of the office. For example, within the period of one month, the United States lost two presidents with the deaths of President Truman and President Johnson.

Name changes often occur in the conversion of an individual from one life to what he perceives as a new life. Thus Elijah Poole became known to the world as Elijah Muhammad and Cassius Clay became Muhammad Ali. Although not as prominent today as in former centuries, the changing of names was a prominent feature in both the Moslem and Christian religions.

Naming that serves the function of transformation or rite of passage from one state to another is frequently accompanied by socially sanctioned ritual. The marriage ceremony, the conferring of degrees, the ordination of ministers, the conferring of titles, the inauguration of officials—all are rituals that are socially sanctioned and often accompanied by great pomp and ceremony. Religious conversion is often accompanied by a change of name in ceremonies of confirmation. The word *christening,* or conferring of a name, entered our common vocabulary, and today we ceremonially christen not only people but also boats, aircraft, and other vehicles and objects.

Reification. Reification has been described as the tendency to make the abstract concrete.[20] Reification can be illustrated as the process whereby we take such terms as democracy, communism, and capitalism and convert them from processes, ideas and styles into supposedly con-

19. Some authors who deal with the transformational power of language are Cassirer, *Language and Myth*, esp. pp. 62–83; Burke, *Rhetoric of Motives*, esp. pp. 10–13; Hugh Dalziel Duncan, *Symbols in Society* (New York: Oxford University Press, 1968), pp. 21–22; and Hugh Dalziel Duncan, *Communication and Social Order* (New York: Bedminster Press, 1962; London: Oxford University Press, 1968), pp. 147, 260.

20. Condon, *Semantics and Communication*, p. 51.

crete objects. Because we have created a term we feel that it must refer to some *thing* when the term may in fact refer only to a broad class of social perceptions or general styles of interaction.

Although reification still plagues us in the realm of political and social action, there have been significant changes in language in the last one hundred years. The prevalence of process philosophy in the physical sciences combined with the Orientalization of Western language have tended to make us more comfortable with language that does not refer to concrete objects. While we tend to look for the concrete in language, to reify, we also feel relatively comfortable discussing the concept of atoms, which are not things but patterns of activity or processes. We are slowly learning to grapple with the concepts of electricity, magnetism and gravity—concepts that are described as field phenomena, concepts whose existence cannot be demonstrated directly by pointing to a concrete object.

SOME NEGATIVE CONSEQUENCES OF NAMING AS ENVIRONMENT

Some aspects of our language environment affect us in negative ways, retarding the development of the self and thereby limiting the individual's contributions to the growth of society. Three such negative aspects of language—racism, sexism, and agism—are prevalent in our language environments.

Racism has probably been one of the most widely discussed problems in our language. Negroes in the United States have found their language environments filled with negative stereotyping, such as the names nigger, boy, Uncle Tom, slave, pickaninny, coon, jungle bunny, etc. Other racial and ethnic groups in our culture have had to cope with similar terms: spick, kike, wop, dago, chink, and polack, to name but a very few.

When we consider such language environments, we can readily discover the limiting, constricting, and socially retarding effects that they have. It has been shown, for example, that children growing up in lower-class black ghettos drew pictures of themselves that had few limbs, no fingers, no mouths or eyes or ears. Their self-images were severely restricted when compared with self-images of white middle-class children of the same age. When the black children were given intensive redefinitions of the key term in their language environment (changing "Black is bad" to "Black is beautiful"), their pictures of themselves began to contain more representations of limbs, mouths, eyes and ears.[21] Other people tell us who we are, and we tend to believe them.

21. CBS Television Network, "Of Black America: Black History—Lost, Stolen, or Strayed," 2 July 1968, Executive Producer, Perry Wolff.

We extend ourselves into friendly language environments; we withdraw from hostile ones.

In more recent years, our concern for sexism in language has become almost as prominent as our concern for racism. Many of the typical Dick and Jane readers for elementary school children portrayed girls as weak, emotional, unable to cope with problems, in need of their brothers' protection, and concerned only with housework and motherhood as future goals. The same books portrayed boys as strong, brave, unemotional, able to cope with problems, protective of their sisters, and considering a wide variety of exciting professions. These stereotypes both typified and reinforced the language environment of most children in our society.[22]

The effects of this language environment are similar to those of racism in many ways. Women often score lower than men on measures of self (self-image, self-confidence, self-worth, self-perception, etc.). Because of the sexist language environment, many women even today find it difficult to conceive of themselves as mentally and emotionally capable of engaging in business and social interactions with males as complete equals. The effects of sexism on men in our society are equally important. Many men react to the stress of having to maintain a "macho" image—of always having to appear to be strong, completely controlled, dominating, aggressive, unemotional. Some social scientists believe that the early age at which men die and the higher incidence of heart attacks among men in their thirties and forties may well be related to these stereotypes in the language environment.[23]

Changes in the language environment are, however, having profound effects in "consciousness raising" of men and women. These changes in the language environment are leading to changes in self-perception and self-image which in turn lead to changes in communication behavior (and vice versa). Textbook publishers have radically revised the Dick and Jane stereotypes, thus changing the language environment of children in significant ways. Likewise, the common vocabulary is beginning to show signs of modifying the way we speak about men and women.

We sometimes think the effects of racism and sexism in language are especially profound because they primarily affect children. But language environments affect each and every one of us. Adults are no less influenced by language environments than are children. An illustration of the effects of language environments on adults can be seen in problems of agism in language.

22. "Sexist Texts," *Time,* 5 November 1973, p. 66. See also Cynthia Eaton and Carol Jacobs, "Princeton: Changing the Textbooks," *American Education* 9 (June 1973): 26–28.
23. See Sidney M. Jourard, *The Transparent Self,* rev. ed. (New York: D. Van Nostrand Co., 1971), pp. 34–41.

Agism in our language environment often gives us a negative view of older people and prevents us from seeing that not all older people behave in the same way.

What images do you associate with the terms *old, aged,* and *elderly?* The chances are extremely high that these words have negative images for you. Our society places its emphasis upon youth. To be beautiful is to be young, not old. Our society does not revere its aged; we separate them from the young in their own cubicles in prison-like institutions that we call "nursing homes" or "homes for the aged." A friend of ours, who is seventy-five years old, berated us one day for referring to him as old or elderly. "Old people are senile and belong in homes," he staunchly insisted, "and I am neither of those. I don't associate with old people, and I don't like to be called old."

Racist, sexist, and agist stereotypes in our language usually have negative consequences in the development of the self and the self-image of the individual. When a person encounters your language as his or her environment, what will he or she find? Will your language imply that he or she is bad, evil, lazy, drunken, dirty, second-class, a sex object, used-up, senile, useless? Or will your language suggest that the person is beautiful, a child of the universe with potential and worth as a human being?

It is difficult to eliminate these negative stereotypes from your language, but it can be done. The first step is to become aware of the stereotypes that you are using. Listen carefully to your own language. Get others to help you identify the terms you use that may have negative or undesirable effects on others. Then substitute more positive words for those you have identified. Change your own vocabulary. And finally, watch the "we-they" division.[24] Whenever you discover yourself referring to "them" as apart from yourself, you are probably bordering on a negative stereotype. "Why don't *they* speak like the rest of us?" Aren't *they* intelligent enough to hold jobs like us?" "Oh, one of my friends is one of *them*." These statements reflect an often unconscious division that implies superiority and inferiority. In order to successfully change your own language, it is necessary to control if not eliminate the we-they distinctions in your use of language.

LANGUAGE AS INSTRUMENT: SCIENCE AND MAGIC

We have looked at how language forms an important environment for every human individual. We have seen how the language environment shapes and molds each person's self-concept. But how do we *use* the language environment to communicate with others? What are the best ways of manipulating this language environment to achieve effective interpersonal communication with other persons?

The answers to these questions would be easier if there were only one commonly accepted theory of language. At this time, however, there are two equally important and widely held views of the nature of language and its use. The two theories appear to be mutually exclusive and contradictory on several key points. So far, it has not been possible to synthesize them into one theory. This does not mean that either theory is wrong; it means that neither of them is fully comprehensive. Each theory explains a different aspect of language that is essential to understanding how we use language in interpersonal communication. It is important to understand both viewpoints, for they suggest quite contradictory ideas about how we ought to use language most effec-

24. See Duncan, *Symbols in Society*, pp. 81–104.

tively in interpersonal transactions. The two basic views of language are the scientific view of language and the magical view of language.

THE SCIENTIFIC VIEW OF LANGUAGE

Most readers will already be familiar with the scientific concepts of language. Science has dominated our formal education systems for the last two hundred years or so. The scientific concept of language follows the basic structures of logic, abstraction, systematization, categorization, and inference that we have been taught from the time we were children. The scientific model of language makes several basic assumptions.

Language is Representational. The first assumption of the scientific view of language is that language *represents* reality. To the traditional scientific mind, reality is "out there," external to the human organism, and is perceived through the organization of sense data. The sense data experienced by the person is not reality itself, but is merely a representation of reality.[25] Scientific theorists of language stress that "the word is not the thing," that "the map is not the territory."[26] Rather, words merely represent reality in the same sense that a map represents (but is not the same as) the territory it portrays.

The reason that words do not equal reality is that all human processes of perception and interpretation, including language, inevitably involve abstraction from what is being perceived. The human organism's perception, organization and categorization of sense data are greatly affected by language. A collection of sense data is grouped together on the basis of some characteristic of the sense data. The collection of sense data is then represented in the mind by a word. Words, or language symbols (whichever term one wishes to use) are in this sense representations of categories of sense data. Because of the nature of representation, the actual sense data is necessarily distorted through imperfections in the sense organs or through individual biases in perception. Therefore, words are not the real world but are representations of the real world mediated by the perception and organization of sense data.

Ogden and Richards first discussed the representational nature of language as involving the word or symbol, its referent, and its reference.[27]

25. See Werner von Heisenberg, *Philosophy and Physics* (New York: Harper Torchbooks, Science Library, 1958); and Arthur Eddington, *The Philosophy of Physical Science* (New York: Macmillan Co., 1939).
26. Condon, *Semantics and Communication*, p. 13; and Chase, *Power of Words*, p. 147.
27. C. K. Ogden and I. A. Richards, *The Meaning of Meaning: A Study of the Influence of Language upon Thought and of the Science of Symbolism* (New York: Harcourt, Brace & World, 1923; Harvest Books, 1946), pp. 1–23. The diagram that follows is adapted from p. 11.

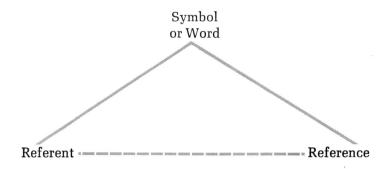

These three elements may be diagramed as a triangle composed of the word, the thing in reality that the word represents (the referent), and the perceptual processes that mediate between the word and the thing the word represents (the reference). Notice that this diagram of language's representational nature illustrates the division between the thing that is represented (the referent) and the individual's mediating processes such as perception, categorization, interpretation, etc., that organize sense data (the reference). The word or symbol not only represents reality (or the thing) but also represents the processes of the mind—our experience of reality. From the scientific point of view, the *meaning* of a word is made up of both the referent and the reference.

A simple example of the representational view of language is based on the statement of general semanticists—primary advocates of the scientific model of language—that the word is not the thing. The word *dog* (symbol) is related both to our idea of a dog (reference) and to the animal itself (referent); however, the word is not the animal. We can talk about dogs all day without actually having such animals present. Furthermore, a mailman who has been bitten by innumerable dogs will probably have quite a different idea (reference) about dogs than a person who owns a prize-winning dog. The scientific view of language tries to account for the similarities and differences in the meaning of the word *dog* to both the mailman and the housewife by dividing the meaning of the word, or symbol, into referent and reference, and by constantly reminding us that when we use language, we are using a *representation* of reality. When we speak, we are abstracting from reality and organizing reality according to our own particular frames of reference.[28] In the transactional model of interpersonal communication, we have called these frames of reference *perspectives*.[29]

Kinds of Abstraction. The second assumption of the scientific view of language is that language may be manipulated to represent various

28. Haney, *Communication and Organizational Behavior*, pp. 63–73.
29. See chapter 4.

kinds of abstraction. One kind of abstraction is neither more nor less representative of reality than any other; they are merely different.

Four kinds of abstraction are usually discussed in the scientific view of language. These are statements of observation, statements of inference, statements of judgment, and tautologies.[30] Each kind of statement represents a slightly different relationship between the word, the referent, and the reference. Each kind of statement emphasizes a different perspective of the user in relationship to the external world.

Statements of observation are statements that place primary emphasis upon describing the objective qualities of the referent, or physical reality. Statements of observation attempt to minimize the influence of the observer—to decrease the amount of inference and judgment that arises from putting sense data into categories. When a person makes a statement of observation, the person is trying to describe what is observed in such a way that all other users of the language may reconstruct the referent.

The statement "The boy is walking" is considered to be a statement of observation. When a user of the language says, "The boy is walking," he or she is minimizing the role of the individual's perceptual process as well as the individual's associations with language. We must recognize, however, that even the statement "The boy is walking" is not completely observational. Inferences and judgments are also implied by the choice of the language. The observer could have said, "The boy is ambling," or "The young male *Homo sapiens* is in locomotion on a horizontal plane at a moderate speed in relation to the ground by means of alternately placing one foot in front of the other." All three statements are observational insofar as they try to emphasize describing the external world more than describing the values, references, and feelings of the observer.

A second kind of abstraction involves inference, the process by which people fill in gaps in the information they encounter in order to make sense out of that information. In *statements of inference,* the perspective of the observer—his prior experiences, attitudes, and values—plays a prominent role. A typical statement of inference would be "The boy is hungry." This language involves more than mere observation of external reality. The boy may be eating rapidly, but this action might reflect that he is late for school and won't get another chance to eat for four hours, rather than any particular hunger at the moment. Hunger is something that cannot be observed *per se;* it can only be inferred or assumed.

30. Condon, *Semantics and Communication,* pp. 81–86. What we term a *statement of observation*—derived from Haney, *Communication and Organizational Behavior,* pp. 185–214—is called a *statement of description* by Condon. Our discussion of the four kinds of abstraction is based largely on these sources.

Inference can be both helpful and unhelpful. Anyone who has worked with computers knows that the computer must be told *exactly* what to do; if there is any omission in the directions it receives, it will be unable to infer what is missing. A person who functioned like a computer would be completely unable to function in human society because he or she would be unable to make sense out of the necessarily incomplete messages he or she would receive. Inference can be inaccurate, however; we can assume that the boy is just rushed when he is actually starving. Incorrect inferences can lead to confusion or incongruency within interpersonal communication transactions.

A third kind of abstraction in the use of language is the *statement of judgment,* which places primary emphasis upon the perspective of the user of language. The speaker is telling us as much about his or her *interpretation* of the external event as he or she is of the external event itself. A typical statement of judgment might be "The girl is sweet." In this statement, there is little emphasis upon describing the person or upon inferential processes. Rather, the speaker is rendering a value judgment, basing the judgment on the references in the speaker's mind. Judgment is necessary, but can be harmful if it is hasty or ill-considered.

A fourth kind of abstraction in the use of language is called a *tautology*. A tautology is a statement that places a definition on sense data that cannot be verified through sense data. The statement "Man is a featherless biped" is often cited as a tautology. The statement is a circular definition that is conceived by the mind and imposed on sense data. In its most abstract form, a tautology may have no referent in physical reality at all. For example, the statement "$A = A$" is a tautology in which A may represent anything and everything in physical reality. But observation, or sense data, is not necessary to verify that "$A = A$." In this kind of abstraction, the meaning of the statement exists apart from the referent.

Arbitrary Relationships Between Words and Things. The third assumption of the scientific view of language is that there is no *necessary* or *inherent* relationship between the word and the thing that the word represents.[31] For instance, the object that you are reading now might just as easily have been called a *bomble* or a *sinthern* as a *book*. From a scientific view of language, what an object, concept, or event is called is a convention of the language community. The object that the English call a *book* is termed *livre* by the French; there is no necessary connection between the word and the thing, only a socially agreed upon connection.

31. C. F. Hockett, "Animal 'Languages' and Human Language," in *The Evolution of Man's Capacity for Culture,* ed. J. N. Spuhler, (Detroit: Wayne State University Press, 1959), pp. 32–38.

SCIENTIFIC USES OF LANGUAGE

The scientific view of language is based on the assumptions that language is representational, involves different kinds of abstraction and has an arbitrary relationship with the things represented. This view has definite implications for the use of language as an instrument of communication.

Index Your Abstractions. Incongruency may arise in transactions when one person is using one kind of abstraction while the other party is perceiving a different kind of abstraction.[32] Paul may interpret Helen's judgments as statements of observation. When he does so, Paul forgets that her statements reflect her value structure and her perspectives on the event being observed. He must also remember that his statements reflect his perspectives on the event and that both their perspectives are abstractions from reality. Paul may see Helen's furniture as *junk* while she sees it as *antiques*. The furniture is neither junk nor antiques and it is both junk and antiques. The words Paul and Helen apply to the furniture represent different abstractions from the furniture and reflect their perspectives on the referent as much as describing the referent itself.

People can reduce misunderstandings in interpersonal transactions by indexing the kinds of abstractions they are using. A husband might say, "My wife does not respect me." To determine the meaning of the statement, the husband and any observer of the statement must index the statement as a statement of judgment. They must realize that the statement involves inferences and systems of values in the husband's interpretation of sense data he experiences in interaction with his wife. The statement "My wife does not respect me" represents the husband's perspectives, his interpretation of his own experiences and his own sense data, as much as it represents his wife's behavior toward him.

When we are faced with difficulties in working out the problems of interpersonal communication in the relationship between a husband and a wife, we must differentiate between statements of judgment and statements of observation. We would ask the husband to abstract from his experience in a different way. We would have him operationalize his judgmental statement, "My wife does not respect me," to a set of statements of description. His statements should answer the question, "What behaviors does your wife engage in that lead you to infer that she does not respect you?"

The responses to this question should be statements of observation. The husband might say: "My wife will begin breakfast without waiting for me to get to the table"; "My wife is always criticizing the way I

---

32. Condon, *Semantics and Communication*, pp. 81–86.

dress"; or "My wife doesn't answer my questions; she ignores me when I want to know something about her activities."

In attempting to resolve difficulties in interpersonal communication between two people, it is usually most productive to attempt to bring the discussion to statements of observation which can be verified by the observations of all parties concerned.[33] Statements of inference and judgment require exploration not only of the observed behaviors, but of the mediational processes and value systems of the people involved. Such explorations are most fruitful in improving the communication health of individuals or dyads when they are based upon agreement at the observational level of abstraction.

The most difficult kind of abstraction to deal with in interpersonal conflicts is the tautology. Oftentimes difficulties in communication take the form of spirals that are based on tautologies; one person in the dyad defines the problem completely in terms of itself. This creates a kind of vicious cycle that prevents any other person from effectively interacting with the individual. When one or both parties in an interpersonal transaction are dealing with their relationship at the strictly tautological level, it becomes very difficult to break into the closed circle of thinking that perpetuates the problems.

Archie might describe his wife, Edith, by using a tautology.

> Archie: *My wife is a dingbat. I just can't deal with her sometimes, you know?*
>
> Observer: *What makes you say your wife is a dingbat?*
>
> Archie: *Because she is.*
>
> Observer: *What do you mean by the word dingbat?*
>
> Archie: *A dingbat is Edith, my wife.*
>
> Observer: *But how does she act that makes you think she's a dingbat?*
>
> Archie: *Well, she just acts like a dingbat, you know.*

The observer in the dialogue is trying to locate some reference or referent for the term Archie is using. The observer's probes are designed to try to get Archie to break out of defining the situation completely in terms of tautological abstractions and to redefine the situation in terms of statements of judgment, inference, or observation that can be explored in a more empirical way.

The goal of the scientific use of abstractions in language is to make language consensual—to ground our use of language in experience that can be mutually validated and to draw relationships between words and

---

33. Haney, *Communication and Organizational Behavior*, pp. 185–214.

referents that can be derived by an empirical system of logic.

Manage Inference. One of the most important insights we can gain about our own interpersonal communication involves the concept of inference. *Whenever we communicate in an interpersonal situation we are involved in the process of managing inferences.* To become more effective in our interpersonal communication, whether it be between parent and child, between husband and wife, or between employer and employee, we must learn to manage the inference process more effectively. While this section focuses upon drawing inferences from the use of language in interpersonal communication, the same principle can be applied to the management of inferences in the use of the other message systems—space, sexuality, and gesture.

The success we have in managing interpersonal communication depends upon both our *acuity* in interpreting the elements of communication for ourselves and our *facility* in structuring the perceptions of others in interpersonal transactions.

The following incident typifies the need to manage inferences. A student enters his instructor's office. After the exchange of greetings, the instructor and the student seat themselves. The instructor asks, "And what can I do for you today?" The student responds with something to the effect that he wishes to discuss the mark he received on an examination or a paper. The conversation proceeds for several minutes focusing upon the student's performance on the item in question. They discuss points of difference in interpreting the student's paper. During the conversation the student becomes more and more animated and his statements become stronger. Finally the student says, "Well, I think that you have something against me and that it is showing in your reading of my paper."

At this point the instructor should realize that the subject of the interview is not the paper or even the grade. The "real" communication between instructor and student may be about their own interpersonal relationships, their feelings of trust and distrust, their feelings of warmth and hostility. Or the discussion may lead to considering the student's entire program or to the discovery that the student is flunking out, is not meeting the minimum requirements of his program, or has marital, romantic, or financial problems that are significantly interfering with his performance in the classroom.

This type of incident is very commonly experienced by professionals, such as doctors, lawyers, ministers, counselors, and teachers. The client initiates a conference. The acute listener rapidly discovers meanings within the communication situation that indicate that the stated purpose for the conference is not the real purpose for the conference. It then becomes the task of the professional person to structure his own inferences about the client's behavior to determine a way to manage the interview and bring to light what the other person really came to talk about.

The person who is involved in counseling, clinical, or advising relationships with others must be attuned to the processes of inference and abstraction to be successful in interpersonal communication. He or she must listen for a variety of possible meanings; the person should not assume that the initial inference or the most obvious inference about the nature of the communication is always accurate. The person who is most successful in managing his interpersonal communication transactions is usually the person who realizes that every word or gesture, every statement or action can lead to a variety of inferences. The most successful communicators can sort through the variety of possible inferences and discover which set of inferences is most meaningful in the specific encounter.

What is involved in the management of the inference process? There are ways that each of us can better manage the inferences that others draw about us from our communication with them.

1. *Be aware of the other person's perspectives.* Every person perceives communication from a different set of perspectives. In order to manage the inferences that other people draw about us, we must realize that they do not necessarily see us as we see ourselves. They will not see us meaning precisely the same thing that we see ourselves meaning when we communicate. We must empathize, trying to envision the other's perspectives, in order to communicate more effectively.

2. *Highlight the significant points of meaning.* We must communicate in ways that indicate what is important to us and what is unimportant to us. One branch manager of a company failed to do this; he was forever calling the central office to complain about every little inconvenience in his office. Eventually the people in the central office came to discount everything the manager complained about. They could not infer what problems were important to the manager and what problems were trivial to him. Furthermore, because the manager complained about everything in the same harried manner, people in the central office gradually inferred that the manager was incompetent in distinguishing between important and trivial matters of administration.

Sometimes we can highlight really important issues by repeating them or by giving them special emphasis. If Bob mentions his wife's health a number of times during a conversation with Mike, Mike is more likely to infer that the health of Bob's wife is meaningful to Bob at this particular time. The number of times a given matter is emphasized and the stress the language is given become guiding factors in the inferences others may draw from the situation.

3. *Avoid stereotypic uses of language.* These lead the listener to infer more than is intended. The three guidelines for correcting negative stereotyping discussed earlier can be useful in checking the inferences that you and others make. By using *etc.* you can avoid the allness syndrome. Both you and others will realize that you are not saying all there is to say about the subject being discussed. By indexing you can avoid the indiscrimination syndrome and keep yourself and others from inferring that what you say about one person or object generalizes to all members of the set of persons or objects. By time indexing you can indicate to yourself and others that people and things change over time. What you say to be true now is not necessarily what was true at a former time, and vice versa.

The scientific use of language has had tremendous positive consequences. The rise of modern science and technology—with all of its power to harness nature for man's benefit—has been built upon the idea that reality is "out there," that language only represents reality, that language involves various kinds of abstraction, and that the relationship between words and real things is arbitrary. We have discussed how the scientific use of language can help improve interpersonal communication. The difficulties with the scientific approach to language, however, are best seen in light of the magical view of language.

THE MAGICAL VIEW OF LANGUAGE

While science is commonly accepted in our society, magic is not. Magic is most widely seen as the production of some effect (like making a rabbit appear in a hat) by using some special gesture (like passing a hand over the hat) or uttering special words (like *abra cadabra*). When we are dealing with the relationship between words and the inanimate world, science is more efficient than magic. Uttering words does not make the rain fall, for example, because there is no apparent connection between the words and the rain. But in human affairs, and in interpersonal communication in particular, language is used more as magic than as science. By uttering the words "John, please bring me the paper," we render important changes in the environment; John does get up and bring the paper. The relationship between people and language is not the same as the relationship between rain and language. By uttering words we can unleash great power in interpersonal relations; by uttering words we can affect ourselves and others. And we can best understand this phenomena by understanding language as magic.[34]

34. A few of the many authors who explore the magical dimension of language are Richard Bandler and John Grinder, *The Structure of Magic: A Book about Language and Therapy* (Palo Alto, Calif.: Science and Behavior Books, 1975); and Burke, *Permanence and Change.*

There are three basic assumptions in the magical model of language. The first assumption is that language is constitutive. The second is that language possesses an unconscious dimension which operates in all human interactions. The third is that the way language embodies reality is meaningful; in other words, meaning exists in the way language constitutes reality for its users.

Language is Constitutive. Cassirer, Jung, Levi-Strauss, Duncan, and others who discuss language as magic point out that for most people language embodies or *constitutes reality*.[35] Words do not represent some reality "out there"; words have a reality, a meaning, and power in themselves. When we use words, we use them as if they were the thing. Words are effective in interpersonal communication—words have power to effect changes in the social environment—only as long as the words embody reality for their users.

We can understand how language embodies reality more clearly by looking at the way we use language magically. Any viewer of the children's television show "Captain Kangaroo" knows that the two magic phrases are *please* and *thank you*. We teach children that they can obtain what they want more readily if they use the word *please*. Using *thank you* after receiving something will increase the likelihood of its being offered again. Children are taught that they may increase their control over their social environments by uttering these words. And this is, of course, what magic is all about—uttering words to control environments.

The comedian George Carlin has pointed out that we will not allow seven words to be uttered on television because of the constitutive nature of language.[36] The words one cannot say on television point to sexual organs, sexual intercourse, or other bodily functions. When Carlin's routine on these words is played to a mixed audience, there is often an emotional reaction involving tension-release, nervousness, and some offense. People are not reacting to organs, events, or bodily functions but to the words themselves. The people who will discuss "sexual intercourse," "defecation," or "urinary elimination," may become offended when someone says "fuck," "shit," or "piss." People don't react to some "reality" represented by the words; they react to the words themselves. The words constitute a reality for the users; words possess an emotional power.

Other examples of the constitutive nature of language abound. The ancient Hebrews (and many of their modern descendants) believed that

35. See Cassirer, *Language and Myth;* Carl G. Jung, ed., *Man and His Symbols* (London, Aldus Books, 1964; New York: Dell Publishing Co., Laurel Edition, 1968), esp. pp. 1–94; Levi-Strauss, *The Savage Mind;* and Duncan, *Symbols in Society.*

36. George Carlin, "Class Clown," published by Dead Sea Music, BMI: Little David Records distributed by Atlantic Recording Corp., New York, 1972.

to know or utter a person's name was to have power over the person; hence, they did not utter the name of God because He was the all-powerful One who summoned men (not vice versa).[37] The Christian invokes Christ's name to call forth his presence based upon the promise of Jesus that "where two or three are gathered in my name, there am I in the midst of them." The magical view of language is found not just in religion but also in law; a person whose name has been damaged can sue the person who damaged it. This concept of libel assumes that to damage a person's name is to damage the person.

Language Has an Unconscious Dimension. The second assumption of the magical model of language is that language always possesses an unconscious dimension.[38] A word or symbol possesses its own history, identity, and meaning. The user of a word does not create the word; words transcend any particular individual. They are cultural phenomena existing before the individual was born and existing after the individual

37. See the discussion of the phenomenon by Cassirer, *Language and Myth*, pp. 44–62.
38. Carl G. Jung, "Approaching the Unconscious," in *Man and His Symbols*, ed. Carl G. Jung, pp. 1–94. See also Theodore Thass-Thienemann, *Symbolic Behavior* (New York: Washington Square Press, 1968).

Remember Captain Kangaroo telling you to use the magic words please *and* thank you?

dies. Thus, the meaning of words exists apart from the use any particular individual makes of them. The meaning of words exists in the collective or social environment. When we speak a word, we call forth its meaning from what Jung has termed the *collective unconscious*.[39]

When we use language we are not always aware of all the meanings of the words.[40] Sometimes the unconscious meaning of language guides our use of language. It is very common, for example, for a person to use a word in a perfectly correct sense but be unable to say what the word means. Words can guide our behavior even though we do not know either the referents or the references in the scientific sense of language.

We were reminded of this point once when we were reading an article on radical revolution. What is the meaning of the term *radical*? We could use the word correctly but could not define it. We then discovered that *radical* could be used in several different contexts with the same basic meaning. For instance, we say, "Radical four is two, radical nine is three"; we also say, "Marx is an advocate of radical revolution." We found that the word *radical* means "root." Thus, we can translate those statements into "the square root of nine is three" and "Marx advocates a return to the roots of social order." Once the meaning of the word was called into consciousness, it made sense to us. But for nearly twenty years we had both been using the word with its meaning only unconsciously defined.

The study of the unconscious dimensions of language and their effect on interpersonal communication is a fascinating and well-documented area of study. Anyone interested in reading more on the subject should refer to the writings of Carl Jung and his students or of the psychoanalytic linguist Theodore Thass-Thienemann.[41]

Meaning Exists in Language. From the scientific point of view, meaning is arbitrary; it exists in the user of the language, not in the language itself. The scientist says, "Words don't mean, people do." From the magical point of view, meaning is not arbitrary. The "magician" argues that words have inherent meanings that we invoke when we speak. For the magician, meaning does not exist in people, but in the way words constitute reality for their users. Because the meaning exists in the word itself, the individual does not have the power to change the meaning of words at whim. When a person tries to speak in this way, we call the person autistic, or withdrawn from reality. Such a person's language loses its meaning.

39. Calvin S. Hall and Vernon J. Nordby, *A Primer of Jungian Psychology* (New York: New American Library, Mentor Books, 1973), pp. 38–53.

40. Thass-Thienemann, *Symbolic Behavior,* pp. 76–93.

41. Thass-Thienemann, *Symbolic Behavior;* and the same author's *The Subconscious Language* (New York: Washington Square Press, 1967).

Freud believed that all symbols, and consequently all language, are extensions of the body and bodily functions. All symbols could therefore be analyzed in terms of parts of the body (such as the genitals, the breasts, the mouth, the anus), bodily functions (such as defecation, urination, eating), or physical relationships (such as sexual intercourse).[42] In a psychoanalytic interpretation of a poem or a story or a dream, a cane or walking stick may be seen as a symbol of a penis. An artist's retreat to a cloistered attic may be interpreted as a symbolic retreat to the womb. By analyzing all language along these dimensions, Freud was able to draw a relationship between dreams and conscious behavior. This symbolic interpretation is an extremely powerful method of analyzing language.

More recent theorists, including the speech pathologist Clyde Rousey, argue that the sounds of a word are also extensions of bodily functions.[43] The harsh k sounds at the beginning and ending of the word cock make the word extremely aggressive. The elongated sounds in the word mood are seductive. A person who uses language that has a great deal of harsh articulations (k, t, d, p) may be seen as unconsciously hostile and sexually aggressive; a person using the labial sounds (m, n, oo, u) may be seen as unconsciously sexually seductive. Rousey has shown that careful analysis of language sounds can be useful in diagnosing various psychological conditions and patterns of interaction.

MAGICAL USES OF LANGUAGE

In Childhood Development. The way we use language in interpersonal communication usually involves language as magic. For the infant there must be a magical relationship between its cry and the production of the nipple.[44] From the infant's point of view, the cry causes the nipple to appear. Children encounter constant reinforcement of similar magical relationships as they begin to use language; children learn that words can produce changes in the environment that mere action cannot. A child may point and wave its arms when hungry. But it may not be fed until it utters the word *milk* or *thirsty.* A parent may physically restrain a child reaching for a glass of milk until the child utters the word *please.* Words magically change the motion in the environment to action directed toward some desired end. The magical power of words is emphasized throughout the child's socialization.

42. Charles Brenner, *An Elementary Textbook of Psychoanalysis* (New York: International Universities Press, 1955; Garden City, N.Y.: Doubleday & Co., Anchor Books, 1957), p. 57.
43. Clyde Rousey and Alice E. Moriarity, *Diagnostic Implications of Speech Sounds: The Reflections of Developmental Conflict and Trauma,* with an Introduction by Peter Ostwald (Springfield, Ill.: C. C. Thomas, 1966).
44. Sullivan, *Interpersonal Theory of Psychiatry,* pp. 69–70.

Often the use of the words *I'm sorry* illustrates the *morbid* use of the magical powers of language.[45] Because of the magical qualities of language, it is easy for a very young child to come to believe that uttering the phrase literally abolishes the act. The child may knock over a lamp which falls to the floor and breaks. By crying and saying, "I'm sorry," the child avoids anxiety brought on by the conseqeunces (a distraught parent and physical or social punishment). Under certain kinds of reinforcement by the parent, the child comes to believe and to act as if the lamp were never broken. This behavior frequently continues into adulthood. Many adults act as if uttering the words *I'm sorry* somehow obliterates their actions and eliminates the consequences of those actions.

The words *I'm sorry* lose their morbidity if parents carefully teach the child to distinguish between the act and how the child feels about the act. The words do not eliminate the act; they express feelings about the act.

Please, thank you, and *I'm sorry* represent significant examples of the magical use of language in the socialization of children in our culture. The three phrases serve three different functions: to persuade others to do something for or in relationship to us; to confirm social acceptance of the acts of others in relationship to ourselves; and to express our feelings and emotions in relationship to an act. Whenever we use language to serve one of those functions, we invoke its magical qualities to manipulate our environment.

In Persuasion. All persuasion uses language in a magical sense. There are two aspects of persuasion that make it magical. First, persuasion assumes that the words we utter can somehow create transformations in the social environment. Second, when we engage in persuasion we structure our manipulation of events through magical rather than scientific thinking.

Persuasion involves the use of language as an instrument to manipulate the environment. When I speak persuasively, I speak to achieve some purpose. When I try to persuade you to do something, I employ language as if the words had the power to alter your perceptions and to generate social and physical action. Persuasion is an attempt to use language to transform elements in the environment by restructuring social perceptions and thereby restructuring social actions.

In Ritual. Probably the most powerful and prominent use of language as magic occurs in rituals. In rites of passage from one state to another, the utterance of words transforms a person's existence. In societies throughout the world, the marriage ceremony is a widely observed ritual that relies on the magical power of language. Other magical

45. Sullivan, *Interpersonal Theory of Psychiatry*, pp. 201–14.

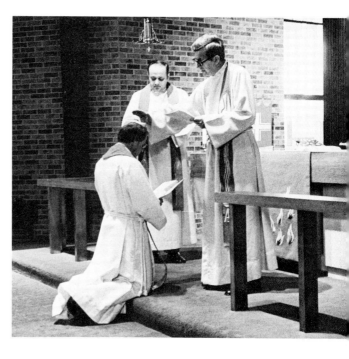

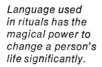

*Language used
in rituals has the
magical power to
change a person's
life significantly.*

words as rites of passage are found in the rituals of baptism, confirmation, and bar mitzvah.

The awarding of degrees (an ironic practice used by supposedly scientific institutions) is another exercise of the magical power of language. We do not graduate with the M.A., the B.A., or even the high school diploma until words confirm our passage from one state of knowledge into another. The university transforms an individual from Mr., Miss, or Mrs., to Doctor by the utterance of words. A person may have the same knowledge, wisdom and insight before the ceremony as after, but words must confirm the state of knowledge. The doors of employment and opportunity in our society remain relatively closed to those people for whom the words have not been uttered. Regardless of how scientific we may perceive ourselves to be, the stark reality remains that we do not admit people into the fellowship of even the most scientific of communities (perhaps particularly in the most scientific of communities) until words have worked their magic.

Words in the rituals of life create and maintain social order and the roles within it.[46] The service of ordination of ministers, priests, and rabbis is an example of role creation through the ritual utterance of words. When a person is ordained, he or she assumes a different role and can perform ceremonies and other social functions that had been

46. See Duncan, *Symbols in Society,* esp. pp. 110–23; see also Duncan, *Communication and Social Order,* p. 144.

previously denied to him or her. A person becomes president of the United States because we name that person president. The powers of the role disappear with the utterance of words of resignation—as we witnessed in the transfer of office from Richard Nixon to Gerald Ford.

Words maintain roles through the process of *mystification*.[47] When we don't understand words, we find them mysterious, so we tend to place our faith in the user of the mysterious words. A role has authority in direct proportion to the mystery surrounding the role. With careful study most persons can become capable of doing at least some of the work of a lawyer, for instance. For just any person to read the law books and write wills, deeds, or contracts, however, demystifies the role. A role that can be undertaken by anyone loses its mystery and to that extent loses its authority within the social order.

Each role in society attempts to maintain its position by reserving to itself a set of mysterious terms. Lawyers use legal words; bankers use financial words; doctors use medical words; teachers use educational jargon; ministers pronounce words of blessing, union, and comfort; judges pronounce sentences. Bankers, for example, create mystery about their roles by using the mysterious language of finance—loans, mortgages, debentures, interest compounded quarterly, securities, trusts, credit. To the extent that we find this language mysterious, we tend to place our faith in bankers. They have the words; they must know what they are doing. The same is true of the psychiatrists who make pronouncements about the id, the ego, catharsis, repression, sublimation, schizophrenia, paranoia, depression, mania. All such words are designed to create mystery and to maintain the authority of a role within the social order.

In Healing. An intriguing aspect of language is its power to heal.[48] The healing power of religion, counseling, psychotherapy, etc., rests largely upon the magical power of words. The spoken and written word can bring about remarkable transformations in human outlooks. The meaning of life appears to be bound up in the ways in which language is used and misused. We should not belittle the magical power of language in the realm of the human psyche or spirit.

A chaplain of a large medical center related the following experience of the magical power of language to heal. One day a man came to the chaplain's office requesting that the chaplain counsel the man's wife. The woman felt an overwhelming but unfocused guilt in her life. Several doctors, psychiatrists, and counselors had been unable to help her. The chaplain agreed to counsel the woman, who came to his office the fol-

47. Burke, *Rhetoric of Motives,* pp. 114–27.
48. Jerome D. Frank, *Persuasion and Healing: A Comparative Study of Psychotherapy* (Baltimore: Johns Hopkins Press, 1961; New York: Schocken Books, 1963).

lowing day. Their discussion convinced the chaplain that she was, indeed, suffering from a debilitating sense of guilt and shame about her whole life rather than about any particular act she had committed. After careful consideration, the chaplain took her to the hospital chapel, had her kneel at the altar rail, and read her the words of forgiveness and absolution from the communion ritual in the hymnal. She seemed greatly relieved and departed.

A few days later, the husband came to the chaplain, thanking him profusely for the miracle of the wife's recovery. The husband testified that, for the first time in years, the terrible weight of guilt had dropped from her shoulders; she was like a new person. The "miracle" was accomplished through language—in this case, ritual language. The woman experienced the words of forgiveness as real; she felt forgiven. Healing words, whether in a ritual, a speech, a therapy session, or a conversation with a friend, have the power to change lives.

Surely one of the most important tasks of students of interpersonal communication is to examine carefully ways people use the magical power of language to hurt and to heal. One basic key to mental health lies in the way we communicate with each other, person to person. Our goal in the study of interpersonal communication should be to discover ways to produce healthier and more meaningful lives for ourselves and for others through our communication.

MISUSES OF LANGUAGE

Both the scientific and magical qualities of language are subject to misuse. Those misuses have serious consequences for the development of the individual and the future of the human race, so an awareness of them is extremely important.

Scientific Misuse. The greatest danger of the scientific view of language arises from the assumption that the connection between the word and what it represents is arbitrary. Some people misuse language by refusing to name an act, event, or object what it plainly seems to be. Assuming that there is no necessary connection between the word and the thing, they apply different words to things than are usually applied. The ultimate consequence of such language misuse is the destruction of the social order, since social order is built upon social agreement about the meaning of words in communication.

In the United States we have witnessed firsthand the consequences of the scientific misuse of language. For over a decade the American society was torn apart by the arbitrary use of language. Government officials developed the arbitrary use of language with ever-increasing skills, and ever more devastating harm to our social order. Words that people held to have particular meanings suddenly became redefined. There seemed to be no relationship between what people observed and the language with which these observations were discussed.

Acts that to general public perception were bombing raids on civilian targets in North Viet Nam were arbitrarily renamed "protective reaction strikes" by military and government officials. What was commonly viewed as an act of aggression—the sending of American troops into Cambodia—was quickly renamed an "incursion" into enemy held territory. The killing of women and children at My Lai was called a heroic mission by some, murder and unwanton massacre by others. The effects on our social order were severe. Discussion of these events became meaningless when language could be manipulated so arbitrarily. Words appeared to lose their power.

Our society had not had time to recover from the shock of this conflict before it was plunged into the political difficulties generally labeled Watergate. Once again the society became deeply divided, and the fabric of our government stood in jeopardy, when high government officials, skilled in the scientific uses of language, continued to use language as though words had no intrinsic meaning. Specific acts that were declared illegal by the legislative branch of government were simply renamed and continued under those new names by the administrative branch. Such practices culminated in what must be the ultimate in the arbitrary use of language: common lies simply became "inoperative statements."

The potential danger in the scientific use of language is that when words are conceived as merely representing reality, rather than embodying reality, the users of the language may change the relationship between the word and what it represents as they see fit. Unless words possess meaning and power in themselves, we stand in danger of permitting our language to become meaningless. When this happens there is no longer anything to hold society together; social order disappears.

Magical Misuse. Language as magic has been notoriously destructive to human beings and human environments. The magical qualities of language lead to stereotyping, naming, and self-fulfilling prophecies which may be used either for health and growth or for destruction. While naming and stereotyping have positive effects, these same processes allow us to burn witches (because naming a person a witch makes it so) and to kill our fellow men (because calling them enemies makes them enemies).

Another magical misuse of language involves the inappropriate mystification of roles. Salesmen, repairmen, and various professional people may mystify language by using unnecessary jargon to reduce understanding of what they are doing. They could communicate more effectively by putting their technical vocabulary into plain language when talking to the layman—i.e., anyone outside their own roles. While we cannot entirely eliminate mystification without weakening language and destroying social order, we should not use terminology that is more complex or indirect than necessary to communicate and maintain role relationships.

Modern man's dilemma involves reconciling the scientific and magical views of language. Each view describes an essential aspect of language, yet each is incomplete in itself. Furthermore, each view has positive and negative consequences in the use of language. We must attempt to find ways to conceptualize language that are comprehensive and ways to use language that contribute to the growth and health of individuals and society.

SUMMARY

Language is one of the major environmental forces that shape the human being. Language is integral in the formation of the self and in the processes of perception. Naming is the major environmental characteristic of language. Seven functions of naming are: signification, definition, polarization, stereotyping, socialization, transformation, and reification. Naming as an environment has both negative and positive consequences.

There are two basic views of language. The scientific view of language holds that language is essentially representational. A word or a symbol is composed of two elements: the referent (the object or reality to which the word refers and which the word represents symbolically); and the reference (the internalized reactions, interpretations, and meanings of the word to the user). Representational language has various levels of abstraction from reality which form the basis of the processes of inference. In the scientific view, the connection between the word and the object it represents is arbitrary. Problems may arise from the abstraction and arbitrariness of language.

The magical view of language holds that words are constitutive rather than representational. When a word is used, it is a reality. Words carry with them inherent meanings which have been transmitted from generation to generation via language throughout the history of the culture. Language not only embodies the evocation of experience with objects and events; it also carries with it the unconscious meanings attached to words throughout history. The magical view of language is prominent in our legal and political systems today as well as in our everyday use of language. Persuasion, healing, and religion would not be possible without the constitutive nature of language.

QUESTIONS FOR REVIEW

1. What is the twofold relationship between language and perception?
2. What is signification? What is definition? Give an example of each.
3. What three polar dimensions seem to exist in all languages?
4. What are three kinds of stereotyping? Give an example of each.
5. How does language function to maintain racism, sexism, and agism?
6. What is the representational or scientific view of language? What are the three assumptions of this viewpoint?
7. What is the constitutive or magical view of language? What are the three assumptions of this viewpoint?
8. How do we use language as magic in our everyday conversations?

EXPLORATIONS

1. Most names have historical meanings and references. *Dennis,* for example, is derived from Dionysius, the Greek god. *Peter* is an English name which originally meant "rock or stone." Last names also have specific meanings. *Smith* referred to a person who worked with metals; *Miller* referred to a grinder of grains. An interesting exercise for your communication journal is to take your name(s) and the names of other members of your family (or those of your close friends) and look up their historical derivation in any of the numerous books of names available in the library or in various dictionaries.
2. Write down three negative stereotypes you have about yourself (e.g., I'm short-tempered). Next imagine the stereotype to see if the words you have chosen to describe yourself really are "you." Begin this process by carefully describing the specific situations or circumstances in which the stereotype applies to you. Are you short-tempered all of the time, or under certain conditions? What conditions? What behavior indicates that you are short-tempered? In other words, translate the stereotype you have about yourself into descriptive statements of specific behaviors in specific situations. You may be surprised at the insights this simple exercise will generate into the relationship between language and self-concept as well as between language and behavior.
3. A simple but interesting exercise is to experiment with the names that you call your associates. Note the changes in relationships that occur if you start calling your teacher by first name and some of your peers by Mr., Mrs., or Ms. Focus not only on their reactions but on your feelings about changing the names and forms of address.
4. Select two or three meaningful symbols from your environment or your interactions. Why are these symbols meaningful to you? Where

do their meanings come from? Do they come from your use of the symbols, from the community, from historical contexts? Would these symbols be meaningful to someone from a different culture? Does meaning exist in the symbols?

5. Leaf through a magazine and select some symbol of our times. In considering this symbol try to examine the feelings and emotions that exist in the symbol and distinguish them from the feelings and emotions that you have about the symbol. In what ways does the symbol have meanings different from your own reactions to it?

FOR FURTHER READING

Condon, John C., Jr. *Semantics and Communication.* 2d ed. New York: Macmillan Co., 1975.

One of the most widely used textbooks in general semantics, this work is designed to introduce the student to basic concepts in the uses of language. Condon presents the "scientific" model of language as representational of reality. He then presents a number of ways in which we can improve our uses of language through careful application of the scientific model. It is a highly readable book for students and interested laypersons.

Frank, Jerome D. *Persuasion and Healing: A Comparative Study of Psychotherapy.* Baltimore: Johns Hopkins Press, 1961; New York: Schocken Books, 1963.

Psychiatrist Frank examines psychotherapeutic theory and practice as a healing discipline by looking at the common aspects of various forms of contemporary psychotherapy, as well as such other attempts to heal persons as religious healing, the placebo effect in medicine, experimental persuasion studies, religious revivalism and communist thought reform. This examination reveals the larger framework of persuasion in which both mental and spiritual healing occurs.

Haney, William V. *Communication and Organizational Behavior Text and Cases.* rev. ed. Homewood, Ill.: Richard D. Irwin, 1967.

This book presents a discussion of the uses of language from a general semantics perspective. The structure of the book consists of a general discussion of theoretical concepts followed by a series of incidents taken from everyday life, business settings, and history that illustrate each concept.

Ogden, C. K., and Richards, I. A. *The Meaning of Meaning.* New York: Harcourt, Brace & World, 1923; Harvest Books, 1946.

This work contains a set of essays by two of the most prominent semantic/literary critics of the early twentieth century in which they explore the many ways in which meaning has been studied. The book is a rather sophisticated one and should be read primarily by more advanced students.

Thass-Thienemann, Theodore. *Symbolic Behavior.* New York: Washington Square Press, 1968.

This work is a highly original, controversial analysis of symbolic behavior which combines the methodologies of linguistic analysis with psychoanalysis. The result is a fascinating account of the symbolic underworld, unconscious dimensions of language that direct and emerge through human behavior.

Chapter 7

Gesture as a
Primary Message
System

There is a fundamental unity between the verbal and nonverbal aspects of interpersonal communication. The evidence produced by clinical, experimental, and observational research tends to indicate that the distinctions often made between verbal and nonverbal communication are both arbitrary and artificial.[1] Every verbal act contains nonverbal aspects which are essential to the meaning of the verbal act. Likewise, every nonverbal act functions in essentially the same way as a verbal act. Nevertheless, it is useful to distinguish a message system of gesture that is different from the message system of language.

In an interpersonal transaction, any act to which one or both participants can assign either implicit or explicit significance at the denotative and/or metacommunicative levels is a gesture. Let us consider each part of this definition.

In an interpersonal transaction. Gestures are acts that occur within a field of mutual perception. A gesture may be best conceived not as an isolated event that "communicates" something about a person, but as part of an ongoing communicative transaction in which participants exist in relationship to each other.

Any act. Gesture, as we have defined it, is a very broad concept, for we include the possibility that all acts may be gestures.[2] Gesture includes not only what we do, but also what we fail to do. Not doing something is itself an act to which significance can be assigned.

Let us consider a rather famous example. On March 21, 1973, former President Nixon and his advisors discussed the payment of money to Howard Hunt. During the discussion, President Nixon referred to the money and said, "[Well, for Christsake], get it."[3] Various grand juries

1. Ray L. Birdwhistell, "Body Motion," in *The Natural History of the Interview*, 4 vols., ed. Norman A. McQuown (Chicago: University of Chicago Library Microfilm Collection of Manuscripts on Cultural Anthropology, no. 95, ser. 15, 30 June 1971), vol. 1, chap. 3 (not paginated).

2. Paul Watzlawick, Janet Helmick Beavin, and Don D. Jackson, *Pragmatics of Human Communication: A Study of Interactional Patterns, Pathologies, and Paradoxes* (New York: W. W. Norton & Co., 1967), pp. 48–49.

3. Gerald Gold, ed., *The White House Transcripts: Submission of Recorded Presidential Conversations to the Committee on the Judiciary of the House of Representatives by President Richard Nixon* (New York: Bantam Books, 1974), p. 172. (The expletive is deleted in this source.)

interpreted the failure of Nixon's aides to respond to this statement—the act of not questioning the president on the ethics of paying hush money—as acquiescence to an illegal conspiracy.

To which one or both participants. Within an interpersonal transaction it is impossible not to act. Every act of both participants becomes part of the context in which the ongoing communication occurs. It is not necessary that both participants notice or assign significance to an act for that act to influence future events within the transaction. In identifying a gesture, *the intention of the person acting* (either in the sense of the intended meaning or even in the sense of *whether* a person intends an act to have meaning) *is not a relevant issue.*[4]

While conversing with his wife at a cocktail party, a husband's eyes follow the very attractive hostess. The wife may observe the act of looking and may interpret the act as a threat or an insult. To understand the fight that follows, the fact that the wife observed and responded to the husband's act is far more important than the husband's intention.

Can assign either implicit or explicit significance. Since communication involves both behavior and experience of behavior, significance can be assigned to an act in an experiential way (as when a particular act contributes to the interpretation of a message) or in a behavioral way (as when a person responds to an act in a predictable, patterned way). Significance can be assigned whether or not the act was consciously experienced. Participants in a transaction need not be able to interpret or explain an act for that act to be meaningful.

An example of the implicit significance of a gesture was observed by a psychiatrist.[5] When one of his patients, a young schizophrenic girl, would begin talking about sexual fantasies in interview sessions, her mother would rub her finger under her nose. The daughter would change the subject. Subsequent analysis demonstrated that neither the mother nor the daughter was aware of the nose-rubbing act. Although the act was never consciously experienced or interpreted, both participants clearly assigned implicit significance to it.

On the other hand, one or both parties in a communication transaction can assign explicit significance to an act. We say that an act is assigned explicit significance when at least one of the participants consciously perceives and interprets the act.

Those acts that do not contribute to interpretation and are not implicitly assigned significance have no message value in the transaction (although they have message potential). Acts that have message potential but are not assigned significance are not viewed as gestures in a

4. Albert E. Scheflen, "The Significance of Posture in Communication Systems," *Psychiatry* 27 (1964): 318.

5. Flora Davis, *Inside Intuition: What We Know about Nonverbal Communicaton* (New York: McGraw-Hill, 1971, 1972, 1973), pp. 24–25.

particular transaction. To be a gesture an act must be assigned either implicit or explicit significance within a communication transaction.

At the denotative and/or metacommunicative levels. An act can contribute to the significance of a message at any level of meaning. Certain gestures, such as the hitchhiker's pointed thumb, contribute at the denotative level. Other acts are primarily interpretive metacommunication, as when the facial expression of a speaker tells us how to interpret his or her verbal behavior.

DISCRIMINATION AND REGROUPING IN PERCEPTION OF GESTURE

Although this definition of gesture allows any act to become communicative, relatively few of the virtually infinite number of acts that a human being can make are actually assigned explicit or implicit significance. Human beings are not sensitive to all the stimuli that are within range of their senses. In fact, the nervous system may filter out as much as 90 percent of all stimuli that impinge upon the senses. There is an element of choice in the selection of stimuli; the mind is able to honor certain stimuli and to reject others.

The process by which certain stimuli are selected from among all the stimuli that are picked up by the senses is called *discrimination*.[6] In reading this book, you may screen out smells from the kitchen, minor noises from outside, your own physical processes, and so on. Furthermore, as you read this page, you probably don't notice the page number or the minor imperfections on the page. You select and attend to the black letters rather than to the white background; you could, however, attend to either.

Regrouping is the process by which these selected stimuli are gathered together into meaningful patterns.[7] The regrouping process is partly innate; we have an inborn ability, for instance, to group together into different colors the vast quantities of light waves to which the eye is sensitive. The regrouping process is also partly learned; for example, we group together certain sets of sound waves into words that are understandable. As you read this book, you tend to see not isolated letters but patterns of letters that form recognizable words. If you've taken a speed-reading course, you probably don't see isolated words but rather large sequences of words that you have trained yourself to recognize as meaningful patterns.

Discrimination and regrouping are processes that are quite important in understanding the concept of gesture. Within a transaction, the behavior of each participant becomes part of the environmental stimuli that are picked up by the other person's senses. By the process of discrimination, we select and attend to certain behaviors from the continuous behavior of others. By the process of regrouping, we put these behaviors together into recognizable patterns, or *acts,* to which we can assign significance.

The processes of discrimination and regrouping also function in our experience of our own behavior. We discriminate certain of our own behaviors, to which we attend, and we regroup these behaviors into recognizable patterns, or acts. These are the acts of which we are aware, the gestures that we "mean" or "give," according to Goffman.[8] We are not aware of all of our behavior, however; nor do we necessarily experience our own behavior in the same way that others experience our behavior. Others may discriminate and regroup behavior into different acts. Therefore, others may assign significance to acts of which we are not even aware. Goffman has called this the behavior we "give off."

As a message system, gesture forms both an environment in which we grow and an instrument which we can manipulate. The gestural

---

6. Abne M. Eisenberg and Ralph R. Smith, Jr., *Nonverbal Communication* (Indianapolis and New York: Bobbs-Merrill Co., 1971), pp. 56–57.

7. Ibid., p. 57.

8. Erving Goffman, *The Presentation of Self in Everyday Life* (Garden City, N.Y.: Doubleday & Co., Anchor Books, 1959), p. 2.

environment is closely related to the culture in which we grow. Within the context of a specific culture, we learn how to behave, how and what to discriminate, how and into what patterns to regroup, and how to assign significance to acts. Gesture as instrument is also related to the culture. Just as every child in an English-speaking culture learns to speak more or less recognizable English, every child learns how to act, how to respond to acts, and how to interpret acts in ways that are more or less recognizable in that culture.

Behaviors that are discriminated and regrouped into recognizable patterns are, in general, the acts to which a person will assign significance. These are the acts that are gestures or elements of the gestural message system. In our discussion of culture, we speak of significance, not meaning. Significance is, in general, determined by a culture; meaning, however, is created on several levels by participants in a transaction. When we consider gesture as environment, we will be considering those acts to which members of a culture commonly assign specific kinds of significance when those acts occur within transactions. When we consider gesture as instrument, we will be considering the ways participants use or manipulate those acts to which at least one party has assigned significance in a particular transaction.

GESTURE AS ENVIRONMENT

The environmental significance assigned to gestures is learned as the child develops a self, which is a product of interpersonal communication. The young child imitates behavior observed in transactions with significant others. The child later imitates such behavior with understanding. In these early childhood transactions, the child learns the cultural rules by which we act and notice acts as they are manifest in the behavior of significant others in the child's environment.

In the role-playing stage, children begin to incorporate into their own behavior the societal aspects of these cultural rules. They perceive that cultural rules are related to particular situations and learn these new situation-specific rules. The ability to understand and to use particular gestures is greatly refined. It is quite likely that by the role-playing stage children are unconsciously and habitually manifesting only those behaviors that are included in the culture's limited repertoire of gestures. It is also quite likely that by this time both discrimination and regrouping patterns are relatively fixed. In short, by the end of the role-playing stage children have probably learned the "act" aspects of the gestural environment.

There is a simultaneous development in learning the significances assigned to acts. In the earliest stages of child development, the kinds of significances assigned to acts is very limited; many acts are learned with only implicit significance assigned. The implicit significance is that generated by the reinforcing behavior of significant others—behavior of which the child is probably never aware. At some point the child begins to assign explicit significance to acts, at first in a crude and simple way, probably in reference only to particular others encountered in transactions. Certainly by the stage of play, the child has recognized that certain acts are usually considered positive and others are usually considered negative. This positive and negative significance is still quite crude and may be limited to the recognition that Mommy is pleased or Mommy is not pleased.

In the role-playing stage, however, the child begins to recognize that acts are consistently assigned significance, not only in a particular relationship, but in all relationships that he has experienced. This development is accelerated with symbolic role taking. In symbolic role taking the child's understanding is no longer limited to those acts that he directly performs or experiences others performing. Notions of societal significance become refined as does, of course, the child's ability to recognize, interpret, and use gestures in particular transactions.

The development of a particular gesture, the smile, illustrates the sequential development of gesture. The human infant manifests the social smile at about five weeks.[9] The mothering one responds to this smile in a very positive way, with cooing or fondling. From this point on the infant smiles quite frequently. Somewhat later, the child learns both that his or her smile is likely to be responded to with holding and/or playing behaviors and that a smile by a significant other is likely to be followed by such behaviors. Already the child assigns significance to the act of smiling. At some point, the child realizes that a significant other's smile can be interpreted to mean something like "He/she is going to be nice to me." This significance can later be generalized and refined to "He/she is happy or glad."

The child comes to realize that in some settings—for example, in a church—others are not likely to respond positively to the smile and others are not likely to manifest the smile. That is, in the role-playing stage, the child begins to realize that smiling behavior is not consistent with some particular roles and situations.[10] This crude notion is refined over time until the child learns (perhaps without ever being aware of learning it) that there are times and places where we can smile and times and places where we can't. In this sense, the child is learning the

9. Davis, *Inside Intuition*, p. 54. See also Bunny Jacobson et al., "The Affective Component of Speech Communication Development," in R. R. Allen and Kenneth L. Brown, eds., *Developing Communication Competence in Children* (Skokie, Ill.: National Textbook Company, 1976).

10. Davis, *Inside Intuition*, p. 27.

SILENCE

Silences serve a very significant function within interpersonal transactions. People can use silence strategically to make ambiguous comments or to avoid taking responsibility for their part in conflicts ("I didn't even say anything!"). Silences can be interpreted as agreeing, disagreeing, comforting, hurting, pleasant, unpleasant, and so on. In any setting, the act of remaining silent can be assigned significance at any level. In some settings, silence will almost invariably be assigned significance —such as when someone greets you and you remain silent; when someone asks you a question and you remain silent; when someone finishes talking and the silence grows. The meaning ascribed to silence, or the interpretation of a person's silence, very much depends on the context in which it occurs and the behaviors that accompany it. Nevertheless, the act of being silent is an act to which significance can be assigned. Being silent can be a gesture.

societal significance of the smile, so that later in life, observing someone smiling at a funeral, he or she feels, at the very least, that smiling is inappropriate. All acts are assigned this kind of broad societal significance.

Gesture is a message system that is an essential part of the environment of every human being. Beginning in infancy, each person acquires his or her gestures from significant others in the environment. The particular environment, or culture, in which a person is born and/or grows is highly influential in determining the particular set of gestures that an individual will acquire.

In considering gesture as an environment, we limit our discussion to those acts that create and maintain social order. Hugh Dalziel Duncan describes social order in this way: "Social order is expressed through hierarchies which differentiate men into ranks, classes, and status groups, and, at the same time, resolve differentiation through appeals to principles of order which transcend those upon which differentiation is based. Hierarchy is expressed through the symbolization of superiority, inferiority, and equality, and of passage from one to another."[11] Sociologist Erving Goffman views social order as having, fundamentally, two characteristics: a set of underlying ground rules and a set of social routines which are patterned expressions of these rules.[12] We may call the first characteristic *social rules* and the second *social rituals*.

Social rules comprise the code about what is and what is not proper behavior.[13] Social rituals are specific sets of behaviors that serve fairly

11. Hugh Dalziel Duncan, *Symbols in Society* (New York: Oxford University Press, 1958), p. xii (see also pp. 51–53).
12. Erving Goffman, *Relations in Public: Microstudies of the Public Order* (New York: Basic Books, 1971; New York: Harper & Row, Harper Colophon Books, 1972), p. x.
13. Ibid., p. 5.

definite functions in maintaining social rules.[14] Taken together, social rules and social rituals are behaviors that make up what we learn as "good manners." Things we don't do ("don't belch, it's not polite") comprise social rules; things we should do ("say 'please' and you'll get the butter") comprise social rituals.

There are three broad categories of acts that make up our gestural environment. Each category serves a very specific, well-defined function in the development of the self and the maintenance of healthy interpersonal communication. The three categories of environmental gestures are manners and etiquette, gender signals, and locational signals. Each of these categories of acts serves to establish and maintain social order through the regulation of interpersonal communication transactions.

MANNERS AND ETIQUETTE

Etiquette is a class of gestures that involve ceremonial aspects of behavior in certain settings. The whole concept of etiquette is a reflection of a status and class hierarchy.[15] Etiquette provides prescriptions about how we should act. The closer a person's behavior conforms to these standards, the higher will be that person's perceived status in the social

14. Ibid., pp. 62–65.
15. Hugh Dalziel Duncan, *Communication and Social Order* (New York: Bedminster Press, 1962; London: Oxford University Press, 1968), pp. 331–34.

Whether you hold your fork in your right hand or left hand, use chopsticks, or eat with your fingers, your manners at the dinner table reflect your cultural background and your social standing.

hierarchy. A person must acquire these "social refinements" in order to advance in the hierarchy. Etiquette provides one standard by which we evaluate behavior and determine the status and class of the behaver; it provides a set of prescribed behaviors which indicate how "high class" people are different from "low class" people. In this way etiquette reflects and maintains social order in the hierarchial sense.

Addressing Behavior. One form of manners or etiquette which both reflects and maintains social hierarchy is addressing behavior.[16] Addressing behavior refers to the way we address people when they are present. It seems to include two very broad levels: informal address and formal address. First names are less formal than last names; nicknames are less formal than first names. Formal addresses include "Mr. Jones," "Ms. Jones," "Dr. Jones," "Professor Jones," "Father Jones," and "Reverend Doctor Jones."

Learning good manners includes learning to address others properly. How we address others is definitely related to their positions in the hierarchy; how others address us may reflect their view of our positions in the hierarchy. That children address adults in a formal way,

---

 EYE GESTURES

The eyes are quite possibly the most sensitive communicative organs in the body. Eyes communicate through eye contact, gazing patterns, and staring.

Eye contact is certainly one of the most meaningful acts a person can perform; it is also one of the most complex. People avoid prolonged eye contact in almost all settings. One reason for the avoidance of eye contact is that the eye is uniquely and simultaneously the sending organ and the receiving organ. Folklore tells us that the eyes are the windows of the soul. During eye contact we look into and are looked into in a very revealing way.

We are likely to initiate encounters with eye contact; eye contact is a certain sign that mutual perception of perception has

occurred and that the behavior of the other is somehow a response to our presence. It is very difficult not to respond to an address that begins with eye contact.[17] Panhandlers recognize this and use eye contact to initiate encounters in such a way that they may be refused but rarely ignored.

Schizophrenics try very hard to avoid eye contact with everyone. Conversely, psychiatrists working with withdrawn patients will wait several minutes, if necessary, to establish eye contact before attempting to initiate verbal dialogue. Even seriously disturbed persons find it difficult to deliberately avoid others with whom they have established eye contact. Eye contact forces a recognition that the other is human. Protestors frequently make use of this fact in conflicts with the police; after establishing

---

16. Ibid., pp. 288–301.
17. Erving Goffman, *Behavior in Public Places: Notes on the Social Organization of Gatherings* (New York: Macmillan Co., 1963), p. 95.

eye contact police are inclined to be less violent.[18]

Eye contact seems to be assigned significance primarily on the relational level.[19] Eye contact creates union. We can deliberately ignore another until eye contact is established; after that, ignoring the other is virtually impossible. Masters avoid eye contact with servants to maintain proper distancing between them. Waitresses become quite adept at avoiding eye contact with customers for whom they have no time.

We also manipulate the eyes in gazing or looking in interpersonal transactions. There are social rules that regulate gazing patterns in virtually every setting. These rules dictate where we can look, when we can look, for how long we can look, and at whom we can look. Goffman describes the gazing pattern of "civil inattention," by which we register recognition of another's presence with a brief look and indicate a lack of special interest in the other by pointedly looking away or by not looking too long.[20] People are very sensitive to being looked at; sometimes we "feel" we are being looked at long before we see the other looking. Any gazing act that violates the implicit social rules is likely to be assigned significance.

Staring is simply extended gazing. We use staring in fairly recognizable and predictable ways, most frequently to control the behavior of another, or to register disapproval of the behavior of another. Thus, we use staring as a monitor. However, the act of staring can also be assigned relational significance. Goffman describes the "nonperson" at whom we can stare quite easily.[21] We treat them as if they were not persons. Children, servants, cripples, and mentally ill persons are all assigned nonperson status in certain settings, and the act of staring defines the person-nonperson relationship. Of course, for the person-nonperson relationship to be maintained, the nonperson must keep his or her eyes lowered. If the nonperson looks up and establishes eye contact, it threatens the relationship.

---

while adults address children on a first name or nickname basis, reflects relative positions and roles in the hierarchy.

Greetings and Farewells. Greetings and farewells are forms of social rules and rituals that provide "brackets" around particular social activities by marking a change in degree of access. Greetings mark a transition to a condition of increased access; farewells mark a transition to a state of decreased access. Greetings and farewells serve to regulate social transactions so that events proceed in the routine, orderly, predictable way.[22]

Greeting rituals can also reflect and reinforce the hierarchical dimension of social order. One clear example of this is the salute in the

18. Davis, *Inside Intuition*, p. 67.

19. R. V. Exline, "Visual Interaction: The Glances of Power and Preference," in *Nonverbal Communication: Readings and Commentary*, ed. S. Weitz (New York: Oxford University Press, 1974), pp. 65–92.

20. Goffman, *Behavior in Public Places*, pp. 83–88.

21. Ibid., pp. 86–88.

22. Goffman, *Relations in Public*, pp. 73–94.

army by which a subordinate both greets and shows respect to a superior. The magic words *please* and *thank you* bracket potentially annoying or disruptive (but necessary) requests in such a way that the request is made and responded to with as little disturbance to other events as possible. A person politely holding a door open for another indicates the order in which they will go through the door and avoids the clumsy situation in which both or neither will attempt to go first. These forms of manners serve to regulate social transactions so that events proceed smoothly.

Display Acts. Social rules that regulate such acts as facial expressions, postures, vocal loudness, and so on, are called *display rules*.[23] Display rules determine the appropriateness or inappropriateness of an act.

Display rules maintain social order by limiting and regulating the kinds of acts that will normally occur in any social setting. All display acts are regulated by particular display rules. When an act is appropriate—that is, when it doesn't violate display rules—the social dimension of the significance assigned to it may be minimal. When an act violates a display rule, however, the significance assigned to that act is likely to include some reference to its inappropriateness.

Acts that violate social rules threaten the order that such rules maintain; therefore, the violation of a display rule is very likely to be noticed and interpreted. Even when the inappropriate act is excused or ignored (as it is in some situations), it will probably be noticed and assigned significance nevertheless. A person talking in an extremely loud voice on a train or in a closed elevator is usually given stares of disapproval by others around him. People who arrive at formal dinners in informal attire are coldly ignored or openly criticized and are made to feel conspicuous and uncomfortable. A nondrinker at a cocktail party becomes the subject of open comment and discussion because he or she is violating an implicit rule of the occasion. What is important in the last example is the *display* itself. A nondrinker is never noticed if he simply walks around with a glass of cola or ginger ale. The fact that he has a glass in his hands is sufficient conformity to the display rule to receive positive sanction from the group.

Ritual Apologies. Many social rituals serve the function of excusing, explaining, or clarifying the intent when a social rule is broken. Ritual apologies serve to restore social order when a social rule has been violated.[24] Significance may be assigned to a violation of a rule which is then followed by a ritual apology. Such significance will probably be

23. Paul Ekman and Wallace V. Friesen, "The Repertoire of Nonverbal Behavior: Categories, Origins, Usage, and Coding," *Semiotica* 1 (1969): 49–98 (esp. pp. 75–76).
24. Goffman, *Relations in Public*, pp. 108–18.

specifically related to a particular transaction. For example, consider a man who bumps into a woman on the subway, and immediately apologizes. She may assign significance to the act, but in a very personal way ("He's trying to get me to notice him") rather than in a broader way ("He's trying to start trouble").

GENDER SIGNALS

Manners are personal acts that serve the social function of establishing and maintaining social order. Another class of acts are assigned significance in relation to gender distinctions rather than to social order. *Gender signals* are those acts that are recognized by members of a particular culture as connoting either masculinity or femininity. Certain acts are performed in one way by males and in another way by females.

Many gender signals are subtle acts by which we distinguish the male from the female. For example, consider the posture of the standing American male when he is "acting masculine": thighs ten to fifteen degrees apart, pelvis rolled back, arms slightly away from the body. Compare this posture to that of the female "acting feminine": legs close together, pelvis tipped forward, arms close to the body. It seems clear that somehow males learn to stand in a "masculine" way, and females,

We display masculinity and femininity in the way we stand, sit, and walk. These gender signals are learned from our culture.

in a "feminine" way. The American male finds it both physically difficult and psychologically uncomfortable to assume the feminine posture described above.[25]

It seems likely that gender signals arose from the basic need to distinguish male from female. Mankind is a dimorphic (two-sexed) species in which purely physiological features provide no clear distinction between the sexes.[26] There are large-breasted men and small-breasted women, women with deep voices, men with high voices, etc. In order to clearly differentiate the sexes, humans develop what anthropologist Ray Birdwhistell calls tertiary sexual characteristics. These gender signals are organizations of gender display and gender recognition at the level of body position, body movement, and bodily expression. Tertiary sexual characteristics exist in every culture he studied. However, each culture has its own unique expression and definition of these characteristics. Members of every culture can recognize acts that are considered masculine and acts that are considered feminine for that culture.

These subtle tertiary sexual characteristics, together with such things as hair and dress codes and stereotyped sexual role behavior patterns, constitute the class of gender signals. We are not certain how and when they are learned, although there are indications that in the United States they are learned by age four in the South and somewhat later in the Northeast. In general, gender signals seem to provide a basis for distinguishing between members of each sex.

We know very little about the occurrence, function, and significance of gender signals in particular kinds of social transactions, although it is clear that they occur in many noncourting situations. Gender signals are culturally prescribed and learned by members of each culture; they are a part of the gestural environment into which we grow.

LOCATIONAL SIGNALS

A third class of acts that seem to have broad societal significance are those that distinguish between the many regional, ethnic, racial, and class subcultures in a complex society. Just as gender signals serve to distinguish between the sexes, these signals can serve to indicate both the present and the original subcultural location of a member of a culture.[27] We will call this class of acts *locational signals*.

The origin, importance, and use of these locational signals are not clear. Theorists seem to agree that such subcultural gesture variations

25. Davis, *Inside Intuition*, pp. 9–13.

26. Ray L. Birdwhistell, *Kinesics and Context: Essays on Body Motion Communication* (Philadelphia: University of Pennsylvania Press, 1970; New York: Ballantine Books, 1972), pp. 51–54.

27. Albert E. Scheflen, *How Behavior Means* (New York: Gordon and Breach, Science Publishers, 1973; Garden City, N.Y.: Doubleday & Co., Anchor Books, 1974), pp. 97–106.

BODY COVERINGS

We manipulate our body coverings—dress and hair—as gestures. Our use of both dress and hair seem slightly analogous to the role of plumage in animals—which is used primarily in courting, mating, and dominance rituals or displays. We use dress and hair in similar, although more sophisticated, ways.

Dress is very important in defining roles and in labeling social situations. Uniforms almost embody roles. Dress can serve the same symbolic functions as language. Dress can point: the waitress's uniform points out her role. Dress can polarize: there exist clearly different patterns of dress for both the "establishment" and the "counterculture." Dress can transform: the priest's Roman collar transforms him. The act of choosing a dress form is a gesture

which can serve quite important functions in communication.

Hair is related to dress but is somewhat different in that we have fewer day-to-day or situation-to-situation choices possible. Nevertheless, choosing hairstyles and lengths constitute acts to which great significance is assigned, especially today. Hair can influence with whom we interact and how we interact.

Both dress and hair are very important in defining roles and in establishing the context in which communication occurs. We can choose to dress formally or casually, stylishly or sloppily. Choosing body coverings becomes an act to which significance can be assigned. Thus we can use dress and hair instrumentally, as gestures.

---

embody or indicate the value structure of the subculture. Albert Scheflen notes that each subculture develops its own style, which he defines as "a particular way of enacting some customary sequence of behavior,"[28] which is associated, by convention, with particular ideas or meanings.[29] Therefore, if we can identify the locational style of a person and we are familiar with the associations of that particular subculture, we can predict in a fairly accurate way the ideas, meanings, and values of that person. Ideally, of course, if we learn to do this, the locational signals could be valuable communicative tools. What seems to happen, however, is that we learn to differentiate some subcultural styles, at least in a very crude way; but the associations they indicate to us reflect our own stereotypical picture of the ideas, values, and meanings of that subculture, rather than the actual associations of that subculture. For example, the complex, stylized greeting rituals of ghetto blacks are, to them, signs of solidarity, of the closeness that the ghetto can promote; to some white observers, however, black greeting rituals reflect stylized, habitual arrogance.

Social scientists currently know relatively little about the nature of locational signals. Regional dialects and accents are certainly the most

28. Ibid., p. 93.
29. Ibid., p. 105.

well-known kind of locational signal; style, according to Scheflen, is another. Indeed, for many people, even physical features (color of skin, slant of eyes, size of nose, etc.) are locational signals to which significance is assigned. Obviously there is a need to study locational signals in greater depth to determine what they are, how they function, how they arose, how they are assigned significance, what kind of significance they are assigned, and so on.

For purposes of clarity, we have separated manners, gender signals, and locational signals and discussed each separately. Obviously this separation is artificial; there is considerable overlap between these three classes of acts. There are, for example, masculine forms and feminine forms of the same social rituals. Indeed, it seems likely that a large part of the entire class of manners can be divided into those manners that a male learns and those that a female learns. Similarly, there are regional variations in manners, so that some social rituals and social rules are also locational signals. Furthermore, the significance assigned to gender signals and locational signals frequently invokes the concept of social order. Feminists, for example, argue that many gender signals connote the social inferiority of the female and maintain the sexual-social hierarchy. Similarly, the significance assigned to locational signals can invoke hierarchical or regulatory dimensions of social order. Manners, gender signals, and locational signals together form the environment of gesture into which we grow; they are important in shaping our identities as members of a particular rank on the hierarchy, a particular sex, and a particular subculture.

GESTURE AS INSTRUMENT

Our view of gesture as an instrument of communication is based on our previous analysis of primary message systems. The verbal and the nonverbal message systems are not independent systems of communication used for different purposes to communicate different things. They together play roles in conveying or creating meaning in transactions. We recognize, of course, that when the major concern in a particular transaction is the attitude or emotional state of one or both persons, as in courting or lovemaking, nonverbal message systems may assume predominance; when the purpose of the transaction is some sort of information transfer, the verbal message system may be more important. In most of our interpersonal communication transactions, however, all of the message systems together are important in conveying or creating meaning.

No behavior, of and by itself, has meaning, although any behavior can be meaningful insofar as it contributes to the creation of meaning

in transactions. Specific behaviors do not necessarily indicate certain emotions or attitudes, although in some cases they may. A smile may indicate happiness, but it may also indicate fear, resignation, or a variety of other attitudes and emotions. Determining the significance to assign to a behavior depends on both the context in which the behavior occurs and the existential position of the person assigning meaning. When emotional or attitudinal significance is assigned to a behavior, *a specific behavior contributes to the creation of meaning but does not of and by itself contain the meaning.*[30] Significance can be assigned at the denotative and/or the metacommunicative levels. Ambivalent or contradictory behavior is not necessarily dishonest or hidden; it may reflect genuine ambivalence, or it may be used strategically. Above all, the instrumental role of gesture in human communication is complex.

Even though it is not possible to specify the precise meaning of an act, people seem to assign significance to some acts in a fairly consistent way, reflecting that message systems are codified. We can, therefore, consider some acts and the significance that is usually assigned to them. We can also consider the level at which significance is frequently

30. Birdwhistell, *Kinesics and Context*, p. 56.

assigned to these acts. The assigned significance, however, always involves a choice by the assigner, so we can never specify *a priori* the significance or the meaning to be assigned to any act.

DENOTATIVE GESTURES

Many acts are usually assigned denotative significance. While the denotative level of meaning is the literal content, it should not be viewed as being identical with the verbal. Denotative does not imply that the literal content of the message can be clearly translated into linguistic symbols. Indeed some acts are frequently assigned a denotative significance that cannot be clearly translated into language but in some ways contains a very literal content.

In taking this position, it frequently becomes very difficult to divide behavior into the various levels of meaning. Consider the sarcastic message, for example. It is quite difficult to determine whether the vocal component of a sarcastic message is interpretive metacommunication about the verbal component or whether the literal content of a sarcastic message is the sarcasm itself. The meaning of sarcasm depends on other

Each of these common gestures is denotative. Such gestures convey meaning without reference to other message systems.

behaviors that provide interpretive cues and on the nature of the relationship in which the sarcasm occurs.

Emblems and Signs. There are certain kinds of acts to which denotative significance is usually assigned. Sign language includes a set of acts that serve linguistic functions and that seem clearly denotative.[31]

In any culture, there are certain acts that all members of the culture recognize and translate into linguistic symbols in a fairly consistent way. We assign a clear denotative significance to the hitchhiker's pointed thumb, for example. Such acts are known as *emblems*.[32] The emblems that we seem to employ most frequently are obscene. Other acts, such as rubbing the belly (to indicate hunger), inclining the head and cradling the cheek on the hand (to indicate sleep), and performing a hand-to-mouth pantomime (to indicate eating) are also emblems.

Emblems seem to serve as substitutes for words in some settings. Emblems can occur together with verbal expressions and still be assigned denotative significance. For example, the thumb and forefinger held an inch apart, together with the statement "missed it by that much," form the literal content, or the denotative level, of the message. In such a case, the gesture seems to function almost as a phrase in the sentence. So any act that serves as a substitute for words can be, and usually is, assigned denotative significance.

Other Denotative Acts. Denotative significance can be assigned to any kind of act even if the significance is not easily translated into language. Obviously, it is difficult to present examples in writing of acts that seem to be assigned denotative significance if this significance is not easily translatable into words. But let us try.

Jack and Joe are talking about Jill. Jack asks Joe, "What do you think of her figure?" Joe responds simply by smiling. The smile can be assigned a literal significance which is, nevertheless, difficult to transcribe. If considered together with interpretive metacommunicative behaviors such as the duration of the smile and accompanying behaviors such as a shoulder shrug or lifted eyebrows, the act of smiling can contribute to the meaning of this response. Jack will probably understand the meaning of Joe's reply very well. The smile contains the literal level of the response.

A father is lecturing his adolescent son about the importance of school. The son sits in a rather listless slouch. The father interrupts his monologue to command. "And sit up straight." To the father, the son's slouch contains some literal comment about the father's performance.

Peter walks into a room in which Jack, Joe, and Paul are engaged in conversation. Peter says hello to both Jack and Joe but pointedly ignores

31. B. H. Tervoort, "Could There Be a Human Sign Language?" *Semiotica* 9 (1973): 347–82.
32. Ekman and Friesen, "Repertoire of Nonverbal Behavior," pp. 63–68.

Paul. Peter's failure to greet Paul can be assigned literal significance. Peter may provide Paul with some interpretive metacommunicative behaviors, such as a wink, to aid Paul in interpreting the act. But, Paul assigns some literal significance to Peter's act of not saying hello.

INTERPRETIVE GESTURES

Most of us tend to think of gestures as interpretive dimensions of communication transactions. Our usual inclination is to discuss gestures as acts that somehow modify our words.[33] While this is certainly an important function of gestures, it is only one of the many ways in which we use gestures to create interpretive meaning. Gestures create interpretive meaning not only by modifying other message systems such as language and space, but also by defining roles, defining contexts for communication, and controlling the flow of communication within transactions. In each of these functions, gesture as a message system serves to help individuals punctuate their communication.

Defining Roles. As we present ourselves in given roles, we also indicate to others the kinds of roles we'd like them to play, since certain roles go together and certain roles don't. Therefore, as we use gesture to announce our own intended roles, we also influence the others' choice of roles. In this way, we use gesture to define the role relationships of the transaction. For example, the wearing of a uniform is an act that can contribute greatly to the assignment of a role. The choice of greeting, the warmth of the ritual, can influence the assignment of roles; a warm but formal greeting can help one person assign to the other the role of social friend. The act of displaying a law degree prominently in an office can contribute to the labeling of one person's role as lawyer and another's role as client. A person's act of standing in front of the class and introducing himself or herself is important in being assigned the role of teacher. Thus, we can use gesture to "announce" the roles we hope to play and to assign roles to others.

Defining Context of Transactions. We also use gesture to define the context of interpersonal transactions by labeling both the participants' role relationship and the social situation. An integral part of defining the role-relational context involves a mutual labeling of the social situation. We use gesture to "announce" a tentative label for the social situation.[34] People are particular in manipulating acts for this purpose when they anticipate that others may possibly assume a different context than

33. Virginia Satir, *Conjoint Family Therapy: A Guide to Theory and Technique,* rev. ed. (Palo Alto, Calif.: Science and Behavior Books, 1967), pp. 76–79.

34. See Jurgen Ruesch and Gregory Bateson, *Communication: The Social Matrix of Psychiatry* (New York: W. W. Norton & Co., 1968), pp. 28–29.

PROSODY

We perform recognizable acts by manipulating sound. There are two basic components to the spoken message. The first is the linguistic component; the second, known as prosody or paralanguage, is a gestural component of the spoken message.[35] Prosody consists of pitch, tone, loudness, rate of speaking, and related aspects of spoken messages. Prosody may be the first class of communicative acts that we learn. As infants we babble, and in babbling we utter every sound of every language, but in no particular pattern. By the age of six months, however, babbling becomes restricted to the language patterns of the environment, with pitch, rhythm and speed of the babbling reflecting the language of the parents or others in the environment.

Every spoken message has a prosodic component. We associate some of these patterns with arrogance, seriousness, sorrow, compassion, sarcasm, dominance and submission, love, and so on. Prosody can sometimes be the denotative meaning of a message. For example, you can say the word oh to express surprise, sorrow, sexual pleasure, etc. No matter what emotion is being expressed, the linguistic component remains constant; the literal content is conveyed via the prosodic component. In other cases, the prosodic component is used to generate meaning on the metacommunicative levels; it may be used primarily to define roles, modify other message systems, define contexts of communication, or punctuate transactions. »

the one desired. For example, a man invites a woman up to his apartment. There are several possible contexts in which this transaction could occur. Suppose she is his secretary, but he hopes to create a romantic context. He might keep the lights low, dress stylishly, have romantic music playing, and have wine prominently available. Each of these acts are gestures by which he attempts to influence her definition of the role relationship and her labeling of the social situation. Suppose she is his secretary, and he simply wants to get some overtime work done. He's likely to have the room well lit, dress casually, and have coffee brewing. Each of these acts represents a different attempt to define a role relationship and to label a social situation. We seem to manipulate gesture quite frequently, especially when we anticipate some ambiguity in how others may label role relationships and social situations.

Controlling Flow of Events—Monitors. We often use gestures to attempt to control the flow of events within a transaction. Our definition of gesture includes the possibility that significance can be assigned implicitly, or behaviorally, as well as explicitly. We've also argued that

35. See David Crystal, *Prosodic Systems and Intonation in English* (London: Cambridge University Press, 1969); and David Crystal, "Paralinguistics," in *The Body as a Medium of Expression,* ed. Jonathan Benthall and Ted Polhemus (New York: E. P. Dutton & Co., Dutton Paperbacks, 1975), pp. 162–74.

transactions are ordered and that certain kinds of gestures play an important role in maintaining the order.[36]

There are other, less obvious, acts to which implicit significance is frequently assigned, that regulate or maintain order in transactions. These acts have been named *monitors* by Albert Scheflen.[37] Monitors vary in the degree to which they are recognized and interpreted. The mother's nose-rubbing gesture described earlier is a monitor which served a definite communicative function in the particular transaction. Perhaps the most interesting thing about this particular monitor is that even before the psychiatrist had recognized the patterned response to the act, he had begun himself to use it as a monitor to control the direction of the daughter's conversation. The monitor was assigned implicit significance by all participants, and each, on this implicit level, learned to employ it.

Some monitors are more obvious. Goffman discusses the role of staring in maintaining order.[38] We stare at people who are not behaving properly, in an attempt to modify their behavior. Parents monitor their children's behavior by using certain facial expressions or movements of the arms and hands to indicate to the children that they are out of order. It is not unusual for people to use a running stream of facial expressions to monitor their conversations. In general, such monitors can be viewed (on either the implicit or the explicit level) as comments about ongoing behavior or as commands to modify inappropriate behavior. In this way, monitors represent gestural attempts to control the flow of events within a transaction.

We can use gesture to control transactions in many other ways. For example, a person who is about to speak frequently announces that intent by leaning forward and extending the hands and perhaps by audibly drawing a breath. These gestures make the person more obvious or more central. Such behaviors can be viewed as attempts to get the floor without disrupting the verbal flow of other speakers. A person who is finished speaking and is inviting response frequently sits back and makes some kind of opening gesture with the hand. These behaviors indicate what the person intends or expects another person to do next in the transaction. They are attempts to control the flow of events within a transaction.[39]

Of course, any of these behaviors can be assigned significance on

36. Albert E. Scheflen, *Body Language and Social Order: Communication as Behavioral Control,* with Alice Scheflen (Englewood Cliffs, N.J.: Prentice-Hall, 1972), pp. 61–74; and Birdwhistell, "Body Motion."

37. Scheflen, *Body Language and Social Order,* pp. 104–21.

38. Goffman, *Behavior in Public Places,* pp. 87–88.

39. Scheflen, *Body Language and Social Order,* pp. 67–69; and Starkley Duncan, Jr., "Some Signals and Rules for Taking Speaking Turns in Conversations," *Journal of Personality and Social Psychology* 23 (1972): 283–92, reprinted in Weitz, *Nonverbal Communication,* pp. 298–311.

any level and can be used to create meaning. In general, however, they seem to serve the communicative function, not of creating meaning, but of controlling or ordering transactions. At times, a given act may serve both functions. In any case, the work of Scheflen and Birdwhistell indicates that these kinds of acts occur very frequently in transactions and are important because they are responded to in relatively predictable (in some cases almost absolutely predictable) ways.[40] Virtually all acts to which implicit significance is assigned serve to control the flow of events within a transaction.

Modifying Other Message Systems. In the American culture, verbal behavior is seen as the core of any message that involves verbal behavior at all. When verbal behavior is viewed as having literal or denotative significance, accompanying gestural messages are usually seen as having interpretive or relational metacommunicative significance.[41] Facial expression, vocal components (such as the rate of speech, tone, loudness, etc.), gesticulations (such as the waving of arms), a person's demeanor (as in "he seemed very serious")—all are examples of such interpretive acts. Of course, these acts can be assigned significance at any level, depending on the context in which they occur; but usually they seem to be assigned interpretive metacommunicative significance when they accompany speech.

There exists a significant class of gestures that provide clues to the interpretation of the verbal denotative component of a message. These have been investigated by Scheflen, Birdwhistell, and Adam Kendon.[42] They consist, in general, of behaviors of any part of the body that concur in very recognizable ways with verbal behaviors. Kendon, for example, performed a detailed analysis of the behavior of a man speaking. Kendon found that each level of speech, from phrase to sentence to subparagraph to paragraph, was accompanied by a pattern of body motion so that every change, say from sentence to sentence, was marked by a change in body motion. Each subparagraph was marked in this way, as was each paragraph. Kendon's analysis agrees with analyses by Birdwhistell and Scheflen.

Such behaviors seem to punctuate the communication process. Some gestures provide indications about which sequences form different grammatical units and which sequences of words together form a unit for interpretation. People act out the grammatical structure of their

40. Scheflen, *Body Language and Social Order;* and Birdwhistell, "Body Motion."
41. The nonverbal and verbal dimensions of metacommunication are discussed by Satir, *Conjoint Family Therapy,* pp. 76–79.
42. Scheflen, *Body Language and Social Order;* Birdwhistell, *Kinesics and Context;* and Adam Kendon, "The Role of Visible Behaviour in the Organization of Social Interaction," in *Social Communication and Movement: Studies of Interaction and Expression in Man and Chimpanzee,* ed. Mario von Cranach and Ian Vine (London: Academic Press, 1973). See also A. T. Dittmann and L. G. Llewellyn, "Body Movements and Speech Rhythm in Social Conversation," *Journal of Personality and Social Psychology* 11 (1969): 98–106.

words. People even have acts that serve as periods, question marks, and quotation marks. Americans are likely to end statements with a lowering of the head, hands, or eyelids; they are likely to end questions with a lifting of the head, chin, or eyebrows or with a widening of the eyes. People also use certain vocal acts, such as pausing or raising or lowering the voice at the end of a sentence, in the same way and for the same purpose. People also provide behavioral "punctuation" that helps us interpret their words. Some behaviors help us decide, for instance, whether the words *hot dog* should be considered an overheated canine (with the word *hot* separated from *dog* by some subtle behavior) or as something to eat (with the entire phrase behaviorally marked off).[43] If you think punctuation doesn't play an important role in the interpretation of linguistic messages, thinkhowmucheasieritwouldhavebeentoun derstandorinterprettherestofthissentenceifithadbeenproperlypunctuated. In short, punctuation behaviors help us separate communication into meaningful units.

RELATIONAL GESTURES

Any act may also be assigned relational metacommunicative significance; it may be viewed as a comment about the relationship between the participants. Some relational acts serve to maintain the bonds of the participants. Others serve tentatively to suggest subtle shifts in the quality of the relationship during a transaction. Other acts may serve to define the kind of relationship possible for the participants at a particular time. Still other gestures may be reminders of the nature of the ongoing relationship of which a particular encounter is a part.

Courtship behaviors, for example, can be viewed as relational gestures.[44] Preening behaviors, such as combing the hair and straightening the tie, may be tentative invitations to courtship. Preening the other, such as a woman fussing with her husband's tie, may be bond-servicing behaviors—behaviors that remind the other (and any observers) of their special bond.

Courtship behaviors may be accompanied by behavioral qualifiers that indicate that the gestures are not to be taken literally; these are known as quasi-courtship behaviors.[45] Such gestures serve to build rapport or comfortable relationships in many noncourting settings. Although they need not be, these kinds of behaviors frequently are assigned relational metacommunicative significance of servicing the bond between the participants.

43. A similar analysis can be found in Ray Birdwhistell, "Body Motion."
44. Scheflen, *Body Language and Social Order.*
45. Albert E. Scheflen, "Quasi-Courting Behavior in Psychotherapy," *Psychiatry* 28 (August 1965): 245–57.

Gestures can tentatively define a relationship as symmetrical or complementary. Consider the posture of a father when he is going to discipline his fifteen-year-old son who is coming in late. Head high, shoulders back, chest thrown out, spine straightened are gestures typical of a parent emphasizing authority. For this disciplining transaction to proceed with a minimum of conflict, the son must somehow indicate that he accepts his one down position, usually by lowering the shoulders, head, and eyes. If the son stands straight with chin up and looks his father in the eyes, the father is likely to interpret the behavior as defiance. All these behaviors may be viewed as metacommunicative comments about the father-son role relationship.

Gestures can tentatively define the kind of relationship possible in a particular transaction. Arms and legs can serve as barriers which tentatively define the degree to which a person will be accessible in a particular situation. Frequently (but not necessarily), an open posture or position may be assigned relational metacommunicative significance indicating the degree to which a person is accessible.

Open and closed postures suggest how accessible or comfortable a person may be in a given situation.

Behavior can tentatively redefine the quality of a relationship during a transaction. Shifting from an inaccessible to a more accessible posture can be viewed as a tentative redefinition of the quality of the relationship—as an invitation to a more intimate relationship. In general, any shift from one behavior pattern to another can be assigned relational metacommunicative significance indicating a redefinition of the relationship. Psychiatrists, doctors, and businessmen frequently close the chit-chat portion of a session by leaning forward and assuming a businesslike face. Such gestures redefine the role relationship from a social relationship to a business relationship.

Many acts function as reminders of the ongoing relationship. Any in-joke can be assigned this kind of relational significance. Some bond-servicing behaviors may also be assigned relational significance; a wife may groom her husband at a cocktail party if he is paying too much attention to another woman. Consider the case of a priest interviewing a female parishioner who kept manifesting courtship behaviors toward him. Several times during the interview the priest reached up and stroked his Roman collar. This gesture can be viewed as a relational metacomment reminding both the priest and the parishioner of his role requirements and vows and of the role relationship appropriate within that transaction.

Any act may be assigned relational metacommunicative significance. And, of course, any act that contributes to the clarification of the ongoing relationship or the role relationship in a particular transaction contributes to creating and conveying meaning in transactions.

SUMMARY

Gesture is a primary message system utilized in all interpersonal communication transactions and is highly integrated witn language, space, and sexuality. Gesture is any act to which one or both participants in an interpersonal transaction consciously or unconsciously assign denotative or metacommunicative significance.

Gestures form an important environment for each person. The gestural environment includes three categories of gestures that seem to be particularly significant regardless of the culture. These are manners and ettiquette, gender signals, and locational signals. The gestural environment is particularly important in developing and maintaining the self through communication transactions.

People also use gestures as instruments. We manipulate our gestures to communicate specific meanings to others in transactions. Gestures may have denotative, interpretive, and relational significance. Gestures convey literal content, tell the other person how to interpret the entire message, and signify the relationship that exists between the people. Gestures thus define the nature and context of transactions and monitor the flow of interaction within transactions.

QUESTIONS FOR REVIEW

1. What is the definition of a gesture?
2. What are the three divisions of gesture as environment? Give an example of each type of gesture.
3. What is the importance of manners in interpersonal transactions?
4. How can a gesture be denotative?
5. In what ways do gestures create meaning at the interpretive level?
6. How do gestures modify relationships? Give an example.

EXPLORATIONS

1. Take a personal inventory of yourself for your journal. Which parts of you are messages? Does your clothing serve as a signaling system to others to identify you as a student, teacher, businessperson, police officer, etc.? Perhaps your hair makes a statement about who you are. Do you wear jewelry? What does it say about you? What other aspects of your body or accessories may communicate something about you to others?
2. Most of us don't think about locational signals until we find ourselves in groups in which we are a minority. Yet every member of a majority is a minority in another subculture. Try to identify specific kinds of locational signals that you have that would identify you as a member of specific subgroups within our culture. Consider, for example, signals indicating sexual preference. What signals would indicate homosexual preference? What signals would indicate heterosexual preference? (Suppose a "straight" went into a gay bar. What would identify the "straight" from the "gays"?) What signals indicate solidarity or affinity with a black subculture? with an Italian subculture? with a Polish subculture? with a Catholic subculture? with a Jewish subculture? with a Protestant subculture? with the feminist movement? with any other subculture with which you are familiar?
3. In chapter 6 we looked at killer statements. A good companion exercise is to observe your colleagues carefully for a two-hour period. Make a list of the killer gestures that either dismiss another person or serve as a put-down. In doing this simple exercise, you will begin

to become conscious of how much of our gestural behavior can serve as a negative influence in our interpersonal communication. What do you think each of these gestures really mean? Do you think the person making the gesture intended it to be a dismissal reaction, or do you think the person was unconscious of the gesture?

4. Select a companion with whom you will carry on a conversation. Converse about any topic; however, for a period of five to ten minutes you will speak only by repeating selected words or phrases uttered by your companion. The meanings of your part of the conversation should be conveyed solely by the prosody or vocal inflection you give to the words. For example, if your companion should say something like, ". . . and so I think the interest rates on long-term bonds will probably rise in the next quarter," you might respond by saying, "Long term bonds?" Notice that the question is indicated by the vocal inflection. You could also say, "Long term bonds," indicating concern or disgust with your voice. After a few tries, you may find that you are able to carry on an entire conversation and never do more than repeat a couple of words or phrases uttered by your companion!

5. The next time you get on a train or bus, select one person and try to establish eye contact with that person. Once you have established eye contact, experiment with varying the length of time you maintain contact. What kinds of things are communicated by the various lengths of time you maintain eye contact? You will probably discover that a majority of people will not permit themselves to engage you in eye contact more than twice. What can account for this refusal to interact with the eyes?

FOR FURTHER READING

Benthall, Jonathan, and Polhemus, Ted, eds. *The Body as a Medium of Expression.* New York: E. P. Dutton & Co., Dutton Paperbacks, 1975.

This book is a collection of essays about the role of the body in communication. The essays include Birdwhistell's analysis of the way the body has been studied historically, Bates's examination of the communicative dimensions of the hand, and Willis's study of gestural styles in a motorcycle gang. The essays are, for the most part, interesting and insightful.

Mehrabian, Albert. *Silent Messages.* Belmont, Calif.: Wadsworth Publishing Co., 1971.

In this very popular book, Mehrabian presents the typical psychological approach to the study of gesture. He believes that gestures convey three dimensions of feelings and attitudes: like/dislike, status, and responsiveness. He analyzes many types of gestural messages and summarizes much research in the area.

Scheflen, Albert E. *Body Language and Social Order: Communication as Behavioral Control.* With Alice Scheflen. Englewood Cliffs, N.J.: Prentice-Hall, 1972.

Scheflen, Albert E. *How Behavior Means.* New York: Gordon and Breach, Science Publishers, 1973; Garden City, N.Y.: Doubleday & Co., Anchor Books, 1974.

Weitz, Shirley, ed. *Nonverbal Communication: Readings and Commentary.* New York: Oxford University Press, 1974.

This popular book focuses on the social functions of gesture. The concepts are presented in a fairly simple way, and most are illustrated with photographs. Scheflen presents examples of some of the ways that gesture is used to define relationships, to regulate transactions, and to create and maintain social order.

In this fascinating book, Scheflen explores the ways in which we assign meaning to behavior (rather than the assigned meanings themselves). The five sections of the book explore: how gestures identify a referent; how gestures structure communication contexts; gestures that are not necessarily a consequence of the ongoing sequence; gestures that are metacommunicative instructions; and how gestures can be used to alter or manipulate a situation.

This collection of classical studies of nonverbal communication is one of the best on the market. The studies range from excellent and theoretically sound (e.g., Scheflen's paper, "Quasi-Courtship Behavior in Psychotherapy") to some much less sophisticated studies. The areas covered are facial expression, paralanguage, body movement, spatial behavior, and multichannel messages.

Chapter 8

Space as a
Primary Message
System

When we think of the factors involved in interpersonal communication, we are most likely to limit our attention initially to language, verbal gestures, and certain physical gestures. Only very recently has attention been drawn to the concept of space and the role that space plays in interpersonal communication. When we look at the ecology of interpersonal transactions, we discover that space may be one of the most important factors in human communication, in many cases rivaling the influence of language itself. The way that we exist in space and the ways that we utilize space to communicate with others form a major message system used by all persons in all cultures. As a primary message system, space has both environmental and instrumental dimensions.

SPACE AS ENVIRONMENT

Space, as an environment in which we exist, greatly influences us. All organisms occupy space. Every living organism appears to be sensitive to the space in which it exists and extends itself beyond its physical or bodily boundaries to occupy some dimension of the surrounding space. The space that becomes identified with a particular organism may be defined as territory. In other words, it appears that every living organism extends itself by occupying space which becomes the personal territory of the organism.[1] In humans, the territory is culturally defined. A person's perception of the space or territory that the person occupies is more a function of social conditioning than of individual or genetic biological factors.

Most people are aware of some cultural differences in perception of space. Some of us have experienced communication with persons from

1. Robert Ardrey, *The Territorial Imperative* (New York: Atheneum, 1966).

Latin American or Middle Eastern cultures where individuals maintain very close distances for even the most ordinary and impersonal conversations.[2] An American, conversing with a Latin American, a Hungarian, or an Arab, may back up to the wall in an unconscious attempt to maintain a greater social distance than his or her conversational partner is willing to allow. In fact, many Americans find it difficult to speak with South Americans because of the intimate distances that South Americans seem to need to converse with others. Americans are also amazed at the ability of the Japanese to see boundaries within space unrecognizable to Americans.[3] In one sense the Japanese have a unique ability for being in rooms with other persons and simply not hearing that which is socially unacceptable to hear. The traditional Japanese house has rooms that are created by the placement of silk screens, which to our way of thinking artificially partition off spaces. By rearranging the screens, a room can be divided into two rooms; it is apparently possible for a Japanese family or many Japanese families to engage in the most personal activities without being "overhead" by persons in the adjoining "room" on the other side of the silk screen.

SPACE AS INSTRUMENT

Not only do we live within space but we also manipulate space to create messages in our interaction with others. We use space as an instrument of communication. In certain situations the distances that people maintain between them become a more significant message system than language. A common illustration of the use of space is that of a young couple in an automobile. At the beginning of the evening, the boy is driving and the girl is sitting next to the right-hand door. As the evening goes on, the girl moves toward the center of the car, and by the time the evening is almost over, someone in a passing automobile may see two people sitting in the driver's seat! In this very typical situation, space not only acts as the environment in which two people are communicating; space also becomes significant in itself as a message or message system in the interaction between them.

There is a need for extensive research in the area of space as a message system and the effects of space as a communication environment in human development (especially in childhood and early adolescence). There is evidence that spatial relationships are perceived by infants and take on communicative significance very early in life. Yet information on the ways children manipulate space is scarce or simply unavailable.

2. Edward T. Hall, *The Hidden Dimension* (Garden City, N.Y.: Doubleday & Co., Anchor Books, 1969), pp. 159–60; and Edward T. Hall, *The Silent Language* (Garden City, N.Y.: Doubleday & Co., 1959; Greenwich, Conn.: Fawcett Publications, 1959), p. 164.
3. Hall, *Hidden Dimension*, pp. 149–54.

We are sensitive to the space around us. Often we prefer to leave some space between ourselves and other people.

Since the ways in which adults manipulate space to generate meaning have been given more careful attention, our discussion of space will focus on adult-to-adult interpersonal communication patterns.

THE ENVIRONMENT-INSTRUMENT RATIO OF SPACE

In an ecological model of interpersonal communication, the human organism exists in various kinds of environments and manipulates those environments to create meaning in interpersonal transactions. While we have examined both language and gesture as communication environments and communication instruments, it is important in an ecological approach to stress the interrelationship between environment and instrument in the communication process. This interrelationship is particularly strong when we analyze the role of space in interpersonal communication. Space rarely functions solely as environment or as instrument. In most transactions, there is a ratio between space as an environment and space as an instrument of communication. In most interpersonal communication, space affects language, sexuality and gestures as message systems and at the same time acts as a primary message system in itself. Our analysis must take this dual aspect of space into account.

THE DIMENSIONS OF SPACE

Probably the main reason we seek to understand the factors in interpersonal communication is to achieve greater control over communication situations. When we analyze the effects of space as an environment and an instrument of human communication, we are concerned primarily with the question, How can I manipulate space as a message or an environment in order to achieve the control that I seek in this situation? By controlling the elements of a communication situation, how can I most likely generate specific meanings within that situation?

In analyzing the dimensions of space, we can give various suggestions for utilizing the element of space in ways that are most likely to achieve greater control within specific situations. The phrase "most likely to achieve greater control" is used with great care. In manipulating human behavior one can never be absolutely certain of the outcome. Human beings appear to have an ability to transcend any particular situation and spontaneously generate creativity within that situation. We may discuss only the most probable patterns of behavior that can be generated through the instrumental and environmental uses of the dimensions of space in interpersonal communication transactions.

In managing space in interpersonal communication, we should look for certain aspects of space that influence the control of the interaction or that influence the process of communication. The most important dimensions of space are territoriality, density, distance, angle of inclination (relative height), and angle of interaction.

TERRITORIALITY

Characteristics of territoriality. Territoriality is one of the most influential factors in interpersonal communication transactions. *Territoriality* may be defined as the tendency of organisms to own space.[4] It is the biological propensity to possess space. The first characteristic of territoriality is that it acts as an extension of personal space. Each

4. See Ardrey, *Territorial Imperative*, p. 3; Hall, *Hidden Dimension*, pp. 7–10; and Hall, *Silent Language*, p. 51.

organism has a sense of its own selfhood that is identified with a particular space. There is a certain distance around the body of every organism that is perceived as belonging to the organism. This phenomenon becomes generalized in human beings. We not only carry around with us portable space that extends beyond our bodies and which we consider to be part of ourselves; we also lay claim to other areas or parts of space and transform them into our own territory.

Marshall McLuhan has suggested that the automobile is literally an extension of the human body.[5] We tend to make our automobiles part of our personal territories. The automobile becomes an extension of the physical body, the personality, and the perceived self. When an individual is in his or her own automobile, the automobile is his or her territory. Any other person entering that automobile is entering the personal territory of the owner (who is usually the driver). All of the rights and prerogatives of territoriality belong to the owner.

A person's house or apartment, an office, a store, a particular parking place, a desk—all become areas of personal territory to which we lay claim. We become irritated when we find the territory invaded by others. A very common example of this phenomenon occurs in the

5. Marshall McLuhan, *Understanding Media: The Extensions of Man*, 2d ed. (New York: New American Library, Signet Books, 1964), pp. 194–201.

We use markers to indicate that a territory is already occupied and to prevent its invasion.

classroom. After the first week of class, almost every student has staked out his or her own territory in the classroom by claiming a specific chair as his or her own. If someone else takes that chair after a few weeks time, the student may feel irritation, aggravation, a sense of loss. In reality, a personal territory has been invaded by another person.

A second characteristic of territoriality is that it is always well-defined, but it is defined by the culture. The territory that a person can occupy varies from culture to culture. What you and I see as being our territories in this culture might be considered to be improper use of territoriality in another culture.

Third, territoriality always provides a biological advantage to the possessor. If a territory is yours and a stronger person invades it, you have a biological advantage in defending your own territory. Fascinating observations have been made throughout the animal kindom to confirm the principal of biological superiority of the owner of the territory. A stronger stag invading the territory of a weaker stag for a challenge will be at a biological disadvantage. The younger or smaller stag in his own territory will actually emerge as stronger than the larger stag. Conrad Lorenz's studies of fish showed that when a stronger fish (one proven to be stronger in other battles) invaded the territory of a weaker fish, the weaker fish had a biological advantage. The advantage goes to the possessor of the territory.[6] This is very important when we look at the effect of territoriality on interpersonal communication.

Finally, territory is related to position in the social hierarchy. People who are higher in the social hierarchy tend to have larger territories. The palaces of kings, for example, are tremendously large enclosures, as opposed to the cramped housing in the ghettos of every major city in the world. The amount of territory you can occupy, as sanctioned by the culture, is related to where you are in the social hierarchy.

Use of Territoriality. In analyzing interpersonal transactions it is important to keep in mind in whose territory the interaction is taking place. Suppose, for example, that a principal calls a teacher into his or her office. The interaction is taking place in the principal's territory. Since the teacher is not on his or her own ground but on the principal's ground, the advantage associated with territory will go to the principal. The teacher is the "invader" and will be at an automatic disadvantage. On the other hand, if the principal enters the teacher's classroom, the situation tends to be reversed. The teacher will feel a claim to the classroom as his or her own territory and will perceive the principal as the invader. This will give to the teacher both a psychological and biological advantage in their interaction.

6. Conrad Lorenz, *On Aggression* (New York Harcourt, Brace and World, 1966); and Ardrey, *Territorial Imperative*, p. 3.

In neutral territories, people can exchange information or transact business without either person feeling threatened.

The role of territoriality is an extremely critical factor whenever interpersonal interaction is occurring between a superior and a subordinate, a manager and an employee, a doctor and a patient, a therapist and a client, a counselor and a counselee. The interaction takes on specific characteristics that give the advantage to the person who possesses the territory. If you are in a superior position and you wish to counteract the effects of territoriality in a given interaction, then you should move the interaction to neutral territory. For example, if you are a manager of an office and you wish to have a free exchange of ideas with an employee, perhaps the best place to engage in this discussion might be a hallway, a cafeteria, or a lounge, sometimes even a restroom. All of these spaces are considered to be public areas belonging neither to the management nor to the employees. They are neutral territories.

This effect of territory has great implications in the collective bargaining process. A good labor negotiating team will never hold the talks in the offices of the management; nor will a good management team allow the talks to be held in the offices of a labor union. In most cases collective bargaining discussions occur in some neutral setting, such as a hotel, a court house, or other third party location.

These examples illustrate one effect of territoriality as an environment. Occasionally territoriality has some specific effects as a message. For example, if an employee approached a manager in a neutral territory, such as a lounge, to discuss a raise in pay, the manager's response might be, "Why don't you come to my office where we can discuss this?" Now there might be other reasons for the manager moving the discussion to his office. But one reason (whether conscious or not) could very well be that the manager wishes to have the question of raises discussed in his or her own territory (where he or she feels in command of the situation) rather than in neutral territory (where he or she feels a certain lack of control).

When the manager moves the location of the discussion from the hallway to his or her office, the manager is unwittingly using space as an instrument to indicate uncertainty and desire for greater control in responding to the employee's request. At other times, the employee might find the manager very open and willing to discuss many other "private" issues on neutral territory. Thus, the manipulation of territory can take on meaning in itself.

DENSITY

A second dimension of space as a primary message system is density. *Density* may be defined as the person to space ratio. The greater the number of people in a given area, the higher the density within that area. The fewer the number of people in the area, the lower the density. To our knowledge, the effects of density on human transactions have not been systematically or widely investigated. We can, however, make some tentative generalizations.

The first generalization about the effects of density on interpersonal communication is that the reaction to density depends upon the purpose of the communication situation. A number of observers have described the phenomenon of the subway.[7] Whether in England, the Soviet Union, Japan, or the United States, a high density of persons on a subway tends to lead to withdrawal behavior in the riders. As a subway car becomes more and more crowded, people withdraw into themselves; they have minimum interaction with one another, both at the verbal and nonverbal levels. Not only does conversation subside as density increases, but the amount of eye contact also diminishes. This withdrawal has been discussed as a defense mechanism that people employ to protect the sense of self or self-identity as their personal territories become increasingly diminished.

Yet exactly the opposite kinds of behavior are generated in other public situations that have different purposes. It is easier to perform in

7. Robert Sommer, *Personal Space: The Behavioral Basis of Design* (Englewood Cliffs, N.J.: Prentice-Hall, 1969), pp. 28–29, 39–57. See also Erving Goffman, *Relations in Public: Microstudies of the Public Order* (New York: Basic Books, 1971; New York: Harper & Row, Harper Colophon Books, 1972), pp. 28–61; and Hall, *Hidden Dimension*, pp. 118, 146.

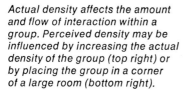

Actual density affects the amount and flow of interaction within a group. Perceived density may be influenced by increasing the actual density of the group (top right) or by placing the group in a corner of a large room (bottom right).

a theater that has standing room only than to perform in a theater that has a sprinkling of filled seats in the audience. It is easier to get great reactions from people in packed auditoriums at political rallies than from people in an auditorium that is only half full.

The principle at work in each of these situations appears to be the opposite of what is at work in the subway situation. Rather than causing the people placed in close proximity to withdraw from one another, the crowding tends to increase the activity of the people. It is easier to present a lecture, a play, or a political speech to an audience of people who do not have large areas of space around them. Effective teachers, performers, and politicians have utilized this principle of control for ages.

Let us examine for a moment a particular instance in which density can be manipulated to generate specific kinds of communication behavior. It is easier to control a classroom for lecture purposes or to generate a discussion when students are placed close together. In general, the closer people are seated to one another, the more group interaction will be generated. It is important, therefore, for a teacher to take this principle into account in arranging a classroom. Suppose, for example, that a teacher has only ten students and the class is assigned to a room that will hold sixty students. In order to increase the interaction among the students and between the students and the instructor, the teacher would be well-advised to arrange the class in a corner of the room so that the vast bulk of the space would be less perceptible to the students.

DISTANCE

The American anthropologist E. T. Hall has provided one of the most extensive analyses of space as a message system.[8] Hall was concerned with discovering how various cultures use space to communicate and

8. Hall, *Hidden Dimension.*

Intimate distance

Personal distance

Social distance

Public distance

how differences in the utilization of space in human communication affects intercultural or cross-cultural communication. In identifying the role of space in cross-cultural communication, Hall postulated four kinds of space.[9] He categorized these according to the average distances that people maintain from each other in their interpersonal interactions and the kinds of activities in which people engage at these various distances. The four kinds of spatial interaction that Hall identified are called intimate, personal, social, and public.

Intimate Distance. Intimate distance is the closest distance that people allow between themselves and others in interpersonal interaction. For most Americans this distance is six to twelve inches. Most individuals perceive this small spatial distance around the body as coexistent with the body itself. Some people even perceive this space as an integral part of the body, depending upon the area of the body involved. Thus, the activities that we allow to occur between ourselves and others at this distance tend to be restricted to activities that most of us would consider intimate.

Most Americans will readily tolerate invasion of the intimate space by their own children, especially infants. We hold infants close to us and allow them to sleep beside us at close distances, maintaining intimate relationships even when they are not in actual physical contact with our bodies. Most of us continue to allow children to maintain very close distances in their interactions with us up to various ages. Generally the maintenance of intimate distinces between parent and child begins to diminish at about the time the child enters elementary school.

Most adult interactions at an intimate distance are sexual in nature. In our culture we associate the intimate distance with sexual interaction. Whispering in the ear, maintaining close facial proximities, or maintaining close body relationships are considered to be intimate interactions.

Personal Distance. Personal distance is identified as a distance of approximately twelve to eighteen inches from the physical surface of the body. The interactions that occur at this distance are viewed in the American culture as being primarily personal in nature. Such interactions are less intimate than those that occur at intimate distances but are still relatively personal.

We utilize personal distance when we engage in personal conversations with friends, when we exchange personal information with colleagues (information that we do not want others to overhear), and when we engage in familial interaction.

Social Distance. Social distance is a space of about eighteen to thirty inches from the body. Social distance is the distance that we most com-

9. Ibid., pp. 113–29.

monly utilize in what might be called social situations. Cocktail parties, job interviews, conversations at desks or water coolers in offices, conversations in hallways, on streets, in supermarkets, post offices, banks, libraries and other institutions—all tend to occur at social distances. At social distances people tend to view their interactions as neither intimate nor personal but as a part of larger patterns of social and cultural interaction. In these situations we are more likely to utilize and invoke socially proper rituals of interaction, such as shaking hands, standing or opening the door for others, and other social courtesies.

Public Distance. Public distance involves distances that exceed thirty to thirty-six inches. In American culture, this is the distance we maintain for public interaction with one another. Communicating person to person in meetings and convention halls, yelling at each other across the street, discussing the weather across the backyard fence, speaking to neighbors while hanging up the clothes or airing bedspreads are kinds of activities that utilize public distance. At public distances we do not perceive the space utilized as an integral part of our bodies or of our self-systems. The space is public territory. Since it belongs to neither occupant, we feel able to move freely within that public space without fear of violating the private territory of other persons with whom we are communicating.

Congruency between Space and Content of Transaction. Probably the most important factor to remember about space, both as an environment and as an instrument of human communication, is the congruency between the message content and the message environment. Effective communication requires congruency between the kind of message or meaning generated and the kind of space used for that interaction. For example, there is a perceived discomfort in a person when another tries to communicate an impersonal message at an intimate distance. There is incongruency when a person discusses the weather or stocks on the New York Exchange or the present state of the government while maintaining a distance of six inches between bodies. Likewise, there is a certain incongruency in saying "I love you" or speaking other intimate language at distances that are normally considered public, such as across the room or across an auditorium. Saying "I love you" standing across the room from another person will probably be perceived as more incongruous than saying "I love you" standing six inches away from that person.

There are a number of communication difficulties that arise from incongruency between the ostensible message and the message generated by the use of space. Salespeople who maintain public distances from their customers will generally have fewer successful sales than salespeople who maintain personal distances from their customers. Therapists, clinicians, psychologists, doctors, and lawyers may often receive different kinds of information from their clients if they conduct their interviews at social distances rather than at personal or intimate distances. Generally speaking, people are more inclined to disclose themselves at personal and intimate distances than at social and public distances; it is incongruent to expect self-disclosure at a public distance. Because many attorneys, medical doctors, bankers, and psychiatrists attempt to deal with personal and intimate affairs of people in space that is perceived by the clients as being social or public, they generate an incongruency between the purpose of the communication and the use of space, which frequently leads to difficulties in communication.

RELATIVE HEIGHT (ANGLE OF INCLINATION)

The relative height of two people communicating with each other can be an important dimension of space affecting their interaction. Relative height by itself probably has little influence on the communication; when combined with other factors in the situation, however, relative height becomes very important.

Relative height combines with hierarchical superiority to influence the patterns of interaction. Relative height is an important consideration when a superior is interacting with a subordinate. The superior can utilize the relationship of higher to lower within the situation with great effect. Generally speaking, the person who is spatially higher in the interaction has the advantage.

Greater height is usually associated with authority in Western cultures. Officers preside from raised desks in Congress; preachers' pulpits are elevated. Honored speakers generally mount the podium, a raised position in an auditorium. At the Olympics the first place winner mounts the highest position on the winner's platform, the second place a lower position, and the third place a still lower position.

That height can become an assertion of one's superiority over others was masterfully portrayed by Charley Chaplin in the movie *The Great Dictator.* In a classic scene, Chaplin portrayed a short German dictator, who was seated at his raised desk; he was conversing with the Italian dictator Busolini, who was seated in an extremely short-legged chair. As long as the Italian dictator remained seated, Chaplin was, of course, in the superior position. A game of musical chairs ensued in which each dictator attempted to maintain a greater height above the other and thus assert his superiority in the situation.

When relative height is combined with territoriality, the effects may be the opposite. The person who is seated in his own territory asserts superiority over the person who is standing in that territory. If a manager calls a subordinate into the manager's office and remains seated while the subordinate is left standing, the relative height acts in combination with territoriality to increase the effects of the territoriality. That the manager remains seated acts to reinforce the perceptions of his or her superiority and the subordinate's inferiority within that situation.

By analyzing the effects of the interaction of relative height with superior status and territory, it is easy to understand why the thrones of virtually every civilization were upon a raised platform in the room. The monarch asserted superiority in the interaction both by ascending the throne, which elevated him above others, and by then remaining seated while the petitioners and the courtiers remained standing. Both of these assertions of superiority—relative height and the seated position—served to reinforce the monarch's status, power, and control over the situation.

The arrangement of the modern courtroom is apparently an extension of the assertion of the superiority of the monarch. In monarchical societies the judge is a representative of the king or the emperor and acts in the ruler's name. Thus the judge, acting in the place of the king, remains seated upon a raised platform during the proceedings while other participants remain standing. The notable exception in American courtrooms is the witness, who is allowed to remain seated while testifying. In the British system, particularly, witnesses are required to stand to give testimony—thus the phrases "to take the stand" and "to stand in the docket."

ANGLE OF INTERACTION

In a series of very simple but important studies, Robert Sommer studied the relationship between dyadic seating arrangements and perceptions of cooperation, competition, and coaction.[10] In these studies Sommer asked people how they would seat themselves in order to compete with each other; how they would seat themselves to cooperate with each other; and how they would seat themselves to coact with each other (that is, do similar things but not be engaged in direct interpersonal interaction).

Sommer's results are significant because they reflect how people perceive various spatial arrangements. Sommer's results do not give us an absolute indicator; but they produce high enough correlations for us to say that, given a specific spatial arrangement, people are likely to perceive certain aspects of that arrangement as influential, both as an environment and as an instrument. These patterns of spatial arrange-

10. Sommer, *Personal Space*, pp. 58–73. Our discussion of angles of interaction is derived largely from this source.

ment may be identified as *angles of interaction.* We have identified four angles of interaction, based on Sommer's findings.

Competitive. When Sommer asked people to indicate how they would seat themselves if they were competing with each other, an extremely high percentage of the subjects took positions opposite each other as illustrated in the diagram.

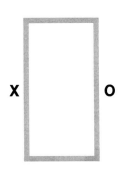

In the American culture competition seems to be associated with face-to-face opposition. We assume this position in basketball, hockey, football, soccer, checkers, poker, and other games of competition. It is significant that when we assume this position in noncompetitive situations, we tend to perceive that situation as somewhat competitive. If a person assumes this face-to-face position in a doctor's office, in a lawyer's office, or with a salesperson, he or she will tend to perceive the doctor, the lawyer, or the salesperson as a competitor rather than a cooperator, because the person perceives the spatial situation as competitive.

Cooperative. When Sommer asked his subjects to seat themselves in a cooperative position, he found two general arrangements that people most frequently perceived as cooperative. The first of these is the diagonal arrangement shown in the diagram.

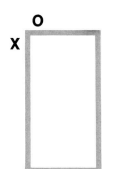

This arrangement allows the communicators to interact face-to-face, yet allows for relative security because of the intervention of the corner of the table or desk between them. While their personal space is not violated, close contact can still be maintained; they can interact at personal and intimate distances across the top of the table.

This position has been found to be the most effective cooperative position for information-gathering interviews, such as in clinics, banks, physicians' offices, and attorneys' offices. This arrangement allows for the exchange of intimate and personal information while maintaining the integrity of the personal territory of both persons in the situation.

Co-optive. The third angle of interaction is the side-by-side position illustrated in the diagram.

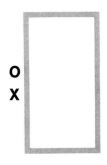

People generally view the side-by-side position as a co-optive position (although some see it as cooperative). In this arrangement the persons interacting are viewed as concentrating on the same task in a position of mutual physical support. There are no defensive barriers between them. It is easier for the two people to touch and to maintain intimate and personal distances. In this angle of interaction it is easier for one person to control or co-opt the other person.

It is sometimes desirable to use both the co-optive and cooperative space in an interview. When a clinician is gathering information from a client, he or she may wish to use the cooperative arrangement. This allows both parties to feel a certain amount of comfort in the situation. The space facilitates the exchange of intimate and personal information but allows the clinician to maintain a certain impersonal distance from the client, thus giving the client a sense of personal security.

Suppose the clinician is an audiologist. After the initial information gathering, the audiologist runs a set of hearing tests in which there is physical contact between the clinician and the client. After the tests are run, the client and the clinician return to the office. At this point it may be desirable for the clinician to utilize the side-by-side co-optive arrangement to discuss the findings of the examination. By switching to the co-optive arrangement, the clinician communicates that the data now belongs to both the client and the clinician. If there are charts or graphs, it is easier to discuss them side-by-side, and in so doing, to give the client a feeling of genuine participation in analyzing the data on his or her own problems.

The co-optive angle of inter-action permits greater control of personal and intimate space in transactions.

While both the diagonal and the side-by-side arrangements are viewed as cooperative, the successful communicator will take into account the specific purpose of the interaction and will select the physical and spatial arrangement that is most conducive to the specific kind of interaction he wishes to generate.

Coactive. The coactive position illustrated in the diagram is rarely used in interpersonal interviews.

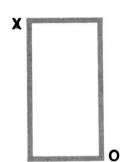

In a coactive position two persons are engaged in similar activities, but their mere physical arrangement tends to work against direct interaction. The two persons may exchange eye contact and dialogue in a coactive position, but neither of these are usually for a prolonged period of time. The coactive position is generally assumed in situations such as testing or in the completion of tasks in which direct and prolonged interaction would be detrimental or excessively time-consuming.

SUMMARY

Space is one of the four primary message systems that both forms an environment which affects all interpersonal communication transactions and can be manipulated to generate specific meanings within transactions. Five dimensions of space are territoriality, density, interpersonal distance, relative height, and angle of interaction. Each of these dimensions of space functions in every interpersonal transaction in which there is physical contact or face-to-face interaction. When we communicate, we should take care to assure that the content of the communication is congruent with the various dimensions of space. Space can modify, amplify, or negate the intended content of a given transaction. We should always be aware of the effects of space (as environment) on our own communication as well as the manipulation of space (as instrument) in specific transactions.

QUESTIONS FOR REVIEW

1. What is territoriality?
2. How does density affect interpersonal communication within groups?
3. What are the four kinds of distance that we utilize in interpersonal communication transactions? Define each.
4. How does variation in angles of inclination (relative heights) affect interpersonal communication transactions?
5. What are the four angles of interaction? What is the importance of each within interpersonal transactions?

EXPLORATIONS

1. Take a personal inventory (perhaps for your journal) of the spatial arrangements that you prefer in your interpersonal transactions with others. For example, do you use cooperative arrangements more frequently than competitive or co-optive interactional arrangements? Do you prefer to be above, at the same eye level, or below those with whom you interact? At what distances do you feel most comfortable?

   Next take an inventory of your personal space. What are the boundaries of your personal territory? How far in front of you does your territory extend? How far at the sides? How far in back of you? Does your territory vary depending upon where you are located (e.g., in church, in an elevator, on a crowded street, on an empty street, etc.)? Try to make a map or graph of the territory that you consider to be a part of "you" that you take with you into your transactions.

2. The next time you enter an elevator, do not turn around and face the door but remain standing looking into the elevator. What are the reactions of the other people in the elevator? Why? In what way are you upsetting their perceptions of space by facing them rather than the door?

3. Do a communication analysis of the spatial arrangements in your home, apartment, or dorm room. What kinds of interaction are permitted? Is the arrangement limited to competitive angles of interaction, or are other angles of interaction permitted and encouraged? What aspects of the arrangement establish who owns the territory? Are there certain "status" positions that emerge out of the physical arrangement (such as being seated at a desk, a chair that dominates the room, the head of a table, etc.)?

   Having conducted a communication analysis of the arrangement of the room(s), analyze the way in which you use these spatial environments to generate specific messages (communication effects) in specific situations. For example, if you have a date coming to the apartment, how do you use the space differently than when your parents visit you? Do you manipulate density, angles of interaction, angles of inclination, and/or other dimensions of space?

4. This is an exercise in territorial invasion. Go to a cafeteria or a library. Select one or more persons who have established a personal territory with markers—objects such as books, briefcases, coats, hats, or umbrellas that are placed to indicate that the occupant does not wish to be bothered. If you are by yourself, occupy the same table in such a way that you remove the person's territorial markers. What are his or her reactions? Why would the person react in this fashion?

An interesting variation on this exercise may be done by a group of people. Again, select someone who has staked out a territory. The first member of your group invades the territory of the target, but infringes only on the periphery. In a moment, a second member of the group joins the table, then a third and a fourth. Each time a new member joins the group, the markers of the target should be moved, and his territory should be visibly reduced or redefined. How does the target react? Why?

FOR FURTHER READING

Ardrey, Robert. *The Territorial Imperative.* New York: Atheneum, 1966.

A former screenplay writer and novelist, Ardrey turned his attention to summarizing the major theoretical and field research literature on human and animal territories. The result was an extremely readable, interesting, and entertaining analysis of what are otherwise highly technical materials.

Hall, Edward T. *The Hidden Dimension.* Garden City, N.Y.: Doubleday & Co., Anchor Books, 1969.

According to Hall, the hidden dimension is space—how human use of space affects interpersonal relations. The science of proxemics studies this spatial usage. Hall discusses how distance and crowding are regulated in animals and humans, how we perceive space, various kinds of distance in human relations, spatial dimensions of intercultural communication, and urban space.

Sommer, Robert. *Personal Space: The Behavioral Basis of Design.* Englewood Cliffs, N.J.: Prentice-Hall, 1969.

Sommer incisively analyzes humans' personal space in a twofold fashion. First, he examines human spatial behavior: spatial values, spatial invasion, privacy, and small group ecology. Second, he looks at some special spatial settings, as in homes for the aged, schools, dormitories, bars, and hotels. His field studies are especially insightful, for they faithfully report the way people utilize space in their everyday settings.

Sommer, Robert. *Tight Spaces: Hard Architecture and How To Humanize It.* Englewood Cliffs, N.J.: Prentice-Hall, 1974.

Modern men and women literally find themselves in some tight spaces, argues Sommer, because they are prisoners of the hard architecture—buildings, furniture, and other spatial settings—which is their own cultural product. Concrete fortress-type office buildings and classrooms, sterile airports, dismal subways, immovable and uncomfortable furniture, and other kinds of hard architecture are contributing to the very social alienation that society should be trying to combat. Sommer most convincingly portrays the power of space as a message system.

Chapter 9

Sexuality as a Primary Message System

While sexual matters are widely discussed in America today, in most textbooks sexuality is not considered a major component of communication. Nevertheless, we believe that sexuality, when properly understood, must be seen as a basic message system in interpersonal communication.

The commonly understood meaning of the names of the other three message systems—language, space, and gesture—provide a fairly adequate image of each respective message system as we have described it. The term *sexuality* is more problematic, however, because of the popular connotations it has—sex manuals, slick magazine foldouts featuring nude or nearly nude models, explicit bedroom scenes in the movies, and so on. While such things obviously involve sex, sexuality as a term and as a message system has a much broader meaning.

We can initially distinguish sexuality (or that which is sexual) from sex in at least three ways. First, sexuality is an aspect of the entire human body, while sex is primarily genital. The term *sexuality* refers to the embodied, physical nature of human beings, not just their genital organs. Second, sexuality is a ever-present condition or state of being, whereas sex is usually a transitory, episodic act. The bodily nature of human existence is a continuing, inescapable condition, only one aspect of which involves "having sex" with another person. Third, sexuality involves all of the individual's relationships, while sex typically focuses on those behaviors that are potentially procreative. All relationships that a person has (with other persons and with the nonhuman environment) are mediated through the body; the reproductive act is merely one kind of bodily or sexual experience.[1]

1. Our view that sexuality refers in the broadest sense to the human being's entire bodily existence (and not just to the act of genital sexual intercourse) is rooted in Freudian thought. See Norman O. Brown, *Life against Death: The Psychoanalytic Meaning of History* (Middletown, Conn.: Wesleyan University Press, 1959), pp. 23–73, 307–22; and Charles Brenner, *An Elementary Textbook of Psychoanalysis* (New York: International Universities Press, 1955; Garden City, N.Y.: Doubleday & Co., Anchor Books, 1957), pp. 22–23.

With this general distinction between the sexual (which is bodily) and sex (which is genital) in mind, we can provide a more specific definition of sexuality upon which this chapter is based. *Sexuality consists of any bodily experience, especially touch, body image, and body rhythm* (both individual and interactional), *that leads to the development of sexual roles and intimacy.*

In actuality, any act or experience has a sexual aspect, just as any act may have a gestural and spatial aspect. Freud saw language as an extension of the human body. Speaking and listening are most certainly bodily activities that can be pleasurable. Gesture likewise is sexual, for every human behavior is bodily. Even the use of space has a sexual dimension, for space can be designed and manipulated to enhance interpersonal distance or intimacy.

While sexuality can be interpreted broadly, we have chosen a definition of sexuality that most usefully distinguishes it from the other three message systems. Tactile body experience, body image, and body rhythm are too important and distinctive in their own right to be included within another message system; they constitute a separate message system. We must remember that while each message system can be analyzed in itself, without reference to other message systems, each message system also reflects and is reflected in all the others. Our definition of sexuality identifies those focal aspects of bodily existence that we believe essentially constitute sexuality as a message system.

THE ENVIRONMENT/INSTRUMENT NATURE OF SEXUALITY

Each of the dimensions of sexuality as a primary message system exists as a significant part of the social environment of every human being. As we shall see, touch, body image, body rhythms, and sexual roles are initially environmental to the human infant and are learned through interpersonal transactions with significant others as the child grows. It may seem strange at first to think of the body as being environmental. We may recall, however, that the infant seems to react to its body as if it were a part of the environment. We seem to actually "grow into" our bodies, and this growth is highly influenced by the nature of our interpersonal transactions with others.

On the other hand we also use our sexuality or bodiliness to successfully integrate interpersonal transactions with others. We manipulate the sexual environment in ways that usually permit transactions to progress toward intimacy or some substitute for intimacy. When there is incongruency between the way we manipulate the sexual message system and the other dimensions of the transaction, we of course have difficulties in communication.

TOUCH AND TACTILITY

One of the principle ways in which we experience our sexuality or bodily nature is through touch. The centrality of touch in human experience is evident in many common expressions.

> We speak of "rubbing" people the wrong way, and "stroking" them the right way. We say of someone that he has "a happy touch," of another that he is "a soft touch," and of still another that he has "the human touch." We get into "touch" or "contact" with others. Some people have to be "handled" carefully ("with kid gloves"). Some are "thick-skinned," others are "thin-skinned," some get "under one's skin," while others remain only "skin-deep," and things are either "palpably" or "tangibly" so or not. Some people are "touchy," that is, oversensitive or easily given to anger. The "feel" of a thing is important to us in more ways than one; and "feeling" for another embodies much of the kind of experience which we have ourselves undergone through the skin. A deeply felt experience is "touching."[2]

Touch is more than a figure of speech; physical contact is an ever-present mode of experiencing the environment. Whether we are being touched by another person, by our clothing, by the wind, or simply by the air in a room, we cannot escape tactility.

The main bodily organ of touch is the skin, which is the earliest of the sensory organs to develop, being functional in the eight-week-old human embryo.[3] The early embryological development of the skin is an indication of the fundamental importance of the skin and touch to the human being throughout life. The skin is the body's largest organ and contains a huge number of sensory receptors capable of receiving stimuli. These sensory capacities of the skin are put to work long before birth, sensing the physical, chemical, and thermal properties of the liquid environment in the mother's womb. During the process of labor or giving birth, the skin of the fetus is stimulated by the contractions of the uterus and the birth canal. This cutaneous stimulation, equivalent to the licking that most other mammals give to their young at birth, is indispensable in preparing all of the infant's sustaining systems to function adequately within atmospheric (as opposed to the previous aquatic) conditions.[4] Such tactile stimulation is essential in activating various aspects of the nervous system, so that the baby will begin to breathe, for instance. If the tactile stimulation provided during labor is insuffi-

2. Ashley Montagu, *Touching: The Human Significance of the Skin* (New York: Columbia University Press, 1971; New York: Harper & Row, Perennial Library, 1972), p. 5.
3. Ibid., p. 1.
4. Ibid., p. 45.

cient to activate respiration, the newborn infant may be slapped on the buttocks (as we have all learned from the movies) or immersed in alternate hot and cold baths (after all, a cold shower *does* make a person take a deep breath!).[5]

Touch is essential not only in activating certain basic bodily processes at birth but also in developing a physically and emotionally healthy human being. Ashley Montagu maintains

> *that cutaneous stimulation in the various forms in which the newborn and young receive it is of prime importance for their healthy physical and behavioral development. It appears probable that for human beings tactile stimulation is of fundamental consequence for the development of healthy emotional or affectional relationships, that "licking," in its actual and in its figurative sense, and love are closely connected; in short, that one learns to love not by instruction but by being loved.*[6]

Since the human infant in the first few months of postnatal life has not yet completed the development that occurs in other higher primates during gestation, the human infant's early postnatal life requires close contact with a mothering one. An essential feature of this contact is literal contact—touch. The baby needs to be handled, stroked, caressed, rocked, cleaned, nursed, and otherwise reassured. Such communication is crucial—not incidental—to the infant's healthy development. Infants placed in the cleanest, most sterile institutional environments often die simply for lack of adequate mothering, or tactile attention; mortality rates for infants in such institutions have been dramatically cut merely by having them regularly picked up and carried around.[7] In a series of famous experiments, psychologist Harry Harlow found that physical contact between infant monkeys and their mothers was extremely important; infant monkeys preferred surrogate cloth monkeys more of the time than they did surrogate wire mothers, even when they were nursed on the wire mothers. The wire mothers simply could not provide the pleasant, intimate body contact that the infant monkeys desired.[8] The human infant is more dependent and less fully developed during the early postnatal period than are monkeys and needs physical contact even more.

Thus one of the basic interpersonal needs (especially of the infant but also of the older child and adult) is touch. The way in which the infant is handled, the amount and character of the tactile communication received from others, is thought to play an important part in physical

5. Ibid., p. 62.
6. Ibid., p. 35.
7. Ibid., pp. 93–95.
8. Ibid., pp. 35–40.

and emotional growth and adjustment.[9] Touch is central to the process by which the self is formed. The handling of the infant, the tactile stimulation of the body, helps the infant to become aware of the nature and extent of its body; without such stimulation, the infant's psychological identification with its body would probably be retarded or damaged. Indeed, clinical study has shown "that the feeling of identity arises from a feeling of contact with the body. To know who one is, the person must be aware of what he feels. This is precisely what is wanting in the schizophrenic,"[10] whose ego is not identified with bodily awareness, and who feels "unembodied." The tactile dimension of interpersonal communication is a transactional process, requiring simultaneous perception by two people of touching and being touched. The lack of adequate tactile communication in infancy can have most profound and distressing results.

The environment of sexuality, considered in terms of the tactile dimension of human bodily existence, differs from culture to culture. Montagu describes different kinds of tactile environments characteristically experienced by infants in different cultures.[11] The Netsilik Eskimo infant experiences almost constant contact with its mother; the infant is carried naked (except for a diaper) inside the mother's parka against the skin of her back, where the infant sleeps, rests when awake, and spends its time except when feeding. The close, intimate contact between mother and child is greatly reassuring to the infant; it is constantly aware of the protective presence of the mother through the touch and warmth of her body, and the child's needs are usually anticipated by the mother tactilely. This early pleasurable tactile experience may well account for the phenomenal ability of the Netsiliks to cope with stress in adult life. Their emotional equilibrium, even in the face of danger, could be based on the predominantly supportive relationships in the culture established initially through tactility in infancy.

The tactile experience of the middle-class American child differs radically from that of the Netsilik infant. The American baby is not continually carried by, or in tactile communication with, the mother; on the contrary, she usually handles the child only to service its physiological needs. Either on schedule, or when the baby cries, she feeds the baby; since bottle-feeding predominates over breast-feeding, a considerable amount of tactility associated with breast-feeding is lost. The mother picks the child up to change a dirty diaper or to bathe it. Most of the time, however, the infant is not in physical contact with anyone; the baby sleeps alone in its own crib and plays alone in its own playpen.

9. Ibid., p. 214.
10. Ibid., p. 235.
11. Ibid., pp. 253–331. The materials on cultural differences and tactility are derived from this source.

Even when the child learns to crawl and to walk, it is touched primarily for feeding, changing, and bathing. The child's pleas to sleep with mother and father, or to be tucked in, or to be told a bedtime story, or to have someone bring a drink of water are usually resisted; these pleas all can be seen as indications that the child is seeking the reassurance that comes from being close to and touching another person upon going to sleep. Even a brief parental compliance with the child's request will usually satisfy him or her. Conventional wisdom indicates, however, that such compliance will spoil the child, just as rocking will spoil the infant; awareness of the child's tactile needs, of the reassuring nature of touch, is minimal in the typical American family.

As we might expect, different tactile environments in infancy contribute to different behavior patterns in childhood and adulthood. One of the possible causes of the seeming coldness and lack of emotionality that characterizes the middle-class English is the restricted tactile expression of love that they receive in infancy.[12] Anglo-Saxon Americans, like their English cousins, are rather restrained in the tactile stimulation of their young and consequently in their adult patterns of touch. Since the infant in America and England is not continually touched by others, it strikes out earlier on its own to explore its surroundings. In contrast, the Japanese infant (who is provided a more reassuring interpersonal tactile environment than are most American infants) has traditionally been more passive in exploring the environment.[13] People's awareness of their bodies and their world, as well as their characteristic ways of expressing themselves to others in interpersonal communication transactions, are all shaped by their early tactile experiences—an essential environmental aspect of human sexuality.

The relative de-emphasis on interpersonal touch in a culture does not mean, however, that such a culture is necessarily less sexual. Americans are typically restrained in touching other people (compared to Latin Americans, for instance), but American culture is very sensual nevertheless. Americans enjoy sitting in nice furniture, walking on plush carpets, riding in sleek cars, living in well-heated and air-conditioned houses, wearing comfortable clothes. Some clothes—underwear, for instance—are worn as much for comfort as for utility; they feel good because they gently press against the skin and genitals. Perhaps Americans compensate for their rather cold interpersonal tactile environment by stressing their material object tactile environment.

Using Touch to Communicate. While we have delineated the difference between sexuality as environment and as instrument, those two aspects of this (or any other) message system are obviously closely re-

12. Ibid., p. 288.
13. Ibid., pp. 295–96.

lated. While touch and physical proximity are interpersonal environments essential to our healthy growth and development, we also use touch and proximity as instruments to establish and maintain satisfactory interpersonal relationships. We use touch to communicate our view of our relationships with other people, touching those whom we love and feel close to more than we touch casual acquaintances. Touch can indicate the status relationship between the communicators. Anyone can touch a baby, for example, but few of us may touch a doctor. Nurses may touch patients, but patients are restricted in touching nurses.[14]

How we touch, as well as whether we touch, is communicative. A tender touch normally indicates positive feelings toward the other, while a hard touch or shove usually expresses negative feelings or hostility—unless it is qualified by a wink or a relational context in which rough horseplay is considered acceptable. Context is always a significant factor in interpreting the meaning of any instrumental communication. Behavior that represents a significant departure from what is usual in the context of a relationship generally has considerable communicative impact. If either of two friends who touch each other mostly in rough horseplay reaches out gently to the other (with an arm around the shoulder or an embrace), that touch is likely to be particularly noticed by the person touched as a sign of affection. In a relationship characterized by gentle touching, a rough touch will likewise receive particular notice; whether that roughness is a sign of hostility or affection will depend upon the relational context in which it is interpreted.

Where we touch others also communicates something. We have already mentioned that patterns of touch are culturally prescribed. Touching that conforms to those patterns is interpreted by the person touched in terms of frequency and manner of touch. The violation of the tactile patterns of a culture or of particular relationship can be especially communicative. When a person who normally touches a friend on the arms or shoulders embraces the friend tightly in a firm but gentle bear hug or places a hand on the friend's stomach, the novelty of the touch is striking and heightens its impact.

The manipulation of proximity (by itself and in conjunction with touch) is also a useful communicative device. By standing or sitting close to other people—close enough to feel their body heat and for them to feel ours—we can communicate camaraderie or affection (provided that such proximity is not mandated by crowded conditions as on a subway). We can also stand close to another person to communicate hostility. When we place ourselves physically close, we usually employ touch to reinforce the message—tender touch if we feel affection, harsh

14. Flora Davis, *Inside Intuition: What We Know about Nonverbal Communication* (New York: McGraw-Hill, 1971, 1972, 1973), p. 157.

touch (through shoving or fighting) if we feel hostility. Touch, of course, requires a certain proximity; we have to be spatially close enough to another person in order to reach out physically to that person. Certain behaviors involving physical closeness and touch are employed to court another person, to indicate a desire to become very close emotionally to that person. Behaviors in which she "makes a pass" at him or he tries to "pick her up" can display courtship patterns. In addition, courtship behaviors can be qualified to indicate that they are intended to lead not to genital sexual intercourse but to some other kind of social relationship. Such qualified courtship behaviors, or quasi-courtship behaviors, are used in establishing rapport in any kind of relationship. Courtly, polite manners as expressed through language and body movement almost always serve to facilitate an interpersonal communication transaction and enhance the relationship of the participants.[15]

Thus human sexuality, or bodily experience, is closely related to patterns of touch. While these patterns vary from culture to culture, in all cultures interpersonal tactility is essential to the maintenance of physical and emotional health.

BODY IMAGE

Another aspect of sexuality, which is related to touch yet distinguishable from it, is body image. Body image is a person's concept or view of the nature of his or her own physical body and its functional value in interpersonal relationships. The image that a person has of his or her

15. Albert E. Scheflen, *Body Language and Social Order: Communication as Behavioral Control,* with Alice Scheflen (Englewood Cliffs, N.J.: Prentice-Hall, 1972), p. 21.

We never see our own bodies directly. Our own body images are derived from our social environment.

body may or may not encompass all parts of the body and may or may not depict the body as socially acceptable or desirable. Body image, therefore, involves the relation of the body to the self and to others, relations that are shaped in part by interpersonal communication transactions.

The first aspect of body image is the relation of the body to the self. The healthiest or most desirable body image probably embraces the entire physical body; a person sees and identifies all parts of his or her body with the self. Of course, everyone sees the self as necessarily connected with the body. But having a fully integrated body image means that the individual experiences the entire body as his or hers. The person *is* his or her body; the person feels *embodied*. According to R. D. Laing, "the embodied person has a sense of being flesh and blood and bones, of being biologically alive and real; he knows himself to be substantial. . . . He is implicated in bodily desire, and the gratification and frustrations of the body. The individual thus has as his starting-point an experience of his body as a base from which he can be a person with other human beings."[16] The fully embodied person, the person with a fully integrated body image, experiences the whole body as "me," has a sense of "ownness" about his body, and can use any part of his body appropriately in any given social situation.

In marked contrast to the embodied person is the unembodied self. "In this position," writes Laing, "the individual experiences his self as being more or less divorced or detached from his body. *The body is felt more as one object among other objects in the world than as the core of the individual's own being.*"[17] A completely unembodied person has a fully dissociated body image; he does not feel related to his body, which he experiences as "not-me." Such an unembodied state is generally indicative of a disturbed individual who has considerable difficulties in living; the completely unembodied person is probably incapable of coping successfully with life.

The completely embodied and entirely unembodied selves are, of course, polar opposites. It is possible for an individual to have a partly dissociated body image, to be partially unembodied. Such a person experiences the self as being closely related to most but not all of the body. Some area or areas of the body are experienced as divorced or detached from his self—as "not-me." The "not-me" is Sullivan's term for the type of early experiences or personifications of the self that are marked by dissociation, intense anxiety, loathing, and dread.[18] The per-

16. R. D. Laing, *The Divided Self: An Existential Study in Sanity and Madness* (Baltimore: Penguin Books, 1965), p. 67.

17. Ibid., p. 69.

18. Harry Stack Sullivan, *The Interpersonal Theory of Psychiatry*, ed. Helen Swick Perry and Mary Ladd Gawel (New York: W. W. Norton & Co., 1953), p. 163.

son with a partly dissociated body image experiences some part of the body as detached from the self, dreads any use of that body part, and becomes extremely anxious when called upon to use it.

We feel more unembodied at some times than at others. The social situation can have a decided influence on this variation in our body image. A person we know usually experiences his hands as his, and can use them in all sorts of activities, such as typing, playing the piano, and writing. But on a basketball court he begins to experience his hands as "not-his," as somehow dissociated from himself. His otherwise-useful hands become awkward, numb, and practically useless. In the social situation of playing basketball, his body image excludes his hands as useful instruments, for whatever reason. So our body images can change from situation to situation. A part of the body that is "me" in most settings can become "not-me" in other settings.

Body image is of central importance in understanding the environmental role of human sexuality in interpersonal communication because our body images are shaped by our communication transactions and in turn shape our future transactions. The process by which the body image is formed is social. While it might initially seem logical to assume that one's body image comes from within one's own body, the body image is largely derived from and maintained through interaction with others. Although we do have an experiential awareness of our body that differs from an outsider's experience of our body, how we experience our body is learned.

For example, if the mothering one has severe anxiety about her infant touching his or her own genitals, that anxiety will probably interfere with the infant's normal and appropriate development of the body image.[19] The infant will come to regard the genitals as "not-me" and will not integrate the genital area into his or her body image and social life. Rather than appropriately learning from the mothering one that society places certain restrictions on the handling of the genitals, the infant in this case learns to dread the genitals. If this kind of pattern continues, the person will not be able to form a satisfactory genital relationship with another person in later life. The person will avoid situations involving genital contact and become anxious when confronted with such situations. Likewise the person whose hands are his everywhere except on the basketball court has probably experienced social criticism or ridicule earlier from others about his awkwardness in that setting and will continue to feel dissociated from his hands in that setting in the future.

So consideration of the first aspect of body image (the relation of the body to the self) leads necessarily to the second aspect (the relation

19. Ibid., p. 145.

of the body to others). The degree to which an individual feels embodied is a function, at least in part, of interaction with significant others from infancy onward. If the child has been allowed to explore his or her own body in a socially normal fashion, and if others have treated him as a normal, fully embodied person by satisfying his need for physical contact (through sports, games, and appropriate demonstration of affection, such as hugging and kissing), then the child will probably develop a fully integrated body image. On the other hand, if others ridicule the child's body, are anxious when in contact with the child, or refrain from touching or standing near him or her, then the child probably either will not develop a fully integrated body image or will be displeased with his body image. In short, the body image is shaped in essentially the same fashion as the self—primarily through social interaction.

One's body image is subject to continuing modification throughout life. If our social relations as adults become increasingly depersonalized as a result of the pressures of a mechanized, highly competitive society, then "our bodies tend to disappear. Not from the other's gaze, or even from our own glance into the mirror. Rather, they vanish from our *experience*. We lose the capacity to experience our bodies as vital, enlivened, and as the centers of our being."[20] As we touch and are touched by fewer and fewer people on less and less of our bodies, our body images shrink so that "we" are essentially cerebral creatures with heads, hands, and arms which are attached to a merely utilitarian torso of which we are only numbly aware.

How we are treated bodily by others has considerable impact upon how we treat ourselves. People with a visible handicap (such as a missing limb) or a behavioral abnormality (such as that associated with some types of mental illness or mental retardation) will usually be avoided by others. The handicapped will be touched less than those who are seen as normal. The interpersonal distances between the handicapped and "normal" people is on the average one foot greater than the distances between "normal" people.[21] The relative body isolation imposed socially on the handicapped is bound to have a negative influence on their own body images. When the handicapped person reaches out to another person to satisfy the need for physical contact and that other person withdraws, the handicapped person will probably experience his own body as undesirable and will either escalate his reaching out or withdraw in despair. In contrast, the person who is treated as if

20. Sidney Jourard, "Out of Touch: The Body Taboo," *New Society,* 9 November 1967, p. 660.
21. U.S., Department of Health, Education, and Welfare, Public Health Service, *Perspectives on Human Deprivation: Biological, Psychological, and Sociological* (Washington, D.C.: Government Printing Office, 1968), pp. 50–56; and R. Kleck et al., "Effects of Stigmatizing Conditions on the Use of Personal Space," *Psychological Reports* 23 (1968): 111–18.

his body were socially acceptable, who is given adequate tactile stimulation, will probably experience his body as desirable and will engage in satisfying tactile behavior with others.

Likewise the person with hands that are relatively dysfunctional in playing basketball will probably continue to experience his hands as "not-his" in that setting unless someone understands his problem and works with him to increase gradually the usefulness of his hands in handling a basketball. His body image will slowly change, so that in his view his hands become embodied in all situations; then his body image will include hands-with-a-basketball as well as hands-at-the-typewriter and hands-at-the-piano.

Using Body Image. A person with a fully integrated body image, an embodied person, will probably feel fairly competent and able to use the whole body in appropriate ways and at appropriate times to move close to others and touch them. Such a person will be able to express himself or herself by manipulating the body in desired ways, such as hugging, kissing, moving close, moving away, and so on. A person with a partly dissociated body image will most likely refrain from moving close to and touching others; such hesitancy might well be interpreted by others as lack of warmth (which *is* what it appears to communicate, regardless of what the person feels or intends to express). So the degree of integration of a person's body image will probably be reflected in the congruency between the person's feelings and behaviors. Although body image cannot be directly observed, it influences our ability to use our bodies instrumentally.

BODY RHYTHM

In addition to touch and body image, body rhythm is an element of human sexuality that has considerable environmental impact upon us. *Body rhythm* is the ordered fluctuation, or time-structured alternation, of regularly occurring and interrelated bodily events, both individual and interpersonal. Body rhythm is analogous to musical rhythm. The rhythm or beat in music is not random or unpatterned; it has a basic pattern indicated by the time signature. Body rhythm is also time structured, with the alternation of the beat characterized by a recognizable pattern (as with the heartbeat). Musical rhythm coordinates all the various musical instruments and their sounds into one coherent whole (an orchestra playing a symphony, for instance); body rhythm coordinates all the various rhythmic elements of the body (heart and circulatory system, lungs and respiratory system, etc.) into a unified, functional, organismic beat. The various elements are brought into synchrony with one another through some basic rhythm. The bodily

Each person has an individual body rhythm which includes all body functions as well as conscious rhythmic movements.

events synchronized by rhythm include our experience, both conscious and unconscious, of the various subsystems of the body (heart, lungs, speech, etc.) and of the body as a whole. Just as different musical instruments vibrate in different ways and yet can be synchronized into one rhythmic whole (a song, concerto, etc.), so individual human bodies have somewhat different bodily rhythms and yet can be synchronized into one interpersonal whole (a conversation, discussion, etc.).

Individual Rhythms. Individual body rhythms are basic to understanding human sexuality as a communicative environment because the human being is a creature whose bodily processes are time structured. The body is not a static entity; it changes and fluctuates over time. The rhythmic ebb and flow within us is our individual biological rhythm—our own body time—of which most of us are ordinarily unaware. These biological rhythms within us are truly myriad. The heart is characterized by one pattern or beat; respiration is characterized by another pattern; and the two are related to each other in healthy people in a heartbeat-to-respiration ratio of four to one.[22] Furthermore, the internal

22. Gay Gaer Luce, *Body Time: Physiological Rhythms and Social Stress* (New York: Pantheon Books, 1971; New York: Bantam Books, 1973), p. 10.

systems of the body generally are regulated by circadian rhythms (*circadian* meaning 'around a day' in length); such internal processes as body temperature, heart rate, metabolism, glandular activity, and cell division all seem to follow daily cycles.[23] As a member of the earthly world of living things, a human's biological processes reflect the twenty-four-hour cycle of day and night. Even though the length of individuals' circadian rhythms may vary (as the length of days varies at different seasons), the approximate cycle that most individuals follow is a daily one. Humans respond to the daily cycle of light and darkness, just as plants do. Even a person placed in a dark mine deep in the earth will continue to manifest circadian rhythms (despite initial variation) in the absence of an observable cycle of day and night. However, when people in far polar regions are deprived of the privilege of observing that cycle, their lives are adversely affected; they become depressed, irritable, and unable to sustain prolonged concentration in the months-long darkness of the Arctic winter.[24] The long process of evolution has implanted circadian rhythms as deeply within humans as in other forms of earthly life; the human body continues to beat with prehistoric rhythms. Our experience of our own bodies necessarily includes these basic body rhythms; our sexuality (or bodiliness) is constituted in part by the rhythms through which our bodies function.

Humans (like other species) have body rhythms that are common to the species, but that differ from species to species and from individual to individual within any given species.[25] Although there are hereditary limits to the range of body rhythms humans can experience, the rhythms of different individuals may vary widely within these limits. For instance, some individuals are commonly called "morning people" because they seem to be alert upon arising and able to function well in the morning. In contrast, other individuals are "night people" who are sluggish in the morning and seem to do their best work at night. Woe to the spouses or roommates who have widely different body rhythms, for the morning person will be energetic and talkative at the very time that the night person is lethargic and sleepy. Because of the many different aspects of body rhythm, there are numerous possible rhythmic combinations between individuals, which can give rise to interpersonal problems. Most of the time, we are not explicitly aware of interpersonal differences in body rhythm; we merely sense vaguely that something is wrong with our relationship. Sometimes we explicitly recognize interpersonal differences in body rhythm, as when the husband realizes that his wife's irritability is the result of her twenty-nine-day menstrual

23. Davis, *Inside Intuition*, p. 132.
24. Joseph Wechnsberg, "A Reporter at Large: Mørketiden," *New Yorker* 18 March 1972, pp. 103–6, 108–10, 112–26.
25. Davis, *Inside Intuition*, p. 132.

cycle (the length of the lunar month) and not of any anger on her part towards him. Interpersonal differences in body rhythm make it important for people to find others whose rhythms complement their own.[26]

Interpersonal Rhythms. Interpersonal, or transactional, body rhythms are significant in the development of both the individual and the individual's social relationships. Our individual body rhythms are shaped not just by heredity but also by our social environment. A baby is soothed and its individual body rhythms influenced when the mother holds the baby on her left side so the baby can detect her heartbeat. Perhaps during the prenatal period, the infant associates the mother's rhythmic heartbeat with lack of tension—an association whose soothing effect continues into postnatal life.[27] In fact, a record of the sounds of a mother's body rhythms (recorded by a tiny microphone placed in her uterus beside the head of her unborn baby) has become a popular bestseller in Japan. The record is an amazingly efficient baby pacifier (stopping 400 out of 550 babies in one nursery experiment from crying and putting 150 of them to sleep).[28] Any mother's individual body rhythms (or aspects of those rhythms) will be communicated to her infant as she holds the infant for feeding, bathing, and so on. If she is anxious, her anxiety will be manifested in her body rhythm, which will convey her anxiety to her infant. If she is calm, her body rhythms will normally be reassuring to her baby. Over a period of time, the nature of the mothering one's body rhythms will modify and shape the infant's body rhythms. Thus, the shaping of the self through social processes occurs in part through the communicative properties of our interpersonal body rhythms.

The influence of interpersonal body rhythms continues to be significant throughout adult life. That fact is not surprising when we reflect upon occasions in which we were upset but were calmed by other people; an individual's more relaxed body rhythms (expressed through speech, body movement, gesture, etc.) can have a relaxing effect on others. Conversely, when someone else becomes alarmed and manifests that alarm in a quicker pulse, rate of respiration, and speech, we tend to become more excited ourselves (with a corresponding increase in our individual body rhythms). We have varying individual body rhythms for varying social situations.[29] A woman might have one characteristic body rhythm while talking with her husband, another while talking with acquaintances in the neighborhood, and yet a third when engaging in

---

26. Ibid., p. 133.
27. Lloyd Shearer, ed., "Parade's Special Intelligence Report: Where to Hold a Baby," *Parade Magazine*, 29 July 1973, p. 19.
28. Lloyd Shearer, ed., "Parade's Special Intelligence Report: Hit Record," *Parade Magazine*, 27 April 1975, p. 4.
29. Davis, *Inside Intuition*, pp. 134–35.

conversation with a favorite aunt. Not all individuals are so flexible, however; some people seem to maintain the same essential body rhythms (whether hyperactive talking or passive withdrawing or something in between) regardless of the demands of the situation. But most of us have a personal repertoire of body rhythms which we manifest selectively (although largely unconsciously) depending upon the person with whom we are at the time.

Interpersonal Synchrony. One of the most intriguing features of interpersonal body rhythms is *interpersonal synchrony* (termed *interactional synchrony* by some writers). Interpersonal synchrony is simply a shared beat between two people in an interpersonal communication transaction.[30] That shared beat has been detected by microanalysis of slowed-down films showing such transactions. Regardless of the culture in which the transaction occurs, interpersonal synchrony occurs whenever people converse. They share the same rhythm, expressed through breath rate, eye blink, speech rate, and other acts. This current, this shared beat, characterizes rapport between two people; movements are literally synchronized at approximately forty-eight beats per second, which some researchers believe is necessary to coordinate any interpersonal transaction.[31]

While interpersonal synchrony is too rapid and too subtle for participants in a transaction to observe consciously, they are aware of it unconsciously. When we are in rapport with others, we tend to know it (although at the time we do not know *how* we know it). Apparently, communicators in rapport are consciously aware of their rapport but not of the nature of the shared beat which underlies it. An individual's body rhythm, which is continually geared to the cadence of his or her own speech,[32] is communicated to others through speech and body motion and mutually adjusted to establish interpersonal synchrony. When such synchrony exists, participants experience the feeling of being in tune with each other. There are "good vibes" between them.

Different interpersonal communication transactions are characterized by different rhythms, depending upon who the communicators are.[33] For example, blacks apparently use their bodies in subtly different ways than whites; black Americans' body rhythms are generally faster and more syncopated and contain considerable small-scale movement. Consequently, transactions between blacks and whites require mutual adjustment to differences in body rhythm and frequently cause some discomfort in the process. Similarly, men and women seem to have different styles of interpersonal synchrony; male-male transac-

30. Ibid., p. 114.
31. Scheflen, *Body Language and Social Order*, p. 53.
32. Davis, *Inside Intuition*, p. 113.
33. Ibid., pp. 117–21.

tions tend to display subdued body motion and only partial synchrony, while male-female and female-female transactions feature more elaborate body motion and more complete synchrony. Furthermore, some transactions are characterized by a rather thorough absence of normal synchrony; one of the participants fails to achieve synchrony between his or her own vocal pattern and body movement, thereby disrupting the development of interpersonal synchrony. Such transactions usually involve one or more participants who are diagnosed as autistic, schizophrenic, or otherwise disturbed. Regardless of the cause of such disturbance, it is almost always manifested in a failure to achieve satisfactory interpersonal synchrony.

Anyone who has ever been in a good dormitory bull session, at a powerful public speech, at a successful concert (folk, rock, classical, or whatever), or at a compelling worship service should be able to recognize the instrumental importance of interpersonal synchrony (through voice and body patterns, music, ritualized speech and movement, etc.). Through the use of rhythm and tension, a common or shared interpersonal cadence is created and intensified, leading hopefully to a climax in which everyone present feels rapport with the others present (dyadic partner, discussion group members, speaker, audience, liturgical leader, or congregation). Our entire communicative lives are oriented towards such transcendence of personal isolation or loneliness and the achievement of the experience of this rapport or communion with others.

SEXUAL ROLES

Human sexuality as a primary message system in interpersonal communication leads to the development of sexual roles. The cultural process by which the individual develops an appropriate sexual role is one example of the environmental dimension of human sexuality. The human species is obviously dimorphic or two-sexed, since the male-female differentiation is functionally essential for reproduction. However, human sexual behavior (as opposed to reproductive sex behavior) is not fundamentally biological; masculine and feminine behaviors are culturally, rather than biologically, determined. In this regard, "it is a great mistake to assume that the behavior which is observed in man is linked to physiology. Studies of culture have shown us that this is usually not the case. Behavior that is exhibited by men in one culture may be classed as feminine in another. All cultures differentiate between men and women, and usually when a given behavior pattern becomes associated with one sex it will be dropped by the other."[34]

34. Edward T. Hall, *The Silent Language* (Garden City, N.Y.: Doubleday & Co., 1959; Greenwich, Conn.: Fawcett Publications, 1959), p. 49.

*Sexual roles
are culturally
defined and
slow to change.*

Americans have traditionally assumed that men are strong, silent, and unemotional, whereas women are weak, talkative, and weepy. But that kind of definition of masculinity and femininity is quite culture bound and culture specific. In contrast, in Iran "men are expected to show their emotions. . . . If they don't, Iranians suspect they are lacking a vital human trait and are not dependable. Iranian men read poetry; they are sensitive and have well-developed intuition and in many cases are not expected to be too logical. They are often seen embracing and holding hands. Women, on the other hand, are considered to be coldly practical. They exhibit many of the characteristics we associate with men in the United States."[35]

The impact of cultural norms upon the development of sexual roles is clearly evident in the patterns of touch that structure our interpersonal tactility. Sidney Jourard has reported that different areas of the body are touched in different frequency by specified kinds of people—i.e., certain areas of an American male's body are touched by his mother, other areas by his father, other areas by a male friend, and still other areas by a female friend. Furthermore, the areas of a female's body that are touched by such people differ from the areas of a male's body that are touched.

35. Ibid., p. 50.

THE BODY AS TOUCHED BY OTHERS

A study conducted by Sidney Jourard revealed that certain areas of the body are touched more frequently than other areas according to the sex and relationship of the people involved.[36] This chart shows the percentage of respondents (based on 168 males and 140 females questioned) who reported being touched in given body areas by mother, father, same sex friend, and opposite sex friend.

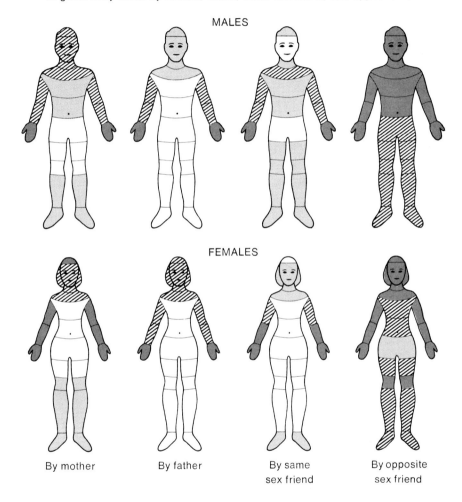

MALES

FEMALES

By mother By father By same sex friend By opposite sex friend

 Indicates 0-25% reported being touched in that area by the relevant person.

Indicates 26-50% reported being touched in that area by the relevant person.

Indicates 51-75% reported being touched in that area by the relevant person.

Indicates 76-100% reported being touched in that area by the relevant person.

36. Jourard, "Out of Touch," pp. 660–62. See also Sidney Jourard, "An Exploratory Study of Body-Accessibility," *British Journal of Social and Clinical Psychology* 5 (1966): 221–31.

Certain generalizations can be made about these patterns of touch. It is a socially acceptable practice for mothers to touch their offspring (whether male or female) on the head, neck, shoulders, arms, hands, lower legs, and feet. Fathers, however, usually touch their children only on the head, neck, shoulders, arms, and hands. In addition, a person can and usually does touch much more of the body of an opposite sex friend than of a same sex friend. An American learns the acceptable cultural patterns of touch by being touched and by observing how others are touched; he develops his sexual role so that it includes the patterns of touch appropriate to his culture and subculture.

One example of the cultural constraints placed on sexual roles involves approved tactile patterns in male-male relationships. "Our culture supports a strong taboo against male-male embraces after the males leave childhood, and especially against male-male kissing. Yet these expressions are unquestioningly meaningful and important to males. Since they cannot secure physical, affectionate contacts in a straightforward manner, they contrive and ritualize situations to obtain them.

In our society, sports is one of few situations in which it is socially acceptable for men to hug and physically show affection for each other.

Scuffling, wrestling, or embracing at the end of a victorious athletic contest allows men to get indirectly what they cannot secure directly."[37] Perhaps one of the reasons for the enormous popularity of contact sports such as football is that the male participants can express themselves openly—encouraging a fellow player by patting him on the rump, hugging a teammate in victory, collapsing in a teammate's arms in despair at defeat, or knocking an opponent silly in anger. Spectators can participate vicariously, thereby finding gratification in seeing others do what culture forbids them to do without suspicion of homosexuality. Before a big sales presentation, a businessman seldom encourages a colleague by patting him on the rump! Nor in most families do father and grown son embrace or kiss after a long absence; they make a handshake do instead. Of course, tactile behavior associated with sexual role differs from culture to culture, and from subculture to subculture. According to Ashley Montagu, "Jews tend to be tactually very demonstrative, and it is considered perfectly normal for an adult male to continue to greet his father with a kiss and an embrace and to do so also on parting. In forty years of close observation I have only once seen an adult American male (in this case in his middle twenties) publicly greet his father with a kiss."[38]

That sexual roles have cultural origins is emphasized in the current attempts to redefine masculine and feminine roles in our society. If sexual roles were limited strictly to genital differentiation, changes in sexual roles would be impossible. Yet we are constantly redefining sexual roles, and the redefinition of sexual roles becomes an extremely important aspect of all interpersonal communication transactions. How we communicate with one another depends to a large extent upon how we define our sexual roles in relation to each other in a particular transaction. We use sexual roles, then, to define the context of our communication with others and thereby to invoke certain sets of rules to govern a particular transaction. Incongruency between sexual roles and the setting or between sexual roles and the content of the communication immediately gives rise to difficulties in communication within that particular transaction.

SEXUALITY AND THE DEVELOPMENT OF INTIMACY

Sexuality or bodily experience plays an essential part in helping us to overcome isolation and loneliness and to achieve unity with other persons through communication. This chapter has focused upon the ways

37. Lester A. Kirkendall, "Sex and Human Wholeness," in *Sexuality: A Search for Perspective*, ed. Donald L. Grummon and Andrew M. Barclay (New York: Van Nostrand Reinhold Co., 1971), pp. 285–86.
38. Montagu, *Touching*, p. 303.

in which sexuality is both an environment in which we communicate and an instrument by which we communicate. The ultimate purpose or goal of interpersonal communication is not just to transmit information or ideas to other people (although that is necessary) but to create and maintain an intimate relationship with somebody. Such love and communion with another is unthinkable and unachievable apart from human sexuality, our bodily experience (developed through touch, body image, and individual and interpersonal body rhythms).

The prototype of intimacy, a kind of close collaboration between two people, is "the act of loving impregnation."[39] This act is obviously impossible apart from the presence and utilization of human sexuality. All aspects of our bodily experience (touch, proximity, body image, body rhythm, sexual role, etc.) are incorporated in genital sexual intercourse. Marriage is the most intimate of all relationships because collaboration is repeatedly consummated by the interpenetration of the bodies of husband and wife. "Having sex" can be the epitome of our experience of human sexuality (as both environment and instrument). But "having sex" does not necessarily produce an intimate relationship; the honest prostitute will be the first to admit that genital sexual intercourse can signify a routine rather than an intimate relationship. Rape features the interpenetration of bodies but not a free and willing collaboration between two people.

Nor do all intimate relationships involve genital sexual intercourse. Intimacy is obviously possible with parents, other relatives, and close friends without any genital relationship being involved or implied. By touching these people in certain ways, by having the "same vibes" as they do (through interpersonal synchrony), by spontaneously expressing ourselves candidly to them, and by accepting them as they accept us, we use all the primary message systems (including sexuality) to create and nurture intimacy. People who experience intimacy only through lustful genital sex will probably have difficulties in living, because they will be unable to be close to anyone that they don't go to bed with. Likewise, people who cannot experience intimacy through lustful genital sex—who for some reason are unable to form satisfactory genital relationships with someone of the opposite sex—will also have difficulties in living, because they will be unable to consummate a loving relationship with the opposite sex by having genital sexual intercourse.[40]

Those people are most fortunate who can use their sexuality in ways that are appropriate to the occasion—who can rightly judge what

---

39. Eric Berne, *Games People Play: The Psychology of Human Relationships* (New York: Grove Press, 1964), p. 18.
40. Sullivan, *Interpersonal Theory of Psychiatry*, pp. 274–76.

the occasion calls for. Hopefully, such people can have an intimate relationship with a spouse (which involves genital sex) and intimate relationships with close friends and relatives (which do not). They will be able to make new friends, utilizing language, space, gesture and sexuality to collaborate with others and cement new bonds of affection. They will be able to maintain valued old relationships by manipulating the message systems in a fashion appropriate to the relational context. Most importantly, they will be able to participate in the creation and maintenance of at least one intimate relationship, which is essential for personal health and well-being.

SUMMARY

Sexuality is one of the primary message systems that functions in every interpersonal communication transaction. Sexuality is distinguished from sex. Sexuality encompasses the whole body; sex is only the genital functioning. Sexuality is ever-present; sex is episodic. Sexuality occurs in all transactions; sex is involved primarily in potentially reproductive acts. There are four aspects of sexuality—touch, body image, body rhythm, and sexual roles.

Touch is one of the major forms of communication. The skin is the largest organ of the body and the largest organ of communication. Without sufficient touch in early interpersonal transactions the human infant may die. Touch is critical to healthy interaction throughout a person's lifetime.

Body image is another aspect of sexuality. The body image is formed primarily through interaction with others. It is also central in guiding the way people interact with others in communication transactions.

Body rhythms form an essential element of every communication transaction. Personal rhythms are associated with individual bodily functioning. Interpersonal body rhythms are manifested in interpersonal synchrony. Such synchrony may often be experienced as "good vibes" and indicates a harmony in the transaction which facilitates a climactic experience. This oneness with another person may be seen as a state of intimacy.

Sexual roles exist in every communication transaction. The communicative dimensions of sexual roles are learned from the society and are subject to change by that society.

QUESTIONS FOR REVIEW

1. Distinguish between sex and sexuality.
2. In what ways is touch important to interpersonal communication?

3. How do we develop our own body images? Why are our body images environmental to us? Where do our body images come from?
4. How do body rhythms affect interpersonal communication?
5. What is interpersonal synchrony? Why is it important to interpersonal communication transactions?
6. In what ways are sexual roles biologically defined? In what ways are they socially or culturally defined? Why is it important to distinguish between the biological and cultural bases of sexual roles?

EXPLORATIONS

1. A valuable journal exercise is the construction of a geographical or geological map of your body. If you did the journal exercise suggested in the explorations for chapter 8, you have already described the boundaries of your body in terms of personal territory. In this exercise, you will map out your body in terms of some of its more prominent transactional features.

    What are the oldest parts of your body? What are the youngest parts of your body? Which are the "hard" parts formed of granite? Which are the "soft" parts formed of sandstone? Which parts are your rivers and streams? Are they swift-running and young (like a mountain spring) or are they languid (like a river near the ocean)? Where are the population centers of your body? Where are the industrial centers? Where are the rural areas, the mountains, the plains, the forests? Where are the untapped resources of your body? Are they on the surface, lying just below the surface (accessible by strip mining), or buried deep (requiring deep mining to bring them to the surface)? Is your body a hospitable land for others? Does it hold out warmth and promise, or is it cold, harsh, and forbidding? What plans would you make for developing this country?

2. With what things about your physical appearance are you satisfied? With what things are you dissatisfied? Which aspects of your physical appearance do you think are attractive to others? Which do you think are unattractive to others? Why? Where did you get your idea of "good looks"? Which aspects of your appearance can you change? Which can you not change?

3. Select a word that you feel best characterizes your feelings about your physical appearance and your body (such as athletic, glamorous, weak, strong, flabby, firm, etc.). Now stand up and assume a body attitude that best reflects the word you have chosen. Next begin to move about the room with each movement reflecting that word. Now choose a word that characterizes your body as you would like it to

be. Assume a body stance that reflects that word; then move around the room with each movement reflecting that attitude. Do the same with several different strengths and weaknesses that you feel your body has. Compare your reactions—both emotional and intellectual —as your body assumes each of the characteristics. Why can't you use your body to reflect strengths at all times?

4. This exercise involves awakening the body. Begin by tapping your face lightly with the tips of the fingers of both hands. Move the tapping down to the neck, the shoulders, the trunk of the body, the hips, the thighs, the calves, and then the ankles; then move back up the body until you reach the head and face again. Awaken your body to the sensations of being touched. You may want to do this to lively music.

5. Sit or stand in front of a full-length mirror. Focus your eyes squarely on your body. Each time you speak a word, make eye contact with your image in the mirror. For a period of two to three minutes, speak aloud positive thoughts about your body. Do not allow yourself to utter criticisms. Notice the changes that take place in your body as you get into this exercise. How would others react to these changes?

FOR FURTHER READING

Brown, Norman O. *Life Against Death: The Psychoanalytic Meaning of History.* Middletown, Conn.: Wesleyan University Press, 1959.

In this remarkable book, Brown reinterprets the fundamental position of psychoanalysis, transforming it from a system limited to dealing with the individual psychic structure to a system capable of dealing with social systems and history. This book is fairly difficult to read but is worth the effort for any student interested in and familiar with the basic psychoanalytic position.

Davis, Flora. *Inside Intuition: What we Know about Nonverbal Communication.* New York: Mc-Graw-Hill, 1971, 1972, 1973.

Although written by a journalist for popular consumption, this book is a solid survey of research in nonverbal communication presented in a very readable style. Davis examines various aspects of what we have called sexuality, such as touch, body rhythm and conversational rhythm, posture, etc. In addition, she discusses numerous types of gestures, such as those of the face, the hands, and the eyes.

Grummon, Donald L., and Barclay, Andrew M. *Sexuality: A Search for Perspective.* New York: Van Nostrand Reinhold Co., 1971.

Based on a colloquy at Michigan State University in 1969, the essays in this collection address a wide variety of issues in the study of human sexuality: sex education, the nature of sexuality (anthropological, biopsychological, etc.), sex and equality, sex and the law, sex and personal development, and others. While some of the articles focus on sex in the reproductive sense, the book provides a well-rounded perspective on sexuality in general.

Luce, Gay Gaer. *Body Time: Physiological Rhythms and Social Stress.* New York: Pantheon Books, 1971; New York: Bantam Books, 1973.

In this book, Luce carefully yet interestingly explores the multitudinous tides and rhythms of the body. Some of the topics covered are work schedules, sleep and dreams, daily changes, sickness and health, and light and darkness. All are discussed in terms of the body's cycles and seasons.

Montagu, Ashley. *Touching: The Human Significance of the Skin.* New York: Columbia University Press, 1971; New York: Harper & Row, Perennial Library, 1972.

Montagu's usual power and clarity of expression pervades this comprehensive and straightforward book about touch. He conveys a wealth of information about touch as it relates to infant care, animal and human development, sex, and cultural patterns of contact.

PART III

Patterns of Interpersonal Communication

Chapter 10

Intimacy in Interpersonal Communication

All people seek to establish intimacy with others through their interpersonal communication transactions; it is central to the growth and fulfillment of every person.[1] Everyone has "the need for intimacy—that is, for collaboration with at least one other person."[2] This collaboration is deeply personal, emotionally gratifying, and mutually rewarding to both parties in a healthy relationship. We need to have people in whom we can candidly confide, with whom we can share our greatest joys and our most disturbing fears, to whom we can talk spontaneously without preoccupation about how we express ourselves or about how we will be received, who will accept us regardless of our weaknesses, and who will likewise share themselves with us. To be fully human each person must, during his or her lifetime, establish intimacy with at least one other human being.

Eric Berne defines intimacy as "the spontaneous, game-free candidness of an aware person, the liberation of the eidetically perceptive, uncorrupted Child in all its naiveté living in the here and now."[3] The interpersonal collaboration designated by the term *intimacy* is spontaneous, freely chosen and expressed by the individual. It is candid and perceptive, free of dishonesty and deviousness (i.e., free of games). It is free from repressive social domination; it is impulsive, self-indulgent, fully alert, and involved in experiencing the activities of the present moment (rather than being preoccupied with the past or immobilized by anxiety about the future). Such intimacy is, or should be, the highest goal of our interpersonal communication.

1. Harry Stack Sullivan, *The Interpersonal Theory of Psychiatry*, ed. Helen Swick Perry and Mary Ladd Gawel (New York: W. W. Norton & Co., 1953), pp. 245–46, 263–71.
2. Ibid., p. 264.
3. Eric Berne, *Games People Play: The Psychology of Human Relationships* (New York: Grove Press, 1964), p. 180.

In defining communication we described loneliness and love as chief motivations in interpersonal communication. Every person seeks to avoid loneliness. The avoidance of loneliness serves as a "push" toward interpersonal interaction. At the other end of the continuum, the avoidance of loneliness finds its fullest release in the establishment of intimacy in loving relationships with other persons. The need for intimacy serves as a "pull" toward interpersonal interaction. It appears, then, that *the establishment and the management of intimacy are basic goals of interpersonal communication.*

Any interpersonal communication transaction may result in the establishment of a state of intimacy between two people. There are numerous barriers, however, that may dictate that other forms of communication behavior are more appropriate or more feasible than the establishment of intimacy. Sometimes a social situation will indicate that intimacy is not appropriate; in other cases one or both parties in the transaction may not be capable of handling intimacy. In such transactions the basic goal of communication becomes the management of substitutes for intimacy (which are called strategies and games) rather than the establishment of intimacy.

One of the great difficulties in discussing intimacy is that, like loneliness, it is an *experience*. Intimacy and loneliness are not behaviors that we can clearly observe; they are experiences derived from and manifest in certain relationships with others. Communication behavior may facilitate or inhibit intimacy, just as communication behavior may perpetuate or overcome loneliness. However, intimacy and loneliness are ultimately experiences through which we perceive and interpret all communication behaviors.

Intimacy is probably first experienced by the infant in the good nipple transactions with the mothering one. In such situations the infant must experience a free, spontaneous, undifferentiated merger of its own experience with that of the mothering one (since the needs of the infant are satisfied and the tensions arising from needs are resolved). This state of intimacy is probably about the closest the human being ever comes to the state of complete euphoria[4]—created by the complete, undifferentiated union of the self with another human being. In adult experience, such states may be momentarily recaptured in loving relationships between friends and within the family, and sometimes in states of orgasm.

As the child matures, the self and multiple perspectives on the self become more and more prominent in the organization of experience. Processes variously described as consciousness, conscience, ego, self-image, defense mechanisms (and similar processes) become dominant

4. Sullivan, *Interpersonal Theory of Psychiatry*, pp. 34–37.

in behavior and experience. Such processes function to defend the self against threat or change by others. The more complicated the experience of self becomes, the more difficult it is to experience union with another person. What is so normal, simple, and spontaneous in the infant's experience becomes complex, infrequent, and difficult to achieve in adult experience.

A WORKING DEFINITION OF INTIMACY

Any technical definition of intimacy is probably insufficient to capture the essence of intimacy (which by its very nature may be uncapturable on paper). For our purposes, we describe intimacy as *a loving collaboration between two people who both understand and feel understood by each other.*

"We need to have people . . . with whom we can share our greatest joys and our most disturbing fears . . ."

There are three distinct facets to this concept of intimacy. First, intimacy as experienced by the human adult may best be described in terms of certain patterns of congruency between the three levels of perspectives experienced by both persons in an interpersonal transaction. The concept of perspectives includes behavior, the way each person perceives behavior, and the way each interprets the behavior of self and the other. Intimacy can probably occur only when there is a high degree of congruency between all these levels of behavior and experience within an interpersonal transaction—that is, when the two persons both understand and feel understood.

Second, intimacy involves a collaboration between the two people in the transaction. Sullivan has said that "intimacy is that type of situation involving two people which permits validation of all components of personal worth. Validation of personal worth requires a type of relationship which I call collaboration, by which I mean clearly formulated adjustments of one's behavior to the expressed needs of the other person in the pursuit of increasingly identical—that is, more and more nearly mutual—satisfactions. . . ."[5] Intimacy cannot be achieved by only one person in a transaction; it requires the collaboration of both partners for its realization. Intimacy cannot be achieved by something that one person does; it is truly a transactional experience.

Third, intimacy is related to love—that concern for the well-being of the other, delighting in his or her presence, integrating one person's own desires and concerns with those of the other.[6] People engage in communication not just to avoid loneliness but also to experience love. Intimacy apart from love is impossible. Thus intimacy can be characterized as the collaborative, loving relationship between two people who understand and feel understood by each other.

AN ILLUSTRATIVE TRANSACTION AND ANALYSIS OF INTIMACY

The situation. Charles and Mary are both in their forties. They are a divorced man and a widow who have been seeing each other with increasing frequency. Although each perceives the other as becoming more serious about their relationship, Mary has avoided close physical contact with Charles. A couple of years ago, Mary developed breast cancer and had her right breast removed. The operation changed Mary's perception of herself from a sexually desirable woman to a person with an incomplete body. While she wants to assume an intimate physical and sexual role with Charles, even to marry him, she is uncertain about how he might react to the information about her operation.

5. Ibid., p. 246.
6. Ibid.; and Berne, *Games People Play*, p. 18.

The transaction. Mary tells Charles about the surgery one evening as they are preparing to dine.

> Mary: *There is something I want you to know. A couple of years ago I had a radical mastectomy and my right breast was removed. Apparently the doctors caught the cancer in time. I really haven't had any more problems with it.*
>
> Charles: *Um. Well, I'm very thankful you took care of yourself and weren't afraid to do what was necessary. We will have to make sure you have regular checkups.*

The transaction reveals an open disclosure of information followed by an appropriate acknowledgment of the information. Charles's reply to Mary acknowledges that he has understood the denotative content of her message; but his reply gives no indication that he understood the relational significance that Mary may attach to the message.

The Experience of Intimacy. If we now look from the communication *behavior* to the communication *experience* of the two people in this transaction, we can outline a conjunction of states that Charles and Mary might experience as intimacy.

Mary:	*Charles:*
perceives her statement as an open, intimate disclosure;	perceives Mary's statement as an open, intimate disclosure;
perceives Charles's response as indicating a mature concern for her as a healthy person;	perceives his response as reassuring Mary of his concern for her as a healthy person;
feels that her fears were unfounded—that the breast removal will not affect her role relationships with Charles;	feels that the removal of Mary's breast in no way adversely affects his role relationships with her;
feels that Charles understands her.	feels that he understands her concerns.

In this illustration, all of the requirements for intimacy in the relationship are present. We can not say that intimacy has been achieved, for that, of course, depends upon the experience of the two parties involved. As observers, however, we can say that the conditions requisite for the achievement of intimacy are present and that the patterns of communication indicate that intimacy has probably been experienced.

We can look at the same transaction between Charles and Mary and imagine that they interpreted the exchange of messages in a different way from that outlined above. If their experience of the transaction were as follows, there would be incongruencies between the various perspectives of Charles and Mary.

Mary:	Charles:
perceives her disclosure as intimate;	perceives Mary's statement as history (people have surgery every day);
perceives Charles's response as indifferent to her feelings about her mastectomy;	perceives his response as reassuring Mary that the past illness does not affect his perceptions of the present relationship;
feels that Charles does not understand her perceptions of her "stigma."	feels that he and Mary have demonstrated that they can exchange information in a mature and rational way.

It is obvious that in this set of experiences, Mary and Charles are not congruent on all levels of perspective. Charles does not understand Mary nor does Mary feel understood by Charles. Even though the behavior of both parties in the transaction is identical to their behavior in the first example, their experience of the communication behavior is significantly different.

When we are attempting to learn how to improve our own interpersonal communication, it is not enough simply to learn a set of behavioral skills. Rewarding interpersonal communication depends as much upon the way we experience the behavior of self and others as it does upon the way we manipulate our own behavior. Mary does not experience intimacy with Charles in the second example because of the stance, or predisposition, that she takes in her anticipation of Charles's response. If Mary's predisposition is to interpret anything Charles may say or do in a negative sense, there is nothing Charles can do in manipulating his own communication behavior that would result in intimacy between them. Mary will have created conditions that prohibit collaboration between her and Charles.

NATURAL BARRIERS TO INTIMACY

Many writers, poets, and scientists as diverse as Wordsworth and Freud have placed a great premium on the intimacy that the human infant seems to experience in the good nipple situation. It has been popular to write about what a wonderful world this would be if we could all live in states of euphoric intimacy with one another—if we could maintain the sort of spontaneous integration of interpersonal transactions that we experience in infancy.

But the world is not a world of just "good nipples." In fact, the structure of interpersonal transactions seems to indicate that a constant state of intimacy is neither biologically possible nor psychologically desirable. There are several critical aspects of interpersonal transactions that either lead to the dissolution of intimacy once it is achieved or serve as natural barriers to establishing intimacy in order to maintain health.

One of the most noticeable features of intimacy in the good nipple transaction between the infant and the mothering one is the tendency of the situation to *disintegrate because it is successful*. The pattern of good nipple situations is the infant's experience of tensions arising from some need, which leads to behavior that evokes appropriate behavior from the mothering one. These behaviors bring about resolution of the tensions and a feeling of satisfaction of the need, which in turn lead to the *natural* disintegration of the interpersonal transaction. Then the infant and the mothering one are both free to engage in other behavior (e.g., sleep or play by the infant, work or conversation by the mothering one). The same pattern occurs throughout life in fulfilling the interpersonal need for intimacy. Once the intimate transaction has been successfully integrated, the tensions arising from the need for intimacy are relieved and the situation tends to dissolve.

Another barrier to intimacy arises from *social rules*. In every culture there are certain social situations in which communication behavior that could lead to intimacy is prohibited or severely restricted. A display of intimacy between a father and his son, for example, might be considered appropriate within the confines of the home but inappropriate in a public setting, such as a crowded supermarket. All social structures (such as the home, the extended family, the community, the state, religious institutions, and social organizations and clubs) generate both implicit and explicit rules that inhibit, restrict, or regulate intimacy in interpersonal transactions.

A third natural barrier to intimacy is *defensiveness*. Defensiveness is the natural tendency of the self to resist perceived threat or change induced by others. Because intimacy is a spontaneous merger of the self with another person, every intimate relationship contains elements of threat to the self. Whenever two people collaborate to create the degree of undifferentiated empathy between them necessary for intimacy to exist, there is a danger that one or both selves will be changed by the experience. Thus, there are both communication climates that create or increase defensiveness and communication climates that are supportive of intimacy.

Jack Gibb has identified six defensive climates and six corresponding supportive climates.[7] *Defensive climates* are characterized by communication behavior that tends to evoke defensiveness by threatening a person's self-image. *Supportive climates* are characterized by behavior that tends to reduce the perceived threat to the self-image and increase trust between the communicators. The six paired categories of perceived communication behavior are as follows:

Categories of Behavior Characteristic of
Supportive and Defensive Climates

Defensive Climates	*Supportive Climates*
1. Evaluation	1. Description
2. Control	2. Problem orientation
3. Strategy	3. Spontaneity
4. Neutrality	4. Empathy
5. Superiority	5. Equality
6. Certainty	6. Provisionalism

Evaluation speech or gestures appear to render judgment on the communication behavior of the other. Gibb observes that "if by expression, manner of speech, tone of voice, or verbal content the sender seems to be evaluating or judging the listener," the listener will go on guard and his or her communication will more likely become defensive.[8] *Description* usually consists of "presentations of feelings, events, perceptions or processes which do not ask or imply that the receiver change behavior or attitude."[9] Such descriptive, neutral communication tends to reduce defensiveness.

Communication that is designed to *control* the other person in the transaction usually evokes resistance. Such control implies that the person being controlled is somehow inadequate, ignorant, immature, unwise, unable to make correct decisions, or holding incorrect or inadequate attitudes. *Problem orientation* is communication designed to assure the other person that there are no hidden motives, that both persons are engaged in a mutual definition of the problem, and that there are no predetermined solutions, attitudes, or methods to be imposed in the transaction.

Strategy is communication behavior that may be perceived as being ambiguous and having multiple motivations. This behavior may involve gimmicks and social deceit. ("Oh, I've got to run. I've got an appointment I had forgotten.") *Spontaneity* is behavior that is free, open, hon-

7. Jack R. Gibb, "Defensive Communication," *The Journal of Communication* 11 (September 1961): 141–48. The six defensive and supportive climates are from this source.
    8. Ibid., pp. 142–43.
    9. Ibid., p. 143.

est, and appropriate to the situation. Spontaneous behavior is defense reducing and is generally a mark of healthy communication.

Neutrality is communicated when one person in the transaction indicates a lack of concern for the other's welfare. *Empathy* for the other's feelings and respect for the other's worth are particularly supportive and defense reducing.

Superiority is communicated when one person implies that he or she is superior in position, power, wealth, intellectual ability, physical characteristics, or in any other way. *Equality* is communicated when one person tries to keep the roles within the transaction on an even level. Even though two roles may be perceived as different, neither role is seen as better than the other role in the transaction.

Certainty is related to dogmatism. When one person is unwilling to consider the other person's perceptions of a situation or unwilling to consider changes in his or her own perceptions, the communication will usually produce defensiveness in the other person. A person reduces defensiveness when he or she communicates a certain *provisionalism*, i.e., a willingness to be open to the other person's views and to be open to change of the person's own perceptions of a situation.

A fourth barrier to intimacy is that, regardless of the communication climate, some people simply have *difficulty in handling intimacy*.[10] Intimacy with another person requires some degree of risk and interpersonal trust. People differ in their abilities to open themselves to interpersonal risk and to handle such risk when it occurs.

Often people who are incapable of handling intimacy have developed an overall pattern of defensiveness in their interpersonal communication. Certainly in particular situations defensiveness is perfectly healthy and necessary for the protection of the self. Anxiety interferes in some situations and must be coped with and defended against. Some people, however, are defensive in situations that do not warrant defensive behavior. In such people, defensiveness may become excessive and may lead to disturbed patterns of communication with others. Excessive defensiveness prohibits the establishment of intimacy.

These four are natural barriers to the maintenance of intimacy in interpersonal transactions: the natural tendency of intimacy to disintegrate once needs are satisfied; social rules regulating intimate behavior; defensiveness in communication; and the inability to handle intimacy when it occurs. We must be careful not to place value judgments on these barriers to intimacy. They are neither good nor bad, healthy nor unhealthy, in and of themselves. These tendencies may be said to be *healthy* when they function to facilitate patterns of growth through interpersonal communication—i.e., when they help to optimize success-

10. Berne, *Games People Play*, p. 61.

"...intimacy is necessary to the healthy growth of the individual..."

ful patterns of living. These tendencies may be said to be *unhealthy* or disturbed when they lead to difficulties in living for a given individual. Recurring, severe difficulties in living show themselves in disturbed communication. The more severe patterns of disturbed communication are usually analyzed as neuroses or psychoses.

One of the major contributions of Transactional Analysis to our understanding of human communication was the discovery that, while intimacy is necessary to the healthy growth of the individual, not all people are equally capable of handling the experience of intimacy. Many people are caught between the push and pull motivation of their interpersonal communication. They cannot tolerate loneliness and will do almost anything, including enduring extreme anxiety, to flee from it. At the same time, they cannot handle intimacy; intimacy becomes as devastating to them as their loneliness. Fortunately, such persons may lead relatively healthy lives by developing patterns of communication that utilize various kinds of interaction as *substitutes for intimacy*. (We shall examine these in detail in chapter 11.) At this point, however, let us look more closely at communication behaviors that usually facilitate the development of intimacy in interpersonal transactions.

COMMUNICATION THAT FACILITATES INTIMACY AND GROWTH

As we have pointed out before, it is easier to illustrate disturbed and pathological communication patterns than to present healthy and "normal" patterns. Communication patterns that facilitate intimacy and growth tend to be known more for what they are not than for what they are. Patterns of communication that can lead to intimacy are not spectacular; they are not dramatic; they do not call attention to themselves. They are not the sort of communication we find in most plays, movies, novels, and stories. But let us look at the positive side. It is possible to identify certain aspects of such communication. What can people do to facilitate intimacy and growth in their own interpersonal communication?

ACKNOWLEDGMENT

The most basic requisite of communication that promotes the development of intimacy is acknowledgment.[11] When people are trying to communicate, they must perceive that their own perceptions are perceived by others. That is to say, there must be some communication behavior that indicates that each person's perceptions are being acknowledged. There does not have to be an expression of agreement, merely some expression of the fact that each person's perceptions have been noted. Let us consider a transaction in which acknowledgment does not occur satisfactorily. A young child comes running in to her mother with a common garden toad.

> Christy: *Mommy! Mommy! Look at what I found in the garden!*
>
> Mother: *Christy, go wash your hands immediately.*

In this example, the mother fails to acknowledge Christy's perceptions of her experience—her joy at discovery, her excitement.

Suppose now that the mother were to respond to Christy with a pattern of communication based upon acknowledgment (which would pro-

---

11. Acknowledgment is discussed in Jurgen Ruesch, *Disturbed Communication: The Clinical Assessment of Normal and Pathological Communicative Behavior* (New York: W. W. Norton & Co., 1957; reprint ed., 1972), pp. 37–38. Our example of Christy and her mother is adapted from Ruesch, pp. 54–55.

mote growth and increase the probability of the mother and child being able to establish intimacy in this transaction).

> Christy: *Mommy! Mommy! Look at what I found in the garden!*
>
> Mother: *Oh, you are excited. Do you know what it is?*
>
> Christy: *No, but look, it jumps when I put it down.*
>
> Mother: *It's a garden toad. I don't like them in the house. Put it back in the garden where you found it. Then come and wash your hands.*

In this example, the mother acknowledges the fact that Christy is communicating with her and acknowledges Christy's perceptions. While the mother obviously does not *agree* with Christy's enthusiasm for toads and would rather be rid of the toad as quickly as possible, the mother's interaction with the child directly acknowledges what the child has communicated to her. Even though the mother and child do not develop a deep intimacy (which might have been possible had they become deeply engrossed in their discussion of the toad), the interaction demonstrates that each person considers the other to be important enough to acknowledge. Such acknowledgment of the other is the first requisite for interpersonal growth and intimacy.

DISCLOSURE OF EXPERIENCE

Most writers in the field of interpersonal communication and interpersonal relations consider disclosure to be another of the basic requisites for the achievement of intimacy. One problem that arises in discussing disclosure, however, is that few authors mean the same thing when they use the term *disclosure*. Definitions of disclosure range from the concept of self-disclosure as the revealing of the "inner" or "real" person to another[12] to the strictly transactional concept of selecting the appropriate role relationship for interaction. For our purposes, we will not talk about *self-disclosure* but will focus on the *disclosure of experience* within the interpersonal transaction (which must, obviously, include the self). The disclosure of experience has two aspects, both of which are essential to the development of intimacy and eventually to healthy communication.

Disclosure of Experience in the Here and Now. One aspect of disclosure is the expression of what a person is feeling, thinking, and experi-

12. Such a view appears to underlie the popular Johari Window discussed in Joseph Luft, *Group Processes: An Introduction to Group Dynamics*, 2d ed. (Palo Alto, Calif.: Mayfield Publishing Co., 1970), pp. 11–20.

encing in the "here and now."[13] There is a sense in which intimacy can be achieved only if both persons involved in an interpersonal transaction are openly, freely, and spontaneously expressing to each other what they are experiencing in the immediate situation. Difficulties in communication occur when a person is trying to communicate one thing while actually feeling or experiencing something else. Prolonged or repetitive disjunction between a person's experience and the person's communication behavior leads to difficulties in living and to deterioration of healthy patterns of interaction.

One frequently finds the communication patterns of homosexuals, for example, disjunctive from their experience. A homosexual may feel an attraction toward another person but may hide any communication of that attraction for fear of rejection or reprisals. Likewise, many homosexuals suppress their natural, and quite normal, communication through touch because "straights" will pull away or display startle reactions when touched by a gay person. Prolonged experience of disjunction between feelings and behavior cannot be healthy; it can only lead to increased difficulties in living.

We may view the disclosure of experience in the here and now by casting our discussion in terms of congruency. *Effective communication leading to growth and intimacy in interpersonal transactions involves the reduction of incongruency between what a person is experiencing and what the person is expressing behaviorally in a given transaction.*

Disclosure does not necessarily entail the revealing of secrets, or discussing the past in intimate detail, or even telling other persons your every impression or evaluation of them. In fact, disclosure frequently means the opposite of each of these, depending upon the context and the appropriateness of such behaviors to the transaction. Disclosure does, however, require careful differentiation of feelings toward persons and events and careful expression of those feelings.

In disclosing experience, carefully distinguish the object or event that gives rise to the feeling. If you are feeling anger, for example, what is the source of the anger? Is it another person? another person's actions? the situation? your own inability to cope with something? Difficulties in interpersonal communication arise when people are not careful to distinguish the source of their feelings. There is a tremendous difference in a child's experience of a transaction when a parent says, "I am angry that you broke my favorite dish," as opposed to when the parent says, "I am angry with you." Pragmatically, it is possible for the child to change the behavior or to prevent such behavior from occurring again; it is difficult if not impossible for the child to perceive any feas-

13. David W. Johnson, *Reaching Out: Interpersonal Effectiveness and Self-Actualization* (Englewood Cliffs, N.J.: Prentice-Hall, 1972), pp. 13, 16.

ible way of changing the self sufficiently to prevent the parent's anger from recurring.

In disclosing experience, express feelings via message systems that most clearly convey the appropriate meaning to the other person in the transaction. If you are feeling anger, it is usually best to acknowledge the anger and its source via the language message system, e.g., to say "I am angry that your message did not get to me yesterday." Failure to express the experience of anger via the language message system may result in the anger being expressed through the gestural, spatial, or sexual message systems, which are more action oriented and in which the meaning of the message may be more ambiguous. When Michael says, "I am angry that your message did not reach me yesterday," Jennifer can interpret with some accuracy the source of the emotion. But if Michael says nothing about his anger and allows it to be expressed through the other message systems, Jennifer may be left with the feeling that Michael is angry (or irritated, or not feeling well, etc.) but may be unable to distinguish the source of Michael's behavior. (Is he upset with *me*? Is the *situation* causing him to act this way? Did *somebody else* do or say something to him?)

Of course, it is not always necessary to articulate every feeling via language. Gestures, manipulation of space, and sexuality can, under some circumstances, be more appropriate and unambiguous than spoken language. Thus, it is important when expressing feelings to select the most appropriate message system.

Disclosure of experience should be congruent with the social situation. Effective communication does not mean "letting it all hang out" all of the time. Communication always occurs within a social context, which has specific role differentiation and specific rules governing the appropriateness of messages. Failure to take the social context into account in disclosure may often result in alienating the other person rather than moving toward intimacy and interpersonal growth.

Selecting Appropriate Roles for Disclosure. Maintaining congruency between experience and behavior is only one aspect of disclosure. Selecting the appropriate role relationship with the other person is a second, equally important aspect of disclosure. The central question in disclosure is not, Am I being honest? or even, Am I being authentic? Rather the central question is, Is this role appropriate for the kind of interaction and mutual perception desired for this transaction? There are guidelines that may help in selecting appropriate roles for disclosure.

Choose role relationships that may be reciprocated by the other person. Authentic communication always involves collaboration between two people in the roles they assume in their interpersonal transactions. Because intimacy involves interexperience (the conjunction of the experience of two people), it is particularly essential that the role relationship selected for disclosure be one that the other person is capable of reciprocating. In the play *The Subject Was Roses*, the son attempts to express his love to his father.

> Timmy: . . . *There was a dream I used to have about you and I. . . . It was always the same. . . . I'd be told that you were dead and I'd run crying into the street. . . . Someone would stop me and ask why I was crying and I'd say, "My father's dead and he never said he loved me."*
>
> John: *(Trying unsuccessfully to shut out Timmy's words.) I only tried to make you stay for her sake.*
>
> . . . .
>
> Timmy: *It's true you've never said you love me. But it's also true that I've never said those words to you.*
>
> John: *I don't know what you're talking about.*
>
> Timmy: *I say them now—*
>
> John:*—I don't know what you're talking about.*
>
> Timmy: *I love you, Pop. (He crosses to center. John's eyes squeeze shut, his entire body stiffens as he fights to repress what he feels.) I love you. (For another moment John continues his losing battle, then overwhelmed, turns, extends his arms. Timmy goes to him. Both in tears, they embrace. . . .)*[14]

In the transaction between Timmy and his father, we see clearly that John behaves at the outset as if he is not capable of handling the intimate role relationship that Timmy is attempting to create. John rejects each of Timmy's initial attempts to assume the intimate role of a son expressing his love for his father. John appears to be threatened by the role that would be required of him in order to validate Timmy's role. In this moving scene we observe the tremendous risk Timmy takes in gambling that his father is capable of reciprocating the role. Imagine for a moment the overpowering emptiness, loneliness, and disconfirmation of self that Timmy would have experienced if his father had refused to turn to him or in any other way acknowledge Timmy's declaration of love. Fortunately, Timmy gambled wisely; John was eventually able to reciprocate to some degree the intimate role relationship.

When we choose the role relationships that we wish to establish in our interpersonal transactions, we should consider whether the other

14. Frank D. Gilroy, *The Subject Was Roses* (New York: Samuel French, 1962), act 2, sc. 4, pp. 70–71.

people are *capable* of reciprocating the role relationships we desire. We cannot achieve intimacy in our relationships with others unless they are willing to collaborate with us in achieving that intimacy.

Choose role relationships that have a reasonable chance of improving the relationship between you and the other person.[15] The particular role chosen for disclosure within a given transaction is appropriate to the degree to which that particular role, or self, may reasonably be expected to improve the ongoing relationship between the two people. In the transaction between Timmy and John, Timmy's choice of role for disclosure presented a reasonable chance that the relationship would be improved by the transaction. Yet in communication counseling, one of the most frequent errors we find is the choice of roles that have little chance of improving relationships. We all encounter people who assume roles of critical employee, arrogant student, sarcastic telephone operator, and so on. Assuming such roles may adequately and accurately disclose a person's feelings but provides little chance of facilitating intimacy or improving relationships in the present or in the future.

Choose role relationships that are congruent with the context of the communication. When you decide to disclose a particular aspect of the self, consider whether the role will violate the rules of the social situation. If the context is a meeting of the board of directors of a bank to discuss raising or lowering interest rates, it would be a violation of the rules implicit in the social situation for one of the members to begin discussing his or her marital problems. The role of troubled husband or wife is inappropriate to this particular context. After the meeting, the same people may gather at their favorite bar or restaurant where they may appropriately discuss that member's marital problems. Each social situation is governed by implicit rules (usually derived from the society or the culture) that indicate the degree to which a given role will be deemed as appropriate by others involved in that situation.

CONFIRMATION OF THE OTHER

While acknowledgment and disclosure are aspects of communication that promote intimacy and healthy interpersonal growth, a third essential component of such communication is confirmation of the other in interpersonal transactions.[16]

When we speak, act, gesture, or communicate in any way, we are asking not only to be acknowledged but to be confirmed in our images of ourselves. Virginia Satir has pointed out that every message we gen-

15. Johnson, *Reaching Out,* pp. 12–13.
16. Paul Watzlawick, Janet Helmick Beavin, and Don D. Jackson, *Pragmatics of Human Communication: A Study of Interactional Patterns, Pathologies, and Paradoxes* (New York: W. W. Norton & Co., 1967), pp. 83–95.

erate in our interpersonal transactions contains a "validate me" aspect.[17] Each message, in effect, generates an implicit request that another person confirm our view of ourselves, of our experience of the world, and of our relationship to the world. We can experience failure to receive confirmation or validation as anything from mildly troublesome to devastating to the self-image. Consider, for example, the transaction that occurs when a thirteen-year-old boy comes running in from school and proudly says to his father:

> Jeff: *Hey, Dad, I beat the captain of the tennis team today!*
>
> Dad: *(Sarcastically) Huh. Some captain you've got.*
>
> Jeff: *(running out the door) Huh. Some father.*

If either person in an interpersonal communication transaction fails to confirm the other, intimacy will probably be impossible. People can achieve intimacy only when each perceives his or her self and view of the world as being confirmed *and* when each is confirming the other's self and view of the world.

Other authors, notably Thomas Harris, have discussed the confirmation of self and other in terms of the phrase "I'm O.K.—You're O.K."[18] The "I'm O.K." position is my confirmation of my self-image. The "You're O.K." position is my confirmation of your self-image. When couched in these terms, we find that to achieve intimacy there must be not only confirmation of the other but also confirmation of the self by the self. If a person does not accept his or her own self-image, it becomes extremely difficult for that person to communicate with others in such a way as to achieve intimacy and interpersonal growth. Thus healthy communication leading toward intimacy must validate not only the other's view of self, but also a person's own view of self. *Healthy communication must begin from the "I'm O.K." position.*[19]

The statement "I'm O.K.—You're O.K." is idealistic. It is necessary for health to adopt the attitude that the self is O.K. and that all others are basically O.K. But we all know from our past experiences that not everybody is O.K. Some people have disturbances in their perceptions of self, in their perceptions of others, in their perceptions of the world, and in their patterns of communication. Some people act in ways that simply are not O.K. They need communication with others that will lead to change. They do not need confirmation of their distorted perceptions and experiences of self.

17. Virginia Satir, *Conjoint Family Therapy: A Guide to Theory and Technique*, rev. ed. (Palo Alto, Calif.: Science and Behavior Books, 1967), p. 81.

18. Thomas A. Harris, *I'm O.K.—You're O.K.* (New York: Harper & Row, 1967; Old Tappan, N.J.: Fleming H. Revell Co., Spire Books, 1973), esp. pp. 74–77.

19. Muriel James and Dorothy Jongeward, *Born To Win: Transactional Analysis with Gestalt Experiments* (Reading, Mass.: Addison-Wesley Publishing Co., 1971), pp. 35–37.

"... one of the chief
features of the experience
of love is the feeling
of unity with the beloved
without loss of either
person's own freedom
and identity."

What do we do when we encounter a person who has disturbed patterns of communication or whose perceptions are not validated by the experience of others? The answers to this question have filled many volumes on the nature of therapeutic communication. Yet one thread appears consistently in virtually all systems of therapeutic communication. What is most essential to therapeutic communication is full acknowledgment of the communication of the person who has difficulties in living. Acknowledging the communication will provide the person some measure of gratification in the transaction. Beyond that we can only attempt to couch our communication in terms that indicate that we accept the person, even though we do not accept his or her perceptions, patterns of interaction, or specific aspects of his or her behavior.

INDEPENDENCE

A fourth characteristic of interpersonal communication required for intimacy and healthy growth has been discussed by Carl Rogers and R. D. Laing as *independence*. Rogers couches the concept of independence in the question "Can I be secure enough in my own person that I can allow the other person to be?"[20] Rogers is pointing to a concept of interpersonal communication in which both parties interact from attitudes of interpersonal security and communicate in such a way that both are always free to become independent individuals.

The unfortunate fact of most interpersonal interaction is that people do not feel secure enough in themselves to permit other people to be independent. People act as if they were afraid that others might reject relationships with them if the others were independent, free to become themselves. Thus, according to Rogers, *courage* is one of the chief requisites of healthy communication.

It is almost paradoxical that we must allow others to be completely free to be themselves before we can achieve the state of intimacy with them. Yet one of the chief features of the experience of love is the feeling of unity with the beloved without loss of either person's own freedom and identity. In the final chapter we shall discuss the paradox of love more fully. Here, it is sufficient to note that it is only by "letting go" of our holds on others that we permit them to be free to truly love us. Once we let go of others, they are free to choose us or reject us. And to allow others to make the choice of accepting or rejecting us requires the greatest of courage.

The British psychiatrists Laing, Phillipson, and Lee have stated this concept in terms of levels of perspective.[21] They point out that when people are free to act with one another, the content of the communication remains at the level of direct perspectives. Healthy, spontaneous interaction that can lead to the achievement of intimacy between two persons is best characterized by the simple, direct statement "I love you." People who meet the test posed by Rogers are able to communicate at the direct level. They are able to interact, and to be content with the knowledge that the other is able to interact, at the level of simple statements of love.

Laing, Phillipson, and Lee point out, however, that our society today is unfortunately characterized by more convoluted patterns of interaction. They find that perhaps a majority of people are too insecure in themselves to permit others to maintain relationships with them at this

---

20. Carl R. Rogers, *On Becoming a Person* (Boston: Houghton Mifflin, 1961), pp. 52–53.
21. R. D. Laing, H. Phillipson, and A. R. Lee, *Interpersonal Perception: A Theory and a Method of Research* (New York: Springer Publishing Co., 1966; New York: Harper & Row, Perennial Library, 1972), pp. 30–45.

direct, free, and spontaneous level of love. Instead, these authors have observed, people tend to place demands upon each other. People are not satisfied with allowing others simply to love them. They demand that others want to love them. Thus, Jack says he loves Jill; Jill says she loves Jack. But neither is happy that the other person simply loves him or her. Jack wants Jill to want to love him; Jill wants Jack to want to love her. And further, although Jack loves Jill, Jack wants Jill to want Jack to want to love her; and although Jill loves Jack, Jill wants Jack to want Jill to want to love him. Their communication is thus designed not so much to express their natural, spontaneous love for each other, but to bind each other to the love relationship with complex demands of wanting to be wanted by each other. Such communication is self-defeating. For when Jack demands that Jill wants Jack to want to love her, he prevents himself from being able to be spontaneous in his love for her (and vice versa). His communication with Jill thus prevents the very state of intimacy that he seeks. Intimacy can occur only when Jack and Jill permit each other the *independence* to love and to be loved.

Rev. Ronald Sunbye has argued that people who communicate with others by saying, "I need you," are really communicating in a way that denies the other person the freedom and independence that are necessary for love to exist.[22] If you say, "I need you," you are commanding me to love you and thereby denying me the independence necessary for intimacy in our transactions. According to Sunbye, the communication of love must take the form of the statement "I don't need you, but I want you very much." When we communicate with others without the injunctions of need, we allow them the independence to choose to love us (or reject us). It is only when our own communication removes the commands from the love of others that intimacy and love are possible.

Fully satisfying and genuine intimacy is always a two-sided operation, with both parties fully and candidly involved. Unfortunately, most of us can handle intimacy only a small part of the time. Many times we engage instead in certain strategies and games to maintain our ties with others. It is to such strategies and games that we turn our attention in the next chapter.

SUMMARY

Intimacy may be described as the loving collaboration between two people who both understand and feel understood by each other. The achievement of intimacy is one of the basic goals of interpersonal communication.

22. The Reverend Ronald Sunbye was pastor of the First Methodist Church, Lawrence, Kansas, in 1966–67 when he delivered a series of sermons on the nature of love, utilizing this theme.

There are four natural barriers to intimacy. First, once intimacy is achieved, the need for intimacy becomes satisfied and the tensions that give rise to the interpersonal situation tend to become resolved. Second, intimacy is highly regulated by social rules that dictate the appropriateness of intimacy. The third barrier to intimacy is defensiveness—the tendency of the self to protect itself from perceived threat or change by others. (Six categories of defensive and supportive climates either inhibit or facilitate intimacy.) Fourth, for some people their inability to handle intimacy is a major barrier to its establishment.

Communication that facilitates intimacy is characterized by acknowledgment, disclosure of experience, confirmation of the other, and independence.

QUESTIONS FOR REVIEW

1. What is intimacy? Why is it a goal of interpersonal communication?
2. What are the natural barriers to intimacy?
3. What are the six defensive climates? Contrast them with the six supportive climates.
4. What is the difference between acknowledging the communication of another person and confirming the content of the communication of another person?
5. Why is disclosure of experience important in interpersonal communication transactions?

EXPLORATIONS

1. Carefully observe your own behavior for an hour. Note the number of times your communication becomes defensive. Then write down the specific statements that evoked defensiveness in you; next write down your own defensive statements. Why were you defensive? Was the defensiveness appropriate? Would a more nondefensive response have been better?
2. Identify one or two specific transactions in which defensive behavior has caused problems. In thinking about that situation, identify how defensive behavior was elicited. How could a supportive climate have prevented the defensiveness? When should defensive behavior not be replaced?
3. Take a specific transaction in which there has been conflict or intimacy. Begin four statements that indicate your feelings about the situation, e.g., "I am happy . . ." or "I am angry . . ." After each statement, try to fill in the specific aspect of the transaction that evoked

the feelings you have listed. For example, "I am happy because you said you liked me." Or "I am angry that you were late for our dinner engagement." Be as specific as you can in analyzing the source of your feelings.

4. Stand face to face with a companion, holding your hands in front of you. Looking eye to eye, begin to mirror each other's movements. Start slowly and keep a continuous motion with the hands. Let the leadership in the situation move back and forth freely. You will soon discover that neither person seems to be leading or following but that the behavior is simply "occurring." Discuss your reactions to the exercise with your companion. In what way was intimacy achieved in this situation?

5. Listen to a five-minute dialogue between two friends. Note the nature of their responses to each other within the transaction. How often did each person acknowledge the communication of the other? How often did each confirm the other? How often did each reject the other? How often did each disconfirm the other?

FOR FURTHER READING

Ginott, Haim G. *Between Parent and Teenager.* New York: Macmillan Co., 1969.

Although presenting a highly diluted theoretical understanding of interpersonal transactions, Ginott's book is nevertheless an excellent collection of transactions, situations, and incidents that are useful for analyzing and understanding interpersonal communication.

Lederer, William J., and Jackson, Don D. *The Mirages of Marriage.* New York: W. W. Norton & Co., 1968.

This excellent book is an analysis of both American marriage and the marital relationship. The authors first present and analyze some of the misconceptions about marriage. Second, they analyze the anatomy of a marriage and some very common destructive elements. Finally, they present ways of evaluating a marriage and offer some ideas about how to make a marriage work.

Rogers, Carl R. *Client-centered Therapy.* Boston: Houghton Mifflin Co., 1951.

An early work by Rogers, this collection of essays describes the client-centered, nondirective technique for dealing with interpersonal relationships in both the clinical and the classroom settings. The essays describe the client-centered technique in dyads, small groups, and classroom groups and present analyses of recorded sessions.

Rogers, Carl R. *On Becoming a Person.* Boston: Houghton Mifflin Co., 1961.

This book is an outstanding collection of talks and essays by the eminent psychologist. The essays "This Is Me" and "Characteristics of a Helping Relationship" have been widely quoted and reprinted. The entire book is recommended for persons interested in learning more about the Rogerian view of interpersonal processes.

Satir, Virginia. *Peoplemaking.* Palo Alto, Calif : Science and Behavior Books, 1972.

This book is about family communication, based on Satir's notions of self-worth, systems, and rules. Satir very clearly and simply presents the theory of the family as a system. She also presents specific exercises designed to improve the quality of family living.

Chapter II

Pseudo-Intimacy: Strategies and Games

While intimacy is sought by all people as a goal of interpersonal communication, there are barriers to achieving intimacy with others. In some cases intimacy is inappropriate because of the social constraints. In other cases, a person cannot overcome his or her defensiveness to permit intimacy to occur. In still other cases, patterns of interaction have become disturbed to the extent that people are simply incapable of handling intense or prolonged states of intimacy. These difficulties in integrating interpersonal situations are reflected in patterns of interpersonal communication designed to provide for the defense of the self by achieving substitutes for intimacy. These patterns of behavior may be called interpersonal *strategies*. Complex and highly structured interpersonal strategies are called *games*.

INCONGRUENCY AND THE PRINCIPLE OF DENIAL

Strategies arise from incongruency within the interpersonal communication transaction. Earlier we discussed the axiom that difficulties in communication may always be traced to incongruency within interpersonal transactions. Incongruency may arise at any number of levels. It may arise between the content and the metacommunicative levels of the message. It may arise between different message systems; there may be a discrepancy between language and gesture, between gesture and space, between language and space, or between sex role and gesture, etc. There may be incongruency between the perspectives, which gives rise to certain kinds of behavior. Or the incongruency may arise from a complex interaction of all of these factors—multiple message systems, multiple levels of meaning, multiple perspectives.

The importance of incongruency between any two or more elements of the interpersonal communication model can best be understood by referring back to another axiom: in an interpersonal communication transaction one cannot not communicate. *When incongruency exists between two or more elements of the interpersonal communication transaction, multiple and contradictory meanings are generated. The person communicating thus has the opportunity to deny the validity of one or more meanings while continuing to communicate.*

The following situation illustrates this *principle of denial.* Suppose Mary says, "I love you very much," while pushing Ken away from her. There is an incongruency between two elements of the transaction,[1] specifically between two message systems. The language system is generating a meaning that is contradictory or incongruent with that of the gestural system. This incongruency permits the person communicating to deny one of the meanings when confronted with the contradiction.[2] If Ken confronts Mary by saying, "Look, Mary, you don't love me because you pushed me away," Mary can say, "But I do love you. I said that I love you, didn't I?"

It is important to recognize the significance of denial of meaning in interpersonal relationships. There has been a distressing tendency in communication literature (and psychiatric literature) to oversimplify obviously complex interpersonal processes. In doing so, many authors analyze communication as if there had to be a single motive to any act. We naively tend to think that we either love someone or hate someone. Even scientists often tend to get caught up in the fallacy of the "either/or." In truth, interpersonal relationships seem to be motivated by the principle of "both/and." Mary can both love Ken and hate Ken, and she can communicate both of these feelings simultaneously. It is fallacious for the scientific observer to point to only one of the meanings generated in the transaction and say that it is the "real" meaning or motive for communication behavior. Both are significant and meaningful, and both are "real" messages.

While a person may be motivated by multiple or ambivalent feelings toward another person, the existence of incongruency between the elements of the transaction permits the communicator to use the incongruency to move toward intimacy while denying doing so, or to vent

---

1. Virginia Satir, *Conjoint Family Therapy: A Guide to Theory and Technique,* rev. ed. (Palo Alto, Calif.: Science and Behavior Books, 1967), pp. 82–84. The example of Mary and Ken is adapted from this source.

2. Ibid., pp. 86–88. It is impossible, however, for the schizophrenic or anyone else to deny successfully that he or she is communicating, as pointed out by Paul Watzlawick, Janet Helmick Beavin, and Don D. Jackson, *Pragmatics of Human Communication: A Study of Interactional Patterns, Pathologies, and Paradoxes* (New York: W. W. Norton & Co., 1967), pp. 50–51, 72–74.

aggression while denying doing so. When Mary is confronted with the discrepancy between her two message systems, she can deny either of the two meanings. She can point to the other message system as conveying the "real" meaning. Such an attempt to deny meaning is possibly the most often used technique for establishing pseudo-intimacy (a substitute for intimacy which defends the self from anxiety while permitting interaction).

Strategic behavior is communication that uses incongruency to deny one or more meanings generated within a particular transaction. In dealing with the concept of strategic behavior in interpersonal communication, it should become clear why it is necessary to develop the complex model and postulate the eight axioms discussed in part 1. It is only when we have an understanding of all the elements of the communication transaction, and of the principles that define the interrelationships between those elements, that it is possible to analyze how people use these elements in strategic interaction. And it is only after we can identify the sources of strategic behavior that we can begin to work to eliminate unnecessary or undesirable incongruencies from our own communication and the communication of others.

STRATEGIES

THE TANGENTIAL RESPONSE

The most common form of strategic behavior in interpersonal communication transactions may be called the *tangential response.*[3] The tangential response is a strategy that permits a person to continue to communicate while refusing to acknowledge the content of the other person's communication. We saw an example of the tangential response in our discussion of acknowledgment. In the example, a girl comes running to show her mother a toad. "Mommy, mommy! Look what I found in the garden!" The mother responds, "Christy, go wash your hands immediately."

In this transaction the mother fails to acknowledge the content of her daughter's communication. Yet, if confronted with the incongruency in her response to the child, the mother would probably deny that she was failing to acknowledge her daughter's communication by pointing to the fact that she did speak to the child. The incongruency, of course, permits the mother to deny parts of her own communication. While the tangential response is the most frequent strategic pattern in inter-

3. Jurgen Ruesch, *Disturbed Communication: The Clinical Assessment of Normal and Pathological Communicative Behavior* (New York: W. W. Norton & Co., 1957; reprint ed., 1972), pp. 54–56, 84–85. See also Jurgen Ruesch, "The Tangential Response," in *Psychopathology of Communication,* ed. P. H. Hoch and J. Zubin (New York: Grune & Stratton, 1958), pp. 37–48.

personal transactions, its effect can be damaging to personal growth and injurious to healthy interaction.

You might want to undertake a short exercise in cataloging tangential responses. Take any fifteen-minute segment of conversation between two people—such as a husband and wife, two close friends, or two people at the office. Listen carefully to their interaction and note each time there is a tangential response. It is important to listen carefully for tangential responses, for they occur so innocuously that it is easy to become oblivious to them. Look at the following conversation between a husband and wife one morning at the breakfast table.

> Husband: *Is the coffee ready? I don't have much time this morning. Gotta catch the eight o'clock bus uptown.*
>
> Wife: *Here's the paper if you want it.*
>
> Husband: *They're predicting rain today.*
>
> Wife: *I won't be here this afternoon. I've got to go over to Harvey's and look for a sweater or something for tonight.*
>
> Husband: *I hope it doesn't rain until I get back. I hate having to walk from building to building in bad weather.*
>
> Wife: *I think I'll look for something in brown to complete my brown outfit. I already have something I can wear in black.*

Notice that the two people are engaged in a face-to-face conversation in which neither person appears to be acknowledging the communication of the other. Each is continuing to conduct his or her own conversation. Each response is tangential to the other person's statement. Yet if either person complained to the other that "We never talk to each other," the result would probably be a very strong denial. "Why, we talked to each other at breakfast this morning. What do you mean we never talk to each other?"

In the conversation between the husband and the wife, each person fails to acknowledge the content of the other's communication. There is a variation of this kind of conversation in which one party seems not even to acknowledge the other person's ability to respond. Such conversations often take this form:

> Husband: *Where are you going today? You said you were going over to Harvey's?*
>
> Wife: *Mmm. Well, I thought I might drive . . .*
>
> Husband: *(Talking over wife's response)* *It's probably going to rain today so be careful . . .*
>
> Wife: *. . . and stop and pick up Helen if she wants to go with me.*

Husband: . . . *not to leave the windows open in the den when you go out.*

To the observer of this transaction, not only are two different conversations going on, but neither party seems to be acknowledging that the other is talking. Not only is there a failure to acknowledge the content of each other's communication; the timing of the remarks indicates a refusal by both parties to acknowledge each other gesturally.

Tangential responses do provide the person who uses them with some communication benefits. The person making the tangential response may feel that the interpersonal transaction has been sufficiently integrated to give him or her some gratification from the interaction. Also, the tangential response does not permit the other person to make a direct response (without actually confronting the person with metacommunication about the tangential nature of the original message, i.e., "What you said was beside the point and did not acknowledge the content of my statements"). Thus, the user of the tangential response may feel that it is a defense of self, which reduces the chances of anxiety entering into the relationship and minimizes the chances of genuine intimacy developing. For some people these substitute forms of gratification may satisfy the need for intimacy. In this sense the tangential response is neither healthy nor unhealthy, but is one of many techniques avaliable for integrating transactions with a minimum opportunity for developing intimacy. Tangential responses are quite common in everyday conversation and are not always unhealthy. Prolonged or excessive reliance on tangential responses, however, would be classified as disturbed communication and would most certainly be indicative of severe difficulties in living.

REJECTION OF THE OTHER

While the tangential response ignores the content and the perceptions communicated in the other person's message, the strategy of *rejection of the other* acknowledges the content of the message but rejects the other's perceptions of the content and/or of the self.[4] In everyday language we might refer to this strategy as the "put-down," but it is a put-down of a particular type.

Let's look at a couple of examples of the strategy of rejection of the other to clarify its characteristics.

Terry has been trying to lose weight and has been very conscious of his body in recent weeks. Happy that he's made some

---

4. See Jurgen Ruesch, *Therapeutic Communication* (New York: W. W. Norton & Co., 1961; reprint ed., 1973), pp. 160–61; and Watzlawick, Beavin, and Jackson, *Pragmatics of Human Communication,* p. 85.

progress, he comes into his room and says to his roommate:

Terry: *I did it! I managed to lose five pounds this week.*
Roommate: *How do you know?*
Terry: *I weighed on the scales in the john.*
Roommate: *Oh, they're probably off by at least five pounds.*

Rhonda has been waiting for several days to see if Jimmie would ask her to the junior-senior prom. When Jimmie finally does ask her, she says to her mother:

Rhonda: *Mom, I'm so excited. I have a date to the prom. Oh, I can wear that white dress now.*
Mother: *Who asked you?*
Rhonda: *Jimmie!*
Mother: *Well, he probably couldn't find anyone else to go with.*

It is difficult to illustrate rejection with printed examples because so much of the essence of rejection lies in verbalized expressions, turns of phrases, accents on particular words, and vocal nuances. It is important to read the above examples out loud, giving the punch lines great care. For the incongruency is between the denotative level and the metacommunication level of the message. If we look strictly at the denotative level as printed here, the responses appear to be plainly and deliberately vicious. Yet if we articulate the lines with the proper amount of lightness and sarcasm, they might readily be passed off as a kind of put-down joke and might be responded to as such by both parties in the transaction.

Even though most examples of rejection of the other take the form of the put-down joke and are usually articulated in a sarcastic or humorous way, the effects of rejection are not humorous. First of all, rejection of the other is a strategy that permits one person to make a statement about another person that can be denied. If Terry turns to his roommate and says, "Why are you being so vicious? Don't you like me?", the roommate can deny the literal content of his message by saying, "Why are you so touchy? Can't you take a joke anymore?"

Second, the strategy of rejection permits the "sender" to place a psychological distance between himself or herself and the "receiver" of the message. Rejection of the other reduces the possibilities of establishing and maintaining an intimate relationship. In this sense, rejection of the other serves as a defense of the self of the "sender."

Third, it is important to examine the consequences of rejection on the person being rejected. In some cases the recipient of a rejecting message may ignore the literal content of the message and attend only to the metacommunication. The recipient's response might be "It was a joke." In other cases, however, the recipient of a rejecting message may be left wondering how much of the rejection was for the sake of humor and how much was really meant as rejection of his or her perceptions and self-image. Repeated encounters with rejection by others may lead to withdrawal from those relationships. The effects of ridicule, a form of rejection, have been well documented; continual encounters with ridicule lead to difficulties in living for an individual. For example, a teenage boy who encounters rejection of self-image every time he attempts to discuss his dating activities with his parents may perceive the parents' strategic communication as disapproval of his dating or as an evaluation of him as sexually undesirable. As a result, he may withdraw from dating.

Again, while rejection of others is not a desirable communication behavior and as a strategy may create difficulties in living for others, it may be an acceptable way for a person to handle the defense of self. For example, a parent may be unable to cope with his or her own anxiety about a teenager's developing sexuality. Strategic communication involving rejection of the other may be the parent's way of coping with his or her own difficulties in living. And while it may not be the best or the healthiest way of interacting, it may be better than no interaction; it may be the result of a desperate attempt by the parent to avoid loneliness. The parent may choose to treat the teenager's sexual life with the humorous put-down (the literal put-down can be denied) and thus face some anxiety in dealing with the subject rather than face the loneliness of having no communication with the teenager.

ONE-UP

Another common form of strategic communication may be called one-up. In this strategy, one communicator attempts to establish and maintain a complementary relationship in which he or she is in the one-up position in situations that do not appropriately call for complementary relationships.[5] The move to the one-up position is made ostensibly on the basis of some disagreement over the content of the transaction; the disagreement over content, however, serves primarily as a vehicle for expressing disagreement or frustration about the relationship through metacommunication. The incongruency in the one-up strategy usually lies between the content and the relational levels of meaning. We have all heard couples engage in the one-up form of interaction. In the following example, a husband and wife are telling a friend about their

5. For a discussion of complementary (and symmetrical) interaction, see Watzlawick, Beavin, and Jackson, *Pragmatics of Human Communication*, pp. 67–70.

recent trip. The husband is trying to describe their experience of getting a flat tire.

> Husband: *Well, we had just gone through this town, Rockville, and we were about . . .*
>
> Wife: *(talking over the husband) Rockland.*
>
> Husband: *. . . five miles out in the country . . . No, it was Rockville.*
>
> Wife: *Rockland. Rockville is in Maryland; we were in Wyoming.*
>
> Husband: *I know we were in Wyoming. We were going to visit your aunt near Jackson.*
>
> Wife: *She lives closer to Wind River Canyon.*

In this transaction the wife makes a series of "corrections" of the husband's story. If confronted with her behavior, she may deny that she is attempting to assert a dominant position over her husband. After all, he is simply incorrect in the content he is communicating. To observers of this transaction, however, it is clear that the interaction between the husband and wife involves far more than disagreement on the content of the discussion. They are, in fact, in disagreement over the nature of their relationship; and they are communicating their disagreement to each other through a strategy, which will permit them to interact without having to confront directly the fact of or the nature of their relational disagreements.

Abandoning the one-up strategy may lead to conditions that promote intimacy and authentic interaction. Suppose that the same couple stopped to examine what they were communicating.

> Husband: *Look, we are digressing. We're not really telling Jim about our trip. We are disagreeing between ourselves. I don't mind that I might be wrong about some of the details and that you are probably right. But I mind that you are continually correcting me.*
>
> Wife: *Maybe I am. . . . I guess that when you start telling a story I get to feeling that I'm left out.*

Such interaction requires a greater level of acknowledgment, disclosure, and confirmation of the other than the strategic interaction of one-up. When two people are openly and honestly confronting each other with their experiences of the relationship, the spontaneous experience of intimacy is more likely to occur. The one-up strategy, through its incongruency and possibilities of denial of communication, permits the two people to interact with each other pseudo-intimately.

VERBALIZERS

Verbalizers are more complex forms of strategic communication that involve various combinations of tangential responses, rejection of the other, and one-up patterns of behavior. Stuart Palmer identifies and describes four distinct kinds of verbalizers: arguing, complaining, gossiping, and disquieting.[6]

Arguing. One of the most common types of verbalizers is perpetually arguing. No matter what people say, the arguer will find some way to take exception. If someone says, "Isn't it a beautiful day?" he may respond, "Oh, I don't know. It's so boring having warm weather in November. It's time we had some snow." Or if someone says, "Don't you love the snow we had last night?" he may respond, "It was O.K. but not as pretty as we had two years ago. Now that was a beautiful snow." (And so on . . .)

Complaining. The complainer refuses to take direct exception in the form of creating an argument. Rather, the strategy of the complainer is to contradict the other person's statements by issuing a complaint. The recipient of the complaint will tend to react by giving sympathy to the complainer, trying to rectify the perceived wrong, or otherwise assuaging the complainer. All these efforts are useless because the complainer will complain about the efforts to correct the situation!

Gossiping. The perpetual gossip is engaging in strategic behavior designed to maintain interaction with another person while keeping that person at a distance. The gossip provides a ready "in" with the other person, but at the same time, the act of gossiping permits the gossiper to avoid the possibilities of intimacy emerging within the relationship.

Palmer has pointed out that the arguer, the gossip, and the complainer are all engaging in patterns of interaction that permit the person to vent aggression while evoking approval. Aggression may be seen as a pseudo-intimate behavior which may be a prelude to intimate behavior. The denial of aggression while venting aggression is really another form of the paradigm of moving toward intimacy—or a substitute for intimacy—while denying making such a move. By verbalizing, a person can engage in aggressive interaction in socially acceptable forms, thus establishing an approved form of interaction and gaining a pseudo-intimate relationship while being able to deny the very act that brings about the relationship, e.g., arguing.

Disquieting. The disquieter is engaged in a slightly different form of interaction. Rather than seeking to gain approval for his actions, the disquieter is seeking to vent aggression while avoiding disapproval. The

6. Stuart Palmer, "Verbalizers," in *Understanding Other People* (New York: Thomas Y. Crowell Co., 1955), reprinted in *Basic Readings in Interpersonal Communication*, ed. Kim Giffin and Bobby R. Patton (New York: Harper & Row, 1971), pp. 200–213.

Gossiping is a strategy that allows people to vent aggression in a socially acceptable form.

disquieter is the person who makes you feel guilty for something you didn't do. For example, Karen and John are talking at the table when Joe approaches them.

> Joe: *Hi, John. Hello, Karen. Listen, I need to talk to you for a few minutes about the booth we're supposed to set up for homecoming. Got a minute?*
>
> John: *Sure, sit down. We were just having a coke.*
>
> Joe: *Oh, I'm sorry. I'll see you some other time. I didn't realize that you were busy.*
>
> John: *We're not busy. We were just sitting here talking.*
>
> Joe: *No, I can't interrupt your conversation. I'll see you sometime when you are not so busy or so tied up with personal affairs.* (He gets up and leaves.)

Incongruency in Verbalizers. Each of the verbalizers is a strategic communication pattern that operates on one or more incongruencies between various elements of the transaction. Each verbalizer provides the person the opportunity to deny that he or she is engaging in the behavior by pointing to the opposite or incongruent element within the message. A person who is arguing with everything another person is saying may strenuously deny that he or she is arguing—creating the paradox of the arguer who is arguing that he or she is not arguing!

We should emphasize that changing the verbalizer patterns requires *both* parties in the transaction to step back and look at their communication. It is not sufficient for one person to point out the behavior to the other. Verbalizers are a transactional phenomenon; they can be effectively overcome only when both parties *agree to communicate about their communication patterns.* We can illustrate this necessity for collaboration with two brief excerpts of dialogue which are typical of the arguing form of the verbalizer.

> Husband: *When did we go to the Thompson's? It was the twenty-eighth, wasn't it?*
>
> Wife: *No, the twenty-seventh. Margo was in town on the twenty-eighth.*
>
> Husband: *But I know it was the twenty-eighth because I just got back from my trip and was in no mood for company. You always seem to be inviting people in or making commitments for us to go out when you know I'll be tired from my trips. Why do you always do things like that?*
>
> Wife: *I don't always do that.*
>
> Husband: *Well, look at it. We had to go to the Thompsons when I got back from New York. Then before that, we had company the day I flew back from Chicago. Who was it, the Johnsons, wasn't it? And when I came back from Philadelphia, it was the Martins.*
>
> Wife: *You invited the Johnsons, remember?*
>
> Husband: *It doesn't make any difference. The point is still the same. You always make commitments when I'm gone.*
>
> Wife: *Why are you arguing with me? You seem very intent on picking an argument today, and I'm not going to let you do it.*

At this point the wife has stepped out of the transaction and has moved to communicate with the husband about their communication itself. If the husband does not agree to collaborate with her, the spiral of arguing may continue.

> Husband: *I'm not arguing. I'm merely pointing out the facts.*
>
> Wife: *But they are not facts. You invited the Johnsons, yet you*

> *seem intent on blaming me for their being here. I didn't do it. That's what I'm telling you.*

> Husband: *You invited the Martins and you made the date with the Thompsons. What do you mean you aren't responsible?*

Instead the husband may join the wife in moving their interaction to a level where they may talk about the incongruencies in their communication. If both parties are able to do this, some level of intimacy may be established and more spontaneous communication may be possible.

> Husband: *I do seem to be arguing with you, don't I?*

> Wife: *Why are you so aggressive toward me today?*

> Husband: *I don't really know. I guess that I just feel that we have not had much time together lately. It would be so nice if we could just have some time alone, to ourselves. Wouldn't it?*

PRAGMATIC PARADOXES AND DOUBLE BINDS

The most complex form of strategic communication is the *pragmatic paradox*.[7] A paradox is a particular form of contradiction arising from incongruency between two or more elements within the transaction. The term *pragmatic* refers to the peculiarly behavioral nature of the paradox, specifically that the message must be denied in order to be implemented, or must be implemented in order to be denied. We may illustrate three variations of the pragmatic paradox by looking at the following situation. Suppose a professor made the following remarks in a large lecture class of 200 people.

> Some of you want to know something about me after being in here for so many days this semester. So let me tell you something about myself. First of all, whenever I talk about myself, I lie. Second, I am very sensitive about losing my hair and going bald, so I never discuss it in public. Third, I am very sensitive in my interactions with people but not with students.

The first paradox, "whenever I talk about myself, I lie," is a logical paradox. The verbal message contradicts itself so that the truth or falsity of the message cannot be logically determined. There are a number of such paradoxes in everyday interpersonal communication, especially

---

7. The concept of pragmatic paradoxes has been discussed extensively by Watzlawick, Beavin, and Jackson, *Pragmatics of Human Communication*, pp. 190, 194–229. See also Jay Haley, *Strategies of Psychotherapy* (New York: Grune & Stratton, 1963); Don D. Jackson, "Interactional Psychotherapy," in *Contemporary Psychotherapies*, ed. Morris I. Stein (Glencoe, Ill.: Free Press, 1962), pp. 256–71; and Paul Watzlawick, "A Review of the Double Bind Theory," *Family Process* 2 (1963): 132–53, reprinted in *Communication, Family, and Marriage: Human Communication*, vol. 1, ed. Don D. Jackson (Palo Alto, Calif.: Science and Behavior Books, 1968), pp. 63–86.

when we examine the incongruencies between multiple message systems. If a person is proclaiming love while pushing the other person away, the message says something about itself that is contradictory with the supposed content of the message. Such behaviors follow the structure of the paradox presented in the first statement.

Other pragmatic paradoxes follow the structure of the second statement, "I am very sensitive about losing my hair . . . so I never discuss it in public." The professor is affirming that he does not do something while he is in fact doing it. The setting and the content of the message contradict each other so that we have to deny either the validity of the message or the validity of the setting in which the message is being generated. Given the message and its context we cannot determine which aspect of the transaction should be attended to and which aspect should be ignored. The person attempting to respond to the entire message must deny the message in order to respond to it.

The third pragmatic paradox arises from incongruency between perspectives. When the professor says, "I am sensitive in my interactions with people but not with students," he violates the perceptions of the recipients of his message, if they are students. The student attending to this message must either deny his or her perceptions of self as a person or deny his or her perceptions of self as a student in order to respond to the message as it was created. From the student's perspectives, the parts of the message cannot be responded to because they contradict each other in such a way that the entire message must be affirmed in order to be denied, or denied in order to be affirmed. The student attending to the message may experience a great sense of frustration, for no appropriate response is possible within the framework of the message as created by the professor. The student must step outside of the framework of the professor's message and comment on the message itself in order to act. Such metacommunication, however, is not always possible in interpersonal relationships.

Paradoxical Injunctions. Many of the difficulties in living that people encounter arise from patterns of interaction known as the *paradoxical injunction.*[8] The paradoxical injunction, which is a particular instance of the pragmatic paradox, arises from the command aspect of a message. In the paradoxical injunction the content or the metacommunication of the message forms a command to engage in certain kinds of behavior that cannot be fulfilled without at the same time denying the command.

One class of paradoxical injunctions takes the form of the command "Be spontaneous!" Now if someone commands you to be spontaneous,

---

8. Watzlawick, Beavin, and Jackson, *Pragmatics of Human Communication*, pp. 194–95; and Viktor E. Frankl, "Paradoxical Intention," *American Journal of Psychotherapy* 14 (1960): 520–35.

there is nothing you can do in response to the command that would, in fact, be spontaneous. For any behavior that you perform in response to the command would be *commanded* behavior and would not, therefore, be *spontaneous*. Any attempt to fulfill the command violates the command.

The "Be spontaneous" paradoxes would be humorous (and are often the basis of comedy in the theatre) if they were not so integral to so many severe problems in communication between husbands and wives, parents and children, lovers, and longtime friends. In these close relationships, the "Be spontaneous" paradox often takes the specific form of the command "Love me." Now, love is a state of intimacy that can only be achieved spontaneously. Love can only be freely given; it cannot be commanded. Thus the command "Love me" is self-defeating for the person making the command, and it is impossible to fulfill for the person of whom it is commanded. Other times the paradoxical injunction takes the form of the command "You ought to love me (look what I've done for you)." Again, there can be no "ought" dimension to love. Binding the other person to you through such injunctions denies that person the freedom to love spontaneously.

Students moving away from home for the first time often encounter another form of the "Be spontaneous" paradox in the form of the injunction "Be independent." Without being aware of the way they are communicating, some parents appear to command their children to be independent of them. Often the student's efforts to assert himself or herself result in parental cries that the student is rejecting the parents, home, or parental value systems. "Look at you. Why do you have that mustache? You're just trying to be like all the other weirdos at school. Why can't you be independent and be neat and cleanshaven like your father?"

Probably one of the most deadly forms of the paradoxical injunction in terms of stifling personal growth takes the form of "I know what's best for you." This form of interaction is probably most frequently found in relationships in which there is a serious dependency, such as between parent and child, between adult and an elderly or incapacitated parent, between an adult and a person who is bedridden, ailing, or otherwise dependent upon the first for basic needs.

> Jane's mother, Ruth, is now sixty-seven years old. Ruth has always lived a very independent life, caring for herself and maintaining her own apartment after the death of her husband five years ago. Ruth recently fell and injured her hip and leg but is determined to maintain her own lifestyle. Jane, however, now sees her mother as reduced to a state of dependency. Since Jane must look after her mother (get her groceries, check on her three

or four times a day, help her with her laundry, make up her bed for her), Jane sees any independence by the mother as an attempt to be troublesome—an "acting out" that we must just come to expect of old people. Jane's attitude is "If I have to look after you, I know what is best for you. If you knew what was best for you, you wouldn't be in this position now, would you?"

It is fairly easy to find real-life patterns of interaction that are similar to the situation between Jane and her mother. Jane's attitude is manifest in almost every sentence and gesture she generates in transactions with her mother. Ruth is caught in the paradoxical situation in which she must strive to accommodate herself to her daughter, for she is grateful that Jane is helping her. But at the same time, Ruth must manifest her own independence if she is to remain a healthy human being. She finds herself caught in the paradoxical injunction set up by Jane. If only Jane knows what is good for Ruth, then Ruth cannot act on her own without violating Jane's perceptions of the situation. Yet without asserting herself, Ruth will remain an invalid. Must she remain an invalid in order to get over her state of invalidism? That is, unfortunately, the structure of many of the communication transactions between people and their elderly parents in our society today.

Double Binds. The double bind is a special case of the pragmatic paradox or the paradoxical injunction.[9] A *double bind* is a pragmatic paradox in which the relationship between the two persons in the transaction is such that neither party can leave the relationship or communicate about the communication that is creating the paradox.

We are reminded of the double bind in which Alice finds herself when she is being brainwashed by the Red and the White Queens.

> "She's all right again now," said the Red Queen. "Do you know languages? What's the French for fiddle-de-dee?"
>
> "Fiddle-de-dee's not English," Alice replied gravely.
>
> "Whoever said it was?" said the Red Queen.
>
> *Alice thought she saw a way out of the difficulty,* this time. "If you tell me what language 'fiddle-de-dee is,' I'll tell you the French for it!" she exclaimed triumphantly.
>
> But the Red Queen drew herself up rather stiffly and said, *"Queens never make bargains."*[10] (Italics ours.)

9. Watzlawick, Beavin, and Jackson, *Pragmatics of Human Communication*, pp. 211–19; Gregory Bateson et al., "Toward a Theory of Schizophrenia," *Behavioral Science* 1 (October 1956): 251–64, reprinted in Jackson, *Communication, Family, and Marriage*, pp. 31–54.

10. Lewis Carroll, *Through the Looking Glass*, as quoted in Watzlawick, Beavin, and Jackson, *Pragmatics of Human Communication*, p. 197. The analysis is based on the latter source.

In this illustration, Alice finds herself in a paradox and attempts to bracket the situation in such a way that she may comment on the paradox created by the Queen's question. This way out is abruptly terminated, however, by the Red Queen's refusal to discuss the nature of the communication itself. "Queens never make bargains." Alice is then in a double bind because she is faced with a paradox about which she is prevented from commenting.

It is uncanny sometimes how much the Wonderland world of Alice approximates the real-life world in which we live. Even when we may be aware that we are in a paradoxical bind in our interpersonal transactions, it is not always possible for us to discuss the binds with those who share them. We just may find ourselves communicating with real-life Red Queens who refuse to make bargains. We must stress once again that it takes two people to resolve any strategic interaction. Both must be willing to step outside of the transaction and examine what is happening from each other's perspectives.

HEALTHY USES OF STRATEGIC COMMUNICATION

Our discussion of strategic communication has emphasized those patterns of interaction that increase defensiveness, produce pseudo-intimacy, and/or are associated with disturbances in communication or difficulties in living with others. We must emphasize, however, that no value judgment should be placed on these strategic patterns of interaction. Strategic communication may be healthy as well as destructive in interpersonal relations. If we are seen as having stressed the unhealthy manifestations of strategic communication too greatly, it is because the authors find it important to observe and correct disturbances in communication whenever possible. We are equally concerned, however, with the identification and use of strategic communication in healthy interpersonal relationships.

There is sometimes a very fine line between the healthy use of strategic communication and disturbed communication. Most forms of humor are based in the tangential response, the rejection of the other, the rejection of the self, the one-up, or some form of the pragmatic paradox. Humor is, of course, essential to healthy communication. The most successful interpersonal communicators have mastered the healthy use of the put-down and the self-deprecating remark to generate laughter and to facilitate the integration of transactions. But where does the put-down or the self-deprecating remark cease to be for fun and begin to reflect the underlying experience of the participants in the transaction?

The answer probably lies very close to the psychoanalytic view of interpersonal communication. In Freud's view, there is no such thing as accidental communication. Even the slip of the tongue and the joke reflect the reality of the experience of the communicants within the transaction. Humor arises from the same incongruency that produces defensiveness. In some senses, humor is always a form of defensiveness —a form of pseudo-intimacy that facilitates interaction but ultimately blocks the movement to states of genuine intimacy. Also, humor is always grounded in the principle of denial. The wisecrack, the sarcastic remark, the put-down of the self or another says one thing on the content level but denies itself on the metacommunication levels. We use humor in interpersonal transactions because humor permits us to communicate things about ourselves, about others, and about our relationships with others that we could not communicate if we could not invoke the principle of denial.

In the previous chapter we stressed that for intimacy to occur, it is necessary that both parties in a transaction be able to cope with the situation. Some people, we pointed out, simply cannot handle intimacy; it overpowers them and reduces their ability to function adequately or appropriately. Thus, we must always make some judgment about the ability of other persons to handle authentic, intimate relationships.

Some of the most successful interpersonal communicators regularly and consciously use strategic communication to help integrate transactions when they see that more spontaneous interaction is not possible. Bill, for example, is a youth counselor at his church. For several years he has been actively engaged in mental health work with both adults and young people. Students are particularly attracted to Bill and find it very easy to communicate with him. When they have problems, they inevitably gravitate toward Bill. Yet Bill uses many forms of strategic communication with the students who come to talk with him. It is easy to find him making a tangential response, rejecting the other, becoming an arguer, or creating various forms of pragmatic paradoxes.

Bill has learned that people who have problems need to preserve some of their defensiveness in order to feel secure in their self-concepts while trying to work out their problems by talking with Bill. He does not try to strip people of these defenses. Rather, Bill uses strategic communication to create specific forms of defensive interaction with such people—to create pseudo-intimacies which serve a purpose until more spontaneous forms of communication are possible.

Marilyn is a teacher who often works with T-groups or sensitivity training groups in her community. Working with people in these settings, Marilyn often uses strategic patterns of communication to produce pseudo-intimate relationships. Such relationships permit people to disclose aspects of the self that they might not reveal in situations in which such disclosure would require intimacy. Marilyn's communication permits other people to maintain their defenses while interacting with her. Marilyn and another person may readily achieve pseudo-intimacy in their transactions, which permits both people to function at a healthy level of interaction. In such cases, strategic communication is a healthy substitute for intimacy.

GAMES

The concept of games in interpersonal communication is important enough that a rather substantial amount of literature has been devoted to the explanation and analysis of games. Eric Berne was one of the major founders of Transactional Analysis, which is concerned with games analysis as a therapeutic technique. Berne's book *Games People Play* was a best-seller for several years.[11] Thomas Harris, a student of Berne, wrote *I'm O.K.—You're O.K.*, which also topped the best-seller list.[12] The basic idea of interpersonal games, then, has already become an integral part of the popular culture and is a concept with which many students may already be somewhat familiar.

According to Berne, games are one way people structure their time between birth and death. Although games are not as growth promoting as intimacy in interpersonal relationships, Berne notes that, because they can serve as substitutes for intimacy, games are "both necessary and desirable." On the other hand, some games may be destructive and may even lead to death. Such destructive games should be minimized or avoided.[13]

Games have five basic characteristics. A game is (1) a highly structured pattern (2) of complementary transactions, (3) with an ulterior motive, (4) leading to a well-defined, dramatic climax known as the payoff, (5) which serves as a substitute for intimacy in interpersonal relations. Let us briefly examine each of the characteristics of games.

The most notable characteristic of games is that they are, indeed, highly structured. Games are readily recognizable by their well-defined patterns of interaction which tend to occur repeatedly so that the relationship between any two given people tends to be characterized by certain games. Two people tend to repeat the same games with each other and to seek other people with whom to play different games.

All games are based on the principle of complementarity, which we introduced in our discussion of punctuation (Axiom VI). A game re-

11. Eric Berne, *Games People Play: The Psychology of Human Relationships* (New York: Grove Press, 1964).
12. Thomas A. Harris, *I'm O.K.—You're O.K.* (New York: Harper & Row, 1967; Old Tappan, N.J.: Fleming H. Revell Co., Spire Books, 1973).
13. See Berne, *Games People Play*, pp. 18–19, for a discussion of structuring time; the necessity and desirability of games is discussed on pp. 48, 171–72; and the five characteristics of games are discussed on p. 48.

quires that one person be one up on the other. Part of the definition of a game is that someone must be "it"; a game requires a victim.[14] If both people are equal—if the transaction is symmetrical—there is no victim. When nobody is "it," the game comes to a standstill.

The following dialogue from *Who's Afraid of Virginia Woolf?* illustrates how a move to establish symmetrical relationships heads off the progress of a game. George and Martha are escalating their one-up strategies into the game "Now I've Got You, You Sonofabitch."[15] (The basic format of NIGYSOB is this: A makes an opening move that appears to be in deference or concession to B, whereupon B uses that move in some dramatic way to "get" A. In other words, A puts himself or herself into a vulnerable position, and B uses that vulnerability to say, "Aha. Now I've got you, you sonofabitch." This dramatic climax of the game is called the *payoff*.) In the play, Martha has just come downstairs. As she enters, George says:

> George: *There you are, my pet.*
>
> Nick: *(Impressed; rising). Well, now. . . .*
>
> George: *Why, Martha . . . your Sunday chapel dress!*
>
> Honey: *(Slightly disapproving). Oh, that's most attractive.*
>
> Martha: *(Showing off). You like it? Good! (To George) What the hell do you mean screaming up the stairs at me like that?*
>
> George: *We got lonely, darling . . . we got lonely for the soft purr of your little voice.*
>
> Martha: *(Deciding not to rise to it.) Oh. Well, then, you just trot over to the barie-poo. . . .*
>
> George: *(Taking the tone from her). . . . and make your little mommy a great big dwink.*[16]

Notice that when George completes Martha's sentence for her, he moves to establish a form of symmetrical relationship, which suspends the game temporarily. A few minutes later, George and Martha pick up the thread of their game, "Now I've Got You, You Sonofabitch." When George agrees to play the game with Martha again, he establishes a complementary relationship by assuming the role of the victim.

> Martha: *George is not preoccupied with* history. . . . *George is preoccupied with the* History Department. *George is preoccupied with the History Department because. . . .*

14. Muriel James and Dorothy Jongeward, *Born to Win: Transactional Analysis with Gestalt Experiments* (Reading, Mass.: Addison-Wesley Publishing Co., 1971), p. 88.

15. Berne, *Games People Play*, pp. 85–87.

16. Edward Albee, *Who's Afraid of Virginia Woolf?* (New York: Atheneum Publishers, 1962; Simon and Shuster, Pocket Books, 1963), act 1, pp. 47–48.

George: . . . *because he is not the History Department, but is only in the History Department. We know, Martha . . . we went all through it while you were upstairs . . . getting up. There's no need to go through it again.*

Martha: *That's right, baby . . . keep it clean. (To the others) George is bogged down in the History Department. He's an old bog in the History Department, that's what George is. A bog. . . . A fen. . . . A G. D. swamp. Ha, ha, ha, HA! A SWAMP! Hey, swamp! Hey SWAMPY!*

George: *(With a great effort controls himself . . . then, as if she had said nothing more than "George, dear" . . . .). Yes, Martha? Can I get you something?*

Martha: *(Amused at his game). Well . . . uh . . . sure, you can light my cigarette, if you're of a mind to.*

George: *(Considers, then moves off). No . . . there are limits. I mean, man can put up with only so much without he descends a rung or two on the old evolutionary ladder . . . (Now a quick aside to Nick) . . . which is up your line . . . (Then back to Martha) . . . sinks, Martha, and it's a funny ladder . . . you can't reverse yourself . . . start back up once you're descending. (Martha blows him an arrogant kiss) Now . . . I'll hold your hand when it's dark and you're afraid of the bogey man, and I'll tote your gin bottles out after midnight, so no one'll see . . . but I will not light your cigarette. And that, as they say, is that. (Brief silence).*

Martha: *(Under her breath). Jesus!*[17]

This time, instead of leveling off, their interaction escalates into a spiral of complementary moves, which suddenly climax in a dramatic payoff.

It Takes Two to Play. Games have ulterior motives. All games are basically dishonest. There is a kind of paradox involved in the dishonest nature of games. While games are ulterior in nature, both parties in a transaction must implicitly agree to play a game. If either party refuses to play by the carefully defined rules, the game cannot progress along the predetermined pattern and the climactic payoff will not be reached. Thus the purpose of the game as a substitute for intimacy is aborted. Berne has pointed out that if one party suddenly refuses to play in the more serious games, the result may be deterioration or even the death of the other partner. In lesser games the result is usually despair or other forms of severe frustration.

17. Ibid., pp. 50–51.

The implicit agreement to play a game can be seen in a typical interaction between two people playing "Why Don't You, Yes But."[18]

> D: *Am I ever hungry. I haven't had a thing to eat all day. Didn't have time for lunch. What do we have in the fridge?*
>
> S: *Oh, I don't know. Lots of things, I guess. (Gets up and opens the door of the refrigerator.) Here's some spareribs left over from Saturday night. I can warm them up for you while you clean up if you want.*
>
> D: *Ugh. Too greasy. No, I don't need indigestion like that tonight.*
>
> S: *Um. Well, if you want something lighter we can cook some eggs. How about an omelet, or scrambled eggs, or eggs and pancakes.*
>
> D: *Pancakes are too messy. I'm not in the mood to clean up the kitchen tonight.*
>
> S: *Well, we can still have eggs. They're not messy.*
>
> D: *I know. They might be all right, but that's really not what I'm hungry for.*
>
> S: *There's some macaroni and cheese. We can heat that.*
>
> D: *Sounds a little heavy. That's messy too. . . . I know. I'm just going to have some pie and ice cream. That will kill my appetite and we can eat later if you get hungry.*

For every helpful suggestion that S makes ("Why don't you . . ."), D has a reason why it won't work ("Yes, but . . ."). Notice that the entire game can be killed before it begins if the two players would exchange something like this:

> D: *Am I ever hungry. I haven't had a thing to eat all day. Didn't have time for lunch. What do we have in the fridge?*
>
> S: *Oh, I don't know. Why don't you find something you like.*

In this transaction, S places the responsibility directly upon D and there is no chance for the series of complementary interactions to emerge. S has refused the invitation to play the game. D will have to make new initiatives if he wants further interaction with S.

Substitutes for Intimacy. Games serve as substitutes for intimacy; they are a complex form of pseudo-intimacy. There are striking similarities between games and intimate behavior. Two people must collaborate as much to produce a successful game as to produce intimacy. Each move in the game may be seen as a stroke, which serves as an extension

---

18. Berne, *Games People Play*, pp. 116–22.

Strategies and games partially fulfill the need for closeness but prevent true intimacy by keeping others at a certain distance.

of actual physical touch (an extension of the sexual message system). Strokes serve to fulfill some of each player's needs for both physical and psychological closeness to another person. But games are designed by the players to prevent true intimacy from developing. Where intimacy is spontaneous and candid, games are highly structured and dishonest. Games permit people to reach the brink of intimacy but permit either or both players to invoke the principle of denial by going for a payoff instead of opening the self to merger with the other. Each can thus deny that he or she needed or wanted an intimate relationship with the other.

BEYOND GAMES

One of the first steps in moving beyond games to game-free intimacy is recognizing when you or others are playing games. An awareness of strategic patterns of interaction and of the nature of games can be useful in detecting when you are setting yourself up to go for a payoff. Awareness of patterns of defensiveness in your own communication and in the communication of others often provides warning signals that a game is beginning or is in progress.

It is more difficult to prescribe what to do to reduce the number of games you play. A frequent question in interpersonal communication courses is, What should I do now that I recognize that my spouse (parent, friend, boss, etc.) is always playing games? The answer to such a question depends upon the value system that each person applies to his or her own life. The answer lies not in the realm of scientific observation but in the realm of philosophy, ethics, and religion. You must consider the consequences that are likely to occur if you refuse to continue games as a pattern of interaction. Oftentimes a refusal to play the games may lead to a breakup of the relationship. Do you value the relationship even with all of the games more than you value not playing games? Sometimes a refusal to play games results in depression or despair for the other person. You have to weigh the relative value of the consequences of refusing the games against the consequences of continuing to play the games. And these are ethical and religious problems.

While games in themselves are not necessarily unhealthy, they are not as desirable (from the authors' point of view) as the spontaneous, game-free integration of interpersonal transactions. From our value systems, we feel that one of the goals of studying interpersonal communication might well be to permit a person to go beyond games—to be able to interact with others in a way that permits the acknowledgement of the other's communication, the confirmation of the other, the disclosure of the self, and the independence of the other to accept or reject that self. Beyond games lies intimacy in interpersonal relationships. Intimacy is a basic goal of interpersonal communication, constantly sought, rarely achieved. Adjusting your own communication toward the goal of intimacy should eventually permit you to be able to manage your own communication behavior and reduce the use of strategies and games. In that direction lies interpersonal growth and improved interpersonal health.

SUMMARY

Strategies and games are patterns of interpersonal communication that utilize incongruency within a transaction to permit the communicator to deny one or more aspects of the message being generated. Complex and highly structured strategies can be analyzed as games.

The most common form of strategic communication behavior is the tangential response—a form of interaction that fails to acknowledge either the content or the metacommunication of a message. Rejection of the other is a strategy that acknowledges the content of the message but denies the other person's self-concept. Rejection of the other underlies many forms of put-down humor in interpersonal transactions.

The one-up strategy is based on the symmetrical-complementary incongruency in punctuating transactions. The interaction tends to escalate because one of the parties is always trying to be one up on the other. Closely related to the one-up strategy are the verbalizers—arguing, gossiping, complaining, and disquieting.

Pragmatic paradoxes and double binds often contain many of the above strategies. The paradoxical injunction is a special form of the pragmatic paradox and is the basis of many serious problems in interpersonal communication. In the double bind, the paradox in the situation is such that neither party can escape from the transaction or metacommunicate about the nature of the paradox or paradoxical injunction.

A game is a highly structured pattern of complementary transactions with an ulterior motive leading to a well-defined, dramatic climax known as the payoff, which serves as a substitute for intimacy.

QUESTIONS FOR REVIEW

1. What is denial within an interpersonal communication transaction? Why does denial depend on the existence of incongruency within the transaction?
2. What is strategic communication?
3. What is the tangential response? Give an example.
4. Give an example of each of the verbalizers: the arguer, the complainer, the gossip, the disquieter.
5. Give an example of a pragmatic paradox or a double bind.
6. What is a paradoxical injunction? Give an example.
7. What are the characteristics of a game?
8. In what ways can strategic communication and interpersonal games be healthy? In what ways can they be unhealthy?
9. What is the difference between intimacy and pseudo-intimacy?

EXPLORATIONS

1. Take an inventory of your interpersonal communication with your spouse or a very close friend. What kinds of interpersonal games do you play? How often do you play "If It Weren't for You," "Why Don't You, Yes But," and "Now I've Got You, You Sonofabitch"? What function do these games serve in your relationship? Are they healthy or unhealthy games?
2. The next time you find yourself arguing with a close friend or your spouse, take a mental inventory of the situation. Is the argument a genuine disagreement? Does it involve misunderstanding? Or is the argument strategic behavior designed to provoke and maintain inter-

action for the sake of interaction? Is either one of you (or both of you) playing at being an arguer? Why?

3. Listen to the conversation of two friends or to a transaction in which you are engaged. How many times in a five-minute period do you engage in one-up? What function does this strategic communication serve in the relationship?

4. Try to identify one or two paradoxical injunctions in which you have found yourself in the last couple of days. Write down the contradictory aspects of the injunction. What is the source of the paradox? How do you feel about the situation? What can you do to remove the paradoxical injunction? Can you metacommunicate with the other person about it? Why or why not?

5. Carefully examine a relationship in which you love the other person. Is your communication designed to make that person love you? Do you impose obligations and demands on that person's love? Do you feel that the other person ought to love you? Do you feel that you have a right to his or her love? Do you communicate these "oughts" and "rights" to that person?

FOR FURTHER READING

Berne, Eric. *Games People Play: The Psychology of Human Relationships.* New York: Grove Press, 1964.

This best-selling book by the originator of Transactional Analysis is both popular and profound. Building upon the foundation of structural analysis (the Parent, Adult, and Child ego states) and Transactional Analysis (patterns of social interaction between people's ego states), Berne details a host of games and other ways of structuring time.

Berne, Eric. *What Do You Say After You Say Hello? The Psychology of Human Destiny.* New York: Grove Press, 1972.

The subtitle explains the book's purpose. The book is a simple and clear analysis of the nature of destiny viewed through the framework of Transactional Analysis. Berne presents the notion of the "script," the unconscious plan by which we each govern our lives. He illustrates how we are influenced by our life scripts.

Harris, Thomas A. *I'm O.K.—You're O.K.* New York: Harper & Row, 1967; Old Tappan, N.J.: Fleming H. Revell Co., Spire Books, 1973.

This book is a basic presentation of Transactional Analysis oriented toward practical personal applications. The book explains the basic T.A. theory of personality (Parent, Adult, and Child) and provides a simple but detailed analysis of the nature and role of the four existential positions in human life (such as "I'm O.K.—You're O.K.").

James, Muriel, and Jongeward, Dorothy. *Born to Win: Transactional Analysis with Gestalt Experiments.* Reading, Mass.: Addison-Wesley Publishing Co., 1971.

One of the best popular expositions of Berne's theory of Transactional Analysis, this book provides an overview of T.A., the life scripts, each of the three ego states, personal and sexual identity, and autonomy. Gestalt experiments based on the work of Fritz Perls supplement the T.A. theory.

Chapter 12

Healthy
Communication
and the
Transcendent Self

Americans today seem to be preoccupied with the notion of health, both physical and mental. They are concerned not just with eating and exercising properly, but also with becoming "real" persons, with relating well to others. The popularity of human relations training, of the encounter group movement, of various kinds of therapies, and of numerous philosophies of personal growth and heightened awareness reflects the current American penchant for health in personal life and interpersonal relationships. This interest in improving the self and relationships with others is one reason for examining the nature of healthy communication.

A second reason for considering healthy communication is that the logic of our transactional approach to human communication requires it. In this book, we have advocated a transactional model of interpersonal communication, presented a series of axioms about such communication, delineated four basic message systems which function both environmentally and instrumentally, and described both intimacy and pseudo-intimacy (including strategies and games). But we must still examine what optimal interpersonal communication is like, whether it is intimate or strategic, and how it utilizes the various message systems. What are the characteristics of healthy interpersonal communication? In this chapter, we shall provide one answer to that complex question— first by defining and exemplifying healthy communication and second by discussing the relationship of healthy communication to the self.

CHARACTERISTICS OF HEALTHY COMMUNICATION

The difficulty of describing healthy communication is evident in the literature of the various mental health disciplines. Psychiatric terminology, for instance, makes abundant reference to abnormality and pathology and only infrequently deals with desirable and healthy behaviors. Psychiatry (like medicine in general) began and developed primarily as the study of pathology—probably because disturbances in communication are typically more identifiable, more patterned, and more susceptible to categorization than healthy communication.

Health has traditionally been conceptualized as the *absence* of illness or pathology. Indeed, there is no single content that necessarily characterizes all healthy communication. Healthy ways of communicating vary widely from person to person; person A can exhibit communicative behaviors quite different from those of person B, yet both persons' communication can be said to be healthy. This range and diversity of communication behaviors that are healthy make definition of the term difficult.[1]

Nevertheless, there remains a need for trying to conceptualize the essential qualities of healthy interpersonal communication if we are to try to understand and improve our own transactions with others. One definition appears to recognize both the complexity and uniqueness of healthy communication, which promotes optimal interpersonal growth with the fewest difficulties in living. We may say that *healthy communication is comprised primarily of patterns of behavior characterized by acknowledgment, appropriateness, efficiency, and flexibility, and patterns of experience characterized by gratification.*[2] Let us look at each part of this definition to understand it better.

PATTERNS OF BEHAVIOR AND EXPERIENCE

The content of healthy interpersonal communication transactions can and does vary widely. *What* people communicate about is usually irrelevant to their communication health. *How* people communicate is the essence of the concept of health. Healthy communication transactions have in common certain structural and functional characteristics. Thus, while the content of any particular transaction is situation-specific, there are identifiable characteristics of patterns of behavior and experience that are healthy.

In describing healthy communication we are not concerned with all behavior and all experience. In our discussion of Axiom II we indicated that all behavior is potentially meaningful and therefore potentially communicative; one cannot not communicate, just as one cannot not behave. In our study of interpersonal communication, however, we are

1. Jurgen Ruesch and Gregory Bateson, *Communication: The Social Matrix of Psychiatry* (New York: W. W. Norton & Co., 1951; reprint ed., 1968), pp. 233–35.

2. Jurgen Ruesch, *Disturbed Communication: The Clinical Assessment of Normal and Pathological Communicative Behavior* (New York: W. W. Norton & Co., 1957; reprint ed., 1972), pp. 34–36.

concerned only with those patterns of behavior and experience that are meaningful in interpersonal transactions. And in identifying healthy communication, we are concerned only with those patterns of behavior that are characterized by acknowledgment, appropriateness, efficiency, and flexibility, and those patterns of experience that are characterized by gratification.

ACKNOWLEDGMENT

To have healthy interpersonal communication, a person must acknowledge the communication of others. Healthy communication is characterized by the ability of the communicator to acknowledge in his or her own communication the content of the communication of the other person in the transaction.[3] Denotative acknowledgment expresses or discloses recognition of some act or experience of the other. Giving a denotative response to a denotative message explicitly recognizes that another person's statement or gesture has specific content.

At dinner a wife might say, "I'm getting so bored staying at home every day. I'm thinking of looking for a job." To acknowledge her statement, the husband would have to indicate in some fashion his awareness of the content of the wife's message. He could say, "Well, what kind of work are you interested in?" Or he could say, "What's so boring about staying here? I wish I could stay around the house all day!" Both comments acknowledge that he recognizes *what* she has said. Whether the acknowledgment is positive or negative—i.e., whether he seems to agree or disagree with her—is immaterial, since in either case he permits her to know that he has heard what she said.

The husband could behave differently and not acknowledge her statement. One form of such failure to acknowledge is the tangential response (discussed in chapter 11). For instance, when the wife says, "I'm thinking of looking for a job," the husband could respond, "Please pass the gravy, dear." The husband's comment recognizes the wife's presence, but does not acknowledge the content of her communication.

A similar kind of tangential response (as opposed to acknowledgment) often occurs in certain encounter groups in which expression of emotion and recognition of intent is prized. John might say, "What do we really want to accomplish this session, anyway?" Mary might respond, "John, you sound hostile." Mary's response is tangential because it ignores the content of John's statement. It would have been healthier for her to acknowledge his remark by saying, "I really don't know what the group wants to accomplish tonight, but I think you sound very hos-

3. See ibid., pp. 37–38, 53–55.

tile." Rather than ignoring the content of John's remark, Mary can acknowledge it and then shift to the new topic of John's hostility. Failure to acknowledge the content of another person's communication is disjunctive, confusing, and unhealthy.

Besides acknowledging the content (or denotative level) of the other's communication, a person may also acknowledge the interpretive level of meaning. In other words, the person can state how he or she feels the other's message was to be interpreted. For instance, the husband in the earlier example could respond to his wife by acknowledging how he thinks she meant for him to interpret her remark. He might say, "I think you're really more interested in just getting out of the routine of housework than you are in getting a job." Oftentimes acknowledgment of the interpretive level of meaning is indicated by phrases such as, "I hear you saying that . . ." or "Do you mean by that . . ." or "Are you saying that . . ."

Acknowledgment of the interpretive level of meaning is healthy because it helps to avoid misunderstanding. Too often when people are uncertain about the meaning of a message, they fail to check their interpretations of the message with the other person. Consequently, what a person thinks another means may not necessarily be what the other means at all. The husband's comment about his interpretation of the wife's remark indicates to her what he thought she meant (that she wants mostly to get out of the house regardless of whether she gets a job). If the wife actually intended to convey the idea that she doesn't mind doing housework but really does want a job, she is now enabled (by the husband's acknowledgment of the interpretive level of her remark) to discern that he misunderstands her. She may then reiterate or amplify her intended meaning to try to reach understanding with her husband.

Acknowledgment of the relational aspects of messages are also usually healthy. The husband, for instance, can make explicit what he thinks his wife's comment indicates about her relationship with him. He might respond to her by saying, "I'm glad you feel free to talk about this with me." This statement not only acknowledges what implications he thinks the content of her remark has for their relationship, but also expresses his solidarity with her. Occasionally it is reassuring to let others know that we see their behaviors as strengthening the relationships between us. It should be noted, however, that excessive needs by either party in a dyad continually to reaffirm or redefine the relationship are not healthy. Excessive acknowledgment of the relational level of meaning is characteristic of disturbed relationships.

Obviously one cannot acknowledge the content or denotative level, the interpretive level, and the relational level all at the same time with equal explicitness. For example, the husband will have to choose whether to acknowledge the content itself ("Well, what kind of work? . . ."); the interpretation of the content ("I hear you saying that you want . . ."); or the relationship ("I'm glad you feel free to talk about this . . ."). Which of these he decides to emphasize will depend upon his judgment about their relative appropriateness.

While the preceding examples have shown only acknowledgment that occurs through the language message system, acknowledgment may come through other message systems as well. A glance, a smile, a flick of the wrist, a certain vocal intonation, or any number of other gestures can communicate acknowledgment of content, interpretation, or relationship to the other person. Healthy communication often relies upon acknowledgment through these message systems to indicate how a message is perceived. A knowing look, an in joke, a pat on the shoulder, or some such gesture is used more frequently than language to acknowledge relational levels of meaning in most healthy transactions. Ultimately, healthy communication involves all the message systems and all levels of meaning that are congruent with one another and appropriate to the situation.

APPROPRIATENESS

In healthy interpersonal communication, the participants select message systems and levels of meaning that are appropriate to the communication situation. Appropriateness refers to the aptness or suitability of any communicative act at any given point in a transaction. Such suitability is obviously closely related to how participants punctuate their communication by labeling the social situation and defining roles and rules. A communicative act is appropriate: if it fits the social situation as labeled by the participants and their society; if it suits the respective roles they have assumed; and if it is compatible with the rules of the social situation. An inappropriate communicative act or message is one that is incompatible with the social situation, its roles, and its rules.

Appropriateness has both a qualitative and a quantitative dimension.[4] *Qualitatively* appropriate communication is suitable in *kind or type* of role and message. If Jim and Mary work at adjacent desks in an office, their communication, if healthy, will be qualitatively appropriate. If Jim asks, "What time is it?" we would expect Mary to respond by giving him the correct time—"It's three o'clock." Their label of the social situation (office work situation), their own roles within it (coworkers), and certain accompanying rules (polite and efficient response

4. Ibid., pp. 32–33, 41, 53.

to requests made by colleagues)—all indicate that a request for the correct time should be answered honestly and directly.

If, however, Jim and Mary have recently had a long conversation over lunch about Jim's preoccupation with the time of day and his need to focus on his work rather than on the clock, Mary might answer his request for the time by saying, "Remember what we talked about at lunch?" In this case, her role relationship with him is such that her response can be about their prior conversation and still be healthy. In contrast, a response of the wrong kind or type might be "It's Tuesday," or "It's December," or even "It's pink." The first two responses give the time, not of the clock, but of the week and of the year; the third gives not the time but a color, which is really beside the point. All three responses would normally be considered to be qualitatively inappropriate.

Role definitions can also be qualitatively appropriate or inappropriate, just as a response can be appropriate or inappropriate. Suppose Tim is talking with Aunt Helen right after Uncle Herb's funeral. If she says, "He was such a wonderful person," the right kind of response by Tim would probably be, "Yes, he certainly was." The role relationship of Tim to Helen is that of supportive nephew to bereaved aunt. If, however, Tim replied, "He was a stingy old grouch," that response would probably be qualitatively inappropriate. The role of disgruntled nephew just doesn't seem appropriate when talking with a grieving aunt immediately after her husband's funeral. The rules of the social situation defined as a funeral usually preclude such comments. Thus, the qualitative appropriateness of a message depends on the social situation, the role relationship of the communicators, and the rules established by the situation and role relationships.

Eric Berne's concept of the *crossed transaction* is probably the most popular conceptualization of qualitatively inappropriate communication (which he indicates causes most of the social disruption around the globe).[5] Jim and Mary at their office desks can nicely illustrate this type of foul-up. If Jim asks for the correct time, and Mary provides it, that transaction is healthy and is not crossed. He makes a request for information (assuming the role of Adult) and she provides an answer (assuming the role of Adult). If, however, Mary responds, "Why don't you get a watch of your own?" (assuming the role of Parent) or "Why do you always pick on me?" (assuming the role of Child), the transaction becomes crossed (his Adult request being crossed by the Parent or Child response). Such qualitatively inappropriate communication produces difficulties in living and blocks the development of healthy communication.

5. See Eric Berne, *Games People Play: The Psychology of Human Relationships* (New York: Grove Press, 1964), pp. 30–32, 49.

In addition to this qualitative dimension, appropriateness has a quantitative aspect. *Quantitatively* appropriate communication is suitable in *amount or degree* and in *timing*. The amount or degree of a response can vary widely from deficient to excessive. If Jim asks Mary for the time and she doesn't say anything at all, her response would be seen as quite deficient—minimal to the point of absence! If, on the other hand, she responds, "It's three o'clock in Philadelphia, two o'clock in Chicago, one o'clock in Denver, twelve noon in San Francisco, nine o'clock in London. . . .", her response would normally be perceived as excessive. Similarly, when greeting someone with the ritual, "How are you today?" no one wants to be given a complete medical profile in return! Such a response is quantitatively inappropriate. "Fine" or "Tired" is all that we really want to hear.

Timing is also an important feature of quantitative appropriateness. In healthy communication, a message (whether initiating something or responding to something else) should occur at the right time. Recommendations for a graduate student do no good if they are made after the deadline for admission to graduate school. A message can also be too early. If Tim wants to encourage his just widowed Aunt Helen to sell her home and move into an apartment, his suggestion should be appropriately timed. It should come when she is able to handle such practical matters, not when she is in shock over her husband's death.

Healthy communication is characterized by saying or doing the right thing at the right time in the right amount according to the requirements of the situation.

EFFICIENCY

In healthy interpersonal communication, the participants reach their goals efficiently. Efficient communication is displayed in the ability to reach or to attain the goals of communication with the least amount of wasted effort.[6] Efficient communication is relatively thrifty (parsimonious) in its expression. The very emphasis upon efficiency in communication assumes that communication is efficient *for* something, whether or not that goal or purpose is consciously perceived by the communicators. The goal of a given communication transaction can range from the simple transfer of information to the establishment or maintenance of a relationship. Communication can establish intimacy or merely provide the communicators with something to do during a certain interval

6. See Ruesch, *Disturbed Communication*, p. 35; and Eric Berne, *The Structure and Dynamics of Organizations and Groups* (Philadelphia: Lippincott, 1963; New York: Ballantine Books, 1973), p. 318.

of time. Whatever the communicative goal or task, efficient communication helps them reach that goal in an economical fashion.

Efficiency in denotative expression via any message system is expected in healthy communication. Language usage should be syntactically and semantically accurate within the idiom of the user's subculture. In other words, language operations should employ normal English sentence structure (in an English-speaking culture) and words that are meaningful within that structure. Messages that are highly garbled, repetitive, or wordy would not be considered typical of healthy communication.

Efficiency in communication does not necessarily require unambiguousness. While clarity of expression is often desired and frequently extolled, complete clarity is undesirable when the purpose of the communicator is to protect his or her self-image or to develop a relationship by keeping the possible meanings of the message somewhat obscure.[7] If Jim thinks Mary is very attractive and wants to ask her for a date, he might do so efficiently by saying very directly, "Mary, you're a very attractive person whom I'd love to take to dinner tonight." But, if Jim thinks such a statement would embarrass Mary, or if he feels self-conscious in making that statement, or if he feels that he would be unable to handle her possible rejection of his offer, then it would be more efficient for him to be a bit ambiguous. For instance, he might say, "Did you hear about that new Italian restaurant that opened up downtown?" with the hope that Mary might express interest and he could then ask her to have dinner there with him. Complete clarity in expressing motives and emotions is possible only when people are open to developing intimacy within the transaction. In most social situations, some ambiguity about feelings and motives may be desirable for efficient maintenance of relationships.

One indication of inefficient communication is the presence of behaviors by one individual that lead the other person to experience him or her as unfocused, as not fully present, or as "not there."[8] Such a lack of focus can range from the complete blankness of a person who is in shock to the momentary unawareness of someone who is preoccupied with other issues or whose mind begins to wander. Such momentary lapses do not usually have serious consequences unless they are highly repetitive or occur at a crucial moment in a transaction. When someone is unable, for whatever reason, to keep his or her attention focused on the present transaction and the issues relevant to it at that time, his or her communicative behavior is inefficient.

7. See Virginia Satir, *Conjoint Family Therapy: A Guide to Theory and Technique*, rev. ed. (Palo Alto, Calif.: Science and Behavior Books, 1967), p. 73.
8. Jurgen Ruesch, *Therapeutic Communication* (New York: W. W. Norton & Co., 1961; reprint ed., 1973), pp. 84–85.

FLEXIBILITY

In healthy interpersonal communication, the participants can be flexible in modifying role relationships, adapting to new rules, and establishing new communication goals. Flexibility is the capability to adapt communication to changing circumstances and new situations. Flexible communicators realize that roles and rules can be modified.[9] As a transaction proceeds and a relationship develops, roles can change and new rules can be adopted. If Jim and Mary are dating, they will probably discover that the dating situation has roles and rules that are quite different from those of their job situation—and they will be flexible in choosing the communication behavior appropriate to the situation. Rules that characterize their own relationship will develop, which they will modify as they see fit.

Furthermore, flexible communication can also involve substituting people in roles—either by switching roles or by changing who plays them. In healthy communication between marital partners, for example, the husband is sometimes the "little boy" who tells his troubles to his "mother" (wife); but sometimes the roles are switched, so that she plays the "child" who seeks out her "father" (husband) for support. At other times, the husband-wife pair might enact friend-friend or lover-lover roles. Yet they each have their own friends with whom they enact friend-friend roles. Thus, both partners are flexible in substituting one role for another within their relationship and in playing some of the same roles with people outside the marriage relationship.

The reevaluation and changing of goals is another aspect of flexibility. While the comprehensive goal of maintaining a relationship might remain fairly constant over time, the specific goals of various communication transactions will probably need reevaluating and changing as time passes. A couple who has been married one week will have different communicative goals than a couple married one decade. The relationship between spouses—or any two people, for that matter—will not grow and mature unless they are willing to adapt their goals to reflect their own individual and relational needs.

No one of the four characteristics of healthy communication behavior is sufficient in itself to define communication health. All four must be present in some fashion for healthy communication to occur. Undue emphasis on any one of these characteristics to the exclusion of the others is unwise and unhealthy. Efficiency, for instance, is not the sole criterion of healthy communication. A communication system can be quite efficient and still be very disturbed or pathological. Many disturbed relationships, full of destructive games, are efficiently main-

9. Ruesch, *Disturbed Communication*, pp. 35–36.

tained by the participants, often with a highly exaggerated need for controlling the transactions. Such communication is most inflexible, since games are by definition highly structured, lacking in spontaneity. Despite the efficiency of certain destructive games, their inflexibility disqualifies them from the realm of healthy communication. Likewise, acknowledgment and appropriateness must also be present in healthy communication transactions. These four characteristics have been separated in our discussion solely for the purpose of analysis.

GRATIFICATION

In healthy interpersonal communication, both parties in a transaction experience the communication as gratifying. Healthy communication consists of more than certain patterns of behavior; it includes patterns of experience characterized by gratification. One of the most important criteria of healthy communication is that it is gratifying for the participants.[10] Of course, the subjective feeling of pleasure or gratification can occur even in very destructive games, if the players have a distorted sense of pleasure. Gratification over another person's misfortune, or with a payoff in a game played at another person's expense, is unhealthy. Healthy gratification, on the other hand, is related to particular patterns of experience: intimacy, agreement, understanding, and realization of understanding. These experiential patterns of interaction are usually gratifying in and of themselves, for they indicate similarities between the communicators' perspectives, which draw people together and release tension when that similarity is successfully communicated.

Of course, *intimacy* is probably the most gratifying result of successful interpersonal communication. It is also gratifying to *agree* genuinely with someone else, particularly when both communicators acknowledge and consciously perceive that agreement. Such acknowledgment involves *understanding*, the congruency of one person's metaperspective with another person's direct perspective. It is particularly pleasurable not just to agree, but to know that we agree—i.e., to understand that we agree. While both agreement and understanding are gratifying patterns of experience, understanding is more crucial to healthy communication than agreement. Disagreement between two people is acceptable, as long as they both understand that they disagree. A healthy interpersonal communication transaction involving disagreement will feature bilateral understanding. If only one party understands that they disagree (while the second misunderstands, thinking that they agree), an unhealthy and lopsided spiral of perspectives will develop. The resulting incongruency between perspectives will be frustrating rather than gratifying.

10. Ibid., p. 36.

Even if two people disagree and misunderstand that they disagree, gratification can still occur if they realize that they misunderstand each other. Suppose that Jim and Mary disagree over the issue of whether he should buy a new car. Jim thinks he should; Mary thinks he should not. But Jim misunderstands, because he believes that Mary thinks he should buy a car. Likewise, Mary misunderstands, believing that Jim thinks he shouldn't buy a car. That situation has highly disjunctive perspectives and will probably lead to considerable frustration when Jim heads for the automobile dealer's showroom—*unless* each of them comes to a realization of their misunderstanding. If Jim realizes that he misunderstands Mary, and if Mary realizes that she misunderstands Jim, then there is a good possibility that they can work their way out of their confusion. *Realization of understanding* is always gratifying and is particularly essential when patterns of incongruency exist at lower levels of experience (disagreement and misunderstanding).

ILLUSTRATIONS OF HEALTHY AND UNHEALTHY COMMUNICATION

Examples of healthy communication are not usually found in drama because healthy communication is not really dramatic on the stage. On the other hand, examples of unhealthy communication abound. An example of unhealthy communication from the play *Twigs* will serve to illustrate the nature of healthy communication by contrast. The following excerpt of dialogue from *Twigs* involves three characters: Celia, a middle-aged woman, in a florid print dress, with dyed red hair and too much makeup; Phil, her husband, a civilian who works at the PX of a local army base; and Swede, their friend and Phil's former army buddy of more than a dozen years ago. Swede is visiting Celia and Phil for Thanksgiving; Phil and Swede are drinking beer in the kitchen.

(1) Swede: *We put quite a few away in our day, huh, Phil?*

(2) Phil: *I know my limit though.*

(3) Celia: *Me too. A goose-egg. None. That's how many is my limit. . . .*

(4) Phil: *(Interrupting) Why don't ya' be quiet for a minute? Christ!*

(5) Celia: *Oh.*

(6) Phil: *On and on and on.*

(7) Celia: *(Embarrassed, quietly) Sorry.*

(8) Phil: *Always gotta be the center of every conversation.*

(9) Celia: *(A slight pause) Could I explain it, Phil? I was jist gonna ask Swede if he missed the Army, is all. I didn't want to be the center.*

(10) Phil: *(Quickly) Alright. Of course he misses the Army. For Chrissake, the questions she asks a person.*

(11) Swede: *Wasn't a bad life. Never hear no complaints from me.*

(12) Phil: *Us master sargeants had it terrific. Right, Swede? I never was even that anxious to retire as a matter a' fact. Mandatory. I never wanted to, though.*

(13) Swede: *I coulda' put in a few more. At the time—it seemed different.*

(14) Phil: *Leavin' the army to me was like—leavin' my life.*

(15) Swede: *It's just that there's never nothin' to do now.*

(16) Celia: *Did you know I had a nervous breakdown, Swede?*

(17) Swede: *(Not quite sure what to say) Yeah.*

(18) Celia: *I had two of 'em, did ya' know that? I think the last one was the only really bad one, though. They was only two years apart.*

. . . .

But I had a psychiatrist and all, like some rich lady. Dr. Cohn. I never liked anybody so much as him in my life. He explained a lot about so many things. So interestin'. (Phil gets up and crosses U.) Like he said I always wanted approval, see. That's what he said. First from my mother then from my husband. And that is the truth. He said I try too hard for approval. The reason I really married Phil is because he was so strict and dominant and strong—like my mother.

(19) Phil: *(Speaks from U.) Why don't ya' just shut up? What the hell does Swede care? I hope ya' don't go around tellin' people all that crap, for Chrissake. Sounds like some doctor, huh, Swede? Me and her mother alike. Jesus Christ.*[11]

The interpersonal communication in this dialogue exhibits patterns of behavior and experience that are decidedly unhealthy. Phil consistently fails to acknowledge Celia's relational needs in this conversation. When she tries several times to include herself in the discussion (lines

11. Abridged from George Furth, *Twigs* (New York: Samuel French, 1972), act 1, sc. 2, pp. 33–34.

3, 16, and 18), Phil fails to understand, and consequently to acknowledge, that her communicative behavior is designed to satisfy her need for inclusion, not to interrupt Phil and Swede *per se*. Of course, Celia's initiating the subject of her nervous breakdown (lines 16 and 18) would normally be seen as inappropriate at that point in a reunion with an old friend (in the middle of Phil and Swede's reminiscing about army life).

While Phil criticizes Celia (lines 4 and 19) for the inappropriateness of what she has said, his response is itself inappropriate both qualitatively and quantitatively. He apparently does not understand that Celia doesn't have a very extensive repertoire of topics; she is rather inflexible (as her mental history corroborates) in her role relationships and inflexible in the way she attempts to integrate herself with others to satisfy her needs for inclusion. She apparently has a long history of interrupting conversations with inappropriate comments at inopportune times. Had Phil been able to perceive and acknowledge her inflexibility and her need to participate in the conversation, he might have been able to avoid the added embarrassment and inappropriateness of his curt dismissal of her remarks (lines 4 and 19). But Phil is himself inflexible—"dominant and strong," as Celia says. He needs to maintain a certain control over the social situation and to banish remarks that he considers inappropriate. Phil's inflexibility, on top of Celia's, further diminishes the potential for communication health. Rather than creating a situation in which her remarks could be seen and acknowledged as appropriate, his own remarks (lines 4 and 19) are themselves inappropriate and inflexible.

The communication between Celia and Phil is efficient, but not in the way that they probably recognize or desire it to be. Celia's statements clearly indicate (to the observer but not to Phil) her need to be a part of the conversation. Phil's remarks are (likewise to the observer but not to Celia) a clear indication of his desire to talk with Swede without Celia's inappropriate intrusions. Yet neither seems to agree with or acknowledge the other's communicative purposes. Phil and Celia's communication is remarkably efficient in implicitly defining the nature of their relationship—and the nature of their interaction as a game. Celia will do what she has to do in order to be recognized, but at the expense of having Phil reprimand her. Phil will reprimand her in order to maintain the appropriateness of his conversation with Swede, regardless of whether Celia is embarrassed in the process. Apparently, Celia and Phil are used to this kind of communicative pattern and perpetuate it. Given the highly structured and recurring nature of the interaction, we could say that Celia and Phil are engaged in a form of the game "Kick Me," in which Celia's interruptions and Phil's put-downs serve as a substitute for intimacy in their relationship.

Even in this brief excerpt, the frustration that Celia and Phil (and even Swede) feel is apparent. The interpersonal communication is not gratifying or pleasant. It is frustrating and unhealthy.

Quite different from Celia and Phil's interpersonal communication patterns are those of Dorothy and Lou. Dorothy is one of Celia's older sisters, who is having dinner at home with her husband, Lou, on Thanksgiving evening in celebration of their twenty-fifth anniversary. The following two segments of dialogue illustrate their healthy communication.

(1) Dorothy: . . . *You know what really stuck in my mind? Something goofy? Mary and Eddie. Remember when we stopped at their house that time we drove out to Brookfield to see Mrs. Blanger? Remember how right in the middle of a conversation, for no reason, he'd call, "Mary?" And she'd say, "What?" Then he'd say, "Hi." And then she'd say, "Hi." Do you remember that Lou? How they'd do that right in the middle of a conversation.*

(2) Lou: *Mary and Eddie Langley?*

(3) Dorothy: *Lou, yes. Be sensible. What other Mary and Eddie do we know?*

(4) Lou: *You* did *that. You* did *that to me.*

(5) Dorothy: *What?*

(6) Lou: *You used to say "Lou, Lou, hi, hi."*

(7) Dorothy: *I did not.*

(8) Lou: *You most certainly did. You'd say "Lou, Lou, hi, hi."*

(9) Dorothy: *I did not.*

(10) Lou: *I can hear you saying it. "Lou, Lou, hi, hi." You most certainly did.*

(11) Dorothy: *(Pause) I did do it to you.*

(12) Lou: *Sure.*

(13) Dorothy: *What does it mean? What did it mean to you when I said that to you? Lou? Lou?*

(14) Lou: *What?*

(15) Dorothy: *(Smiles) Hi.*

(16) Lou: *Oh, for godsake.*

(17) Dorothy: *I think it means like, I know you're here, or hello, or just I love you. . . .*[12]

12. Ibid., act 2, sc. 1, pp. 50–51.

The second excerpt of dialogue is from the end of Dorothy and Lou's scene.

(18) Dorothy: *Lou, don't laugh or anything. I mean this will sound funny but it's true.*

(19) Lou: *What?*

(20) Dorothy: *You're my best friend.*
     (They sit in silence, quietly holding each other. Then Lou puts his arms around her, giving her a big kiss on the cheek. Suddenly she screams and jumps up.)

(21) Lou: *What, for Chrissake? You know, you're heavy.*

(22) Dorothy: *Shush. The champagne. The French champagne. (Brings the bottle to the table to Lou and she crosses U.L. to get the glasses. Lou begins to open the bottle. After a moment.)*

(23) Lou: *(Under his breath) Dorothy?*

(24) Dorothy: *(Crossing with the glasses) What?*

(25) Lou: *I didn't say anything.*

(26) Dorothy: *Oh, I thought you said something. (She stands behind him for a minute and watches him.) Lou?*

(27) Lou: *What?*

(28) Dorothy: *(A radiant smile) Hi!*

(29) Lou: *Hi. For Chrissake, hi.*

(30) Dorothy: *(Crossing down with the glasses) Oh, Lou, you're just terrific.*[13]

There is abundant evidence of healthy communication patterns in this dialogue between Dorothy and Lou. Their conversation seems appropriate to the social situation of a low-key anniversary dinner at home. They give acknowledgment in several ways. Dorothy acknowledges denotative meaning when she realizes and admits that she had said "hi" to Lou as Lou stated (line 11). Dorothy both requests (line 13) and acknowledges (line 17) interpretation of the meaning of that little ritual. Dorothy and Lou acknowledge their relationship both denotatively (lines 17, 20, and 30) and metacommunicatively through the repetition of the ritual (lines 15, 28, and 29). Their communication is efficient in focusing on the issue of their relationship on the occasion of their anniversary. They express the nature of their relationship in a clear, straightforward way (lines 20 and 30) and in a more ritualized and symbolic way (lines 28 and 29). In this case, the repetition of the word

13. Ibid., p. 64.

hi is neither inefficient nor inappropriate for it signifies the love they have for each other and does so in a type of communicative shorthand that could be employed even in the company of other people. Dorothy and Lou are also flexible in their communication, for they do not use the ritual continually; they use it selectively and appropriately. Their communication is apparently quite gratifying for them: they come to agreement, seem to understand, and realize that they understand each other. Their communication patterns are designed to permit the development of intimacy. The absence of strategic behavior between them indicates that both are capable of handling intimacy and finding it gratifying.

Congruency and Healthy Communication. It should be apparent that healthy communication promotes congruency of various types. By definition, healthy communication features congruency between communication behaviors and (1) their meaning (through acknowledgment); (2) the social situation with its attendant roles and rules (appropriateness); (3) the achievement of purpose (efficiency); (4) changing circumstances (flexibility); and (5) such patterns of experience as agreement, understanding, and realization of understanding (gratification).

While such congruency is rarely complete, it is enhanced by healthy communicative exchanges, sometimes culminating in intimacy—that state of relatively high congruency between behavior and experience marked by spontaneity and awareness. Healthy communication thus enhances the establishment and maintenance of optimal relationships with self and with others—featuring pseudo-intimate, strategic communication patterns when necessary, and intimate, game-free communication whenever feasible. Such communication, consisting of the behavioral and experiential patterns described, encourages personal and interpersonal growth and minimizes difficulties in living.

THE TRANSCENDENT SELF

In exploring the nature of interpersonal communication and its function in human relationships, we are led to confront several basic questions. The problem of defining health and healthy communication in particular raises questions about the goals of communication. Healthy communication promotes growth, but growth toward what end? toward what goal? for what purpose? The scientific observer can define healthy communication and its characteristics only if he or she first has some basic beliefs as to the goal of communication. In this closing section, we want to articulate more precisely some of the basic assumptions that have guided us in structuring the model presented and in making our observations of interpersonal communication.

Throughout this book we have held that the self is created and maintained through interpersonal communication transactions. The infant does not come into the world as a fully formed person, only with the potential for learning the significance and use of message systems. The interpersonal transactions within the context of the family, community, and society are then responsible for shaping the self, the perceptions of self, and the perceptions of others. On the other hand, we must now observe that the individual is not completely determined. There is evidence to indicate that the individual decides what perspectives he or she will adopt in interacting with others. To say that the self is molded by forces that form the environment of the self, and at the same time assert that the self has the freedom to adopt a view of life and the universe that transcends the social environment, is to confront a basic paradox in the nature of interpersonal communication.

The paradox should be closely examined for it sheds a great deal of light upon the nature of communication and its functions in life (not only for human beings but for all living creatures). Our reasons for examining the self as a creation of interpersonal transactions have been extensively presented in the preceding chapters. Yet equally compelling are the reasons for concluding that the individual's perspectives are in some measure free from social constraints.

One of the most striking illustrations of the apparent freedom to transcend socially imposed constraints by adopting a life perspective of one's own is found in the experience of bottoming out, or hitting bottom, as it is sometimes known. Many who read this will have experienced what we are talking about; others will have friends or members of their family who have had the experience. For some, imagination and empathy will have to serve to aid understanding. *Bottoming out* occurs when a person feels that he or she has come to the end—that the only escape is into insanity or suicide, alcoholism or drug addiction, or similar acts. At this point, the individual is confronted very squarely with the self apart from all interaction with the social environment. At the moment of confronting the self there is a tremendous sense of isolation —loneliness in the most overpowering sense—and tremendous feelings of alienation from all social contacts.

What is important is that the *decision* not to commit suicide, or to come out of insanity, or to come back from alcoholism, or to abandon drug addiction appears to be a uniquely *individual* one. Such decisions are made by the self confronting the self. Interpersonal transactions have little influence upon such decisions, although they may support the individual once a decision has been reached.

The same is true of persons experiencing severe physical illness who reach a point where they decide either to live or to die. Stewart Alsop, the nationally known columnist who died recently from a rare form of cancer, reported just such an experience.[14] While in a kind of hallucination in his hospital room, he imagined that he was on a train that was pulling into the Baltimore train station. Lurching and falling, he staggered to the door of his compartment to get off the train, all the while cursing the deplorable roughness of the tracks (which he assumed to be the cause of his own unsteady gait upon arising from his hospital bed). Looking out of the door onto the station platform (actually the hall outside his hospital room), he thought it appeared quite foreboding. So he decided not to get off in Baltimore, and instead went unsteadily back to bed (with bruises to show the next morning for his efforts). Alsop was convinced afterwards that if he had decided in his experience to leave the train in Baltimore, he would have been, in effect, deciding to die. But he recovered enough to write the column in which this experience was reported. Strange as this incident may sound, those who have had such experiences are quite convinced of their validity.

The experience of having a freedom of choice about one's own life is not limited to those who have been at death's door. Most people experience themselves as making choices, as deciding what to do or what to believe. These choices often oppose the social milieu or the current social values. Such choices sometimes require the individual to extend or go outside of the prevailing norms for social roles and rules in interaction with others.

The psychologist Rollo May has characterized this aspect of human interaction as "the continuing rebel." The rebel in society is one who senses injustice and "take[s] a stand against it in the form of I-will-be-destroyed-rather-than-submit."[15] The rebel's choice transcends society's norms and pressures. Such rebellion functions as an indispensable force in society without which dynamic social change would give way to stultifying conformity. If all people were the same, society would rapidly die. In our definition of communication we indicated that there must be both unification and differentiation. While the creation and maintenance of the self serves a tremendous unifying function in society, the continually rebellious nature of the individual provides the differentiation that is equally necessary.

The rebel needs society as much as society needs the rebel. If the rebel shapes society, it also shapes him or her. Not only is the selfhood of the rebel (and all people are in a sense the rebel) molded by interpersonal communication transactions, but the very possibility of rebellion is imaged for the rebel in the social environment. A person learns *how* to rebel through the images of rebellion that exist in the person's

14. Stewart Alsop, "I Didn't Stop in Baltimore," *Newsweek*, 11 March 1974, p. 92.
15. Rollo May, *Power and Innocence: A Search for the Sources of Violence* (New York: W. W. Norton & Co., 1972), p. 220.

smaller social circles and in the models provided by the heroic rebellions learned about in history, mythology, and religious rituals of society. Society provides the models by which the individual is guided in making decisions about how to view life and how to act, including how to transcend the forces that create and shape the self. Within social influence, then, lies the paradox of transcendence that permits the individual to retain a spark of freedom to choose one model over another, to adopt this life perspective rather than some other one.

The social environment provides not only patterns for conformity and rebellion (unity with and transcendence of the social unit), but also provides the individual with a variety of attitudes toward life and its communication processes. From all of the attitudes modeled in the social environment, each person chooses a *stance,* an existential position, from which all of his or her behavior derives and through which all experience flows. The stance each person takes determines the way he or she will experience all behavior of self and others. This stance is not something that can be proved to be true or false, right or wrong, but is something that has meaning for the person, which can be communicated to others. To adopt a stance is to take an existential leap of faith. All evidence related to the stance, when gathered together, is still inconclusive. The individual must make a judgment without proof of its correctness. The basis of all experience, and of all observation of ourselves and others, is an act of faith. Scientific observation can only tell us how to observe the communication behavior of others. Which communication behaviors to observe and what they mean are questions based in prior beliefs, derived not from science but from religion, ethics, theology, or philosophy in general.

In the Preface of this book we described an exercise in the giving and receiving of coins.[16] There we observed that the same act may have several distinctly opposite meanings. If we each have one coin to give to a person, we must make a choice. If you did not give your coin to me, I can experience that act as a communication of trust. I can say, "Isn't it wonderful that you felt so secure in our relationship that you felt free to give your coin to Shane and not to me." Or I can experience your act as rejection of our relationship. I can say, "You rejected me. You didn't think enough of me to give me your coin. That is a poor way to tell me you are losing interest in our relationship." On the other hand, suppose you did give your coin to me. I can also attribute different meanings to that act. I can experience that act as binding me to you. I can say, "I'm sorry that you do not feel secure enough in our relationship to feel free to give your coin to Shane." Or I can experience your giving me the coin as an act of love and affection. The particular experience I have of the

16. J. William Pfeiffer and John E. Jones, *A Handbook of Structured Experiences for Human Relations Training* (Iowa City, Iowa: University Associates Press, 1969), pp. 113–15.

communication act depends on the stance that I take.

The experience you have of any communication act depends on the stance that you take. If you see the world as "not O.K." and rejecting you, you will experience the communication of others as rejecting you. If you think I am a liar, there is literally no way in which I can communicate to you that I am not lying and that you can trust me. On the other hand, if you see the world as accepting and basically loving, and if you see me as trustworthy, there is little that I can do for which you would not probably give me the benefit of the doubt. *The meaning of our communication behavior depends upon the stance from which that behavior is observed.*

One of the dominant terms in communication studies in recent years has been *self-actualization.* This concept was popularized by Maslow who postulated that the goal of all personal and interpersonal functioning is the enhancement of the individual so that he or she can achieve his or her full potential.[17] Unfortunately, many people interpret the term *self-actualization* quite literally. They assume that somewhere there is a self that exists prior to social interaction and that the goal of all communication is to create conditions favorable to the growth and development of that "inner person." In communication studies, the emphasis upon self-actualization has been translated into enhancement of private experience—the acknowledgment of a person's own feelings, thoughts and emotions.

As helpful and attractive as the concept of self-actualization is, it falls short of characterizing the basic goals of persons. Peter Marin delineates this idea when he says that:

> *human fulfillment hinges on much more than our usual notions of private pleasure or self-actualization, for both of those in their richest forms are impossible without communion and community, an acknowledgment of liability, and a significant role in both the polis and the moral world. To be deprived of those is to be deprived of a part of the self, and to turn away from them is to betray not only the world but also the self, for it is only in the realm in which others exist that one can come to understand the ways in which the nature of each individual existence is in many ways a collective act, the result of countless other lives.*[18]

A person cannot be "actualized" in isolation from other persons. The fullest and most complete "actualization of the self" is impossible apart from the self's interexperience with other people. The growth of the individual always takes place in history, in a concrete place and an

17. Abraham H. Maslow, *Motivation and Personality,* 2d ed. (New York: Harper & Row, 1970).
18. Peter Marin, "The New Narcissism," *Harper's,* October 1975, p. 55.

actual time. The historical community in which the individual lives, communicates, and dies—rather than the individual's self—must be the chief concern of the individual. In the words of Viktor Frankl, holder of Freud's chair at the University of Vienna and founder of logotherapy, "the real aim of human existence cannot be found in what is called self-actualization. Human existence is essentially self-transcendence rather than self-actualization."[19] The goal of individual functioning is largely the growth and enhancement of that which is external to the individual —people in one's environment, one's community, one's society, one's world, one's God.

Emphasizing that the locus of personal efforts is in the larger universe does not deny the worth of the individual but enhances it by recognizing its true character—that man is the creature whose healthy functioning and individual growth require concern for others rather than preoccupation with self.

Each self is created by the environment and is continuously shaped by the environment. Yet each of us helps to shape the environment which shapes us. Every message is an act that instrumentally changes the social environment. Once we have created messages they are no longer simply our private instruments for changing the environment; the messages become a part of our own environment, and we adapt to our own messages. Thus, we ourselves become changed by our own messages.

The healthy individual shows a kind of transcendent self in his or her interpersonal transactions. Most of us spend our lives being shaped by others—what others think of us, what others think we should do, how others think we should act, and so on. Once in a while, however, we become privileged to meet someone who seems to transcend this kind of interaction with others. This person somehow stands apart; he or she has a kind of aura—an inner serenity which comes through and says, "I am at peace with the world." This person has learned the secret of the transcendent self—the ability to transcend, or go beyond, the strict confines of social interaction. The self-transcendent person is not afraid to tell the world who he or she is. The self-transcendent person declares to all, "You may accept me or reject me. I can deal with either because I know that I am accepted by the universe," (or life, or God, or whatever other ultimate value term the person supplies as the basis of his or her life stance). It is perhaps the ultimate paradox, taught by many major religions of the world, that by losing the self in the social environment, an individual finally transcends that environment. This paradox is surely the key to understanding the relationship between

19. Viktor E. Frankl, *Man's Search for Meaning: An Introduction to Logotherapy* (New York: Washington Square Press, 1963), p. 175.

interpersonal communication transactions and society and social interaction.

We began our inquiry with science and scientific observation. In describing interpersonal communication transactions we moved from describing how transactions function to prescribing how a healthy transaction *should* function. In doing so, we moved from science into the realm of religion and ethics. How each person should communicate with others depends upon the value system he or she holds. The *goal* of interpersonal communication seems to be a value question rather than an observational one. Our inquiry into the nature of interpersonal communication thus ends by pointing back to the humanistic tradition with its questions on the nature of man, the goal of life, and the nature of meaning. We have tried to describe *how* we create meaning in our transactions; the question of *what* is meaningful must be answered by each person in his or her own search for a life stance that will guide all interaction with others.

QUESTIONS FOR REVIEW

1. What are the characteristics of healthy communication?
2. Why is acknowledgment important to communication health?
3. How can you tell if a given message or communication behavior is appropriate? Who determines the appropriateness of communication behavior to a given interpersonal communication transaction?
4. What does it mean to say that healthy communication is efficient?
5. In what way is healthy communication flexible? When can flexibility be unhealthy or pathological?
6. What is gratification? Why is it important to healthy communication?
7. What is a stance? Why is the stance important to understanding a person's interpersonal communication?
8. What is meant by self-transcendence? Why is it important to interpersonal communication?

EXPLORATIONS

1. Make a list (for your journal) of two or three occasions on which you think your communication (or someone else's) was truly healthy. Note the ways in which it was characterized by acknowledgment, appropriateness, efficiency, flexibility, and gratification.
2. Choose one interpersonal communication transaction that you see as among the most gratifying you have ever experienced. Try to think back to that occasion, to relive that experience in your mind as much as possible. What made it so gratifying? Was it intimate? Was it

game-free? What patterns of experience (agreement, understanding, etc.) were present? How important was the other person to the experience? What essential communicative contributions did he or she make to the success of the transaction? If that person is accessible to you now, and if you think it would be appropriate, talk with the person about the experience. See what insight the two of you together can generate on the nature of that gratifying experience.

3. The next time you are at a party or other gathering at which people have a chance to talk informally in pairs or small groups, try to observe unobtrusively a pair who are deep in conversation. Note what they are doing that indicates their involvement with each other (using the message systems discussed earlier in this book). In what ways is their communication healthy or unhealthy?

4. Think of an experience of self-transcendence that you have had. Did it occur while you were alone, in conversation, in a counseling setting, in a drug-induced state, at a public meeting (religious, theatrical, etc.), or elsewhere? Write a one- or two-page narrative of that experience, with as much detail as you are able to provide. Then reflect on the ways in which that experience was both a transcendence of your social environment and an outgrowth of it. What influence has that experience had on your daily life and communication behavior since it occurred? Do you know anyone who has had a similar experience with whom you could talk and explore the dynamics of self-transcendence?

FOR FURTHER READING

Frankl, Viktor E. *Man's Search for Meaning: An Introduction to Logotherapy.* New York: Washington Square Press, 1963.

Psychiatrist Viktor Frankl is a man who lost everything except his life at the hands of the Nazis. In the first part of this book, Frankl recounts his experiences in a concentration camp. Out of the experience, Frankl has constructed an existential analysis called logotherapy (explained in the second part of the book), which attempts to help a person discover the meaning of his or her own concrete life. This is a book that anyone searching for meaning in life should examine.

Oden, Thomas C. *Game-Free: The Meaning of Intimacy.* New York: Dell Publishing Co., Delta Books, 1974.

The usually separate subjects of Transactional Analysis, interpersonal communication, and theology are synthesized here in an exciting and novel way to produce an insightful analysis of game-free intimacy.

Ruesch, Jurgen, *Disturbed Communication: The Clinical Assessment of Normal and Pathological Communicative Behavior.* New York: W. W. Norton & Co., 1957; reprint ed., 1972.

Psychiatrist Ruesch utilizes an information theory model of communication to analyze various communication pathologies observable in a clinic or other setting. He also provides a detailed guide to clinical observation of disturbed and undisturbed communication.

Ruesch, Jurgen. *Therapeutic Communication.* New York: W. W. Norton & Co., 1961; reprint ed., 1973.

Using the same basic information theory model as in the preceding book, Ruesch describes the framework of therapy, how to recognize disturbed communicative behavior, and what the therapist should do communicatively. His summary of the principles of human communication and of therapeutic communication is especially good.

Watzlawick, Paul; Weakland, John; and Fisch, Richard. *Change: Principles of Problem Formation and Problem Resolution.* New York: W. W. Norton & Co., 1974.

Using group theory and the theory of logical types, the authors discuss how to formulate and resolve problems. The distinction between first-order and second-order change allows them to provide a most insightful analysis, especially of the art of reframing. This book offers one very profound approach to transcending a given problem or situation.

INDEX

For providing the photographs on the pages indicated, acknowledgment is made to the following: CBS Television Network, 189; Editorial Photocolor Archives, 4 (Dan O'Neill), 28 (left—Dan O'Neill), 28 (top right—Newsphoto), 73 (Roberto Borea), 84 (J. Lukas), 152 (Dan O'Neill), 153 (left—Newsphoto), 208 (Alain Keler), 312 (Ellen Levine); Rohn Engh, 100, 110; F.A.O. Photo, 209 (P. Boonserm); Emil Fray, 86 (top left), 177 (right); Freelance Photo Guild, 324 (Llewellyn); Gregg Gizyn, 115–21, 123; GTE Automatic Electric, 16 (Nora Davis); Peter Kiar, 38, 230; Frederic Lewis, 21 (left); NASA, 21 (right); National 4-H Service Committee Inc., 153 (right); Marc Rattner, 263; James L. Shaffer, 86 (right), 193 (left); Dennis R. Smith, 43 (left), 45 (right), 48, 52, 134, 135, 137, 239, 240 (top left), 246; Stock, Boston, Inc., 43 (right—Thomas H. Brooks), 128 (Owen Franken), 235 (Donald Patterson, Jr.), 237 (Ellis Herwig), 278 (Owen Franken); United Press International, 28 (bottom right), 45 (left), 65, 68, 82, 83, 86 (bottom left), 164, 200, 258, 270; Van Cleve Photography, 193 (right—Bill Means), 281 (Rohn Engh), 296 (Roy N. Miller III). Photographs not otherwise credited were provided by Don and Renee Walkoe.